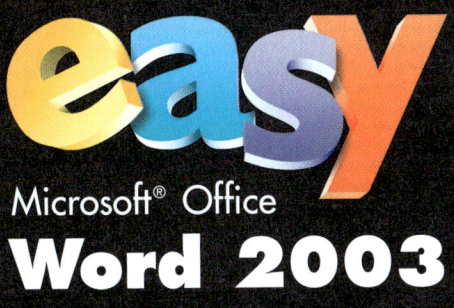

easy
Microsoft® Office
Word 2003

Heidi Steele

D1808940

Contents

Bulk Sales

Que offers excellent discounts on this book when ordered in quantity for bulk purchases or special sales. For more information, please contact:

U.S. Corporate and Government Sales
1-800-382-3419
corpsales@pearsontechgroup.com

For sales outside of the U.S., please contact:

International Sales
+1-317-581-3793
international@pearsontechgroup.com

Associate Publisher
Greg Wiegand

Acquisitions Editor
Michelle Newcomb

Development Editor
Kate Shoup Welsh

Managing Editor
Charlotte Clapp

Project Editor
Tricia Liebig

Production Editor
Benjamin Berg

Indexer
Mandie Frank

Proofreader
Linda Seifert

Technical Editor
Bill Bruns

Team Coordinator
Sharry Lee Gregory
Cari Skaggs

Interior Designers
Gary Adair
Anne Jones

Cover Designer
Anne Jones

Page Layout
Eric S. Miller

Graphics
Tammy Graham

About the Author

Heidi Steele is a freelance writer and software trainer. She specializes in demystifying computer concepts and making programs such as Word accessible to home users and professionals alike. Heidi Steele is the author of numerous other computer books, including *Easy Word 2000* and *Sams Teach Yourself Word 2000 in 24 Hours*. She lives in Port Orchard, Washington.

Dedication

This book is dedicated to my mother, Candace Steele, who is one of the most thoughtful people I'll ever know.

Acknowledgments

My acquisitions editor Michelle Newcomb and development editor Kate Shoup Welsh were both wonderful to work with—engaged, cheerful, and fully cognizant of the challenges of writing and caring for a toddler at the same time. Thanks also to my project editor Tricia Liebig, my technical editor Bill Bruns, and my copy editor Ben Berg for their excellent advice and assistance. On the home front, my partner Doug Urner contributed photographs and sample documents, while keeping me going with his usual warmth, support, and chocolates doled out at steady intervals. Chris Smith graciously allowed me to use his gardening articles as examples in this book, and Deborah Craig once again permitted me to use her paper on Imogen Cunningham. Finally, Chung Yen Shih Chen spent many an hour playing with my son Gaelan and teaching him Chinese while I deepened my relationship with the keyboard in the upstairs office.

We Want to Hear from You!

As the reader of this book, *you* are our most important critic and commentator. We value your opinion and want to know what we're doing right, what we could do better, what areas you'd like to see us publish in, and any other words of wisdom you're willing to pass our way.

As an associate publisher for Que, I welcome your comments. You can email or write me directly to let me know what you did or didn't like about this book—as well as what we can do to make our books better.

Please note that I cannot help you with technical problems related to the *topic* of this book. We do have a User Services group, however, where I will forward specific technical questions related to the book.

When you write, please be sure to include this book's title and author as well as your name, email address, and phone number. I will carefully review your comments and share them with the author and editors who worked on the book.

Email: feedback@quepublishing.com

Mail: Greg Wiegand
            Que Publishing
            800 E. 96th Street
            Indianapolis, IN 46240 USA

For more information about this book or another Que title, visit our Web site at www.quepublishing.com. Type the ISBN (excluding hyphens) or the title of a book in the Search field to find the page you're looking for.

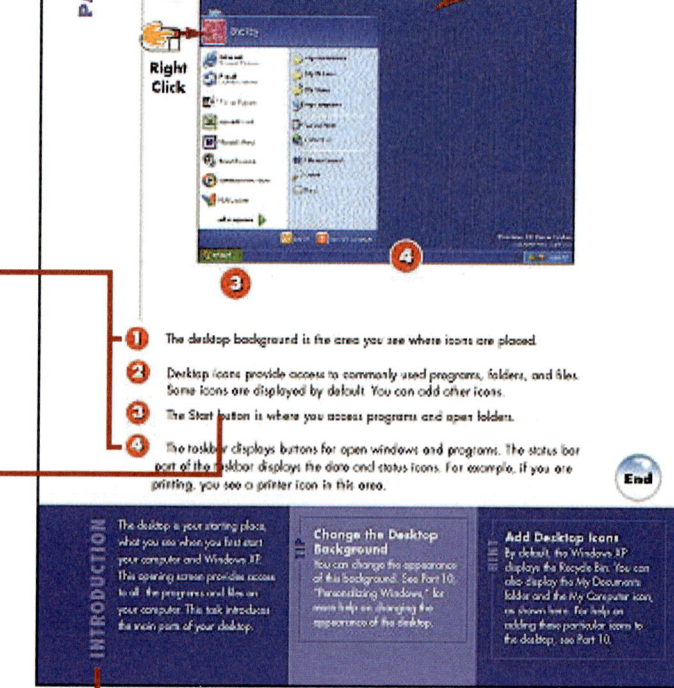

1 Each step is fully illustrated to show you how it looks onscreen.

It's as Easy as 1-2-3
Each part of this book is made up of a series of short, instructional lessons, designed to help you understand basic information that you need to get the most out of your computer hardware and software.

2 Each task includes a series of quick, easy steps designed to guide you through the procedure.

3 Items that you select or click in menus, dialog boxes, tabs, and windows are shown in **bold**.

Introductions explain what you will learn in each task, and **Tips and Hints** give you a heads-up for any extra information you may need while working through the task.

drag

drop

How to Drag:
Point to the starting place or object. Hold down the mouse button (right or left per instructions), move the mouse to the new location, then release the button.

See next page:
If you see this symbol, it means the task you're working on continues on the next page.

End Task:
Task is complete.

Selection:
Highlights the area onscreen discussed in the step or task.

Click:
Click the left mouse button once.

Right-click:
Click the right mouse button once.

Click & Type:
Click once where indicated and begin typing to enter your text or data.

Double-click:
Click the left mouse button twice in rapid succession.

Pointer Arrow:
Highlights an item on the screen you need to point to or focus on in the step or task.

Introduction

Learning to use Word doesn't have to be an agonizing, drawn-out process. *Easy Microsoft Office Word 2003* distills the key skills for you and presents them in colorful, visual steps. This book assumes that you view Word as a tool for getting your work done—no more, no less. You don't see learning a software program as an end in itself. Consequently, this book won't lead you into every nook and cranny of the program. You won't learn five ways of doing the same thing. You will, however, learn the fastest, most straightforward techniques, and you will certainly learn the shortcuts that are truly helpful.

Easy Microsoft Office Word 2003 is a book for beginners. It doesn't assume that you have ever used a word-processing program such as Word before or that you are familiar with Windows. You can use this book regardless of whether you're using Windows 98, Windows Me, or Windows XP.

The foundation for *Easy Microsoft Office Word 2003* is many years "on the front lines" teaching Word classes to beginners. The explanations in this book have been refined in the classroom on thousands of people like you, who want to get up and running in Word without making it a lifetime project. *Easy Microsoft Office Word 2003* does not merely provide stock explanations of how the program is supposed to work, but rather explains how it actually behaves from your viewpoint. If a particular nuance of Word behavior is confusing to most people in the classroom, it's explained here as well, on the assumption that it might be perplexing to you too.

Easy Microsoft Office Word 2003 is intended to be a both a tutorial and a reference. Feel free to flip to the exact task that you need to learn about at the moment. Of course, if you have the time, you can certainly work through the tasks sequentially, but it's not necessary to do so. You don't have to take time out from your day for "study sessions," but can instead apply the instructions in this book to your own documents, dipping into the various tasks as needed.

Word is an intuitive, powerful program, and learning to use it can (and should) be fun. Enjoy!

Acquainting Yourself with Word

Learning a new program is a bit like driving into a new town. You can guess where to find some things right away, but others you may have to putter around a while to locate. In this part, you get help with this process by taking a tour of the Word environment. You'll get a sense of where the various tools are and how to use them. After you know the general contours of the program, you'll be all set to delve into the specific skills required to create documents.

The Word Window

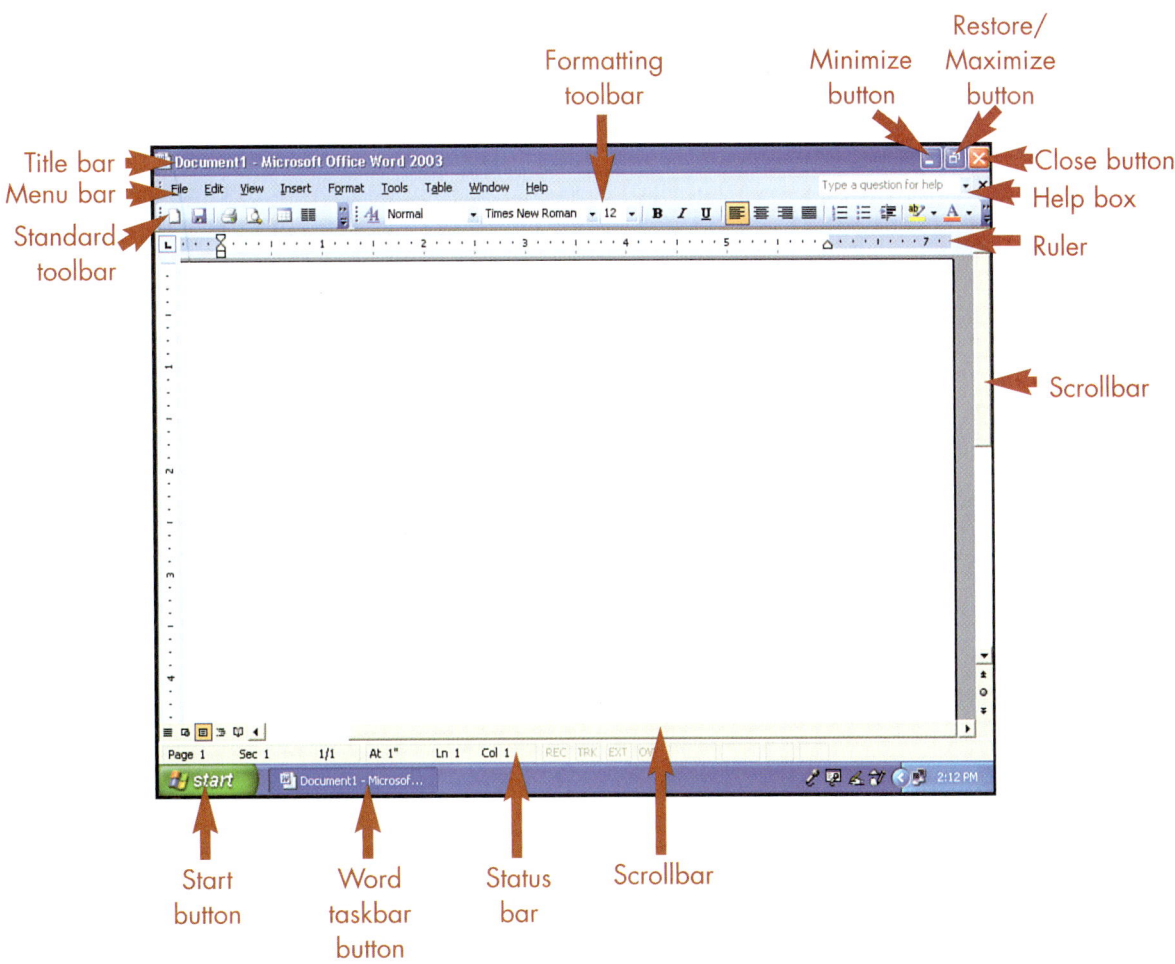

Formatting toolbar

Minimize button

Restore/ Maximize button

Title bar

Menu bar

Standard toolbar

Close button

Help box

Ruler

Scrollbar

Start button

Word taskbar button

Status bar

Scrollbar

Starting Word

Start

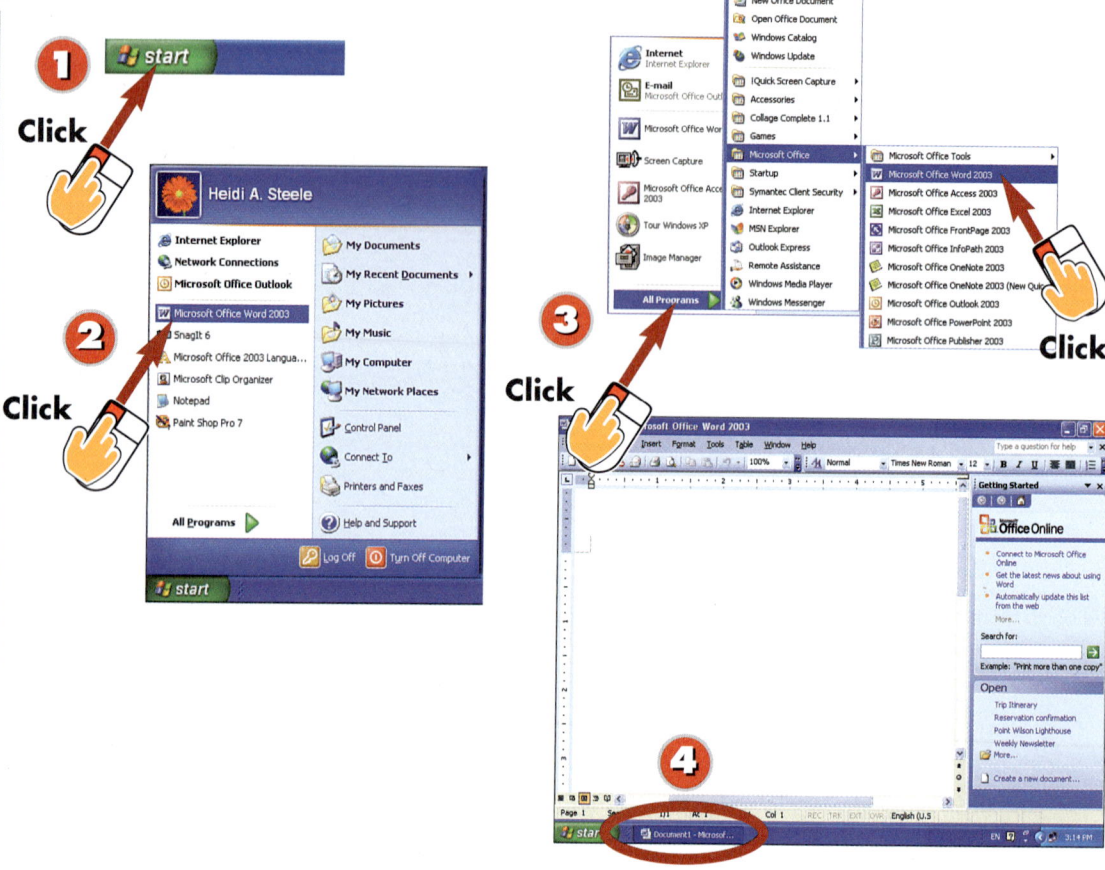

Click

Click

Click

Click

① Click the **Start** button.

② If you see **Microsoft Office Word** in the main Start menu, click it.

③ If you don't see Microsoft Word in the main Start menu, point to **All Programs**, **Microsoft Office**, and then **Microsoft Office Word 2003**.

④ The Word window opens and a Word button appears on the taskbar.

When you want to use Word to create or revise a document, you must ask Windows to start it for you. Once Word has been started, you can tell it is open, even if it's hidden behind other windows, because a button bearing the Word icon appears on the taskbar at the bottom of your screen. An additional taskbar button appears for each Word document that you start or open.

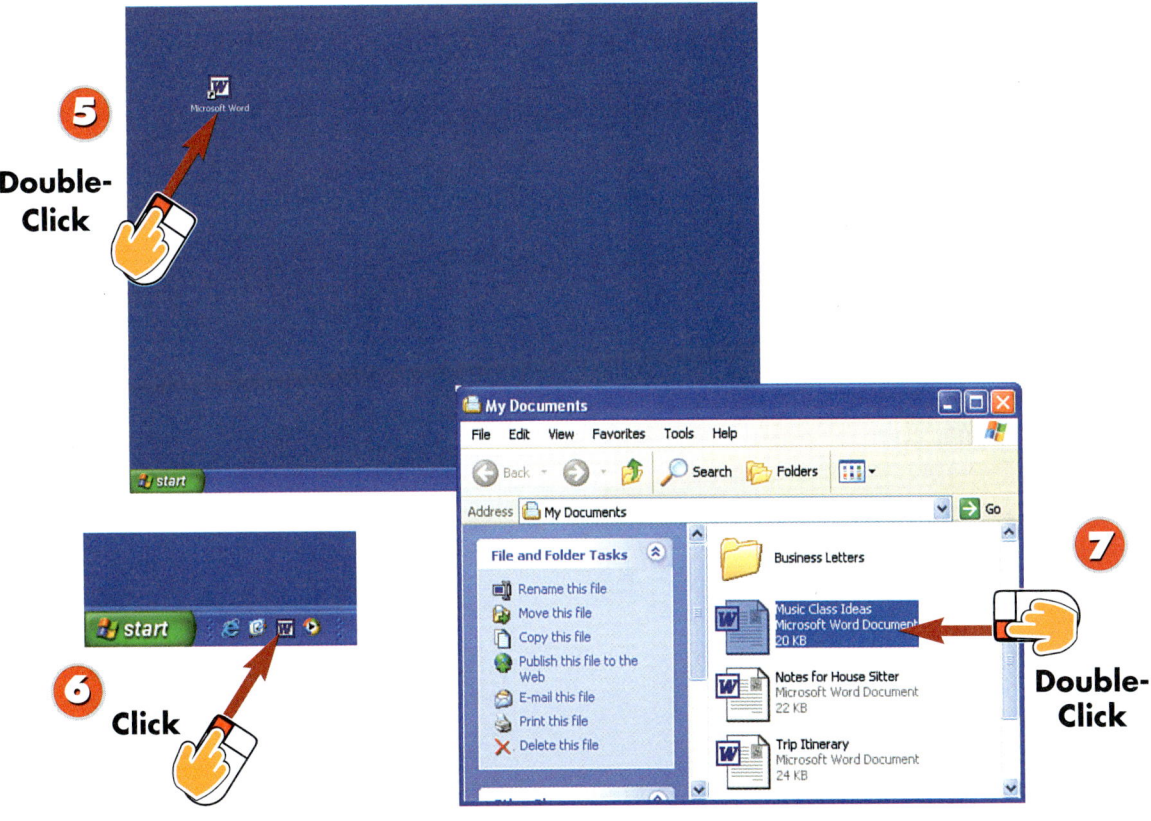

⑤ Depending on your setup, you may have a shortcut icon for Word on your Windows desktop. If you do, you can double-click it to start the program.

⑥ You may see a button with the Word icon on the left side of your taskbar. Clicking this button also starts Word.

⑦ You can also double-click any Word document icon, either on your Windows desktop or in a folder, to start Word and open the document.

End

Double-Clicking Versus Single-Clicking

By default, you must double-click an icon to open the program or document that corresponds with it (see steps 5 and 7). Depending on your setup, however, only a single-click may be required. If so, your mouse pointer will look like a pointing hand instead of a white arrow when you rest it over an icon.

Working with the Word Window

Start

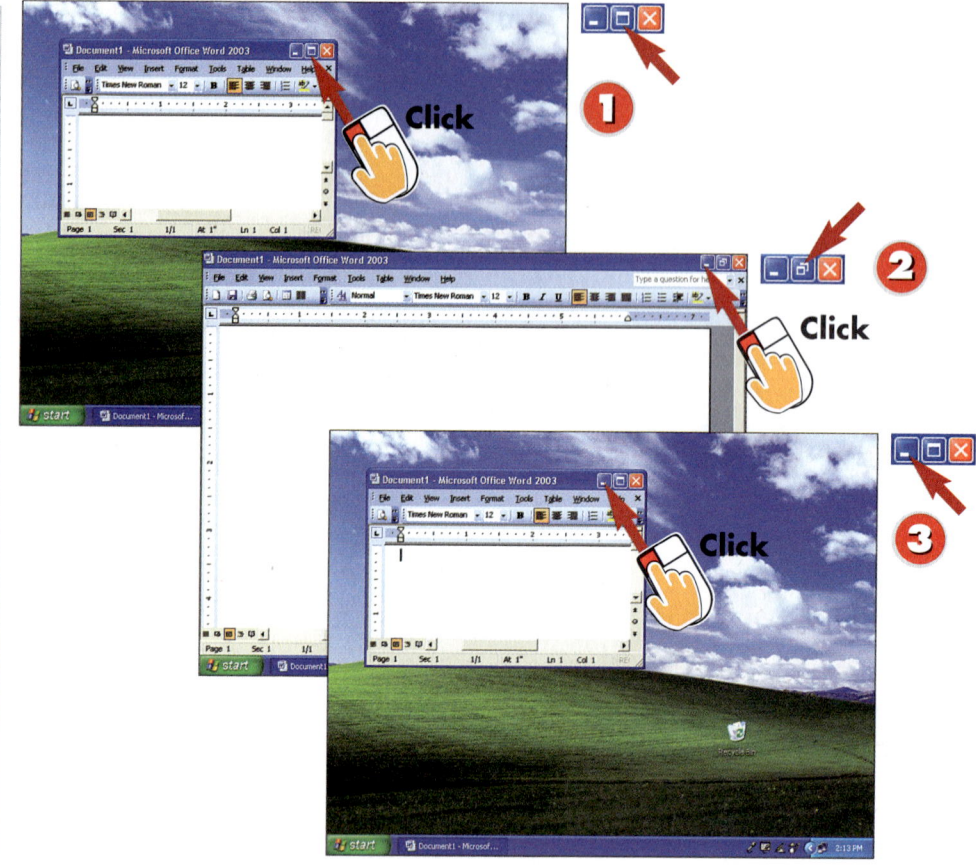

1 Click the Word window's **Maximize** button to make the window fill the screen.

2 When the window is maximized, the Maximize button is replaced by a **Restore** button. Click it to restore the window to its previous size.

3 Click the **Minimize** button to temporarily hide the window.

You can change the appearance of the Word window in a variety of ways. For example, you can make it fill up the screen to give you more room to work, or make it disappear temporarily so that you can see what's behind it on the Windows desktop. You can also move the Word window around on your desktop, or adjust its size in other ways.

TIP

Closing a Window
The Minimize, Restore/ Maximize, and Close buttons that you use in this task control the entire Word window. The Close button directly beneath them closes the document only, leaving the Word window open.

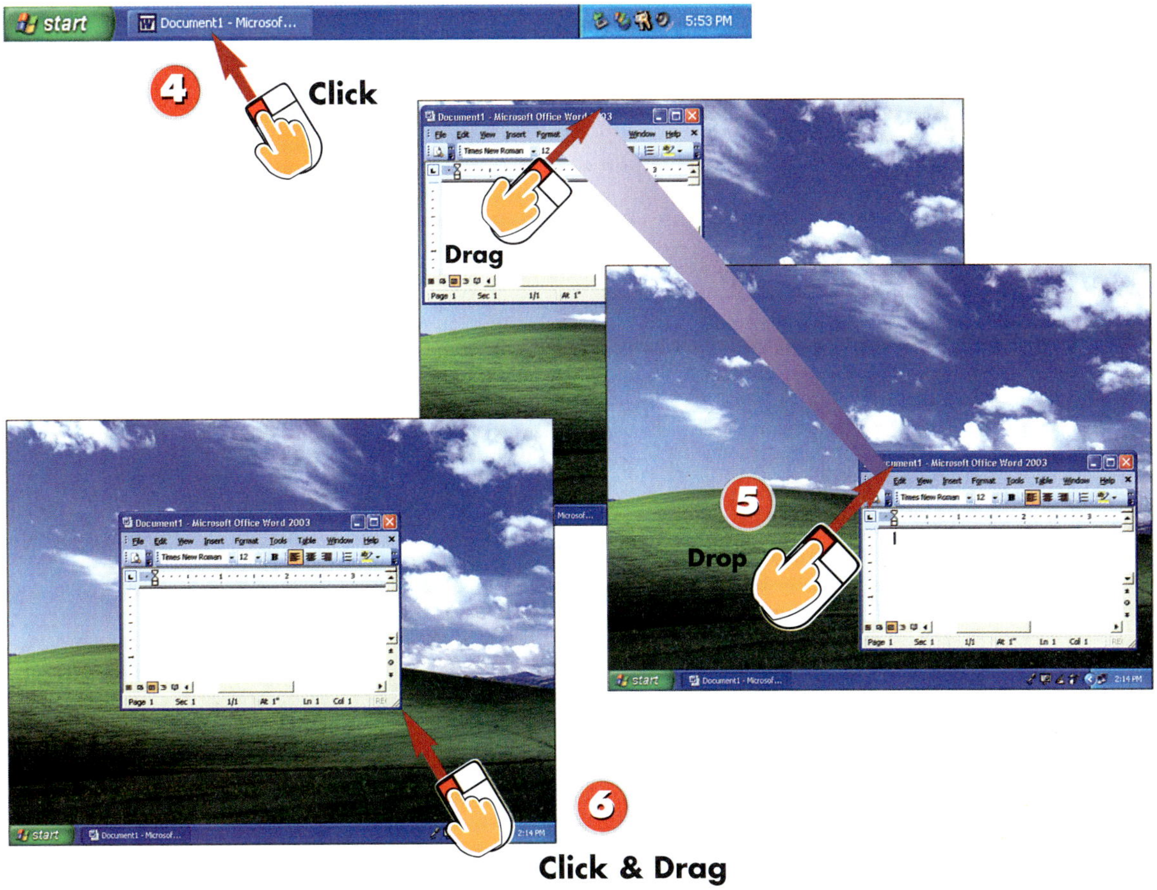

Click

Drag

Drop

Click & Drag

4 Click the window's taskbar button to bring the window back.

5 To move the window, point to its title bar, press and hold down the left mouse button, drag the window to a different location onscreen, and release the mouse button.

6 To resize the Word window, first point to a corner of the window. The mouse pointer becomes a diagonal black arrow. Drag in the desired direction to enlarge or shrink the window.

End

Using Pull-Down Menus

Start

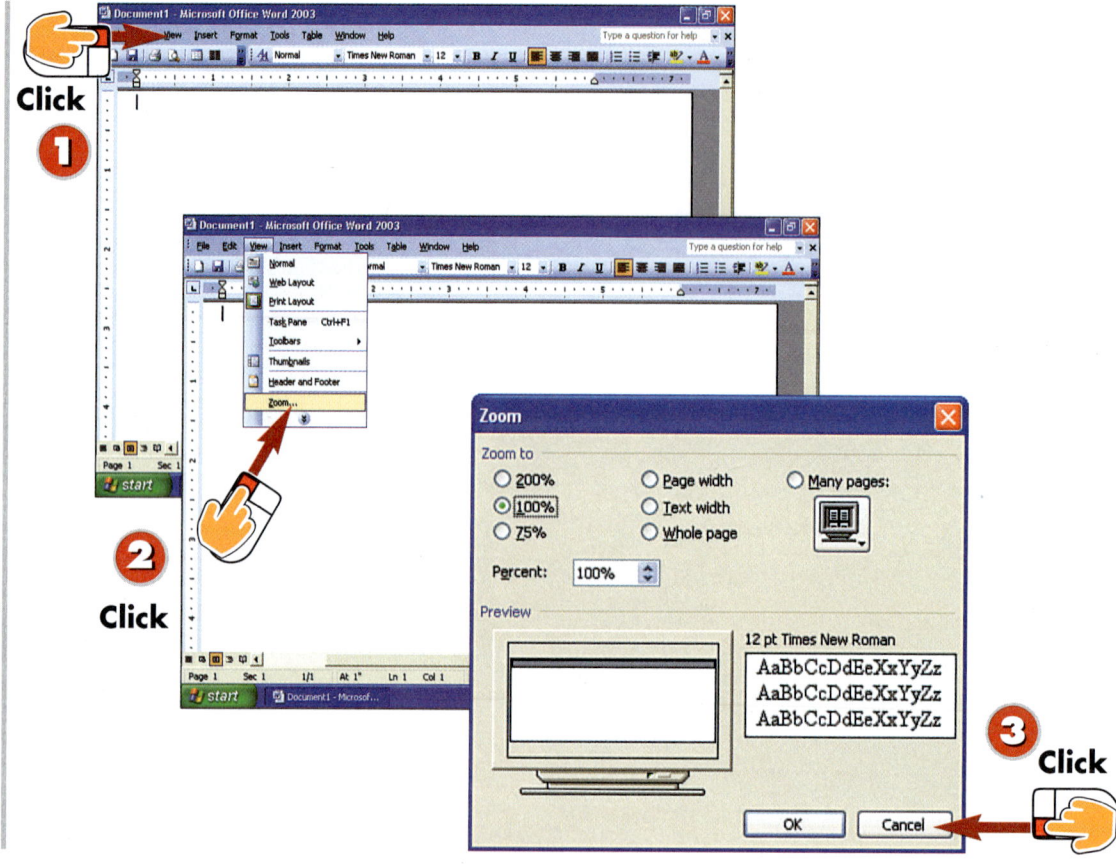

Click ❶

Click ❷

Click ❸

❶ Click the **View** menu to pull it down.

❷ Look at the **Zoom** command. It is followed by three dots (…) to indicate that by selecting it, you will open a dialog box. Click the command.

❸ The Zoom dialog box opens. Click the **Cancel** button to close it.

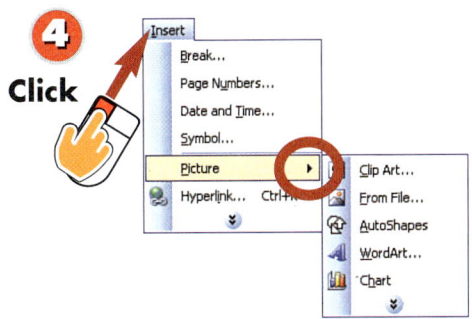

Click

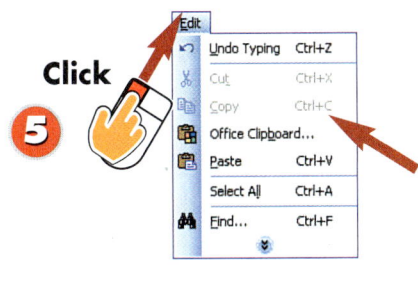

Click

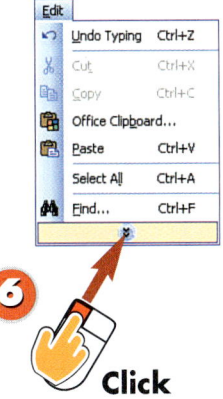

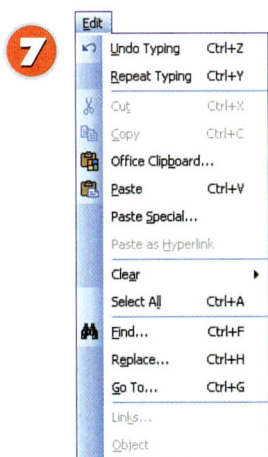

Click

4. Click the **Insert** menu, and then point to **Picture**. The small triangle to the right of the Picture command indicates that a submenu will appear. Click outside the Insert menu to close it.

5. Click the **Edit** menu. The grayed-out commands are not currently available.

6. Point to the **Expand** arrow at the bottom of the Edit menu. (Alternatively, you can rest your mouse pointer over the menu name for a few seconds.)

7. The menu expands to show you all of its commands. Click outside the menu to close it.

End

Customizing Menus

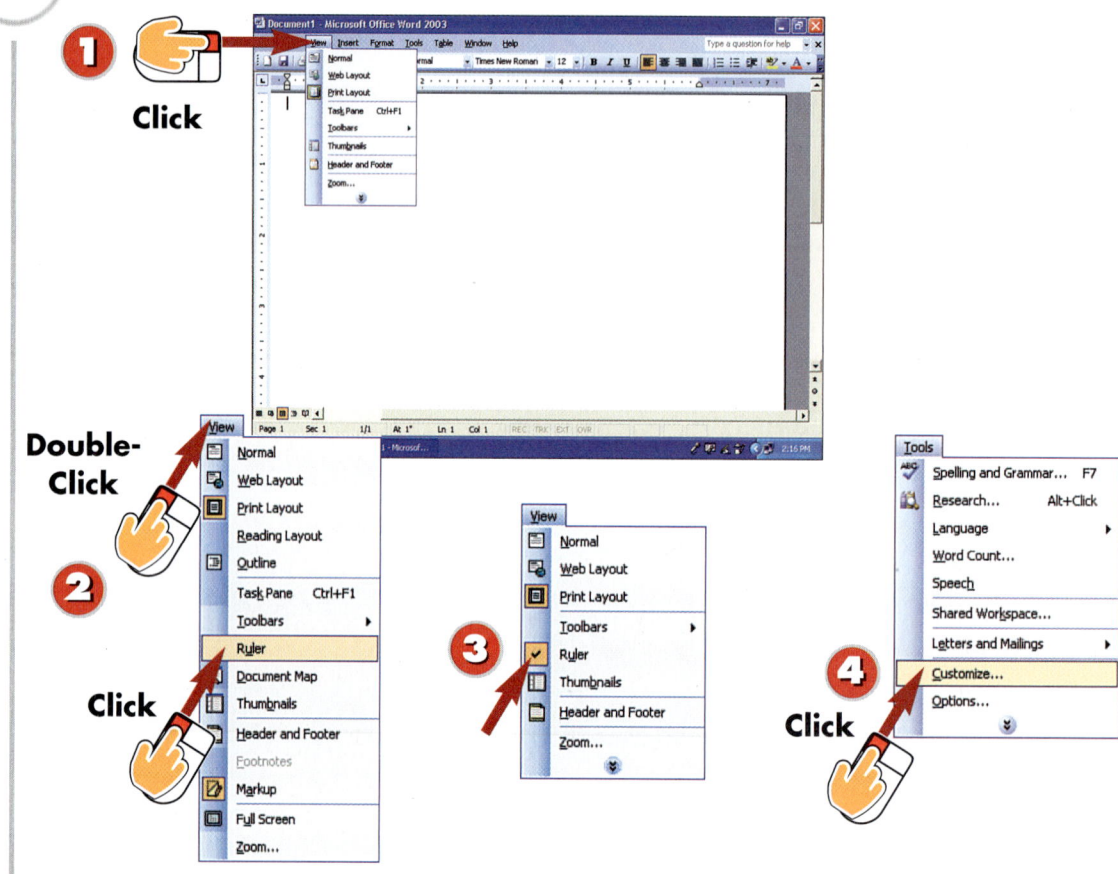

Click the **View** menu. The short menu appears by default. Click outside of the menu to close it.

Double-click the **View** menu to display the full menu. Click the **Ruler** command, which wasn't visible in the short menu.

Click the **View** menu again. The Ruler command is now included in the short menu because you just used it.

To turn off personal menus, open the **Tools** menu and choose **Customize**.

INTRODUCTION

Word assumes that you want to use its personal menus feature. When this feature is enabled, clicking a menu name displays a short menu that contains only the commands you use frequently. Word gives you three ways to expand the menu to display all of its commands. (You learned two ways in the previous task, and you'll learn the third here.) In this task, you practice using personal menus, and you learn how to turn off the feature if you'd rather see the full menus by default.

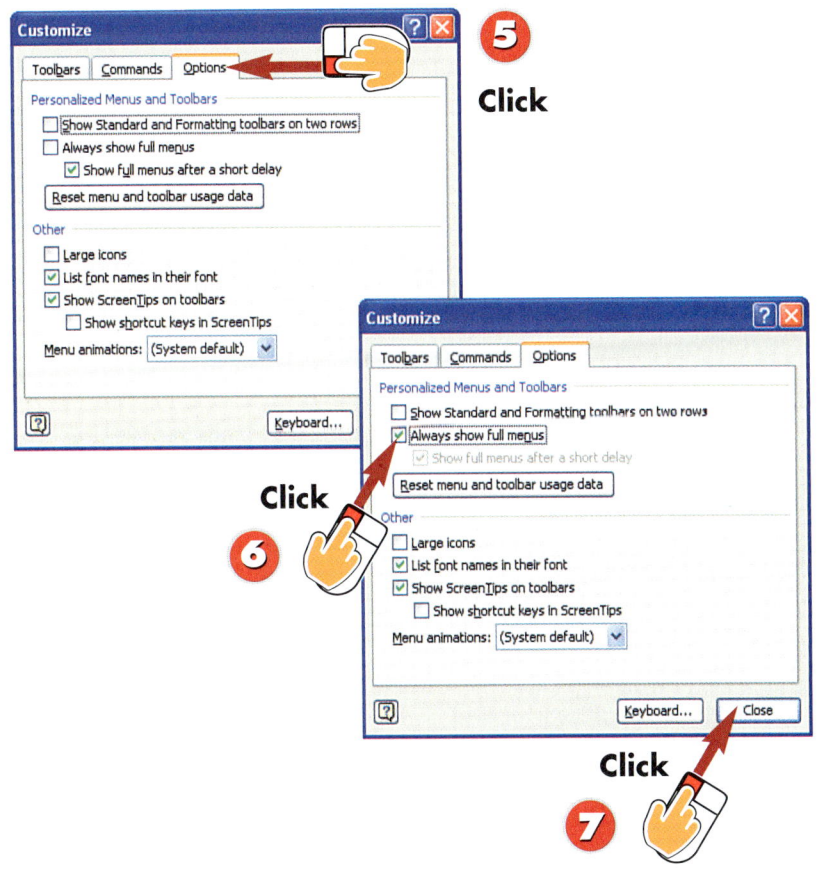

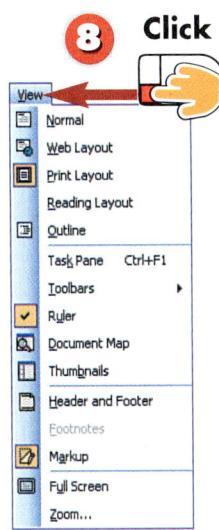

Click 5

Click 8

Click 6

Click 7

5   Click the **Options** tab.

6   Click the **Always show full menus** check box to put a check mark in it.

7   Click the **Close** button.

8   Open the **View** menu a final time. Now the full menu appears by default.

End

Managing Personal Menus
The remaining tasks in this book assume that Word's personal menus feature is turned off. To turn it back on, repeat steps 4 through 7, but clear the **Always show full menus** check box.

Right-Clicking to Display Menus

Start

1
Right Click

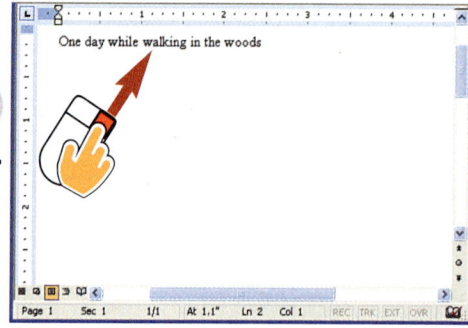

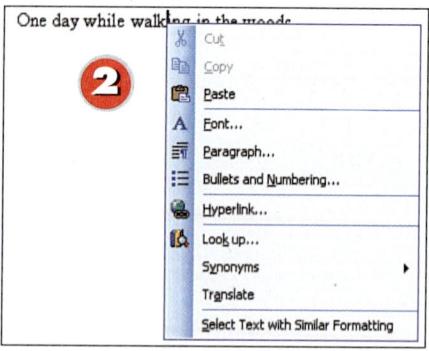
2

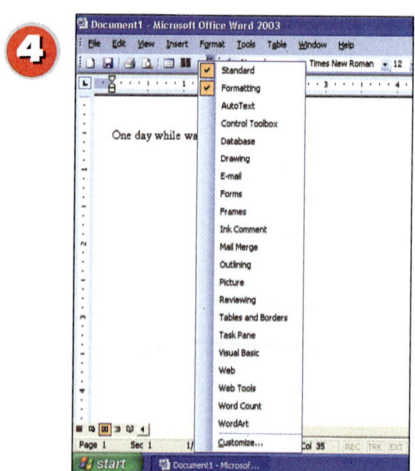
4

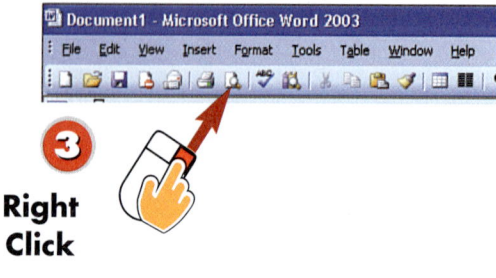
3
Right Click

1 Type a few words in your document, and then right-click anywhere on the text.

2 A context menu appears with commands for working with text. Click outside the menu to close it.

3 Right-click any one of the toolbars in the Word window.

4 This time, the context menu lists your available toolbars. Click outside the menu to close it.

End

INTRODUCTION

In addition to using the pull-down menus at the top of the Word window, you can also use context menus to issue commands. These are small menus that you display by clicking with the right-hand mouse button. The commands in a context menu vary depending on where you right-click. For example, if you right-click text, you get commands for editing and formatting text. If you right-click a toolbar, you get a list of toolbars that you can display or hide (see "Working with Toolbars" later in this part for more information about toolbars). To choose a command in a context menu, simply left-click it.

TIP

Using Word's Main Menus
If you forget to use shortcut menus, don't worry about it. All of the commands in these menus are also available in the pull-down menu system.

Hiding the Ruler

Start

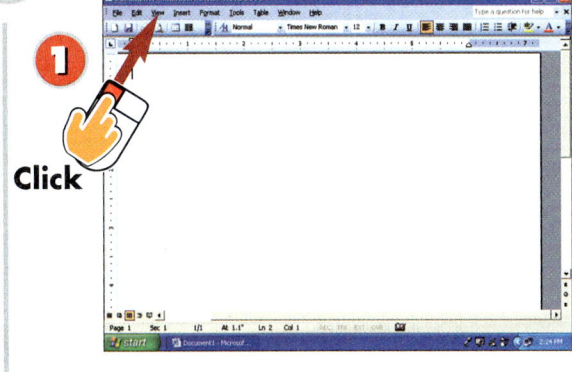

Click

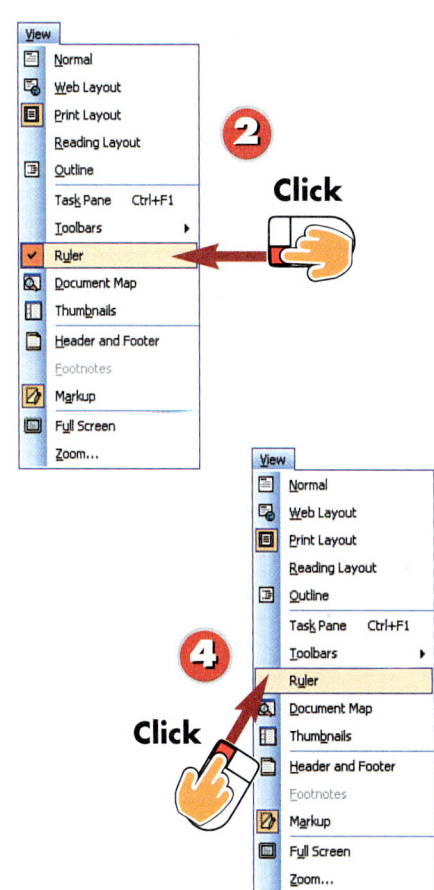

Click

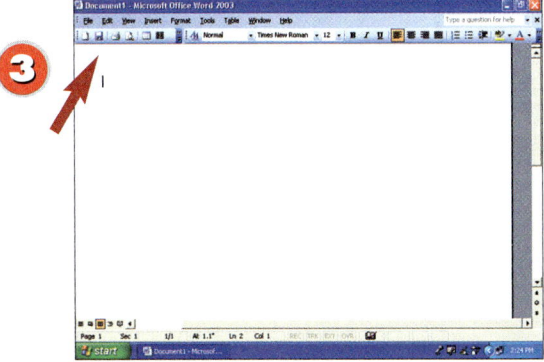

Click

1 Click **View** in the menu bar.

2 The check mark next to the Ruler command tells you that the rulers are currently displayed. Click the **Ruler** command.

3 The rulers are now hidden.

4 Open the **View** menu and choose **Ruler** again to bring the rulers back.

End

INTRODUCTION

By default, a horizontal ruler appears underneath the toolbars in the Word window, and a vertical ruler appears on the left edge of any documents open in that window. You can use these rulers to quickly adjust tabs, indents, and margins (you'll learn about these formatting techniques in Parts 6 and 7). You might want to hide them, however, so that you can see more of your document. You can easily display them again whenever you like.

Working with Dialog Boxes

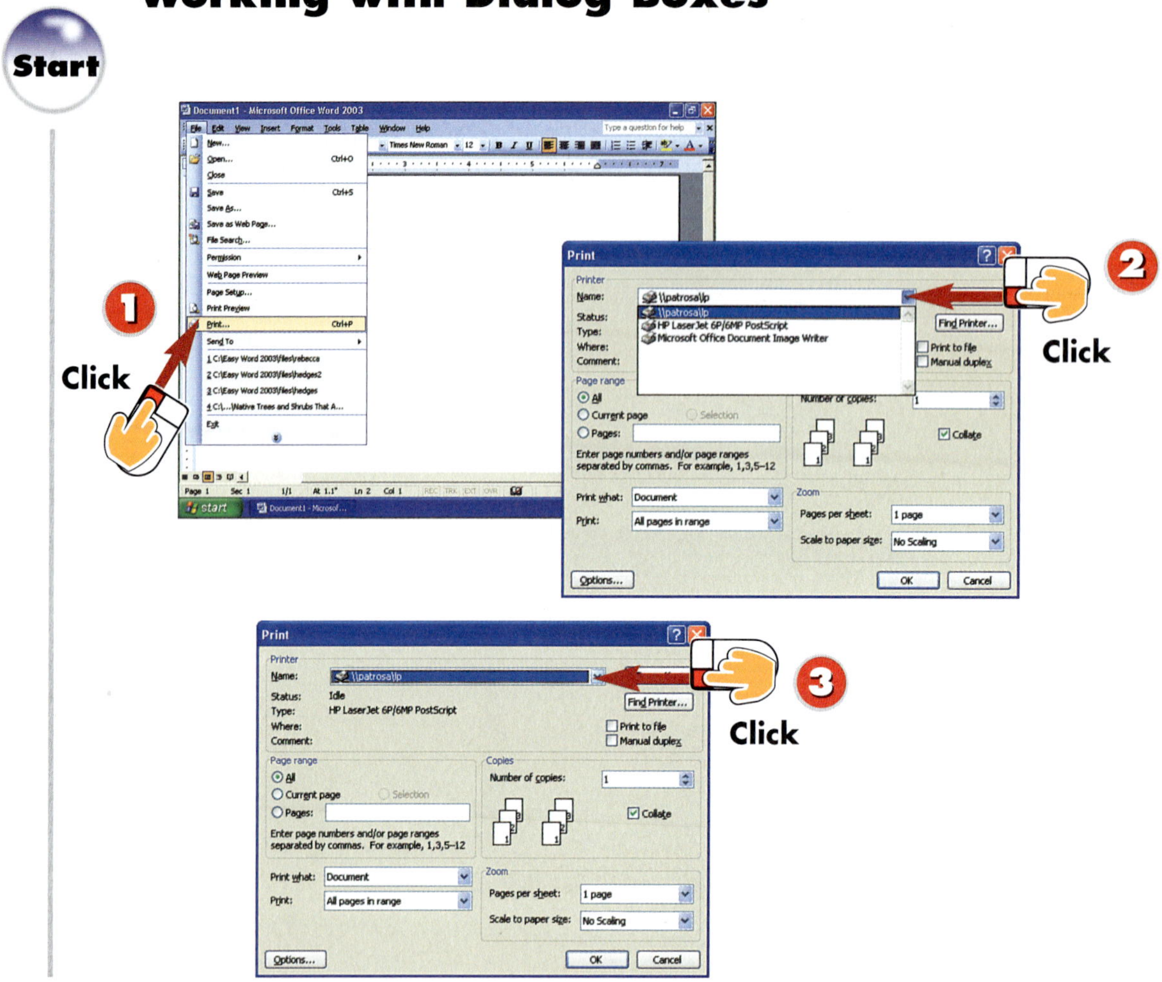

Start

Click

Click

Click

1 Open the **File** menu and choose **Print** to display the Print dialog box.

2 Click the **down arrow** to the right of the **Name** box to display a drop-down list of installed printers.

3 Click the **down arrow** again to close the list without making a selection.

INTRODUCTION

All of Word's menu commands that are followed by an ellipses (...) lead to a dialog box, most of which give you options for specifying exactly what you want to do before Word actually performs the command. Once you've made your selections in a dialog box, you click the OK button to tell Word to carry out the command. If you decide not to go ahead with a command, you can back out of the dialog box by clicking the Cancel button. Here you take a quick look at the elements commonly found in dialog boxes, using the Print dialog box as an example.

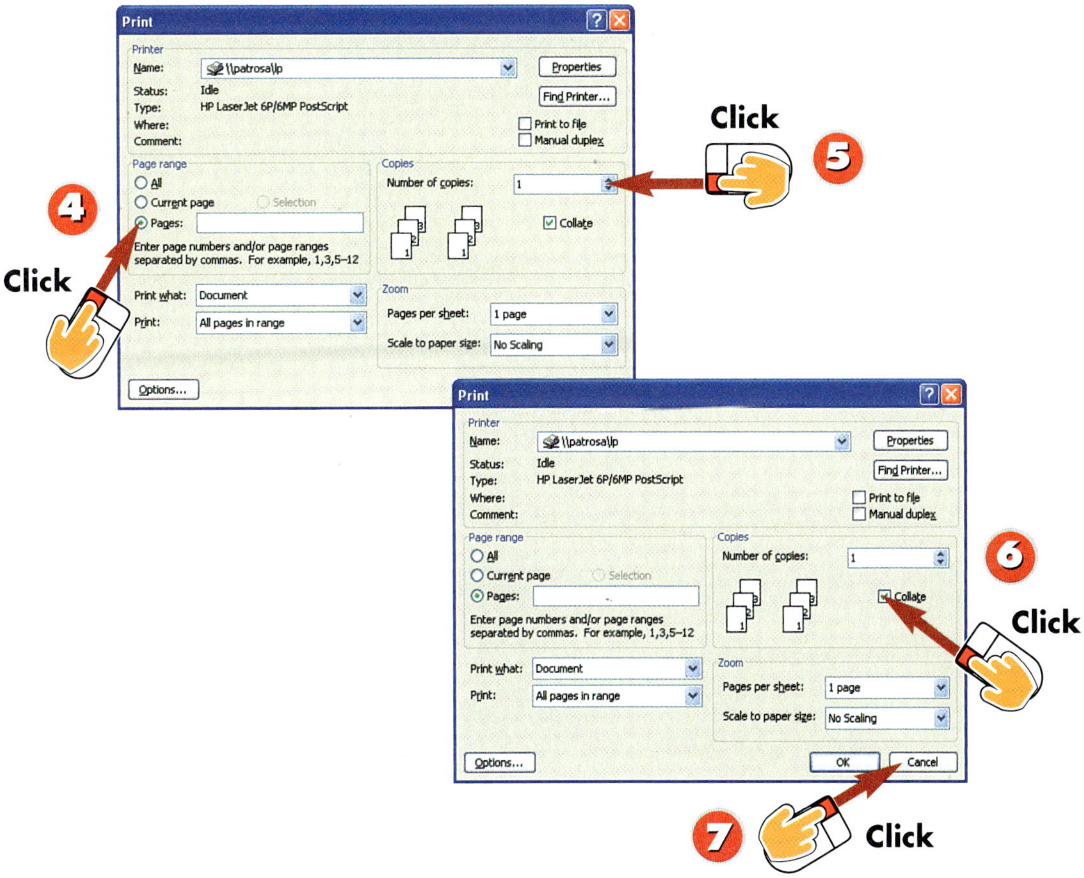

Click ⑤

Click ④

⑥ **Click**

⑦ **Click**

④ Click the **Pages** option button to select it. The text box to its right lets you type the page numbers you want to print.

⑤ Click the up or down spinner arrows to the right of the **Number of copies** box to increase or decrease the number of copies printed.

⑥ Click the **Collate** check box twice to clear the check box and then mark it again.

⑦ Click the **Cancel** button to close the Print dialog box without printing your document.

End

Selecting Options

TIP

If you see a group of option buttons (buttons that are circular in shape) in a dialog box, you can mark only one of them. In contrast, if you see a group of check boxes (buttons that are square in shape), you can mark as many of them as you like.

Working with Toolbars

Start

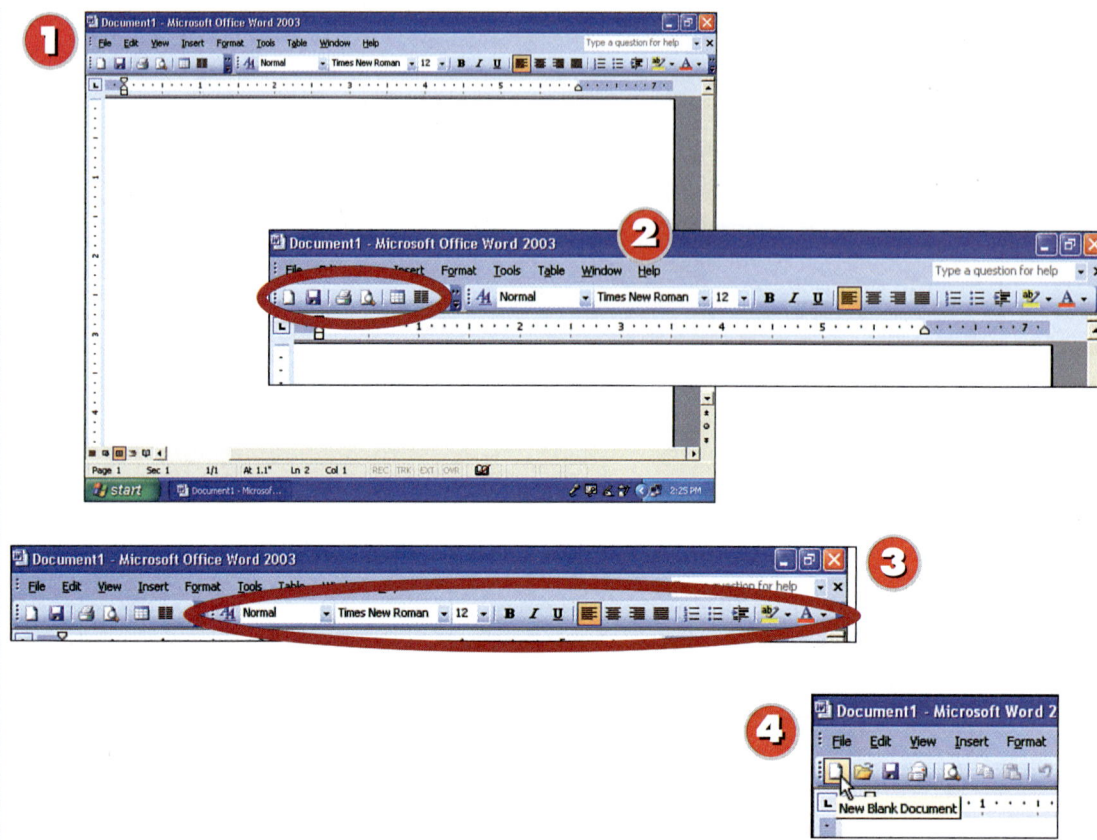

1. By default, the Standard and Formatting toolbars share the same row. The Standard toolbar is on the left and the Formatting toolbar is on the right.

2. The Standard toolbar contains buttons for creating, saving, and opening documents, as well as for performing common editing tasks.

3. The Formatting toolbar contains buttons for formatting your text.

4. Point to the leftmost toolbar button in the Standard toolbar. A ScreenTip appears, displaying the name of the button. All toolbar buttons have ScreenTips.

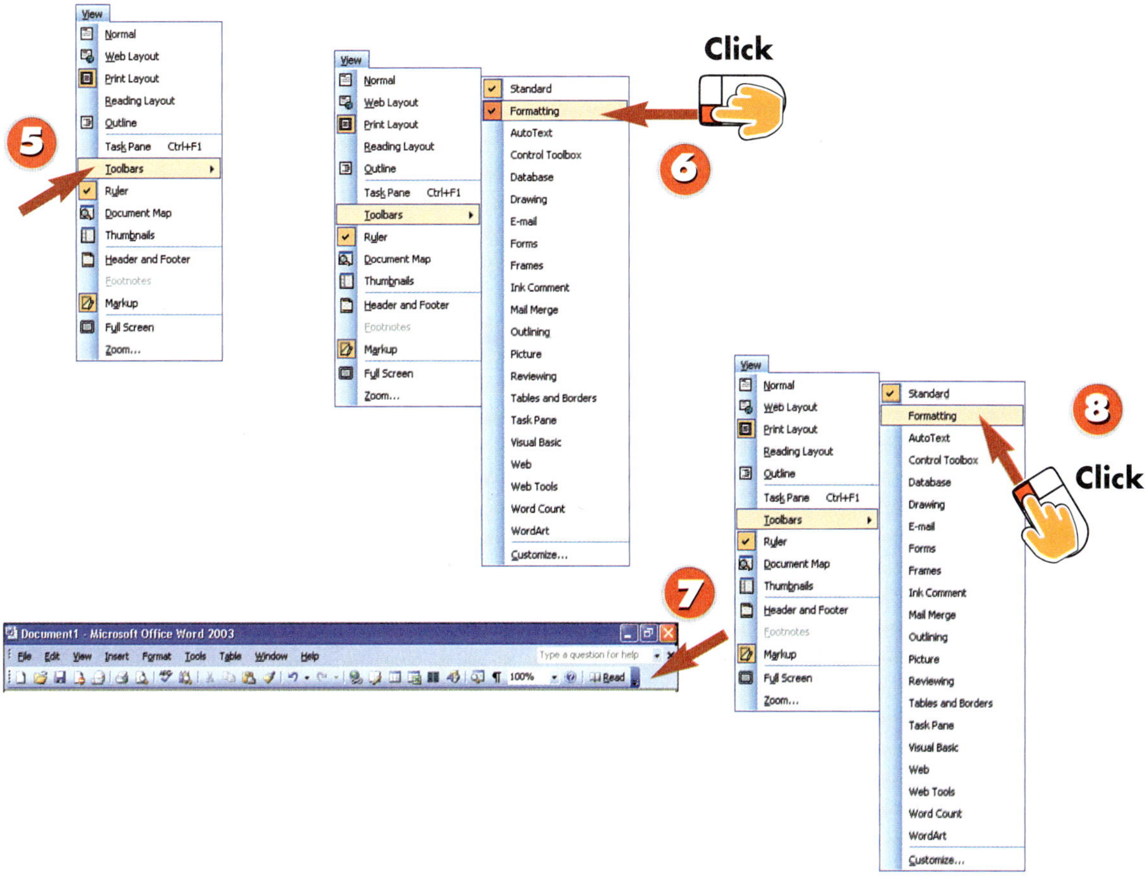

Click

Click

Document1 - Microsoft Office Word 2003

File Edit View Insert Format Tools Table Window Help

Type a question for help

100%   Read

5 Open the **View** menu and choose **Toolbars**.

6 Notice that the Standard and Formatting toolbars have check marks next to them. Click **Formatting**.

7 The Formatting toolbar is now hidden, and all the buttons in the Standard toolbar are displayed now that there is room for them.

8 Open the **View** menu and choose **Toolbars**, and click **Formatting** again to bring the toolbar back.

End

Viewing Additional Buttons

When the Standard and Formatting toolbars share the same row, there isn't room to display all of their buttons at the same time. See the next task to learn how to bring hidden buttons into view.

TIP

Personalizing Word Toolbars

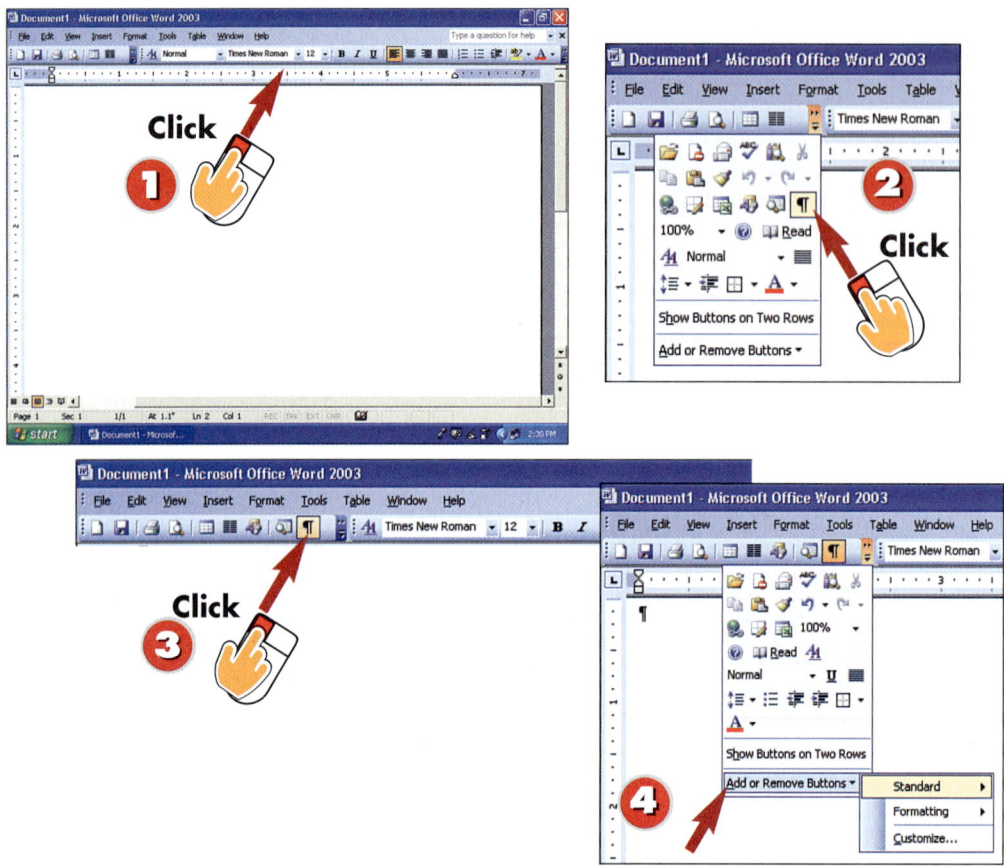

1 Click the **Toolbar Options** arrow at the right end of the Standard toolbar.

2 The Toolbar Options list contains the buttons that don't fit on the visible part of the toolbar. Click the **Show/Hide** button.

3 The **Show/Hide** button is now visible, and the feature is turned on; click the button again to turn the feature off. (See "Seeing Paragraph, Tab, and Space Marks" in Part 3.)

4 To add a new button to the Standard toolbar, click the **Toolbar Options** arrow, and then point to **Add or Remove Buttons**. A submenu appears.

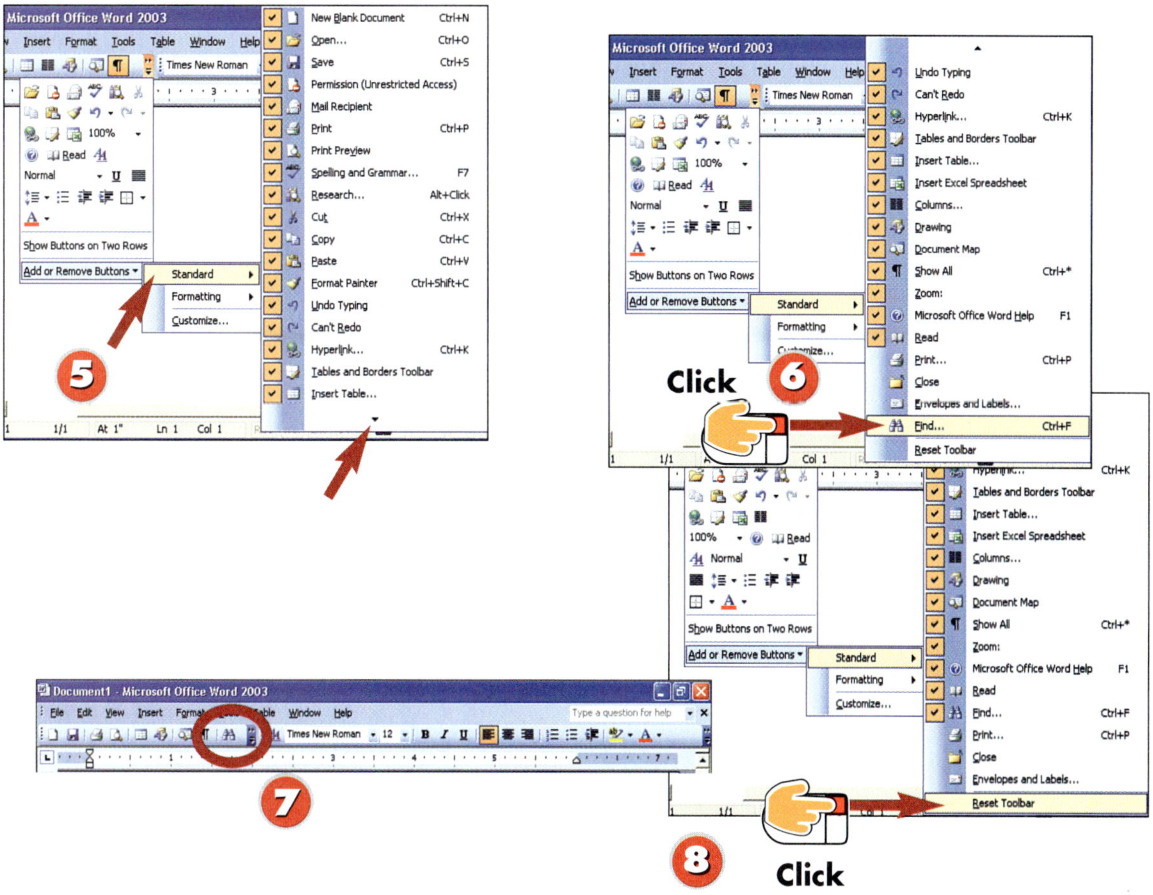

Click

Click

5 Point to **Standard** to display all the buttons you can add to the Standard toolbar. If necessary, click the **down arrow** to bring them all into view.

6 Buttons that don't have check marks are not currently included in the toolbar. Click the **Find** button to add it to the toolbar, and then click outside the menu.

7 The Find button is now on the Standard toolbar. (You'll learn about this feature in "Searching for Text" in Part 8.)

8 To reset the Standard toolbar, click the **Toolbar Options** arrow, point to **Add or Remove Buttons**, point to **Standard**, and then click **Reset Toolbar**.

End

Resetting Your Usage Information

TIP

Word tracks your usage of toolbars and personal menus and displays or hides buttons and commands accordingly. To delete this record and restore the default set of visible buttons and commands, choose **Tools**, **Customize**, click the **Options** tab, click the **Reset menu and toolbar usage data** button, click **Yes**, and click **Close**.

Moving Buttons

TIP

You can rearrange the order of the buttons on a toolbar. To move a button, point to it and hold down your **Alt** key as you drag it to the desired position. Then release the **Alt** key and your mouse button at the same time.

Moving Your Toolbars Around

Start

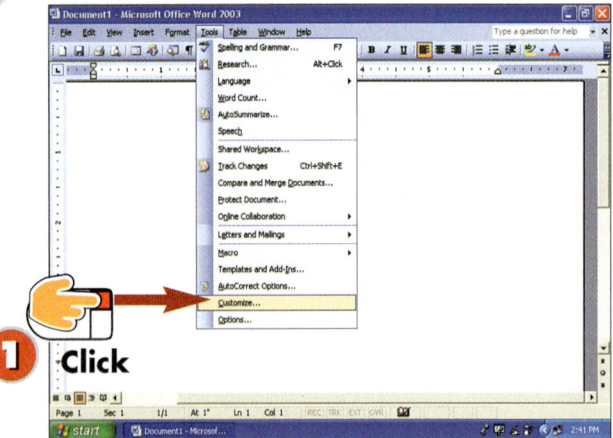

1 Click

2 Click

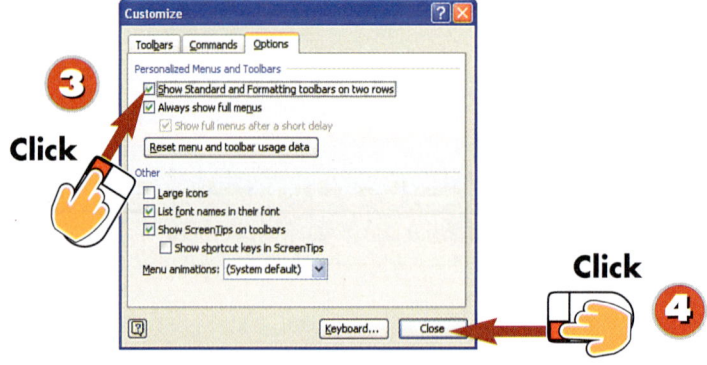

3 Click

4 Click

---

1 Open the **Tools** menu and choose **Customize**.

2 In the Customize dialog box, click the **Options** tab if it is not already in front.

3 Click the **Show Standard and Formatting toolbars on two rows** check box to mark it.

4 Click the **Close** button.

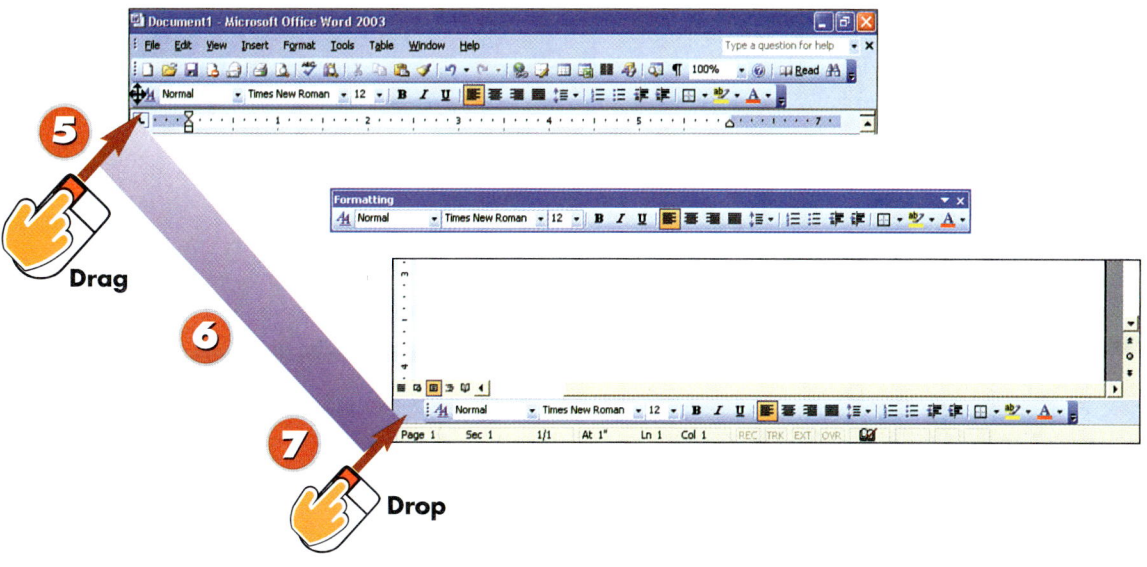

Drag

Drop

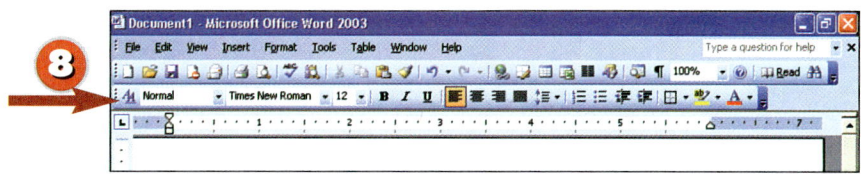

5 The Formatting toolbar appears underneath the Standard toolbar. To move it, point to the vertical line at the left end of the toolbar. The mouse pointer becomes a four-headed arrow.

6 Drag the toolbar into the text area of the window, and release your mouse button. The toolbar is now floating over the window.

7 Point to the title bar of the floating toolbar, and drag down. When the toolbar flattens out along the bottom edge of the window, release the mouse button to dock the toolbar.

8 Drag the Formatting toolbar back up to just beneath the Standard toolbar.

End

TIP

Resizing a Floating Toolbar

When a toolbar is floating, you can resize it to any rectangular shape you like by dragging one of its borders.

TIP

Separating the Standard and Formatting Toolbars

Another way to place the Standard and Formatting toolbars on separate rows is to click the **Toolbar Options** button at the right edge of either toolbar (see the previous task), and then click **Show Buttons on Two Rows**. To make the toolbars share a row again, click a toolbar's **Toolbar Options** button and choose **Show Buttons on One Row**.

Using Task Panes

Start

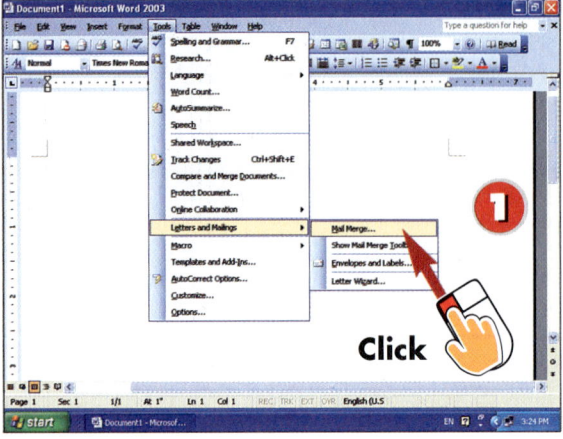

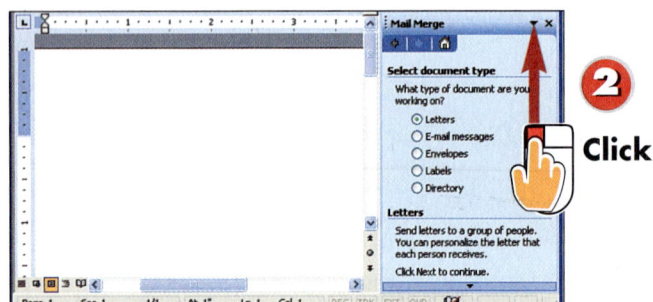

1. Open the **Tools** menu, choose **Letters and Mailings**, and select **Mail Merge**.

2. The Mail Merge task pane appears at the right edge of the Word window to walk you through the steps of producing a mass mailing. Click the **Other Task Panes** button.

3. A list of the other available task panes appears. Choose **Help**.

Click

④ The Word Help task pane appears. If you see a **down arrow** at the bottom of a task pane, you can point to it to move more of the contents into view.

⑤ Point to the **up arrow** at the top of the pane to scroll back to the top of a task pane.

⑥ Click the **Back** and **Forward** buttons to view recently used task panes. Click the **Home** button to display the Getting Started task pane.

⑦ When you are ready to close a task pane, click the **Close** (x) button in the upper-right corner of the pane.

End

TIP

Closing and Displaying Task Panes
You can also close a task pane by opening the **View** menu and choosing **Task Pane**. If no task pane is currently displayed, choose **View**, **Task Pane**. Word displays the task pane you used last.

TIP

Choosing Whether a Task Pane Appears on Startup
By default, the Getting Started task pane appears when you first start Word. It gives you a quick way to open a document, start a new document, or ask for help. If you'd rather not see it on startup, choose **Tools**, **Options** to display the Options dialog box. Click the **View** tab, clear the **Startup Task Pane** check box, and click **OK**.

Getting Help

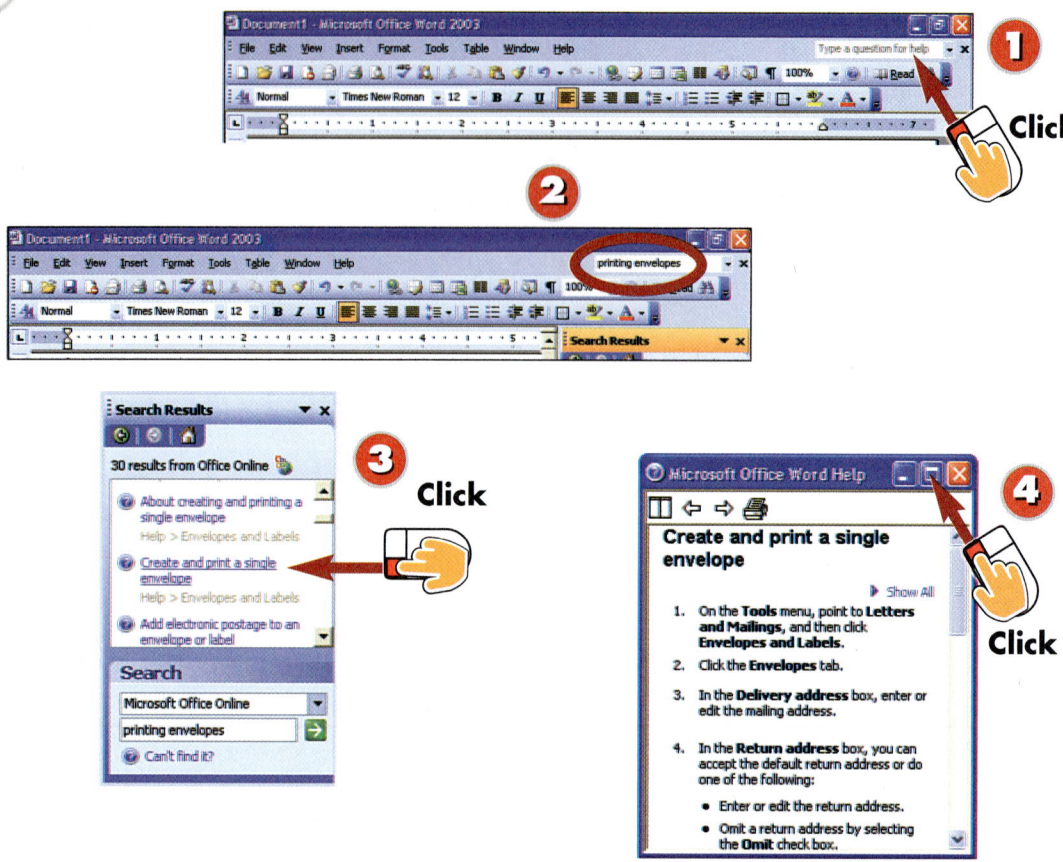

1. Click in the text box in the upper-right corner of the Word window that contains the placeholder text **Type a question for help**.

2. Type **printing envelopes** and press **Enter**.

3. The Search Results task pane appears as Word searches for information about printing envelopes. When the help topics appear, click **Create and print a single envelope**.

4. The Microsoft Office Word Help window opens. Click its **Maximize** button to expand the window.

INTRODUCTION

As you are using Word to do your work, you are bound to come up with questions about how to get certain things done. If you don't feel inclined to ask a co-worker or friend, you can always look up the answers yourself using Word's help system. If your computer is connected to the Internet, Word will access the help information at the Microsoft Office Web site. Otherwise, Word will display the help topics that are stored on your own computer. Either way, you have a fairly good chance of finding the answers you need.

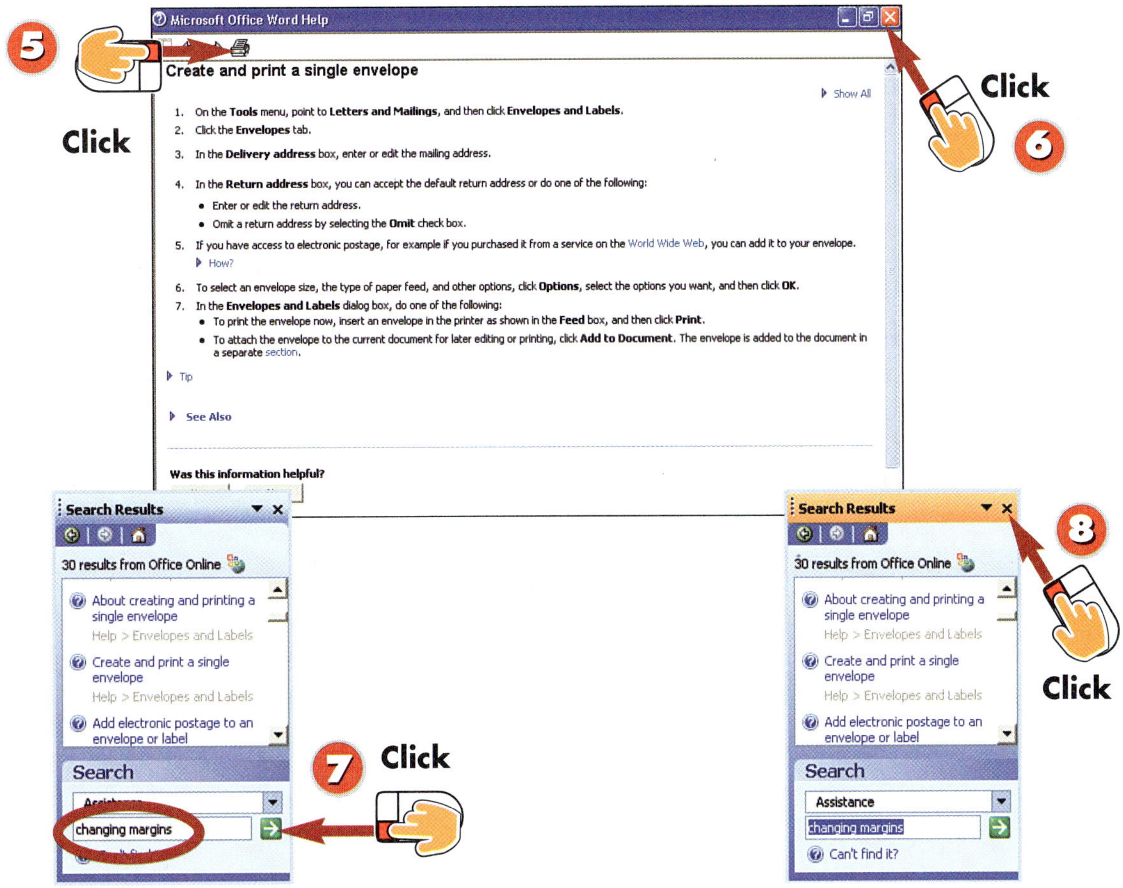

5 **Click**

Microsoft Office Word Help

Create and print a single envelope

▶ Show All

1. On the **Tools** menu, point to **Letters and Mailings**, and then click **Envelopes and Labels**.
2. Click the **Envelopes** tab.
3. In the **Delivery address** box, enter or edit the mailing address.
4. In the **Return address** box, you can accept the default return address or do one of the following:
   - Enter or edit the return address.
   - Omit a return address by selecting the **Omit** check box.
5. If you have access to electronic postage, for example if you purchased it from a service on the World Wide Web, you can add it to your envelope.
   ▶ How?
6. To select an envelope size, the type of paper feed, and other options, click **Options**, select the options you want, and then click **OK**.
7. In the **Envelopes and Labels** dialog box, do one of the following:
   - To print the envelope now, insert an envelope in the printer as shown in the **Feed** box, and then click **Print**.
   - To attach the envelope to the current document for later editing or printing, click **Add to Document**. The envelope is added to the document in a separate section.

▶ Tip

▶ See Also

Was this information helpful?

Click **6**

Search Results ▼ ✕

30 results from Office Online

⑦ About creating and printing a single envelope
Help > Envelopes and Labels

⑦ Create and print a single envelope
Help > Envelopes and Labels

⑦ Add electronic postage to an envelope or label

Search

Assistance

changing margins

7 **Click**

Search Results ▼ ✕ **8**

30 results from Office Online

⑦ About creating and printing a single envelope
Help > Envelopes and Labels

⑦ Create and print a single envelope
Help > Envelopes and Labels

⑦ Add electronic postage to an envelope or label

Click

Search

Assistance

changing margins

⑦ Can't find it?

5 If you want to print the topic, click the **Print** button at the top of the Microsoft Office Word Help window. When you see the Print dialog box, click the **Print** button.

6 Click the **Close** button in the Microsoft Office Word Help window.

7 If you like, you can type another topic to search for help about, and then click the **Start Searching** button.

8 When you are finished, close the Microsoft Word Help window if it's open, and then click the **Close** button in the Search Results task pane to close it.

 **End**

Navigating Help Topics
To move back and forth among the help topics you've displayed since opening the Microsoft Office Word Help window, click the **Back** and **Forward** buttons (the left and right arrows) at the top of the window.

Displaying the Word Help Task Pane
Another way to display the Word Help task pane is to click the **Microsoft Word Help** button in the Standard toolbar (or choose **Help**, **Microsoft Word Help**). If you use this method, you can then type your search text in the **Search** text box and click the **Start Searching** button.

Exiting Word

Start

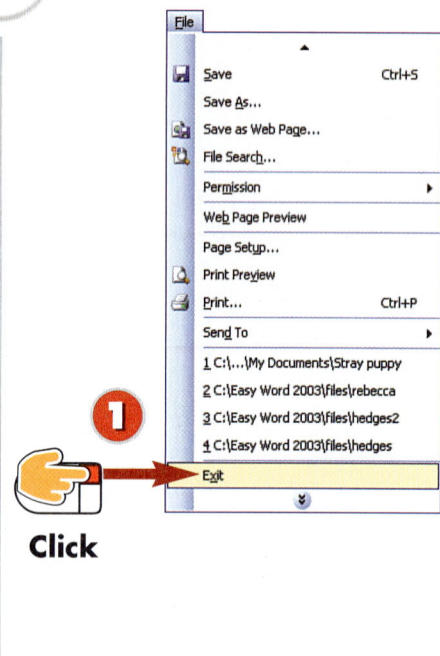

Click

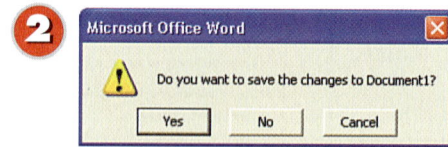

1 Open the **File** menu and choose **Exit**.

2 If Word asks whether to save changes to a document, click **Yes** or **No** depending on what you would like to do. (See "Saving a Document" in Part 4.)

3 All open Word windows close, and no Word buttons remain on the taskbar.

INTRODUCTION

When you are finished working with Word, you need to exit the program. When you issue the command to exit, Word checks to see if you are working on a document that has unsaved changes. If you are, it gives you a chance to save the document before closing it. As soon as you exit Word, the buttons for the Word documents that you had open disappear from the taskbar to let you know that the program is no longer running.

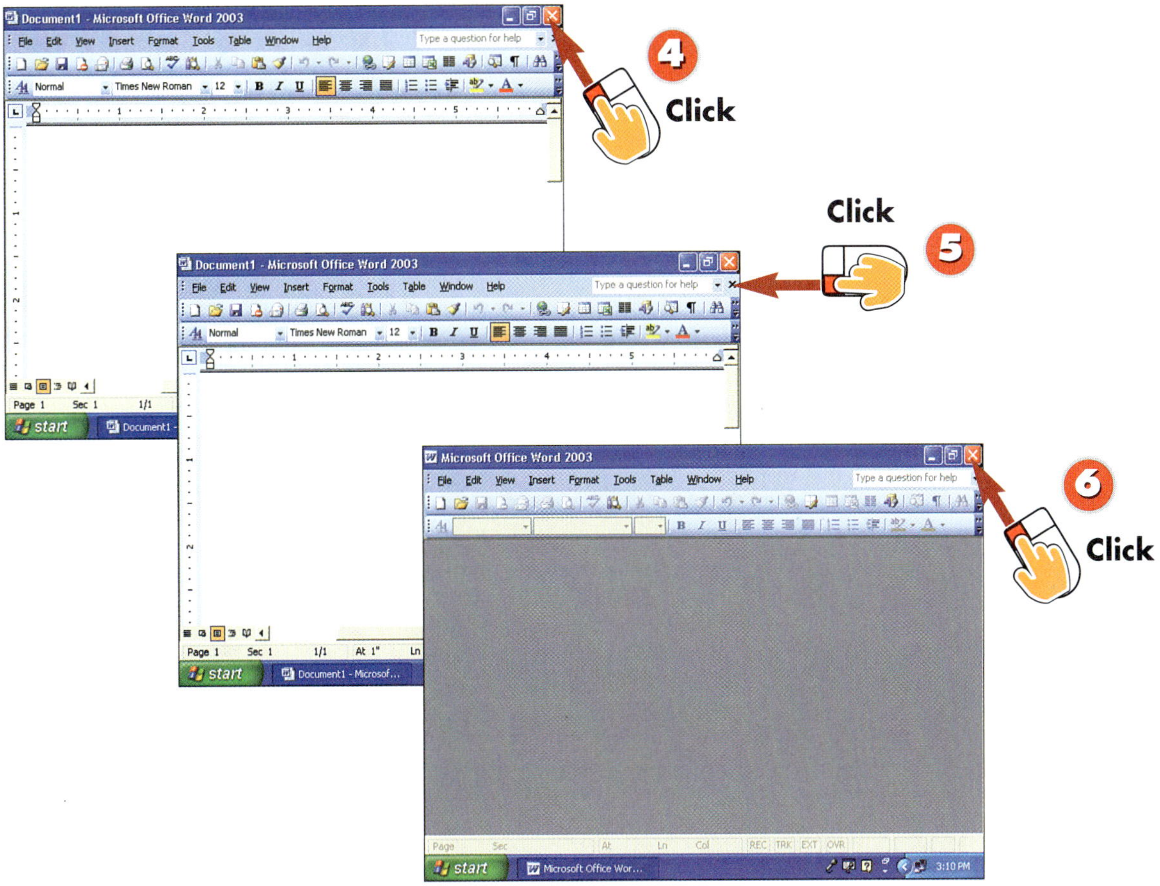

Click

Click

Click

4 Alternatively, you can click the Word window's **Close** button as a shortcut for choosing File, Exit.

5 Click the **Close Window** button if you only want to close the document window, but leave Word open. (This is a shortcut for choosing File, Close.)

6 If you close all of your documents without closing Word, the Word window will be empty. You can then exit Word by clicking the **Close** button (or by choosing **File**, **Exit**).

End

Closing Multiple Word Documents
If you open more than one document at a time, Word by default displays each one in a separate Word window, each with its own taskbar button. Opening the **File** menu and choosing **Exit** or clicking the **Close** button in any Word window closes them all.

Entering Text

Even if you have never used a word-processing program before, you'll feel comfortable typing text in Word in no time. In this part, you learn typing basics, such as when to press Enter and how to move around the document. You also find out how to insert new text into text you have already typed, and how to work with *smart tags*, which are little icons that Microsoft uses to indicate clickable pieces of text in your document.

The Go To Tab of the Find and Replace Dialog Box

Body text

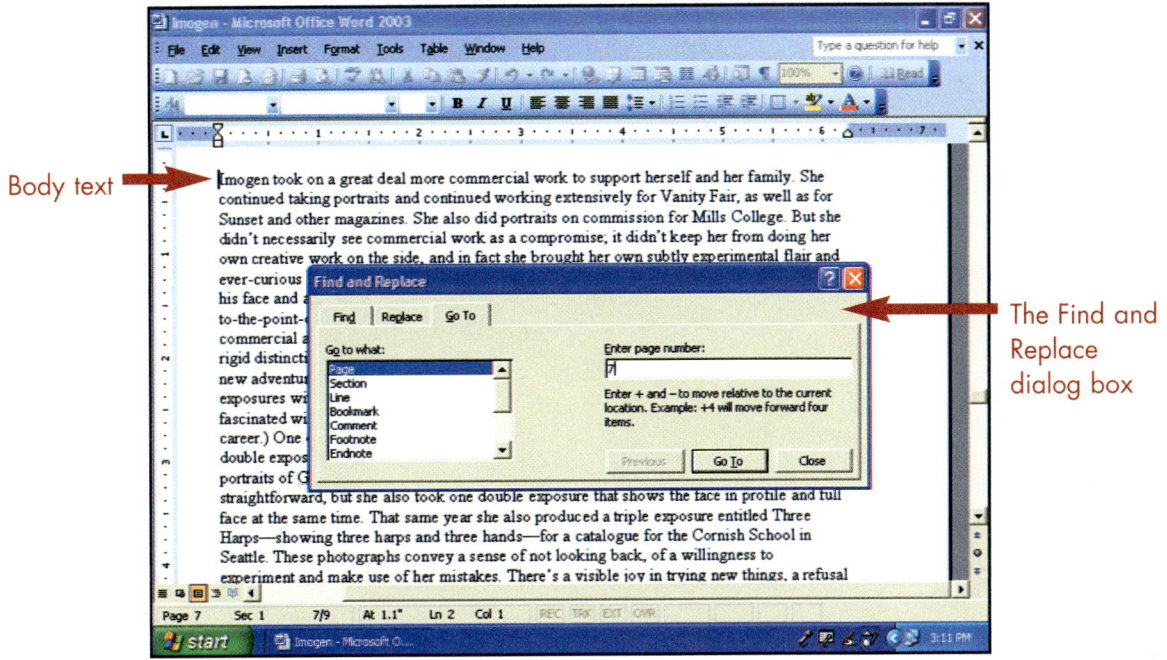

The Find and Replace dialog box

Entering Text

Start

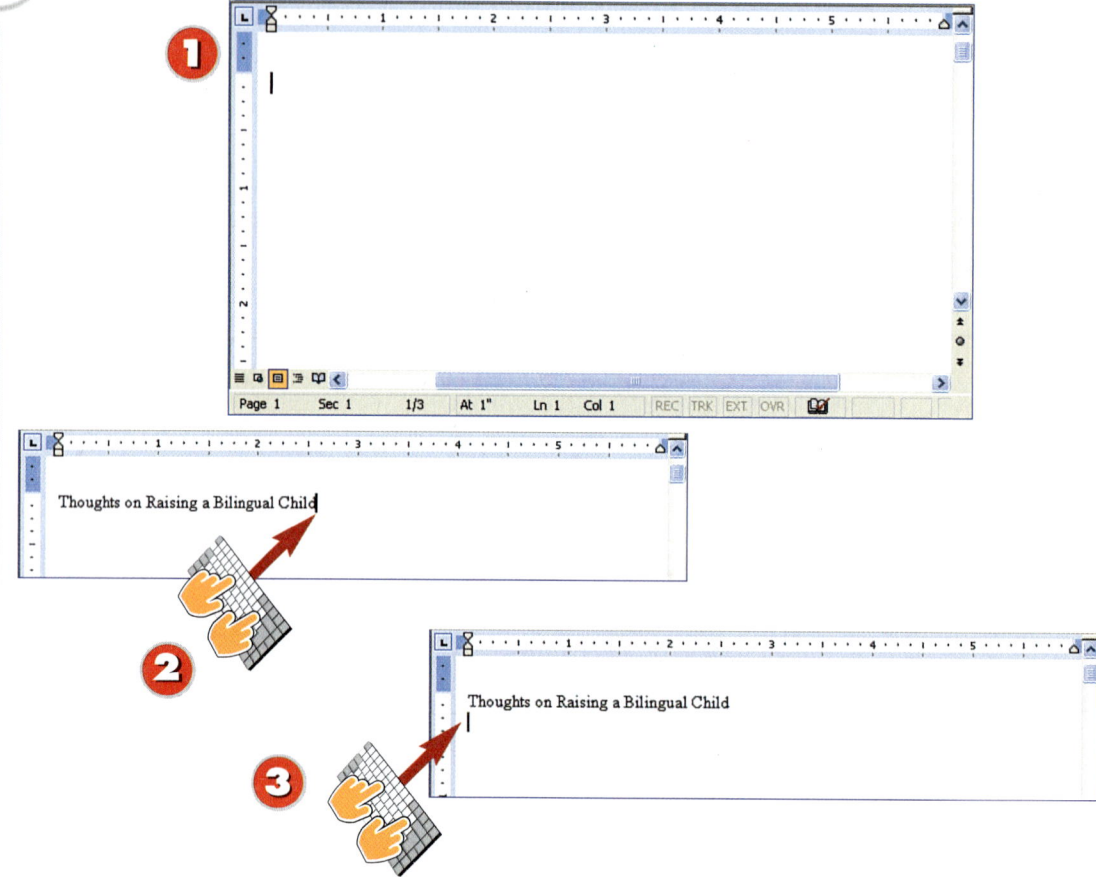

Thoughts on Raising a Bilingual Child

1 Start Word. The flashing vertical bar you see in the blank document is called the *insertion point*.

2 Type a short line of text. As you type, the insertion point shows you where the next character will be inserted.

3 When you want to end a paragraph of text, even if it is only a single line, press **Enter**. The insertion point moves to the next line.

Typing text in a Word document is simple. As soon as you start Word, you can begin typing in the blank document that appears. You don't have to worry about leaving room for margins. Word assumes that you're typing on 8 ½ by 11-inch paper, with 1-inch margins on the top and bottom and 1 ¼-inch margins on the left and right. If you're typing a paragraph that is more than one line long, do not press Enter at the end of each line. Word wraps the text from line to line for you.

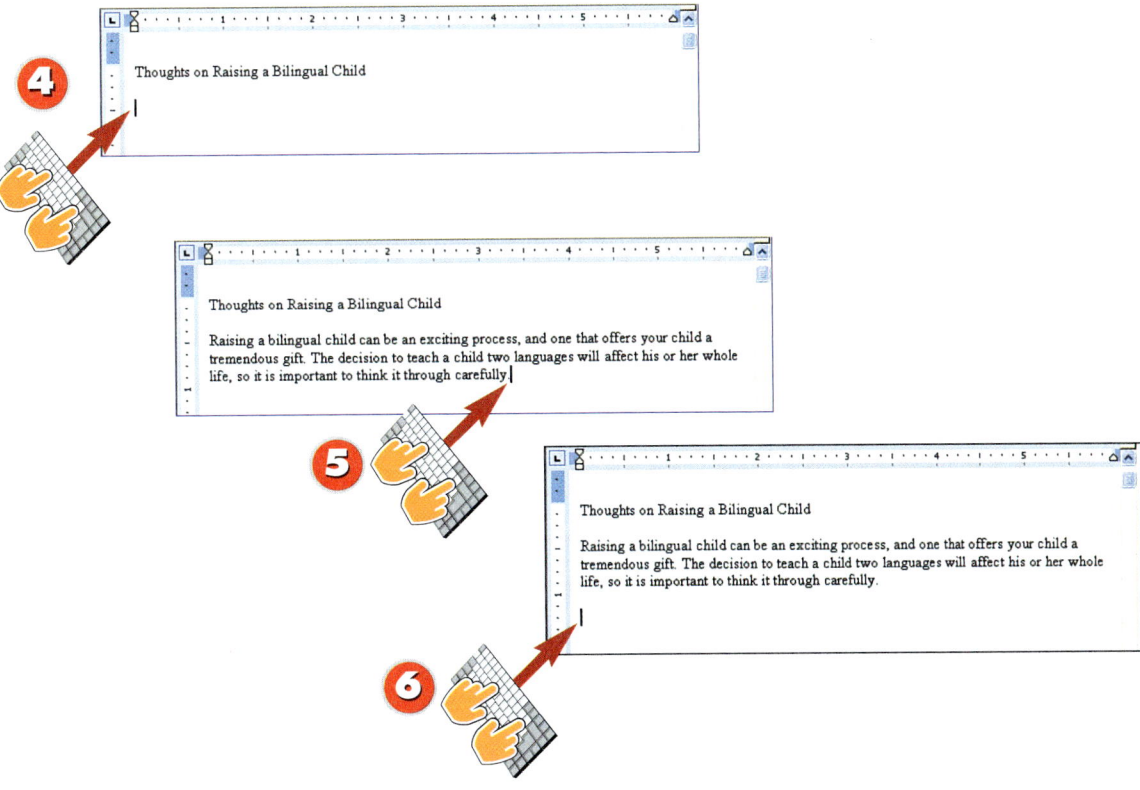

4 Press **Enter** again. When the insertion point is on a new line, pressing Enter creates a blank line.

5 Type a paragraph that is more than one line long, but do not press Enter at the end of each line. Notice that Word wraps the text for you.

6 When you're finished typing the paragraph, press **Enter** to start a new line, or press **Enter** twice if you want to add a blank line.

The I-beam Versus the Insertion Point
The mouse pointer, called the *I-beam*, is often confused with the *insertion point*. The insertion point (sometimes called the *cursor*) shows you where your text will appear when you type. The I-beam just lets you move the insertion point around the document.

Correcting Mistakes as You Type
If you type the wrong character, you can press the **Backspace** key to delete it. You'll learn more about how to delete text in "Deleting Text" in Part 3.

Moving Around the Document with the Mouse

Start

Click

Click & Drag

Click

1. To move to a place that's visible onscreen, first position the I-beam at the desired location. Then, click with your mouse to move the insertion point that location.

2. Click the **down** scroll arrow on the scrollbar to bring the lower part of a long document into view. Click the **Up** scroll arrow to scroll back up.

3. Point to the **scroll box** and drag it up or down the scrollbar to move quickly through a long document.

4. After you've scrolled the document, remember to click to move the insertion point before you start typing.

End

INTRODUCTION

As soon as you've typed some text in a blank document, you need to know how to move the insertion point around within the text to make editing changes. You can move the insertion point by clicking with the mouse or by pressing navigation keys on the keyboard. In this task and the next, you learn how to navigate with the mouse.

TIP

Using the Mouse Wheel

If your mouse has a wheel between the buttons, you can roll the wheel to scroll up and down. If you press the wheel, the mouse pointer changes to two black arrows with a dot in between; you can then scroll by simply moving the mouse without rolling the wheel. To get out of this mode, press the wheel again.

Typing Anywhere on the Page

Start

Double-Click

Last Revision: Spring 2003

2

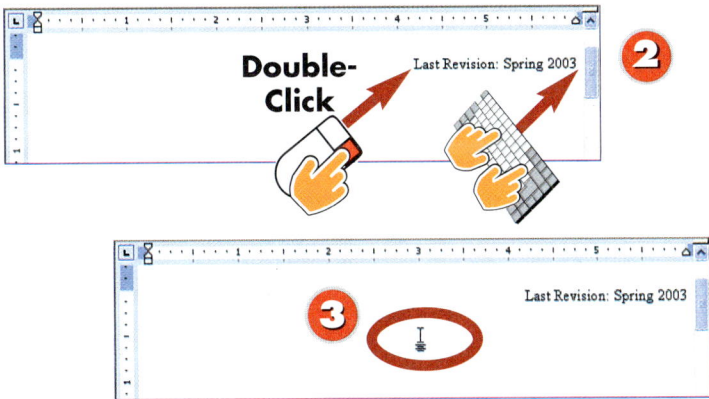

3

Last Revision: Spring 2003

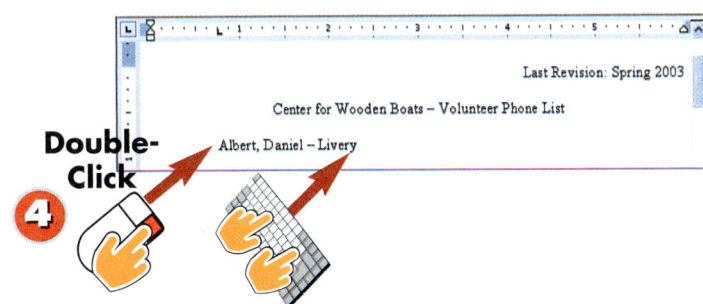

Last Revision: Spring 2003

Center for Wooden Boats – Volunteer Phone List

Albert, Daniel – Livery

Double-Click

4

End

1 To type text that is right-aligned, move your I-beam close to the right margin. After a moment, a special click-and-type icon appears next to the I-beam, indicating right-alignment.

2 Double-click to move the insertion point to the location of the I-beam, and type your text.

3 Move the I-beam to the page's center. The I-beam icon changes to indicate center alignment. Double-click to move the insertion point to the I-beam, and type your text.

4 To type text that is left-aligned on the left side of the page, move your I-beam to where you want to begin typing. Double-click to move the insertion point and type your text.

INTRODUCTION
Word's click-and-type feature lets you start typing in the middle of the page or near the right margin by simply double-clicking at the desired location. Click and type works only in Print Layout and Web Layout views.

TIP
Enabling Click and Type
If double-clicking doesn't move the insertion point, open the **View** menu and choose **Print Layout**. Then choose **Tools**, **Options**. Click the **Edit** tab, mark the **Enable click and type** check box, and click **OK**.

TIP
Left-Aligning Text on the Right Margin
You can also type left-aligned text that is on the right side of the page. Again, move your I-beam to the place where you want to begin typing. Double-click to move the insertion point and type your text.

Moving Around the Document with the Keyboard

Start

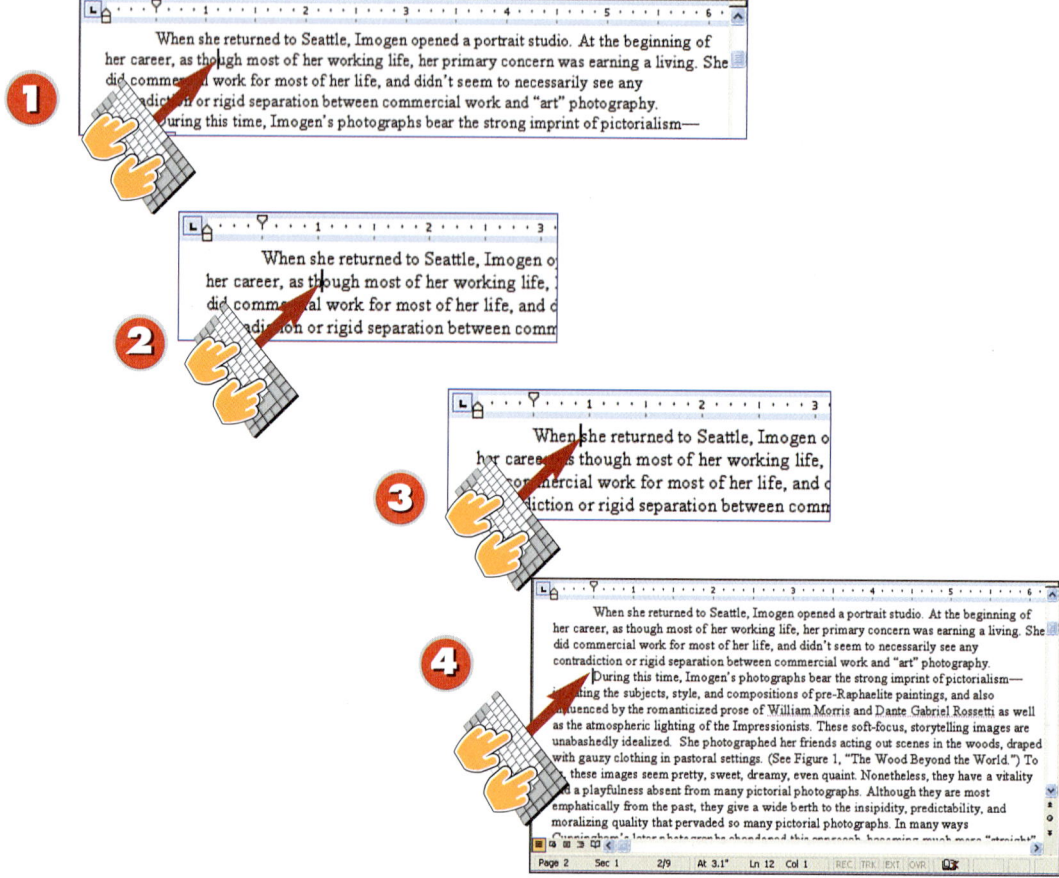

1. Press the **left-** and **right-arrow** keys to move one character to the left or to the right.

2. Press the **up-** and **down-arrow** keys to move one line up or down.

3. Press **Ctrl+left arrow** to move backward through the paragraph, word by word. Press **Ctrl+right arrow** to move forward through the paragraph.

4. Press **Ctrl+up arrow** to move up through the document, paragraph by paragraph. Press **Ctrl+down arrow** to move down through the document.

When navigating with the mouse, you must constantly move your hands away from the keyboard to the mouse and back. When you navigate with the keyboard, however, the insertion point moves as you press the keys. You don't have to click once before you start typing to move the insertion point, as you do when you navigate with the mouse.

TIP

Moving to the Beginning or End of a Line
To move to the beginning of a line, press **Home**. To move to the end of a line, press **End**.

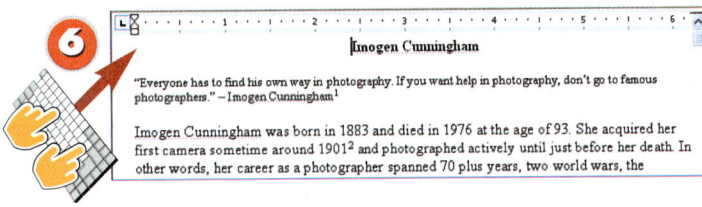

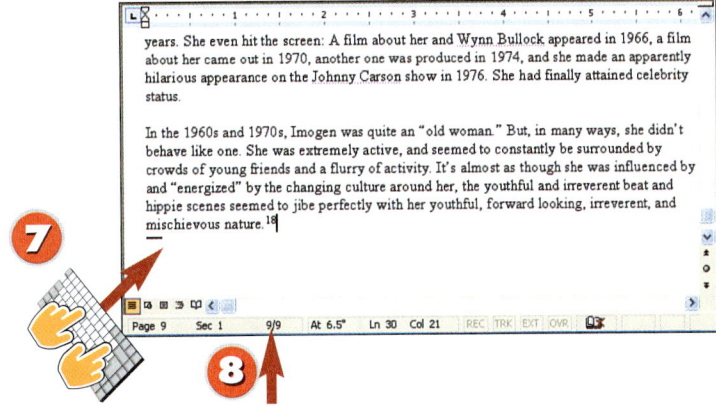

5 Press **Page Down** and **Page Up** to move one screenful of text down or up.

6 Press **Ctrl+Home** to move to the very beginning of the document.

7 Press **Ctrl+End** to move to the very end of the document.

8 You can always tell what page you're on by looking at status bar. Here, the insertion point is on page 9 of a 9-page document.

End

TIP

Pressing Key Combinations
When you press a key combination such as Ctrl+Home, be sure to hold down the first key as you press the second key, and then release both keys.

Getting Back to the Insertion Point
If you have used the mouse pointer to scroll to a different part of your document and want to quickly get back to the insertion point to continue editing where you were, press **Shift+F5**.

Going to a Specific Page

Start

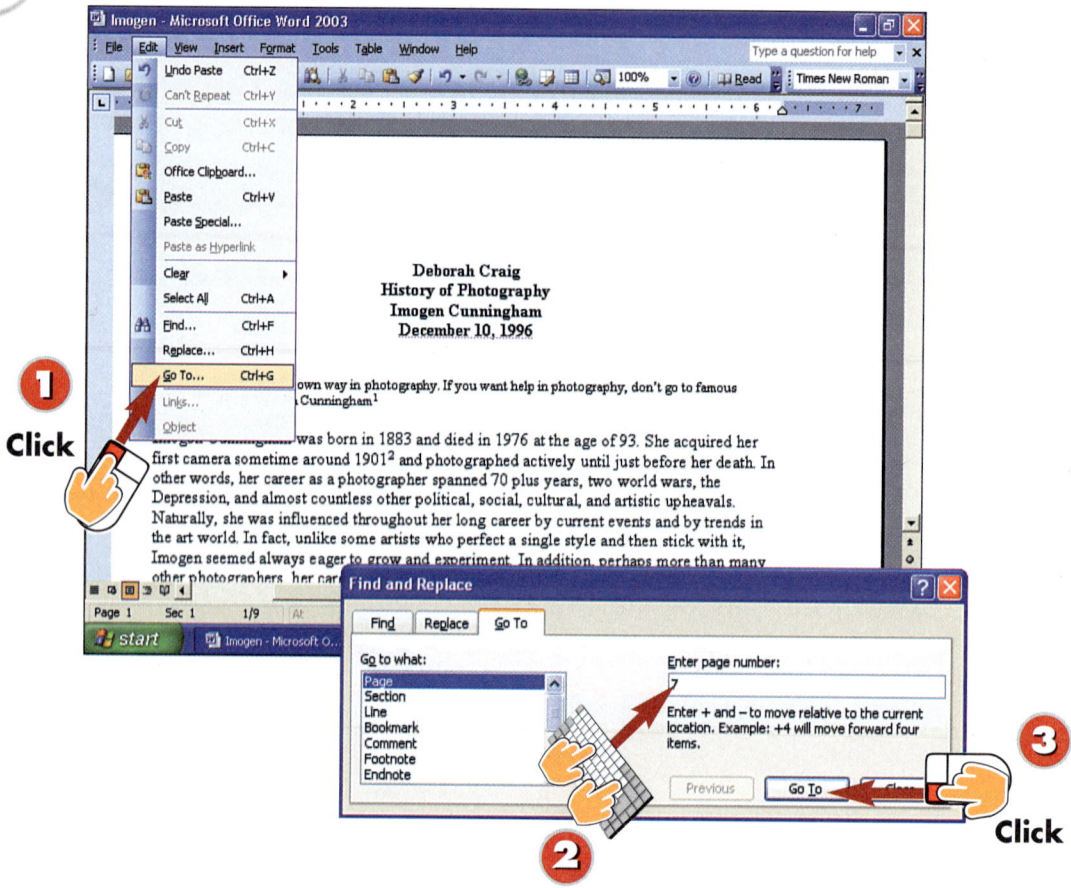

Click

Click

---

1. Open the **Edit** menu and choose **Go To** to display the Go To tab of the Find and Replace dialog box.

2. Type the number of the page you want to display onscreen in the **Enter page number** text box.

3. Click the **Go To** button.

INTRODUCTION

When you're editing a long document, you often need to go to a particular page to make a change. You can, of course, navigate to that page using the standard mouse and keyboard techniques described in the previous two tasks. However, it's often faster to use Word's Go To feature, which allows you to jump directly to any page in your document.

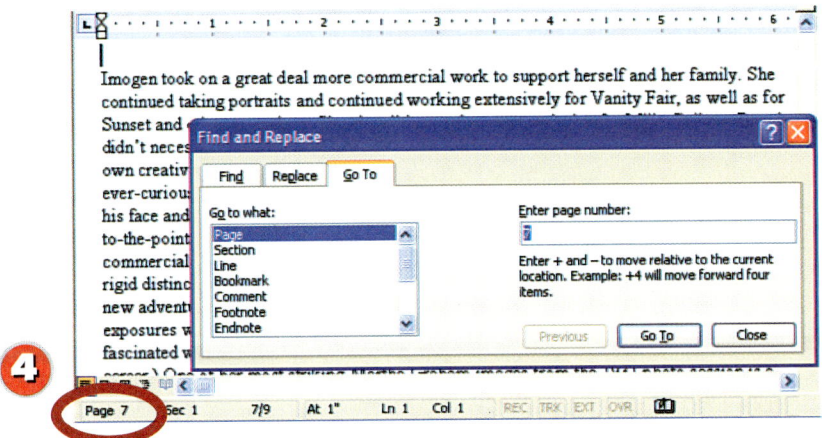

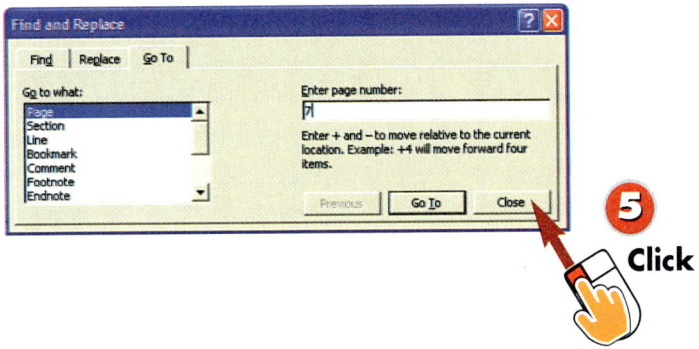

Click

4 Word jumps to that page. (Check the page number in the status bar.) The dialog box remains onscreen so that you can go to another page if desired.

5 When you're finished using Go To, click the **Close** button.

End

Using Go To for Changes
You can use Go To to make editing changes on several pages. Jump to the first page, click outside the dialog box, and make the change in the text. Then click the title bar of the dialog box to reactivate it, jump to the next page, and so on.

Other Uses of the Go To Feature
In addition to jumping to specific pages, the Go To feature also enables you to jump to other items such as comments, footnotes, and endnotes. As you explore Word beyond what is covered in this book, you will likely learn how to use some of these features.

Inserting Text

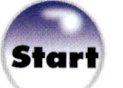

Start

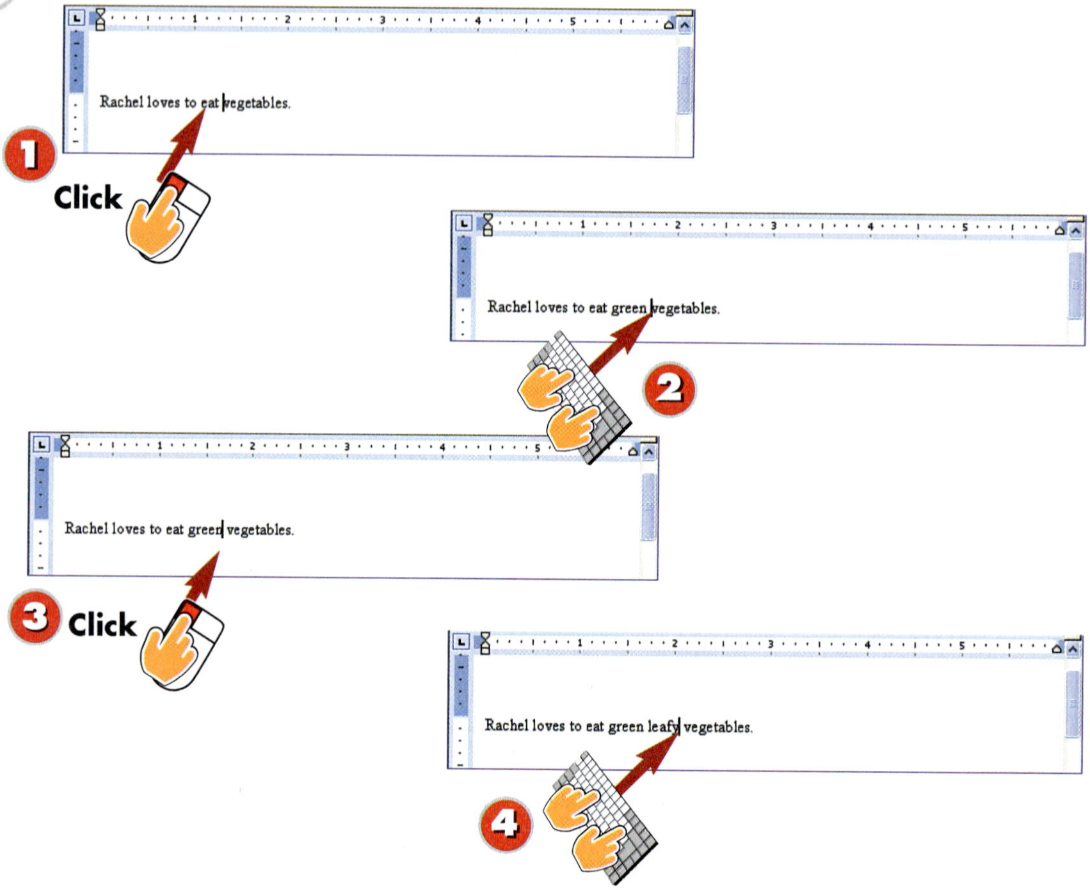
Rachel loves to eat vegetables.
1
Click
Rachel loves to eat green vegetables.
2
Rachel loves to eat green vegetables.
3
Click
Rachel loves to eat green leafy vegetables.
4

1. To insert text between two words that you have already typed, move the insertion point to just before the first letter of the second word.
2. Type your text, and press the **Spacebar**.
3. You can also move the insertion point to just after a word before you begin typing.
4. If you do this, you will need to press the Spacebar first, and then type your text.

End

INTRODUCTION

As you type a document, you'll likely need to add some text here and there. When you type new text, Word pushes the existing text out of the way to make room. Depending on the location of the insertion point when you start typing, you will either need to add a space at the beginning of the insertion or at the end.

TIP

Replacing Text

If you want to *replace* a block of text with new text, it's fastest to *select* (highlight) the existing text first and then type right over it with the new text. See "Deleting Text" in Part 3 for more information.

TIP

Deleting Text As You Type

The default behavior described in this task is *insert* mode. If you press your Insert key, however, Word switches to *overtype* mode. When this mode is active, each character you type *replaces* the character to the right of the insertion point.

Combining and Splitting Paragraphs

Start

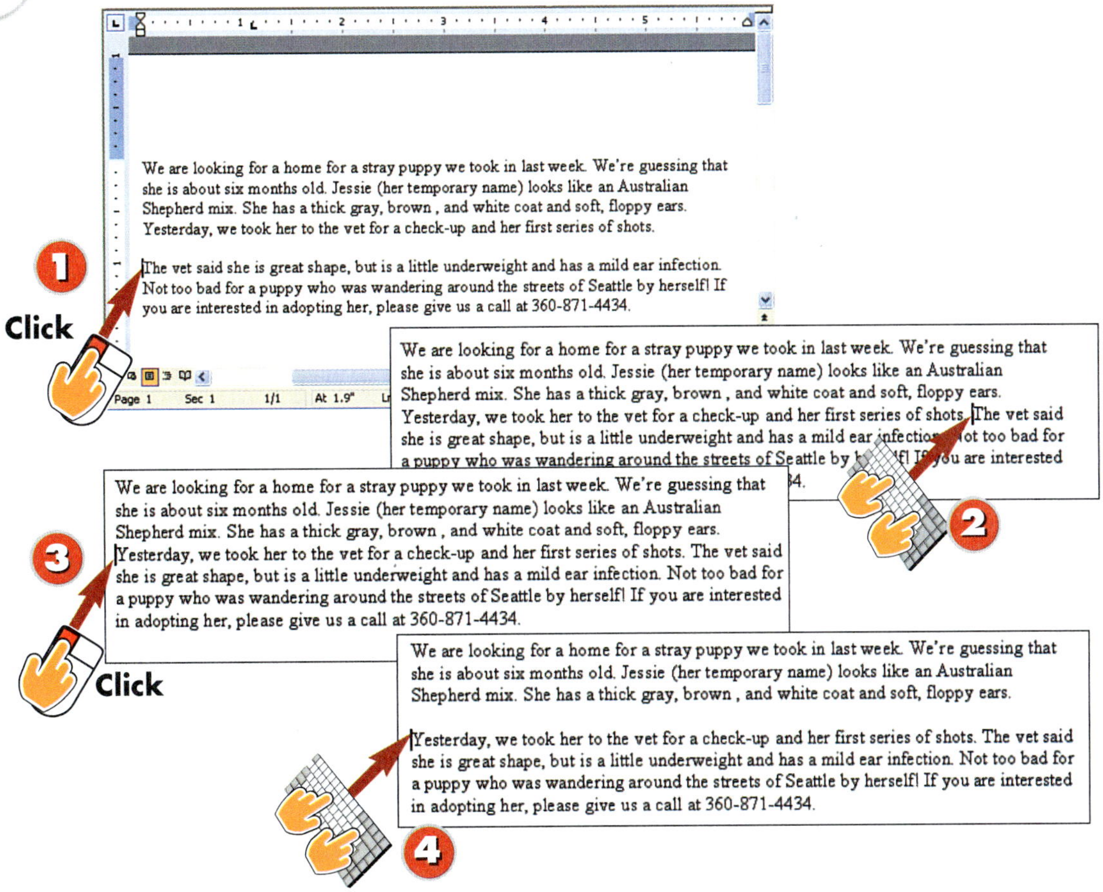

We are looking for a home for a stray puppy we took in last week. We're guessing that she is about six months old. Jessie (her temporary name) looks like an Australian Shepherd mix. She has a thick gray, brown , and white coat and soft, floppy ears. Yesterday, we took her to the vet for a check-up and her first series of shots.

The vet said she is great shape, but is a little underweight and has a mild ear infection. Not too bad for a puppy who was wandering around the streets of Seattle by herself! If you are interested in adopting her, please give us a call at 360-871-4434.

Page 1   Sec 1   1/1   At 1.9"

① Click

We are looking for a home for a stray puppy we took in last week. We're guessing that she is about six months old. Jessie (her temporary name) looks like an Australian Shepherd mix. She has a thick gray, brown , and white coat and soft, floppy ears. Yesterday, we took her to the vet for a check-up and her first series of shots. The vet said she is great shape, but is a little underweight and has a mild ear infection. Not too bad for a puppy who was wandering around the streets of Seattle by herself! If you are interested

②

③

We are looking for a home for a stray puppy we took in last week. We're guessing that she is about six months old. Jessie (her temporary name) looks like an Australian Shepherd mix. She has a thick gray, brown , and white coat and soft, floppy ears. Yesterday, we took her to the vet for a check-up and her first series of shots. The vet said she is great shape, but is a little underweight and has a mild ear infection. Not too bad for a puppy who was wandering around the streets of Seattle by herself! If you are interested in adopting her, please give us a call at 360-871-4434.

Click

We are looking for a home for a stray puppy we took in last week. We're guessing that she is about six months old. Jessie (her temporary name) looks like an Australian Shepherd mix. She has a thick gray, brown , and white coat and soft, floppy ears.

Yesterday, we took her to the vet for a check-up and her first series of shots. The vet said she is great shape, but is a little underweight and has a mild ear infection. Not too bad for a puppy who was wandering around the streets of Seattle by herself! If you are interested in adopting her, please give us a call at 360-871-4434.

④

① To join two paragraphs, move the insertion point to the beginning of the second paragraph.

② Press the **Backspace** key once to join the paragraphs, or twice if there is a blank line between the paragraphs. (You may need to press the **Spacebar** to add a space at the insertion point.)

③ To split one paragraph into two, move the insertion point to just before the first letter of what will become the new paragraph.

④ Press **Enter** once, or twice if you want a blank line between the paragraphs.

End

Working with Smart Tags

Start

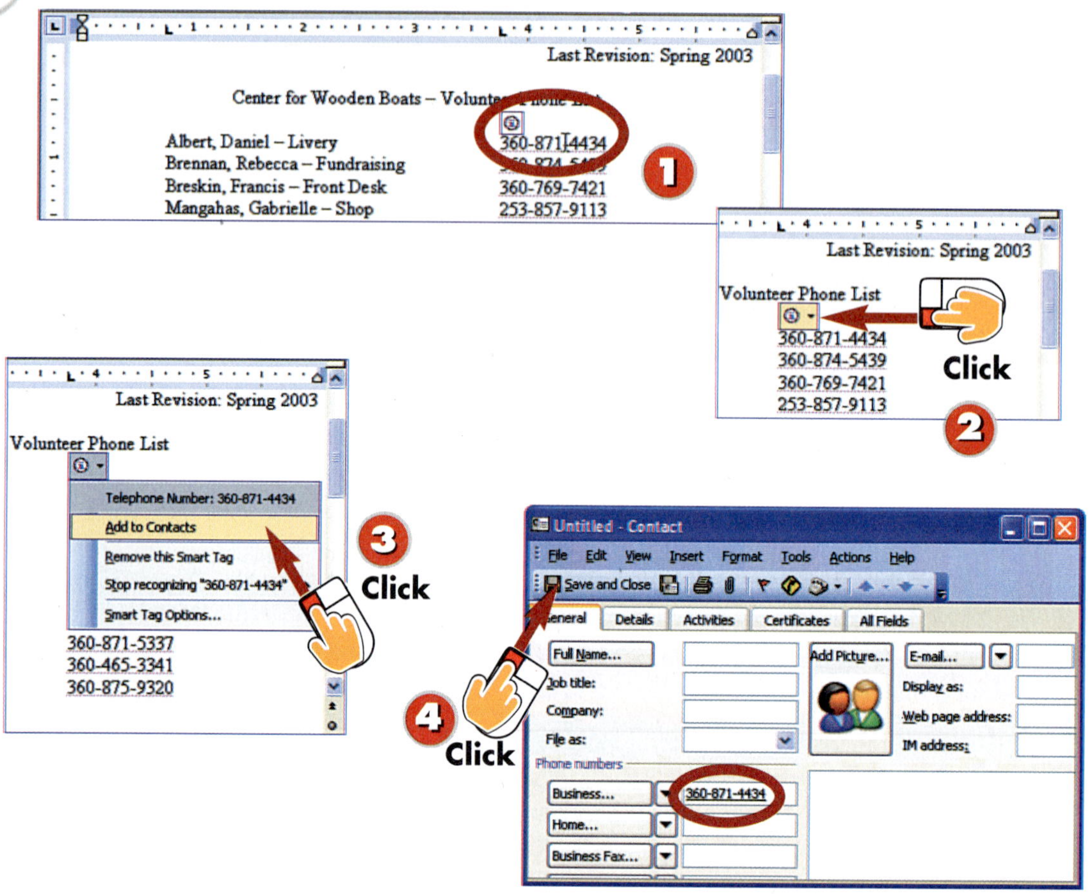

Last Revision: Spring 2003

Center for Wooden Boats — Volunteer Phone List

Albert, Daniel — Livery 360-871-4434 **1**
Brennan, Rebecca — Fundraising 360-874-5439
Breskin, Francis — Front Desk 360-769-7421
Mangahas, Gabrielle — Shop 253-857-9113

Last Revision: Spring 2003

Volunteer Phone List

360-871-4434
360-874-5439
360-769-7421
253-857-9113

Click **2**

Last Revision: Spring 2003

Volunteer Phone List

Telephone Number: 360-871-4434
Add to Contacts
Remove this Smart Tag
Stop recognizing "360-871-4434"
Smart Tag Options...

360-871-5337
360-465-3341
360-875-9320

3 **Click**

Untitled - Contact

File Edit View Insert Format Tools Actions Help

Save and Close

General Details Activities Certificates All Fields

Full Name...   Add Picture... E-mail...
Job title: Display as:
Company: Web page address:
File as: IM address:
Phone numbers
Business... 360-871-4434
Home...
Business Fax...

4 **Click**

1. Move your mouse pointer over purple underlined text (a phone number in this example); a Smart Tag Actions button appears.

2. Point to the Smart Tag Actions button and then click the **down arrow** that appears to its right to display a list of possible actions.

3. Click the action you want to perform. In this example, choose **Add to Contacts** to create a new Outlook contact with this phone number without leaving Word.

4. Outlook's Contact dialog box opens with the phone number inserted. Fill in the person's name and other information, and then click the **Save and Close** button.

Using Additional Buttons

TIP

Two types of buttons may pop up in your text: a lightning bolt and a clipboard. The first is the AutoCorrect Options button; you will learn about it in Part 8. The second is the Paste Options button, which you will learn about in Part 3.

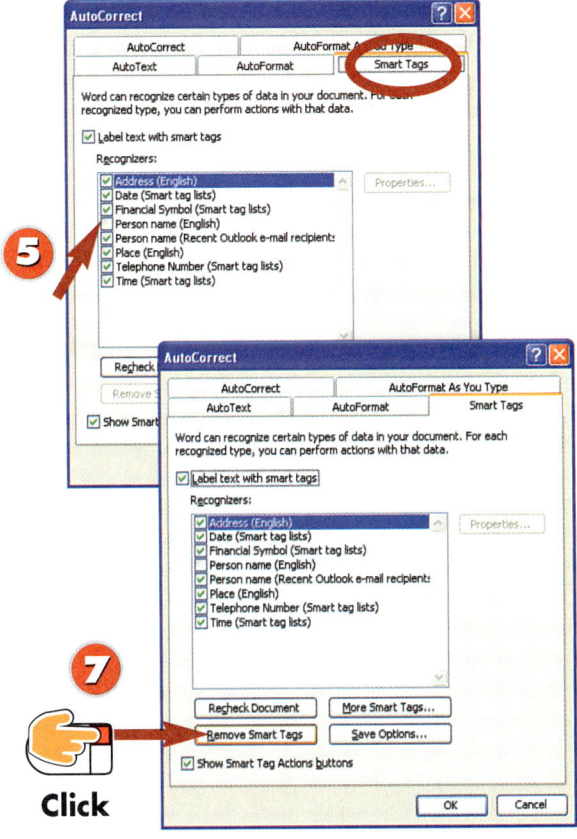

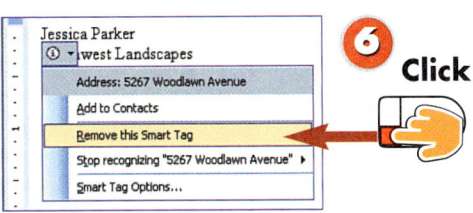

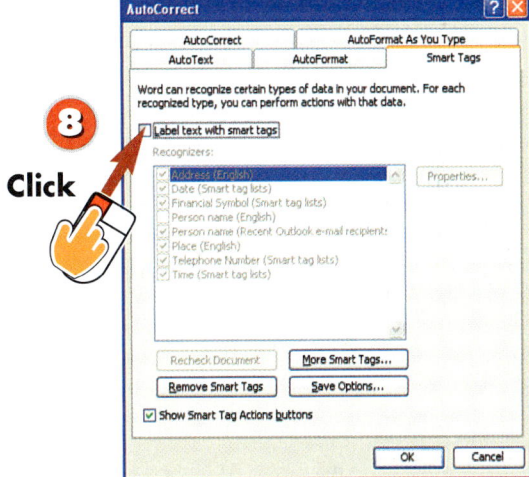

5 To choose what gets marked as smart tags, choose **Tools**, **AutoCorrect Options**, click the **Smart Tags** tab, mark/clear the appropriate options, and click **OK**.

6 To remove an individual smart tag from a piece of text, click the **Smart Tag Actions** button and choose **Remove this Smart Tag**.

7 To remove all smart tags from the current document, choose **Tools**, **AutoCorrect Options**, click the **Smart Tags** tab, click **Remove Smart Tags**, and click **OK**.

8 To turn off the smart tags feature, clear the **Label text with smart tags** check box from the **Smart Tags** tab and click **OK**.

End

Eliminating the Purple Underlines
If you want to use the smart tags feature, but you don't want to see the purple dotted underlines on your text, you can open the **Tools** menu and choose **Options**, click the **View** tab, and clear the **Smart Tags** check box. The Smart Tag Actions button will still appear over text that the smart tags feature has recognized, but you will no longer see purple underlines.

Getting More Smart Tags
Many companies have designed smart tags that you can download from the Web. To see what's available, choose **Tools**, **AutoCorrect Options**, click the **Smart Tags** tab, and click the **More Smart Tags** button.

Editing Text

Word-processing programs would be only be a slight improvement over type-writers if we couldn't use them to revise text. Indeed, the most valuable aspect of using Word is that you can quickly and painlessly edit text you've already typed. The skills you learn here—selecting (highlighting) text, deleting text, cutting and pasting text, undoing actions, and so on—form the foundation of everything else you'll do in Word.

Editing Tools

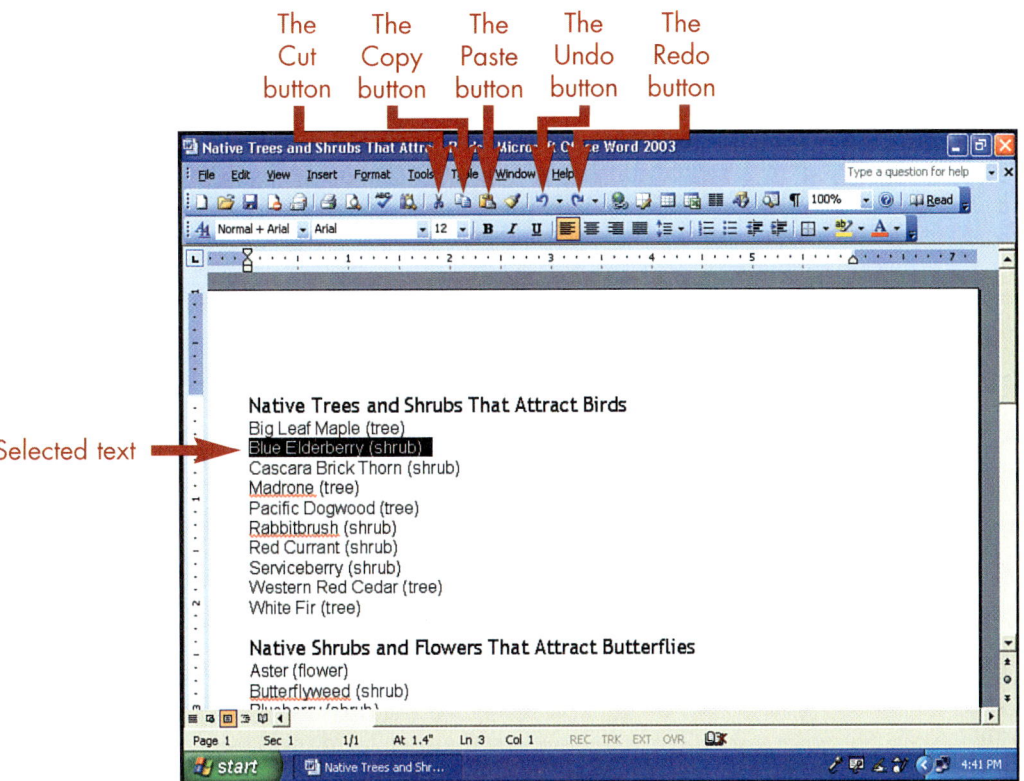

Selecting Text with the Mouse

Start

Depression, and almost countless other political, social, cultural, and artistic upheavals. Naturally, she was influenced throughout her long career by current events and by trends in the art world. In fact, unlike some artists who perfect a single style and then stick with it, Imogen seemed always eager to grow and experiment. In addition, perhaps more than many other photographers, her career and work seem to have been formed by her somewhat unusual family background, individualistic character, and personal circumstances.

Click & Drag

1

2

Depression, and almost countless other political, social, cultural, and artistic upheavals. Naturally, she was influenced throughout her long career by current events and by trends in the art world. In fact, unlike some artists who perfect a single style and then stick with it, Imogen seemed always eager to grow and experiment. In addition, perhaps more than many other photographers, her career and work seem to have been formed by her somewhat unusual family background, individualistic character, and personal circumstances.

Click

Double-Click

3

Depression, and almost countless other political, social, cultural, and artistic upheavals. Naturally, she was influenced throughout her long career by current events and by trends in the art world. In fact, unlike some artists who perfect a single style and then stick with it, Imogen seemed always eager to grow and experiment. In addition, perhaps more than many other photographers, her career and work seem to have been formed by her somewhat unusual family background, individualistic character, and personal circumstances.

1 Position the I-beam at one end of the text that you want to select. Press and hold down your mouse button, drag to the other end of the text, and then release the mouse button.

2 If you selected the wrong amount of text, deselect it by clicking anywhere in the document.

3 To select an individual word, double-click it.

Selecting (or highlighting) text is an essential word-processing skill. In many cases, you must select text before performing a command so Word knows what text you want to affect. For example, you must select text before cutting and pasting or applying many kinds of formatting. In this task, you learn how to select text using the mouse (the next task teaches you how to select with the keyboard).

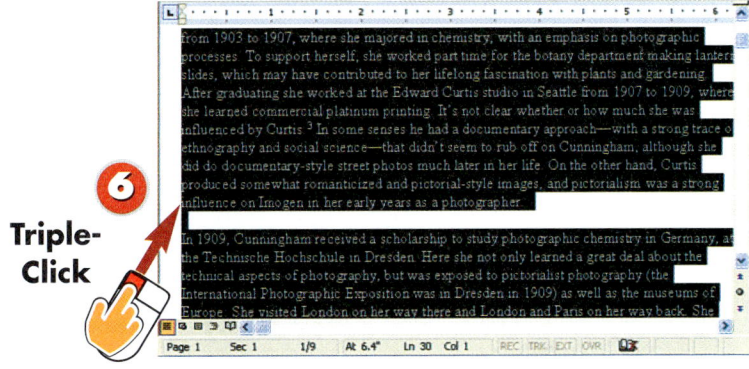

Ctrl + Click

Double-Click

Triple-Click

4 To select a single sentence, hold down the **Ctrl** key as you click anywhere on the sentence. (This only works if no other text is selected.)

5 To select a paragraph, move the mouse pointer to the left of the paragraph and double-click.

6 To select the entire document, move the mouse pointer to the left of the text and triple-click.

End

CAUTION If you have released the mouse button after selecting a block of text, you can't adjust the amount of text that's selected by pointing to it and dragging. If you try to do this, you'll end up *moving* the text instead. You can, however, adjust the selection by using the keyboard (see the next task). If you want to use the mouse to adjust the selection, press the **Shift** key while clicking your mouse (called a **Shift+click**) at the spot you want to extend/shrink the selection to, or click once to deselect the text, and then select again.

CAUTION As you'll see in "Deleting Text" later in this part, when text is selected, any text you type *replaces* the selected text. If you don't want this to happen, deselect the text before typing.

Selecting Text with the Keyboard

Start

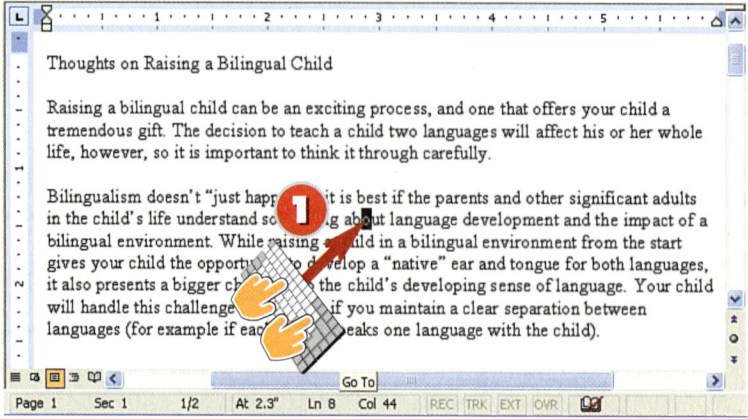

Thoughts on Raising a Bilingual Child

Raising a bilingual child can be an exciting process, and one that offers your child a tremendous gift. The decision to teach a child two languages will affect his or her whole life, however, so it is important to think it through carefully.

Bilingualism doesn't "just happen" — it is best if the parents and other significant adults in the child's life understand something about language development and the impact of a bilingual environment. While raising a child in a bilingual environment from the start gives your child the opportunity to develop a "native" ear and tongue for both languages, it also presents a bigger challenge to the child's developing sense of language. Your child will handle this challenge more easily if you maintain a clear separation between languages (for example if each parent speaks one language with the child).

2 Bilingualism doesn't "just happen" — it is best if the parents and other significant adults in the child's life understand something about language development and the impact of a bilingual environment. While raising a child in a bilingual environment from the start gives your child the opportunity to develop a "native" ear and tongue for both languages, it also presents a bigger challenge to the child's developing sense of language. Your child will handle this challenge more easily if you maintain a clear separation between languages (for example if each parent speaks one language with the child).

3 Bilingualism doesn't "just happen" — it is best if the parents and other significant adults in the child's life understand something about language development and the impact of a bilingual environment. While raising a child in a bilingual environment from the start gives your child the opportunity to develop a "native" ear and tongue for both languages, it also presents a bigger challenge to the child's developing sense of language. Your child will handle this challenge more easily if you maintain a clear separation between languages (for example if each parent speaks one language with the child).

1 Press **Shift+right arrow** to select character by character to the right, or **Shift+left arrow** to select to the left.

2 Press **Shift+Ctrl+right arrow** to select word by word to the right, or **Shift+Ctrl+left arrow** to select to the left.

3 Press **Shift+Ctrl+down arrow** to select down paragraph by paragraph, or **Shift+Ctrl+up arrow** to select up.

INTRODUCTION

Although you'll probably use the mouse to select text most of the time, you may occasionally want to use the keyboard. For example, if you want to select only a few characters, it's usually easiest to use the keyboard. You can also use the keyboard to adjust the size of a selection that you initially made with the mouse. (As mentioned in the preceding task, you can't adjust a selection with the mouse after you've released the mouse button.)

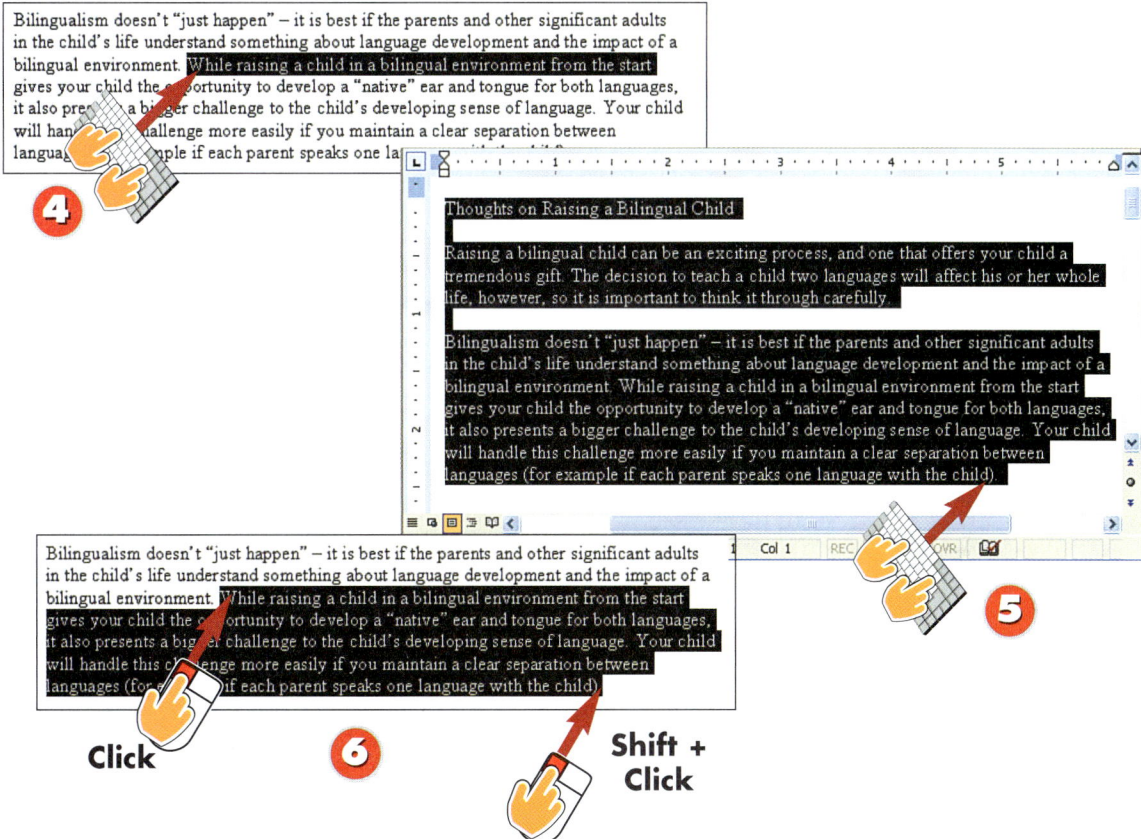

Click

6

Shift + Click

4 Press **Shift+End** to select to the end of the line, or **Shift+Home** to select to the beginning of the line.

5 Press **Shift+Ctrl+End** to select to the end of the document, or **Shift+Ctrl+Home** to select to the beginning of the document.

6 To select any amount of text, click at the beginning of the block of text, and then **Shift+click** at the end of it.

End

Using Multiple-Key Combinations

With the keyboard methods that involve pressing the Shift and/or Ctrl key with another key, keep the Shift and/or Ctrl key held down as you press the arrow keys repeatedly to continue selecting character by character, word by word, and so on.

Deleting Text

Start

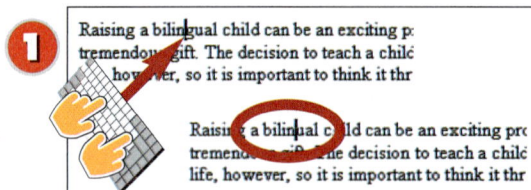

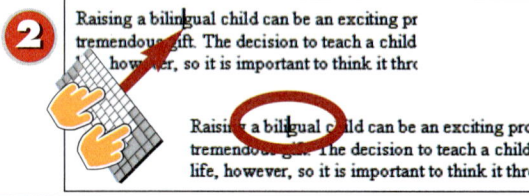

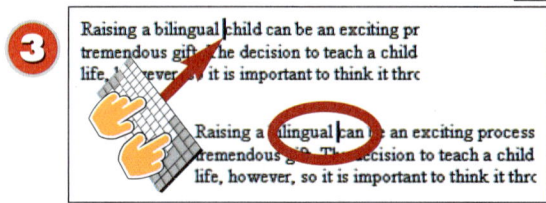

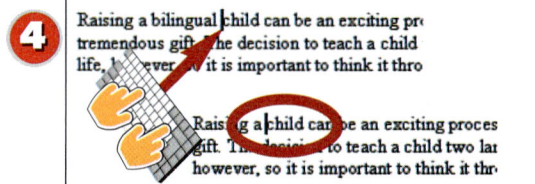

① Press the **Delete** key to delete the character to the right of the insertion point.

② Press the **Backspace** key to delete the character to the left.

③ Press **Ctrl+Delete** to delete the word to the right of the insertion point.

④ Press **Ctrl+Backspace** to delete the word to the left.

INTRODUCTION

It's as important to know how to delete text as it is to insert it. In this task, you learn techniques for deleting that you'll use every time you edit a document.

TIP

Deleting Several Words
To delete several words at once, hold down the **Ctrl** key as you press the **Delete** or **Backspace** key repeatedly.

TIP

Restoring Deleted Text
If you delete text accidentally, you can use the *Undo* feature to get it back. See the next task to learn how.

Bilingualism doesn't "just happen" – it is best if the parents and other significant adults in the child's life understand something about language development and the impact of a bilingual environment. While raising a child in a bilingual environment from the start gives your child the opportunity to develop a "native" ear and tongue for both languages, it also presents a bigger challenge to the child's developing sense of language. Your child will handle this challenge more easily if you maintain a clear separation between languages (for example if each parent speaks one language with the child).

While raising a child in a bilingual environment from the start gives your child the opportunity to develop a "native" ear and tongue for both languages, it also presents a bigger challenge to the child's developing sense of language. Your child will handle this challenge more easily if you maintain a clear separation between languages (for example if each parent speaks one language with the child).

Bilingualism doesn't "just happen" – it is best if the parents and other significant adults in the child's life understand something about language development and the impact of a bilingual environment. While raising a child in a bilingual environment from the start gives your child the opportunity to develop a "native" ear and tongue for both languages, it also presents a bigger challenge to the child's developing sense of language. Your child will handle this challenge more easily if you maintain a clear separation between languages (for example if each parent speaks one language with the child).

Bilingualism doesn't "just happen" – it is best if the parents and other significant adults in the child's life understand something about language acquisition and the impact of a bilingual environment. While raising a child in a bilingual environment from the start gives your child the opportunity to develop a "native" ear and tongue for both languages, it also presents a bigger challenge to the child's developing sense of language. Your child will handle this challenge more easily if you maintain a clear separation between languages (for example if each parent speaks one language with the child).

5 To delete a block of text, first select the text.

6 After the text is selected, press the **Delete** key.

7 To replace existing text with text you type, first select the existing text.

8 After the text is selected, type the new text.

Undoing Mistakes

Start

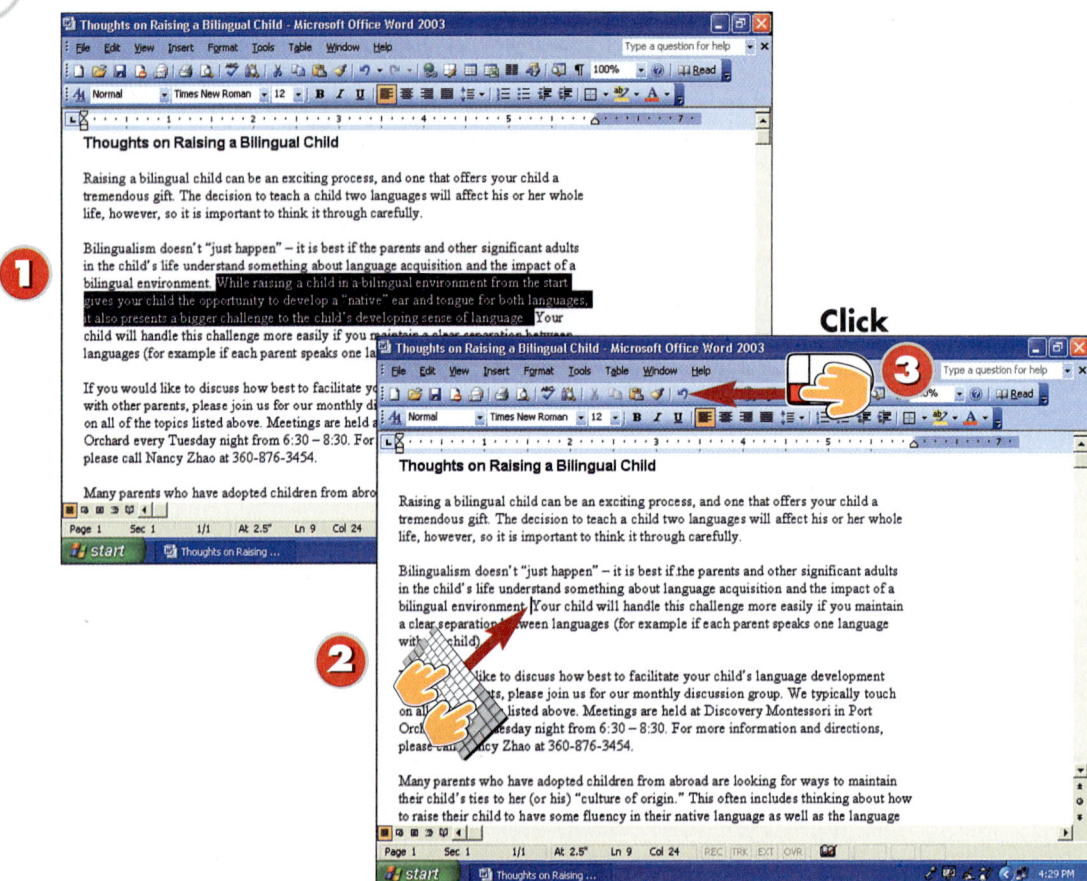

Click

1 To practice using Undo, first type a little text, and then select some of the text that you typed.

2 Press the **Delete** key to delete the selected text.

3 Click the **Undo** button on the Standard toolbar. (Click the button itself, not the down arrow to its right.)

Word lets you undo most actions, including typing, deleting, moving, copying, and formatting text. One of the best aspects of Word's Undo feature is that it lets you undo multiple actions, not just your most recent one. As you experiment with Undo, keep in mind that there are a few actions Word cannot undo, such as opening, saving, or printing a document.

Click

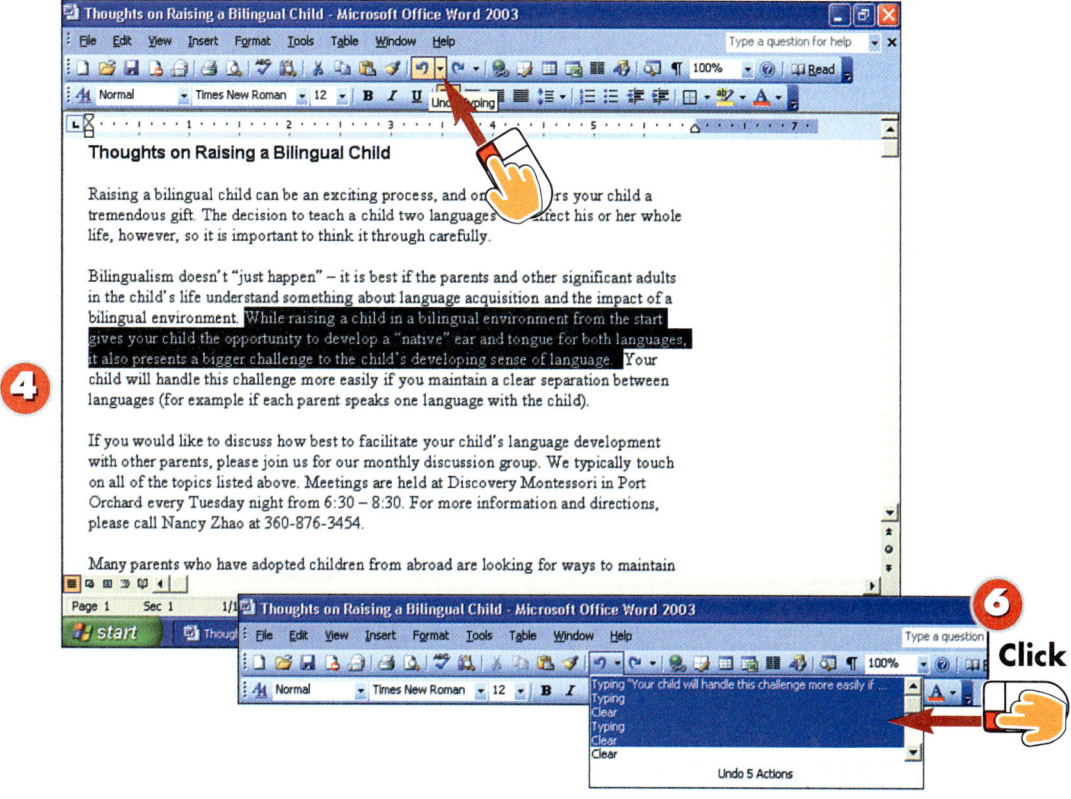

Click

4 Word restores the deleted text. If you keep clicking the **Undo** button, Word reverses previous actions one by one.

5 To undo several actions at once, first click the **down arrow** to the right of the Undo button.

6 Click any action in the list to undo everything back to, and including, the action you click.

End

Using the Redo Button
To the right of the Undo button on the Standard toolbar is the Redo button. Click this button if you have used Undo to reverse an action and then decide that you want to perform the action after all.

Undoing Actions with a Keyboard Shortcut
The keyboard shortcut for clicking the Undo button is **Ctrl+Z**. If you keep pressing Ctrl+Z, Word undoes actions one by one.

Moving Text

Start

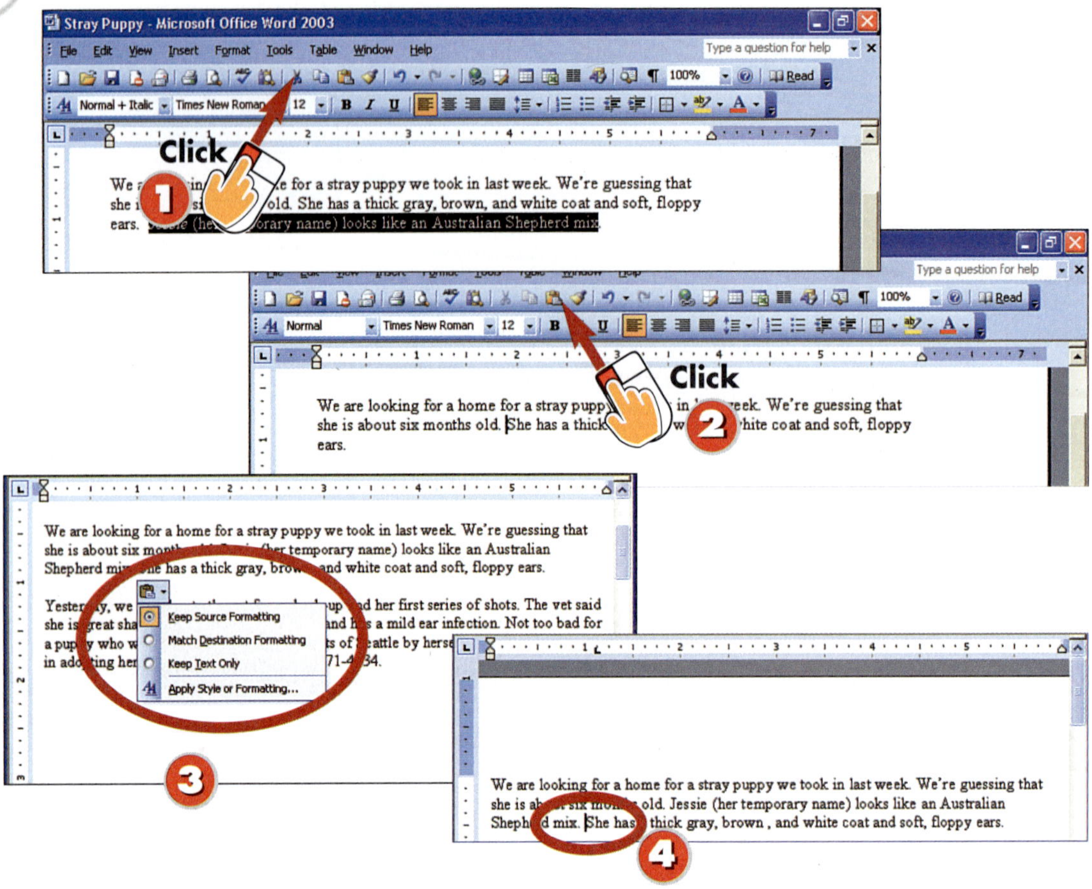

Click 1

Click 2

3

4

1   Select the text that you want to cut and click the **Cut** button on the Standard toolbar.

2   The text disappears from the document. Move the insertion point to the place where you want to move the text and click the **Paste** button on the Standard toolbar.

3   The text is moved to the new location. Point to the **Paste Options** button that pops up and click the **down arrow** that appears to display a list of options.

4   Rather than choosing an option, click outside the Paste Options menu. You may need to add (or remove) a space at the insertion point; doing so removes the Paste Options button.

End

The great thing about using a word-processing program is the ability to cut and paste text from one place in your document to another. When you cut and paste, you remove the text from one location and paste it into another.

Understanding the Paste Options

By default, pasted text keeps its original (source) formatting. If you want the pasted text to take on the formatting of the text into which you pasted it, click **Match Destination Formatting** in the Paste Options menu. To remove all its formatting, choose **Keep Text Only**. To display further formatting options for your pasted text, choose **Apply Style or Formatting**. If you don't want to see Paste Options buttons, open the **Tools** menu and choose **Options**, click the **Edit** tab, clear the **Show Paste Options buttons** check box, and click **OK**.

Copying Text

Start

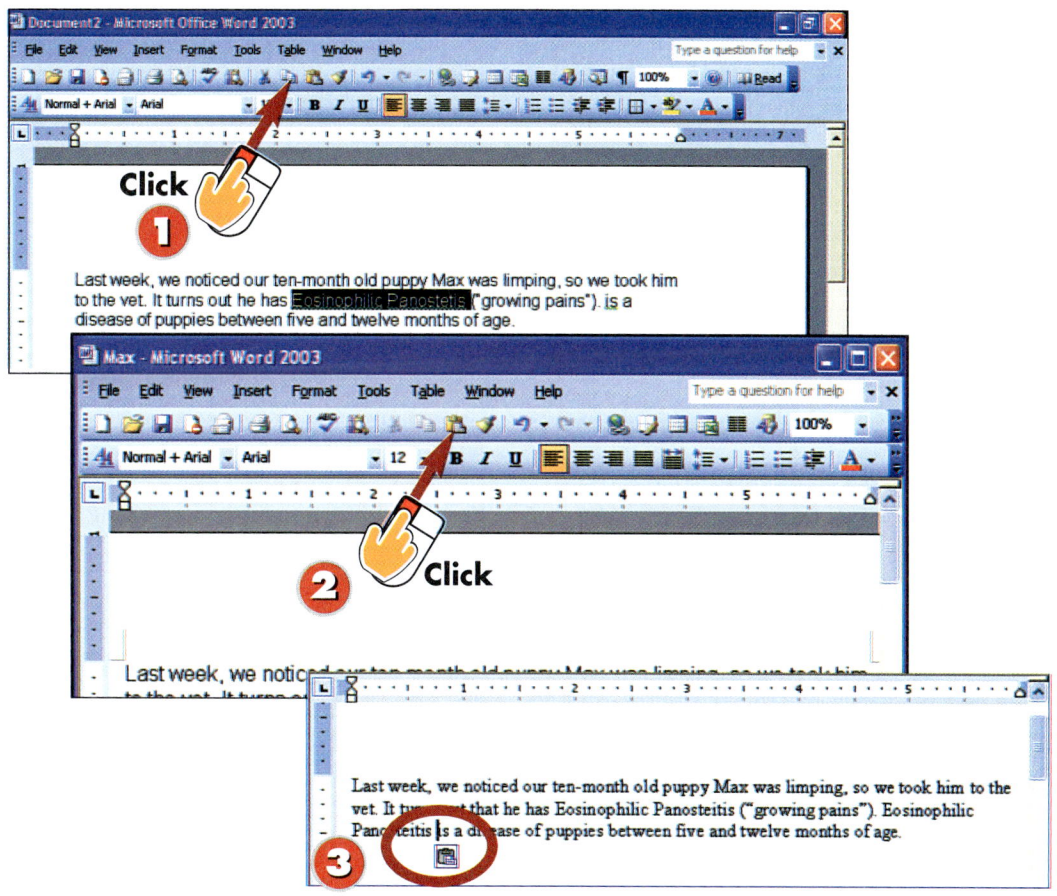

Click ❶

Click ❷

❸

❶ Select the text that you want to copy and click the **Copy** button on the Standard toolbar. The selected text remains in its current location.

❷ Move the insertion point to the place where you want to copy the text and click the **Paste** button on the Standard toolbar.

❸ The text is copied to the new location and the Paste Options button pops up (see the previous task for information about this button). If necessary, adjust spacing at the insertion point.

End

If you have a block of text in one place in your document that you want to copy for use somewhere else, it's much faster to copy it than to type it again. The steps here show you how to copy text from one location to another within the same document.

TIP

The Windows Clipboard

When you copy or cut a block of selected text, it is placed in the *Windows Clipboard*. When you paste the text, Word copies it from the Clipboard into your document—in the same Word document, in another Word document, or in another program in the Office suite. If you want to paste the text into several locations, just move the insertion point to each location and issue the Paste command again. The text is not removed from the Clipboard until you execute the next Copy or Cut command.

Moving or Copying Multiple Items

Start

Click

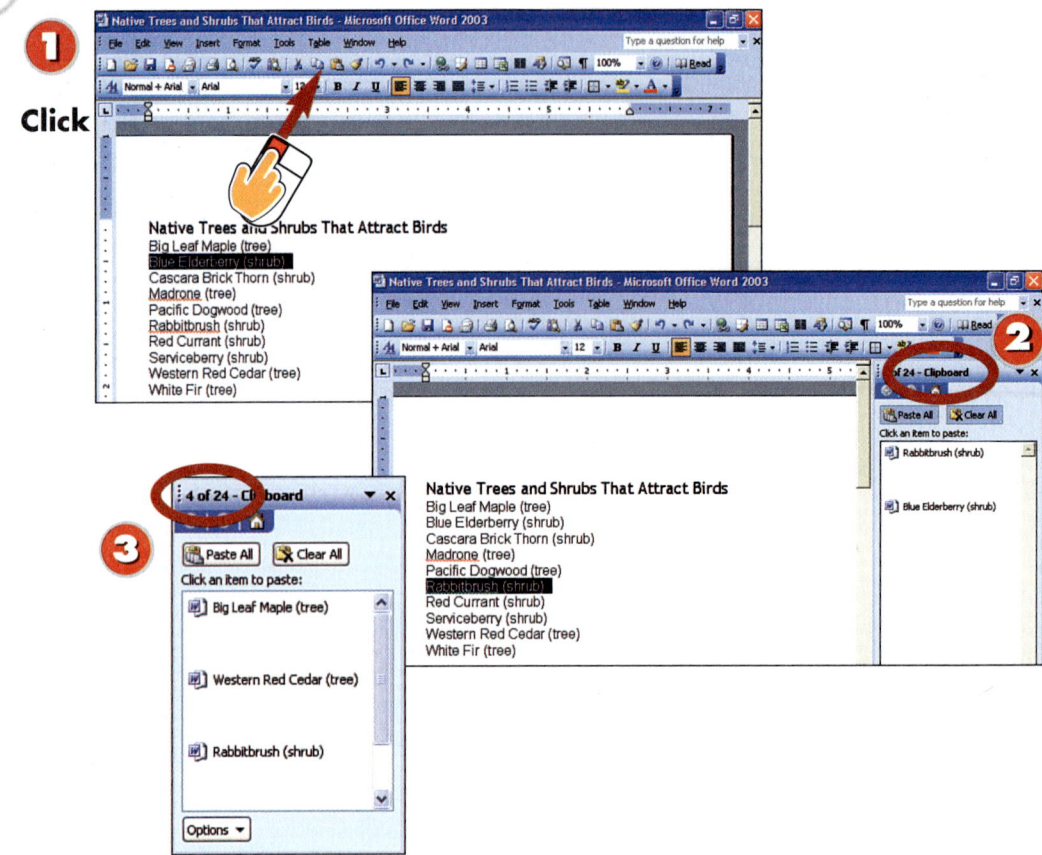

1 Select your first item and click the **Copy** button in the Standard toolbar.

2 Select and copy your second item; the Clipboard task pane opens. Word items are represented in the task pane by Word icons; the Clipboard displays a snippet of text from each item to identify it.

3 If you like, add more items to the Office Clipboard (up to 24). You can add items from any Windows application. The number of items you've added is displayed at the top of the Clipboard.

Most of the time, you only need to cut or copy one piece of text at a time. Occasionally, however, you may need to "collect" a bunch of pieces of text from different places to move or copy. The *Office Clipboard* allows you to do just that. You can collect multiple items of any length (they can come from Word or any other Windows application), and then paste them into a Word document or any other Office document. (This example shows you how to use the Copy command with the Clipboard to copy items, but you can also use the Cut command to move items.)

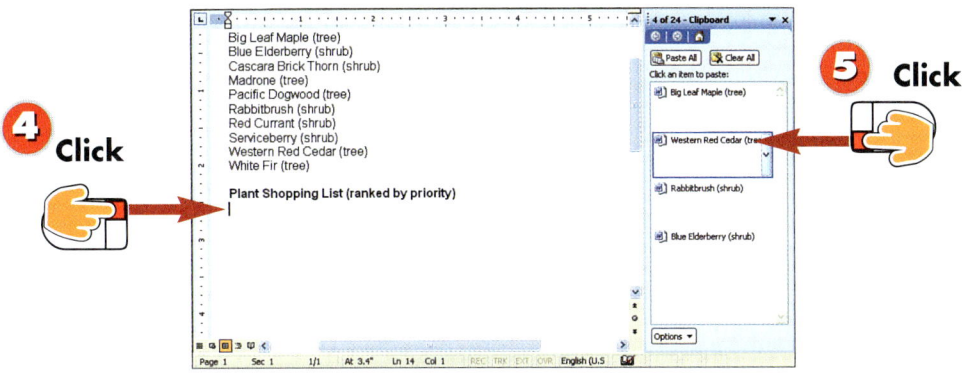

5 Click

4 Click

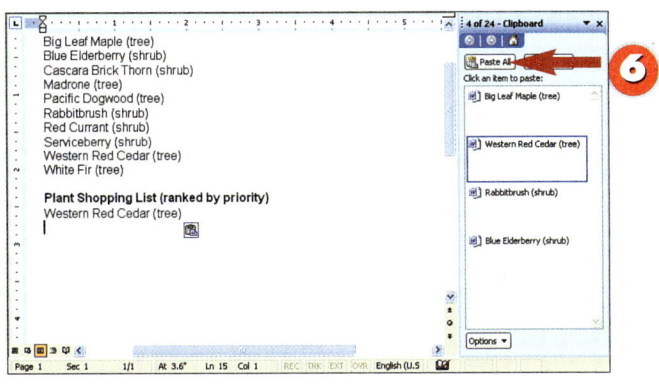

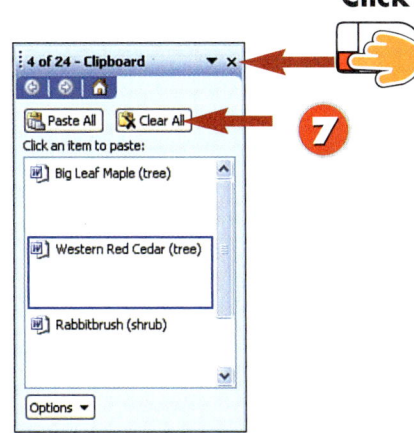

Click

6

7

4 To paste an item on the Clipboard into a document, switch to the desired document and position the insertion point accordingly. (You'll learn how to switch among open documents in Part 4.)

5 Click the item that you want to insert in the Clipboard task pane, and click **Paste** in the list that appears.

6 The item is pasted into your document. To paste all of the items in the Clipboard task pane at once, click the **Paste All** button.

7 To empty the Office Clipboard, click the **Clear All** button. To close the Clipboard task pane, click the **Close** button.

End

Displaying the Clipboard Task Pane
If the Clipboard task pane does not open automatically in Step 2, open the **Edit** menu and choose **Office Clipboard**. To configure the Clipboard task pane to appear automatically when you copy multiple items, click the **Options** button at the bottom of the task pane, and choose **Show Office Clipboard Automatically**.

Inserting a Tab

Start

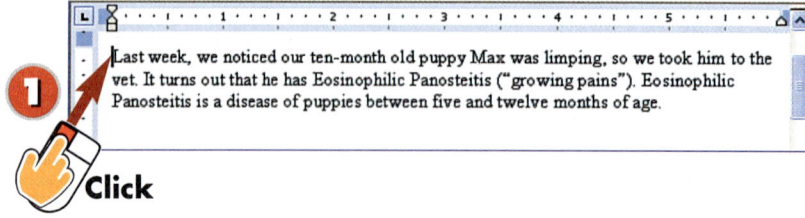

1

Click

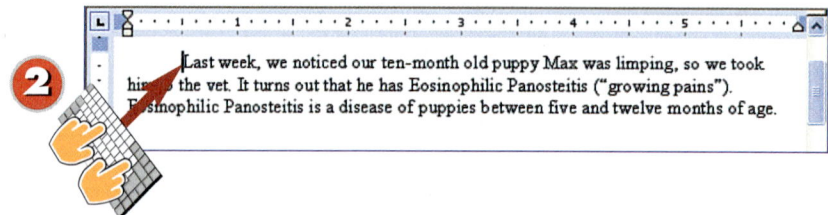

2

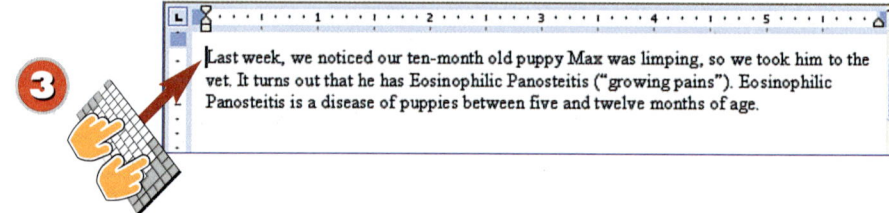

3

1 Move the insertion point to the spot in the document where you want to insert a tab. The faint tick marks along the lower edge of the horizontal ruler represent Word's default tab stops.

2 Press the **Tab** key on your keyboard. Word pushes the text out to the next default tab stop.

3 To remove a tab, make sure that your insertion point is just to the right of the tab, and press the **Backspace** key.

End

When you press the Tab key on your keyboard, Word pushes the text to the right of the insertion point out to the next tab stop. Word's default tabs are set every half inch across the page. These default tabs are all that you need if you just want to indent the first line of your paragraphs. If you want to use tabs to align text more precisely, however, you need to create custom tabs (see "Setting a Custom Left or Right Tab" in Part 6).

Using First-Line Indents
Word may set a *first-line indent* for the paragraph instead of inserting a tab when you press the Tab key at the beginning of a paragraph. The paragraph will look the same either way, and you can remove a first-line indent with the Backspace key.

Seeing Paragraph, Tab, and Space Marks

Start

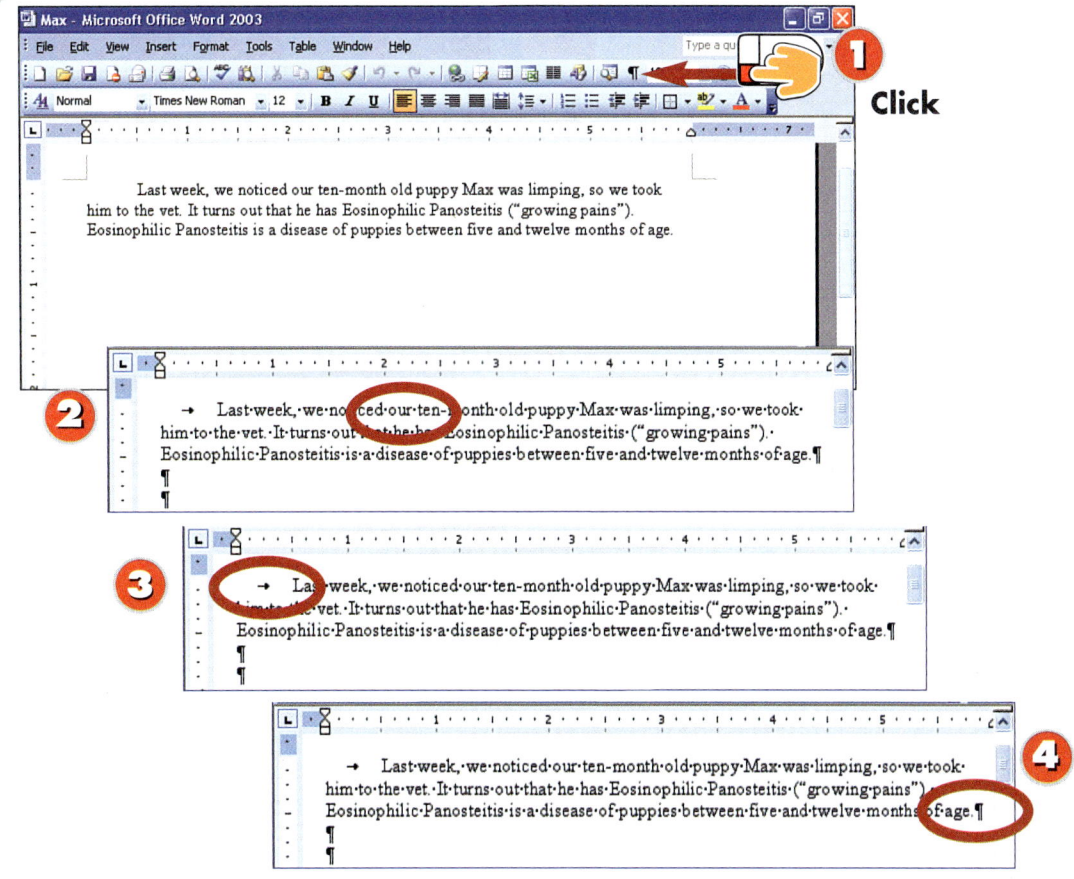

Click

1 Click the **Show/Hide** button on the Standard toolbar.

2 Word uses a dot to show where you pressed the Spacebar.

3 Word uses an arrow to indicate where you pressed the Tab key.

4 Word uses the paragraph mark symbol (¶) to indicate where you pressed Enter to end a paragraph.

End

INTRODUCTION

The Show/Hide button is an extremely handy tool. It displays nonprinting symbols onscreen to show you where you pressed the Spacebar, the Enter key, and the Tab key. You might use this button to check whether you typed an extra space between two words, to see how many blank lines there are between two paragraphs, or to confirm that you inserted only one tab at the beginning of a paragraph.

TIP

Understanding the Show/Hide Button
The Show/Hide button is a *toggle* button. You click it once to turn it on, and again to turn it off. You can turn the Show/Hide button on and off whenever you choose.

Managing Word Documents

Just as a filing cabinet would be of no use if you didn't know how to get files into and out of the drawers, you must understand how to access and store Word documents on your computer system in order to use the program effectively. In this part, you learn elementary yet essential skills, including saving, closing, and opening documents, and creating new ones. In addition, you learn how to "bookmark" folders you use frequently and track down a document that you've misplaced on your computer. You also get pointers on salvaging your work after Word crashes.

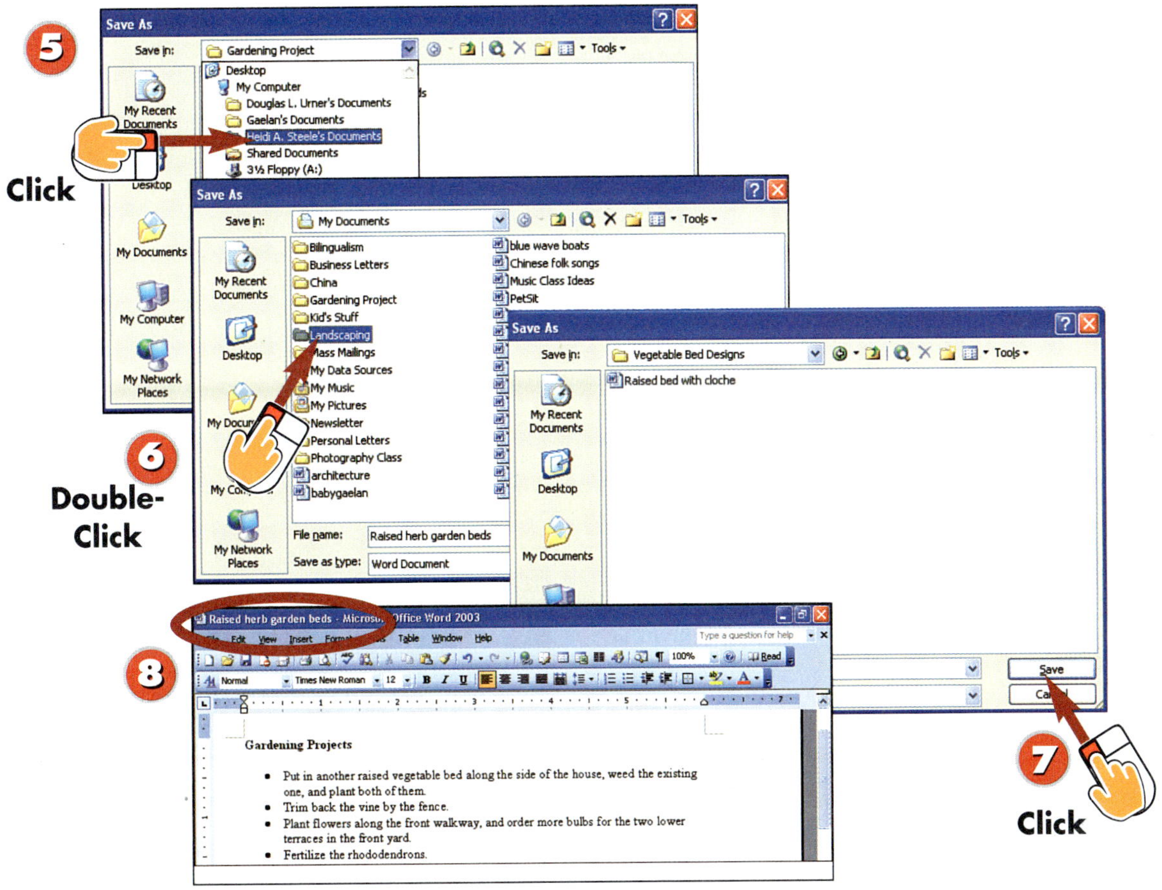

Click

Double-Click

Click

5 To save the file elsewhere, click the **down arrow** to the right of the **Save in** box, and click the entry that contains the folder you want.

6 To save your file in a folder listed under the **Save in** box, double-click the folder to open it (and, if applicable, any of its subfolders).

7 Click the **Save** button.

8 The document's name now appears in the title bar of the Word window.

End

TIP

Overwriting Another Document When You Save
When you try to save a document in a folder that already contains a file with the same name, Word displays a message window with three options: **Replace existing file**, **Save changes with a different name**, and **Merge changes into existing file**. If you want to overwrite the existing file with the file on your screen, choose the first option. If you want to keep the existing file as is and save the file on your screen with a different name, choose the second option. (The third option is beyond the scope of this book.)

Closing a Document

Start

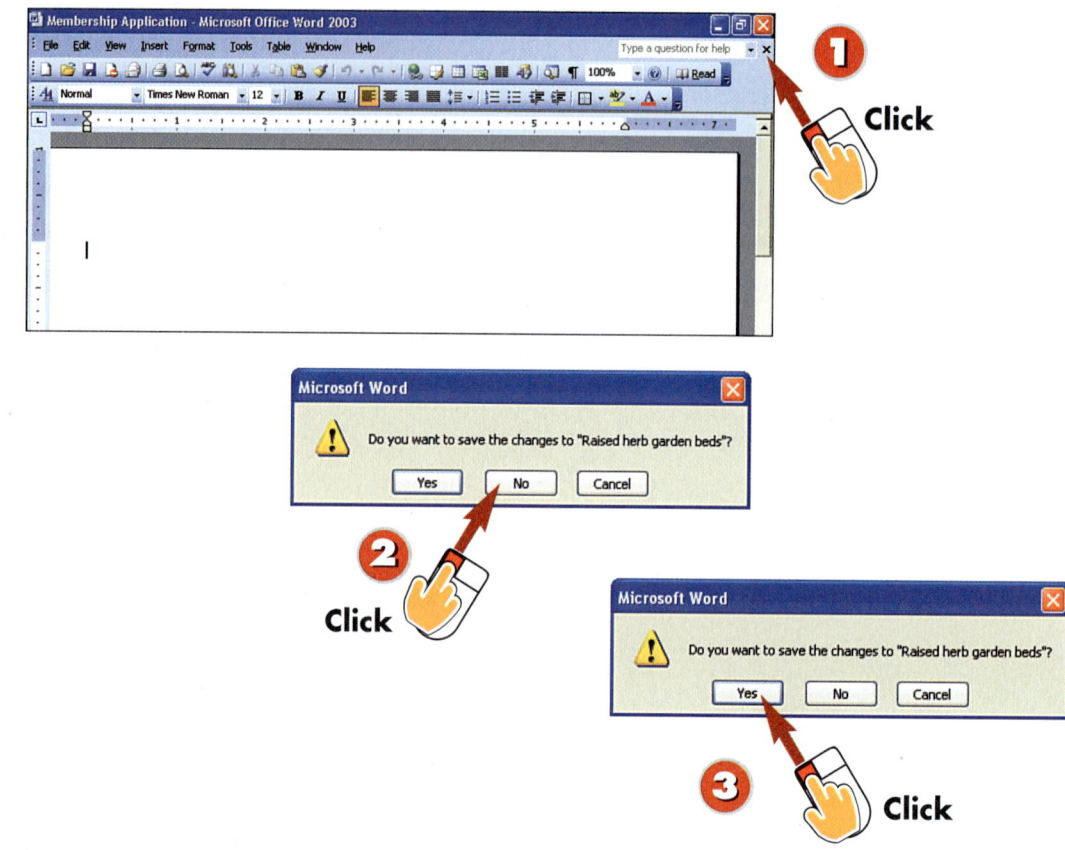

Click

Click

Click

① Click the document's **Close Window** button. If you've saved all your changes, Word closes the document. (If you click the **Close** button in the program window, you will exit Word entirely.)

② If you have unsaved changes, Word asks whether you want to save them. If you don't, click the **No** button. Word closes the document.

③ If you want to save the changes you've made to the document, click the **Yes** button. (Click the **Cancel** button if you decide not to close the document after all.)

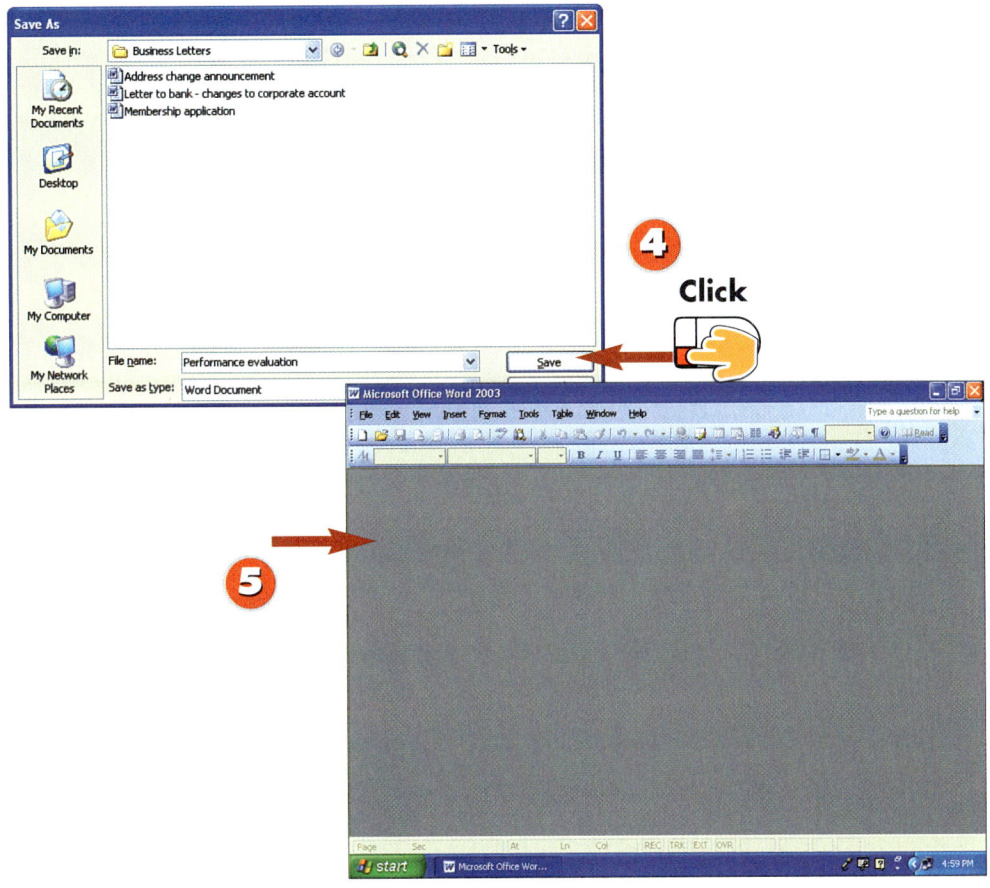

Click

4 If you're saving the document for the first time, Word displays the Save As dialog box. Choose a name and location for the file (see the preceding task), and then click the **Save** button.

5 The document closes, but the Word window remains open to let you start a new document or open an existing one.

End

Closing One of Several Open Documents

TIP
If the document you are closing is one of several you have open, you can click either the program window's **Close** button (the one on top) or the document window's **Close Window** button (the one below) in the upper-right corner of the Word window to close it. That particular document will close, but the others will remain open.

Another Way to Close Your Document

TIP
If you like, you can open the **File** menu and choose **Close** in step 1 instead of clicking the **Close Window** button. The result is the same.

Opening a Document

Start

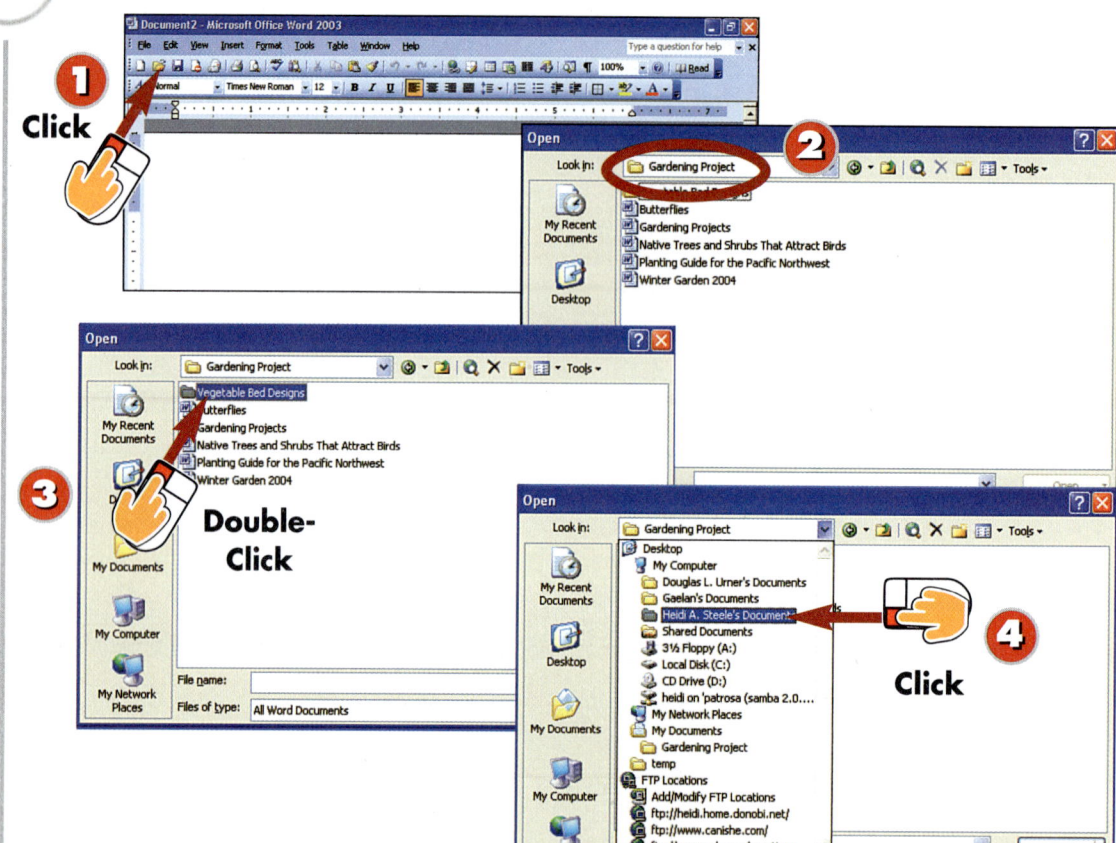

1 Click

2

3 Double-Click

4 Click

---

1 Click the **Open** button in the Standard toolbar to display the Open dialog box.

2 Look at the **Look in** box. If the location listed here is the one that contains your document, skip to step 6.

3 If the folder you want is under the **Look in** box, double-click the folder to open it, and, if applicable, any of its subfolders. Then skip to step 6.

4 To look elsewhere, click the **down arrow** to the right of the **Look in** box, and click the entry that contains the folder you want.

When you want to revise a document that you've previously saved to disk, follow these steps to open it again. You can open as many documents at once as you like, and then use the methods described in the next task to switch back and forth among them.

TIP

Opening a Document Quickly
Word lists the four documents that you've opened most recently at the bottom of the **File** menu and in the **Getting Started** task pane. If your document is in one of these lists, you can just click it to open it instead of following these steps.

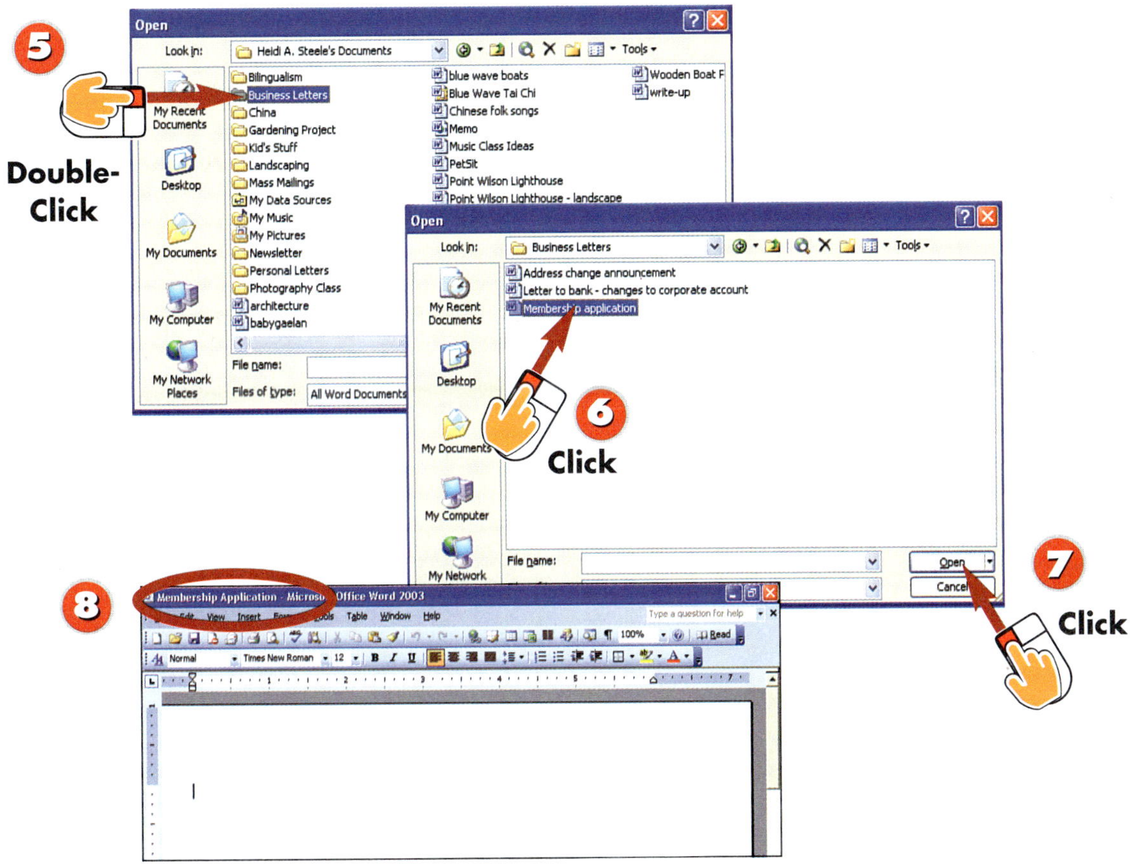

Double-Click

Click

6

Click

7

8

Click

5 As in step 3, double-click folders until the folder that contains the file you want to open is displayed in the **Look in** box.

6 Click the document you want to open.

7 Click the **Open** button. (You can also just double-click the document name.)

8 Word opens the document for you.

End

Previewing Documents

If you need help finding your document, you can use the Preview feature in the Open dialog box. Click the **down arrow** to the right of the **Views** toolbar button at the top of the Open dialog box (this button is immediately to the left of the Tools button), and choose **Preview** in the list that appears. The right side of the Open dialog box becomes a preview pane that shows the contents of the currently selected document.

Switching to Another Open Document

Start

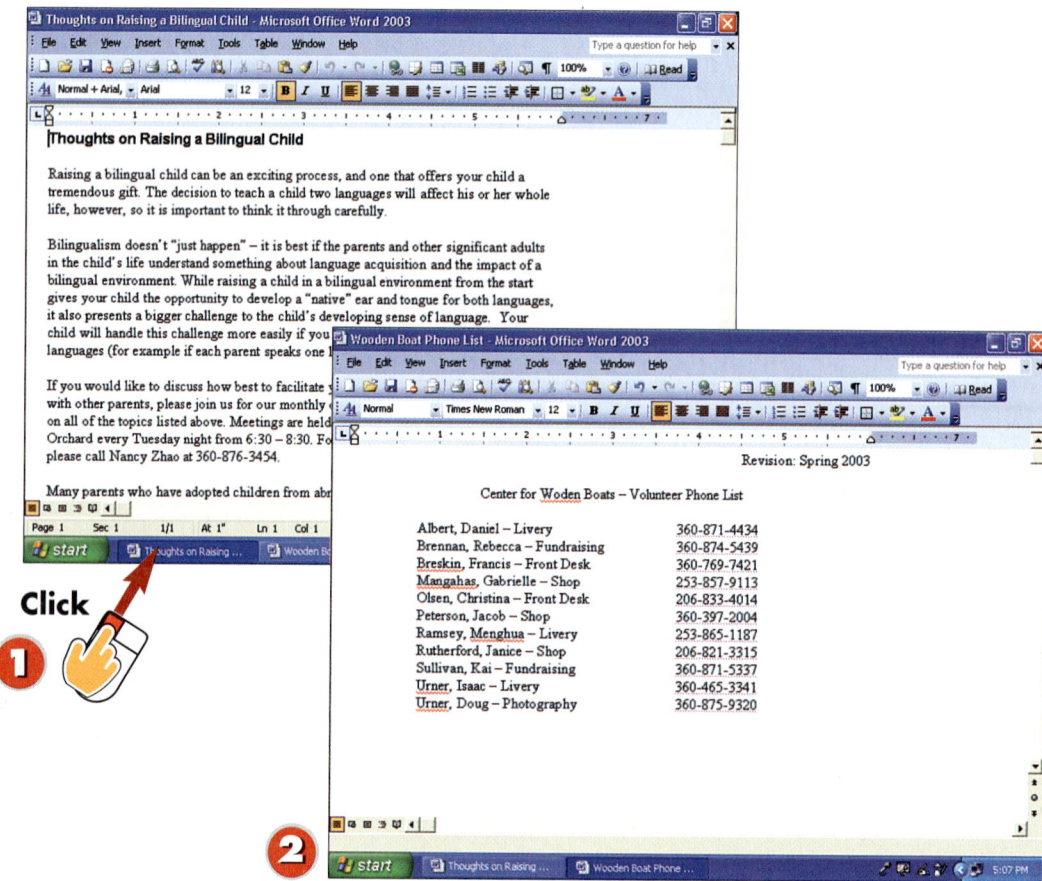

Click
1

2

1. The taskbar at the bottom of your screen contains a button for each Word document that is open. Click the taskbar button for the document that you want to switch to.

2. Word brings that document to the top.

It's quite common to want to work on more than one Word document at the same time. When you have multiple documents open, they stack on top of each other much like a sheets of paper, with the document you are currently working on at the "top" of the stack. It only takes a couple of clicks to bring another document to the top. Word gives you more than one way to do this. Try the methods introduced in this task and then use the one you like the best.

TIP

One Word Taskbar Button
If you would prefer not to see a separate taskbar button for each Word document you have open (see step 1), open the **Tools** menu and choose **Options**. Click the **View** tab, clear the **Windows in Taskbar** check box, and click **OK**.

Click

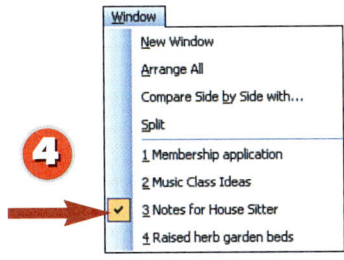

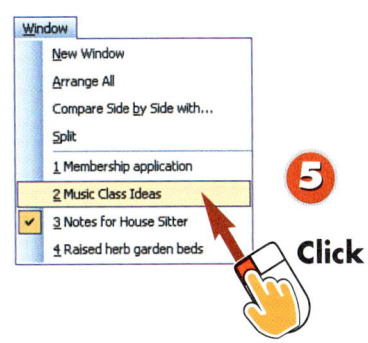

Click

Alternatively, click **Window** in the menu bar.

The Window menu opens. At the bottom of the menu is a list of all your open documents; the current document has a check mark next to it.

Click the document that you want switch to. Word displays the document for you.

End

Using the Keyboard
The keyboard shortcut for switching among open Word documents is **Ctrl+F6**. Each time you press Ctrl+F6, Word brings another open document to the top.

What Happens When the Taskbar Gets Too Crowded
Depending on your display settings and the number of Word documents you have open, Windows may decide that you don't have enough room to display a separate taskbar button for each document. When this happens, it displays only one Word taskbar button that contains a number indicating the number of open documents. When you click the button, a list of all the open documents pops up. To switch to one of the documents, simply click it in the list.

Getting to Your Favorite Folders

Start

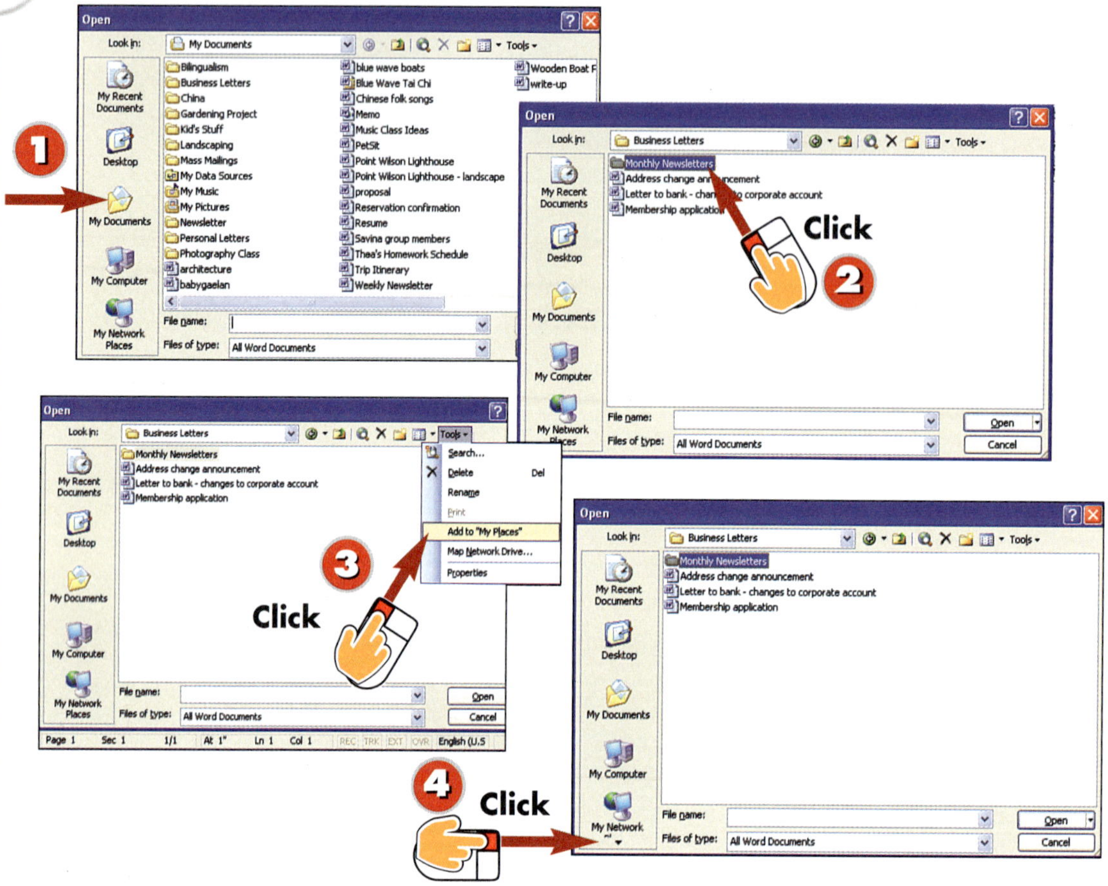

1. Display the Open or Save As dialog box. The Places list is the vertical bar on the left side of the dialog box.

2. Navigate in the Open or Save As dialog box until you see the folder for which you want to create a shortcut in the main part of the dialog box. Click the folder to select it.

3. Click the **Tools** button in the Open or Save As dialog box's toolbar, and click **Add to "My Places"** in the menu that appears.

4. The shortcut is added to the Places list. You may need to click the **down arrow** at the bottom of the list to bring it into view.

If a folder you use frequently is buried deep in the file structure on your hard disk or is on another network computer, it can be time consuming to navigate to it in the Open and Save As dialog boxes. Fortunately, you can avoid this hassle by creating a *shortcut* to the folder. The shortcut, which appears in the Places list on the left side of the Open and Save As dialog boxes, simply points to the folder. Clicking the shortcut opens the folder just as if you clicked the folder itself. For help displaying the Save As and Open dialog boxes, refer to "Saving a Document" and "Opening a Document" earlier in this part.

Click

Click

Click

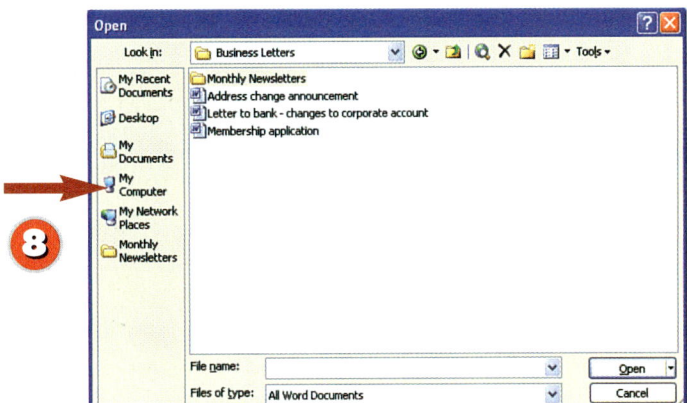

5 To move a shortcut up or down in the Places list, right-click the shortcut and choose **Move Up** or **Move Down**.

6 To remove a shortcut from the Places list, right-click the shortcut and choose **Remove**. This only removes the shortcut, not the folder to which it pointed.

7 If you want to shrink the size of the shortcuts in the Places list so you can see more of them without scrolling, right-click any of them and choose **Small Icons**.

8 The shortcut icons are now smaller. (To restore them to their original size, right-click any one of them and choose **Large Icons**.)

End

Renaming Shortcuts in the Places List

If you want to change the name of a shortcut, right-click the shortcut and choose **Rename**. In the Rename Place dialog box, type a new name and press **Enter**. This only changes the name of the shortcut, not the name of the actual folder. You can rename only those shortcuts that you've added to the Places list, not shortcuts that were there by default.

Starting Additional New Documents

Start

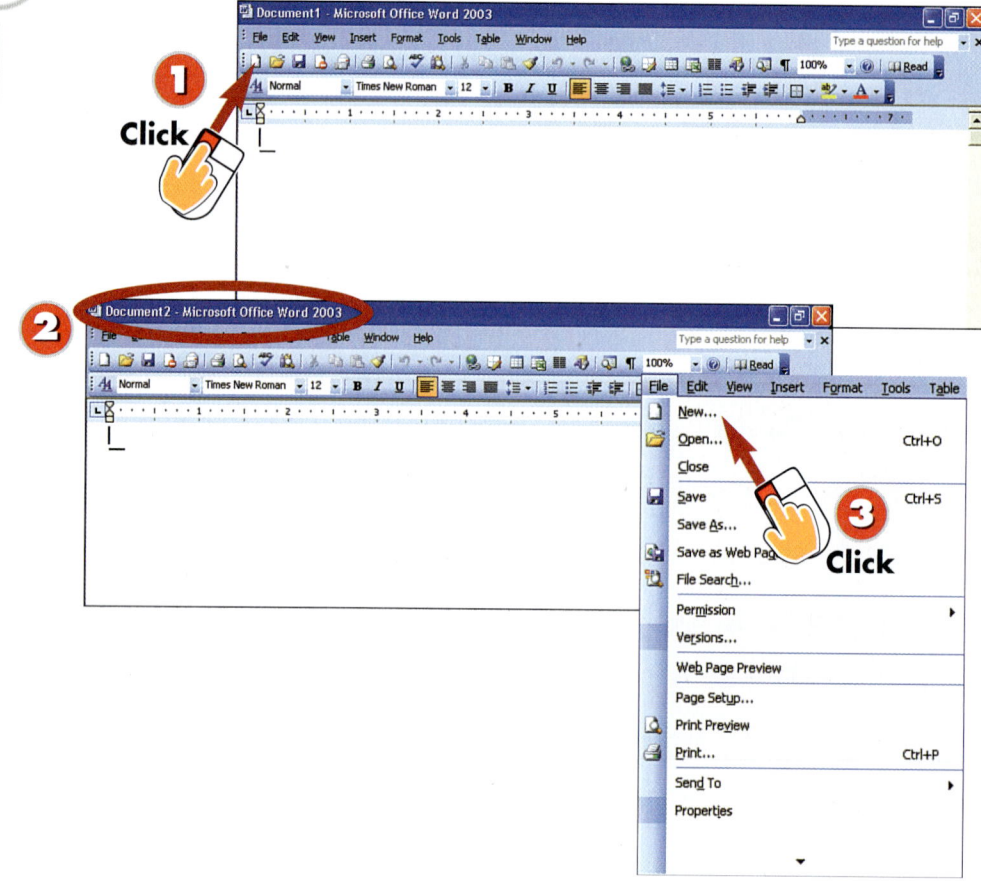

Click

Click

1. With a document already open, click the **New Blank Document** button in the Standard toolbar.

2. A new Word window opens, displaying a new blank document (it is named Document2 because it is the second document you opened in this Word session).

3. This time, open the **File** menu and choose **New** instead of clicking the New Blank Document button.

INTRODUCTION

Each time you start Word, you get a new blank document that has the temporary name Document1 (which you replace the first time you save the document). However, you may at times want to start a second or third document in the same Word session. Word lets you keep multiple documents open at once, each in its own window, so you don't have to close the currently active document before beginning another one.

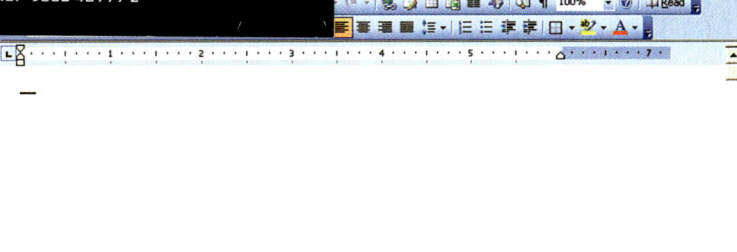

4 The New Document task pane opens. Click **Blank Document** under **New** at the top of the task pane.

5 Word starts a new document, just as if you had clicked the New Blank Document button. (See the next task to find out when the File, New command is useful.)

End

New Document Names

TIP

When you start a new document, its name may be Document2, Document3, and so on. The number in the name does not mean that you have that number of documents currently *open*; it just means that you have *started* that many documents in the current Word session.

72

Standardizing the Look of Your Documents

Start

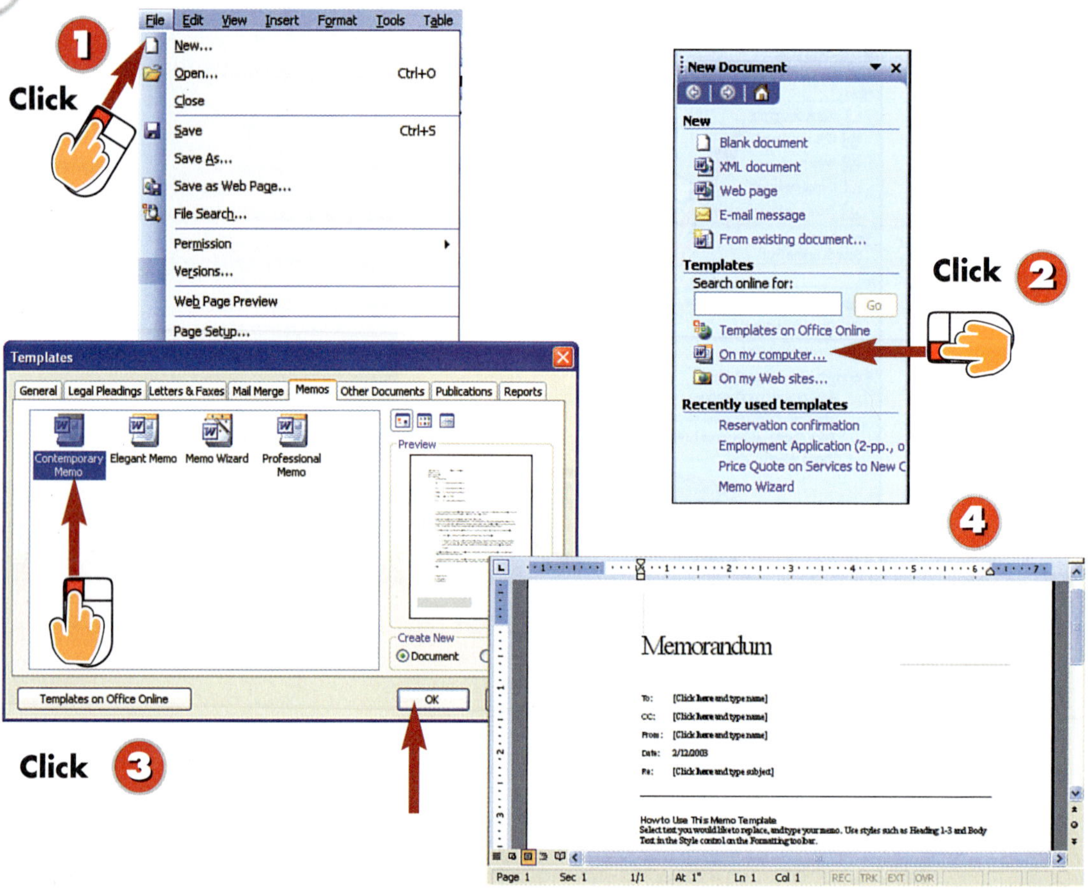

Click 1

Click 2

Click 3

4

Memorandum

To: [Click here and type name]
CC: [Click here and type name]
From: [Click here and type name]
Date: 2/12/2003
Re: [Click here and type subject]

How to Use This Memo Template
Select text you would like to replace, and type your memo. Use styles such as Heading 1-3 and Body Text in the Style control on the Formatting toolbar.

1. Open the **File** menu and choose **New** to display the New Document task pane.

2. In the New Document task pane, under **Templates**, click **On my computer** to open the Templates dialog box.

3. Click the tab that contains the kind of template you want to use (your tabs may differ from those shown here), click a template to select it, and click the **OK** button.

4. Word creates a new document based on the template you chose.

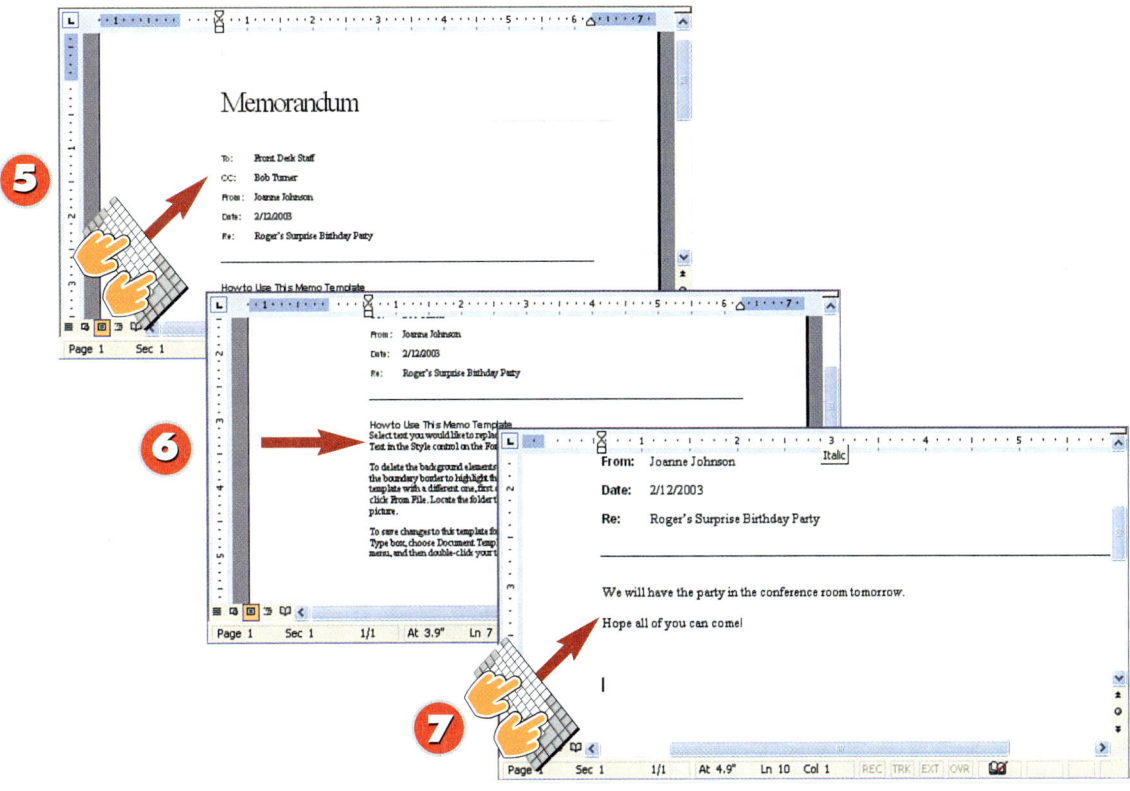

5 If you see **[Click here and type]** instructions, type over them with the text you want in your document.

6 Some templates have instructions on using the template where the body of the document will go. If yours does, first read the information.

7 Select the instructions, and type over them with your text. (Your text replaces the selected instructions.) Optionally save, and then close, the document.

End

Saving Templates
When you save a document that you based on a template, Word saves it separately from the template. The template maintains its original appearance so that you can use it over and over again.

Accessing Your Favorite Templates
Word displays the templates you've used most recently in the **New Document** task pane under **Recently used templates** so that you can access them easily.

Using a Wizard to Create a Document

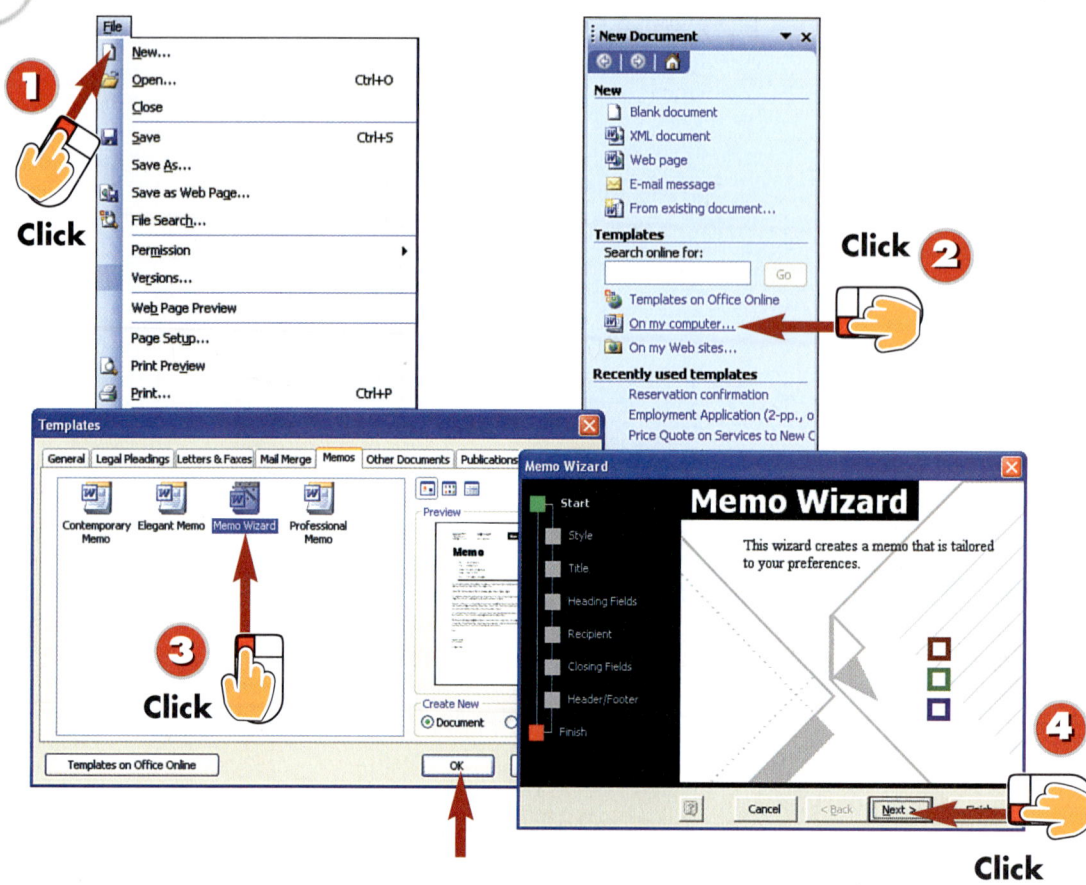

1. Open the **File** menu and choose **New** to display the New Document task pane.

2. In the New Document task pane, under **Templates**, click **On my computer** to open the Templates dialog box.

3. Click the tab that contains the kind of wizard you want to use (your tabs may differ from those shown here), click a wizard to select it, and click the **OK** button.

4. Word displays the first screen of the wizard you selected. Click the **Next** button.

If you'd appreciate a bit more hand-holding than you get with standard templates, try using a *wizard*. Wizards, like other templates, give you "blueprint" text and formatting, but they also ask you questions about what you want to include in the document, and then create just what you asked for. Wizard-generated documents look exactly like documents based on standard templates, complete with "click here" instructions to help you fill in the text.

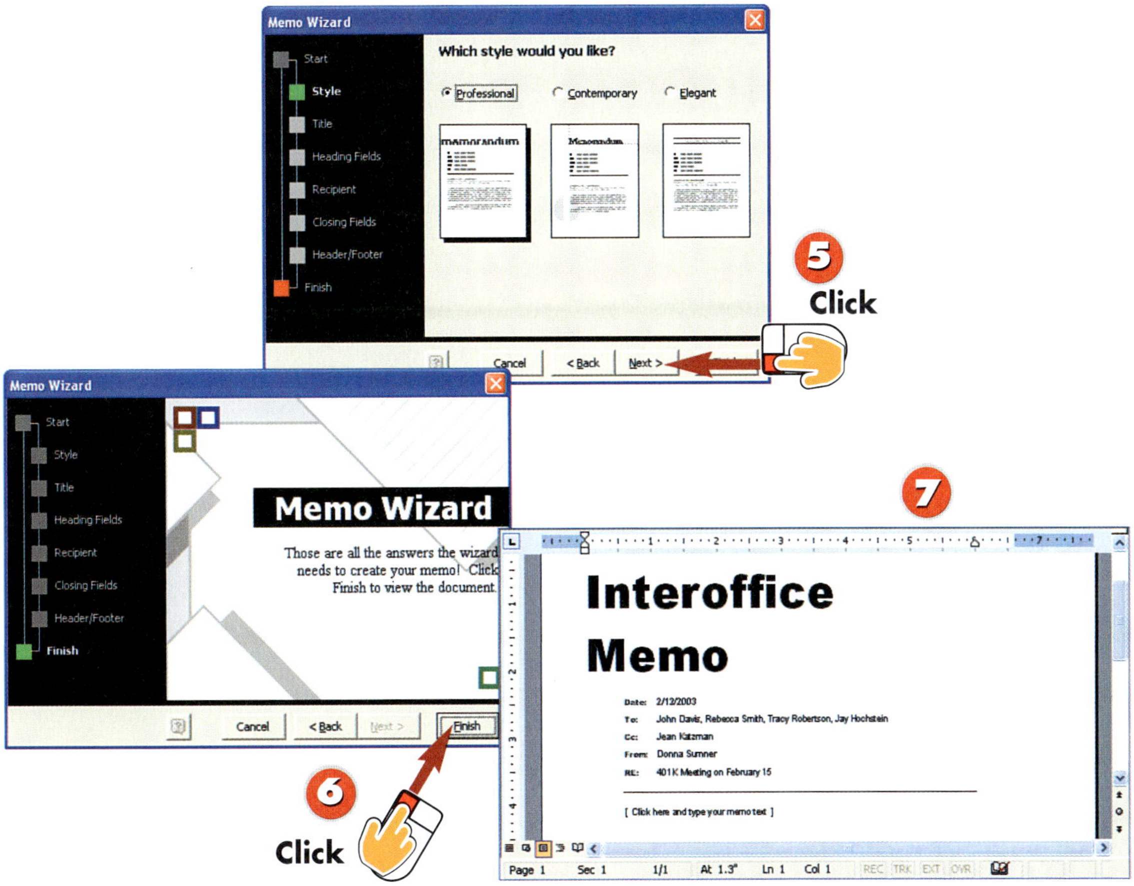

Memo Wizard

Which style would you like?

Start
Style
Title
Heading Fields
Recipient
Closing Fields
Header/Footer
Finish

Professional   Contemporary   Elegant

memorandum

5 **Click**

Cancel   < Back   Next >

Memo Wizard

Start
Style
Title
Heading Fields
Recipient
Closing Fields
Header/Footer
Finish

Memo Wizard

Those are all the answers the wizard needs to create your memo! Click Finish to view the document.

Cancel   < Back   Next >   **Finish**

6 **Click**

Interoffice Memo

Date: 2/12/2003
To: John Davis, Rebecca Smith, Tracy Robertson, Jay Hochstein
Cc: Jean Katzman
From: Donna Sumner
RE: 401K Meeting on February 15

_____

[Click here and type your memo text]

Page 1   Sec 1   1/1   At 1.3"   Ln 1   Col 1   REC   TRK   EXT   OVR

7

---

5 The wizard presents its first question. Choose the option you want, and click **Next** again.

6 Continue answering the wizard's questions. When you reach the last page, click the **Finish** button.

7 In a moment, the document appears. Optionally, fill in the remainder of the text, save it, and close it.

End

Searching for a Document

Start

PART 4

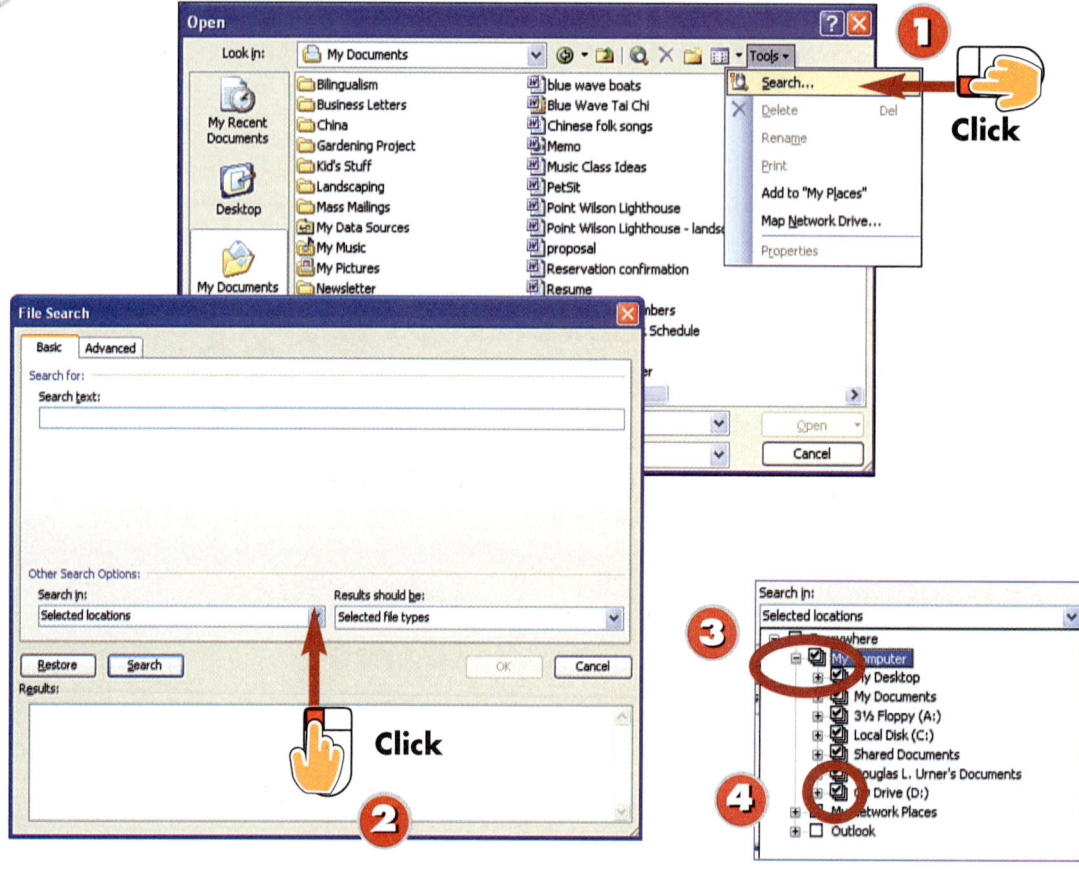

Click

Click

1. In the Open dialog box, click the **Tools** button and choose **Search**. (For help displaying the Open dialog box, refer to "Opening a Document" earlier in this part.)

2. The File Search dialog box opens. In its **Basic** tab, click the **down arrow** next to the **Search in** box to display a drop-down list of locations.

3. To expand a location to see its contents, click the **plus sign** next to it. When a location is expanded, the plus sign changes to a minus sign.

4. A "triple" check mark indicates that Word will search within that location as well as all of its subfolders. Uncheck any locations you want to omit from the search.

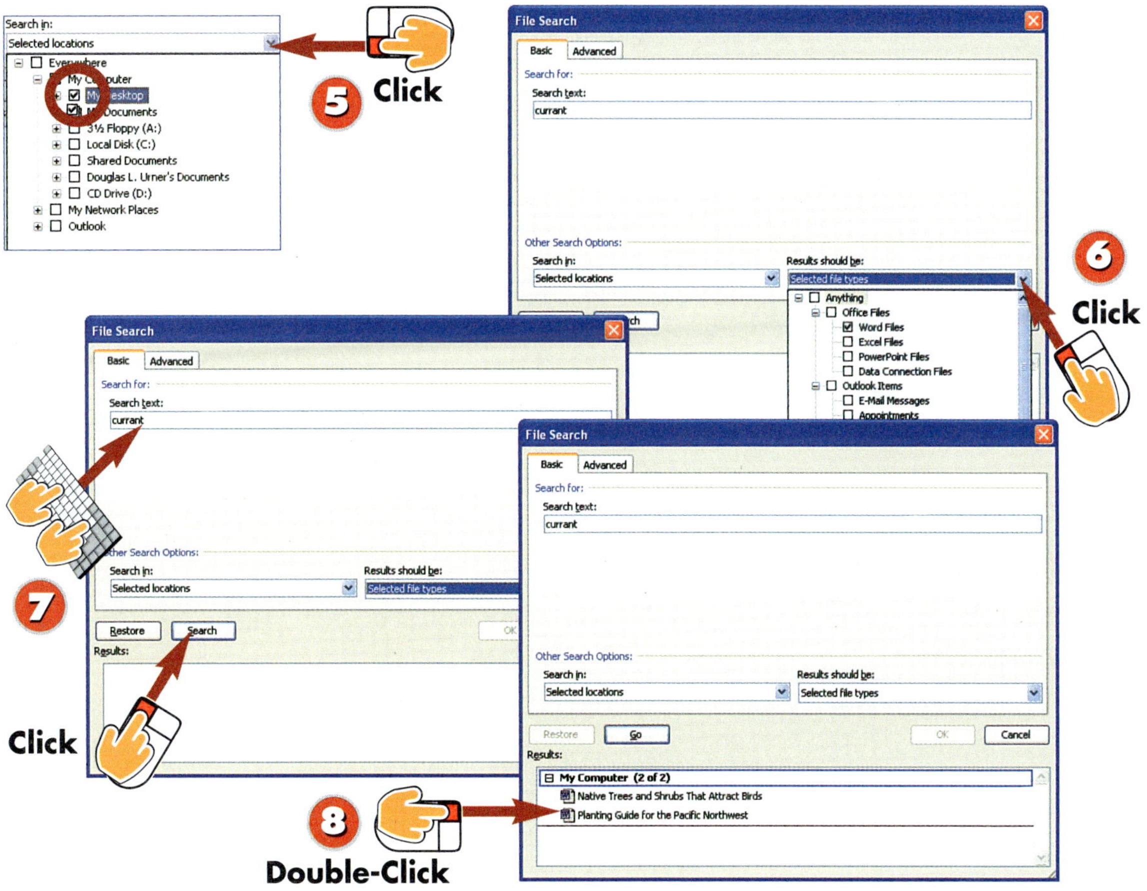

Click

Click

Click

Double-Click

5. To include a location but not its subfolders, clear its check box, and click again to mark it with a "plain" check. When you're ready, click the **down arrow** to close the list.

6. Click the **down arrow** next to the **Results should be** box. Clear all the check boxes except for **Word Files**, and then close the list.

7. In the **Search text** text box, type the text from your document that you want to search for, and then click the **Search** button.

8. Word displays the documents it finds in the **Results** area. Double-click a document to open it.

End

Deciding Where to Search

When deciding where to search, keep in mind that you should include all the locations that could possibly contain your file, while not defining an overly broad search that will take a long time to perform. If you have started a search and then realize that it's too broad, click the **Stop** button (the Search button turns into a Stop button during a search). Once you have narrowed your search locations, click the **Go** button to resume the search (the Stop button becomes a Go button as soon as you stop a search).

Recovering After Word Crashes

Start

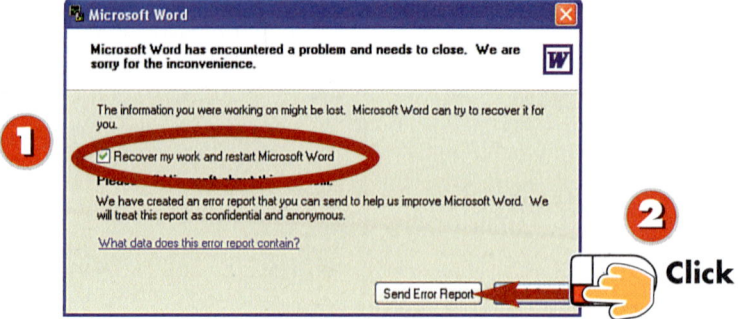

Click

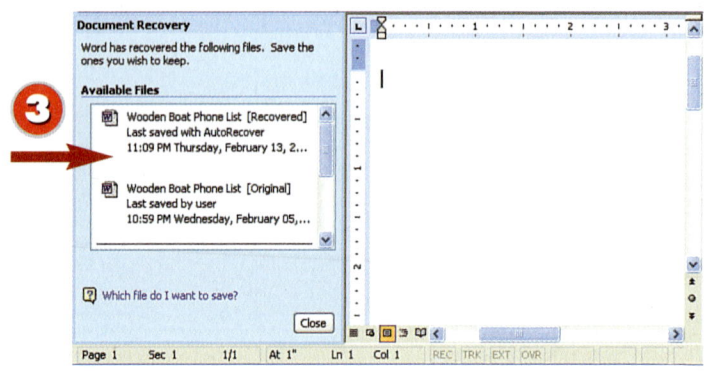

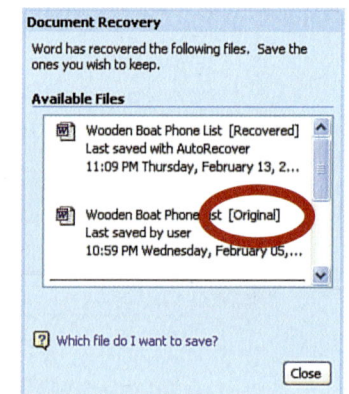

① When Word crashes, it displays an error message, restarts and tries to recover your documents. If you see a check box offering to restart, you can optionally clear it.

② To send Microsoft a report about the crash, click the **Send Error Report** button. Otherwise, click the **Don't Send** button.

③ Word restarts and displays the Document Recovery task pane, which lists all available versions of the documents that were open at the time of the crash.

④ If **[Original]** appears with the document name, either you have made no changes, or you made changes and the original version is displayed along with the recovered version.

Despite your best efforts to close Word and shut down your computer properly, there will be times when something malfunctions and Word simply grinds to a halt. When Word crashes, it displays a message telling you it's done so and politely informs you that you will lose any unsaved work (a compelling reason to save frequently). The next time you start Word, you will have an opportunity to view and save the documents that Word recovered from the crash.

TIP

Sending Error Reports
Microsoft analyzes the error reports it receives from crashes and occasionally provides you with information about how to prevent them.

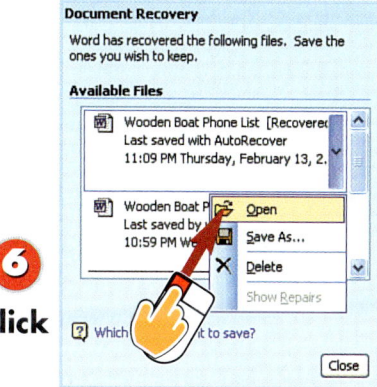

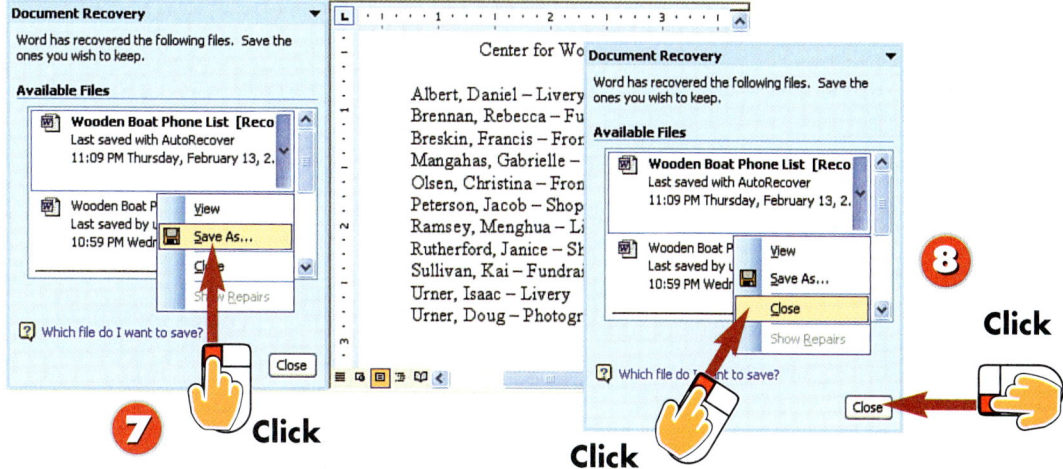

5 If **[Recovered]** appears with the document name, you made changes since you last saved, and Word is offering you the version it saved with its AutoRecover feature.

6 Click a file to open it (or click the **down arrow** and choose **Open**). **Open** changes to **View** in the drop-down list; view each file to see which one contains your changes.

7 To save a file, click the **down arrow** and choose **Save As**. Keep the same name and location to overwrite the original file, or choose a new name and/or location.

8 To close a recovered document, click the **down arrow** and choose **Close**. When you have finished, click the **Close** button to close the Document Recovery task pane.

End

Viewing and Printing
a Document

You can create such a wide variety of documents in Word—from standard letters, memos, and reports to academic papers, flyers, and Web pages—that Word gives you a broad set of choices for viewing documents onscreen and printing them. The first four tasks in this part discuss viewing options; the last three teach you basic printing techniques.

Print Preview and the Print Dialog Box

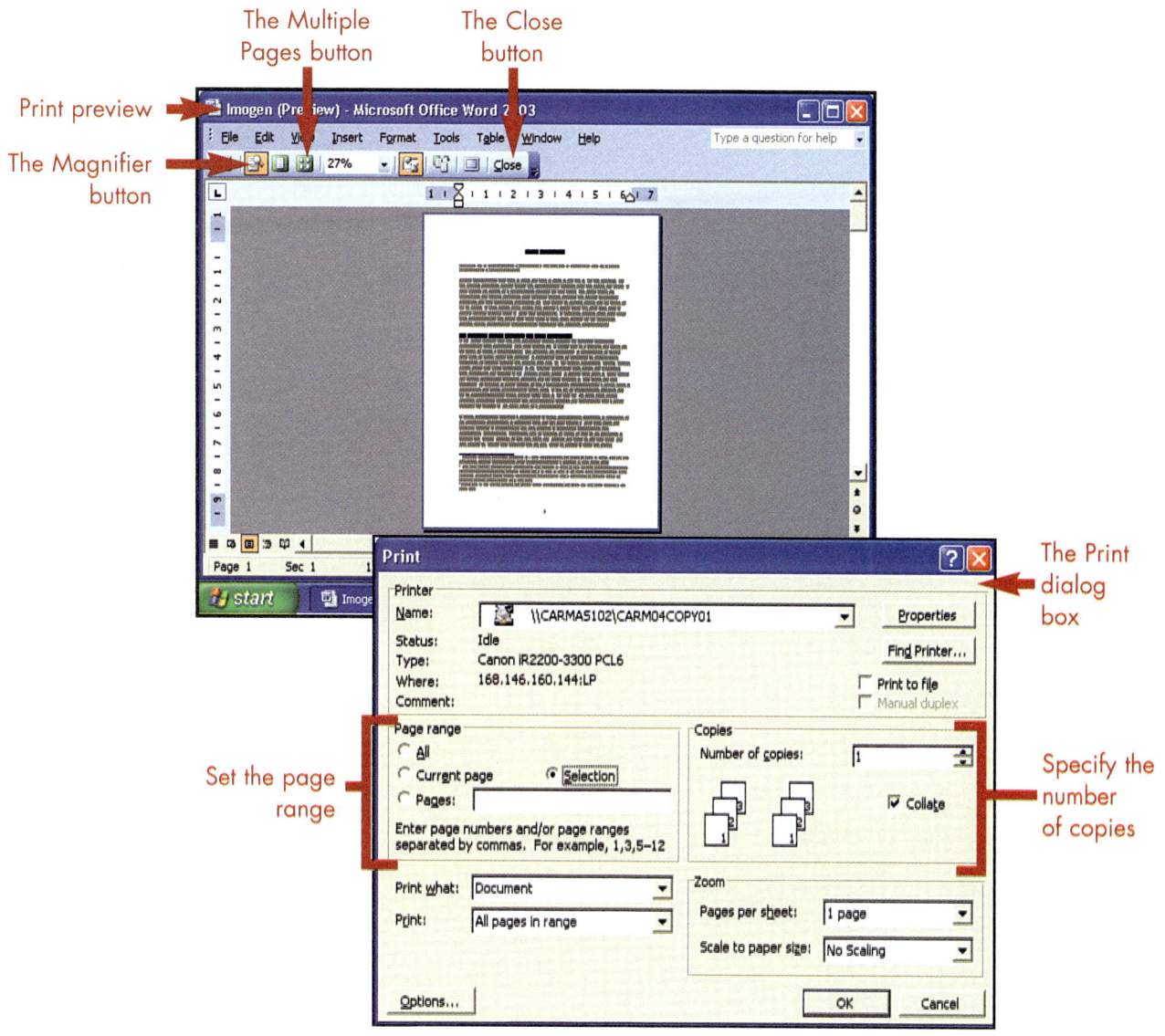

Selecting a View for Your Document

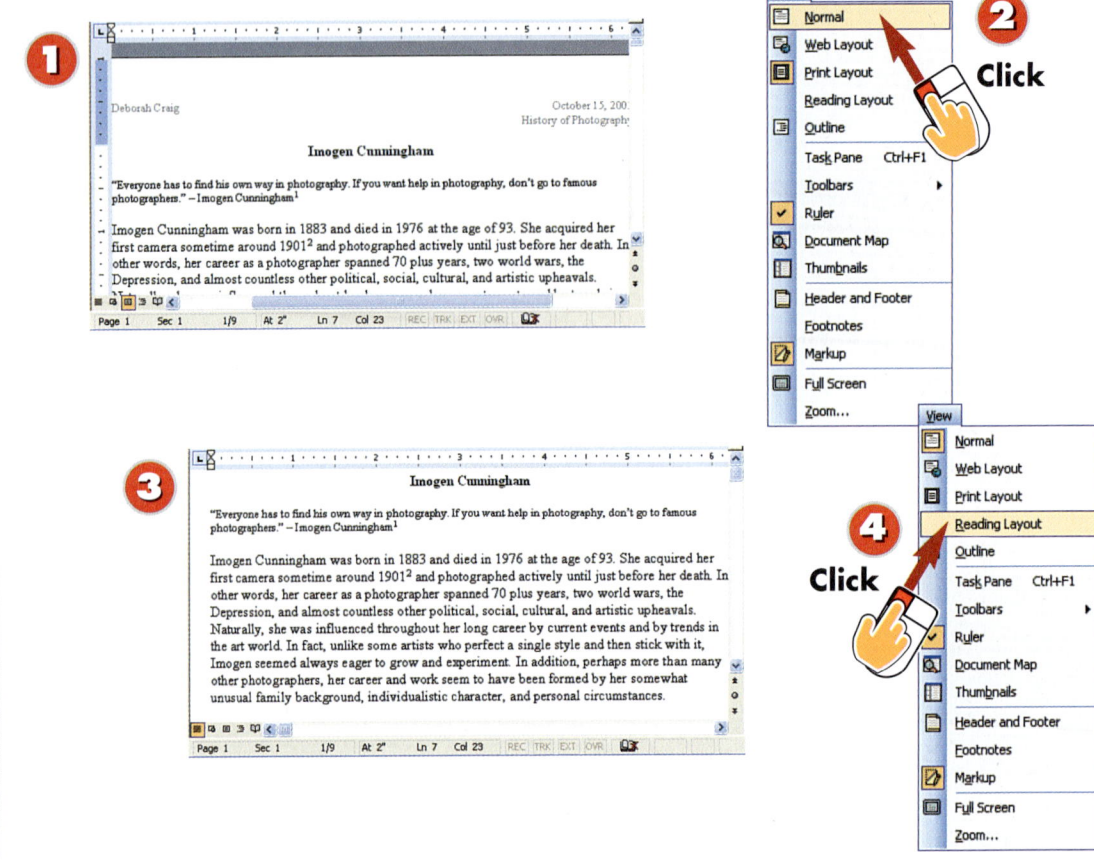

① In Print Layout view, margin areas and vertical and horizontal rulers are visible, as is the edge of the page. (The area off the edge of the page is dark gray.)

② Open the **View** menu and choose **Normal** to switch to Normal view.

③ In Normal view, you can't see the margin areas, and you don't have a vertical ruler.

④ Open the **View** menu and choose **Reading Layout** to switch to Reading Layout view.

INTRODUCTION

Word provides several *views* you can use to work with your documents. *Print Layout* view, the default, shows the margin areas of your document, so you can see things such as page numbers. You need to use this view to work with columns and graphics, among other things. If you are typing a document that doesn't contain a lot of formatting, *Normal view* should work well. This view doesn't show your margin areas, but it gives you an uncluttered view of your text. *Reading Layout* view is useful if you need to read through a long document and want to see the text clearly.

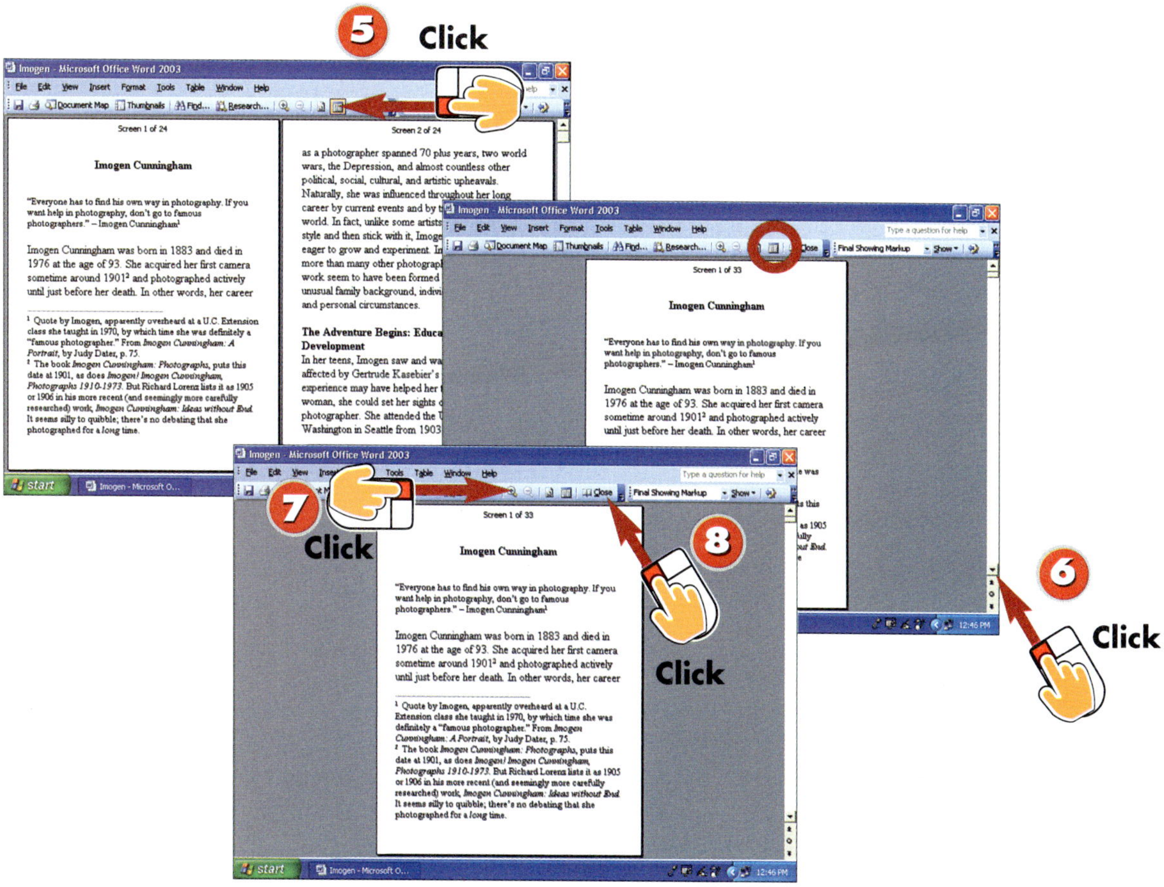

⑤ **Click**

⑦ **Click**

⑧ **Click**

Click

⑥ **Click**

⑤ Text is enlarged, and is displayed in pages. Click the **Allow Multiple Pages** button to switch from displaying two pages to displaying one.

⑥ Click the **down arrow** on the vertical scroll bar to view the next page. To again view two pages at a time, click the **Allow Multiple Pages** button.

⑦ To adjust the size of the text as it's displayed onscreen (this doesn't change how it prints), click the **Increase Text Size** or **Decrease Text Size** button.

⑧ When you are finished, click the **Close** toolbar button to switch back to the previous view.

End

What Is a Screen?

TIP

In Reading Layout view, Word uses the term *screen* to refer to the pages you see on the screen. It does this to help you remember that the amount of text you see on an onscreen page in Reading Layout view doesn't bear any relation to what will appear on the printed page. Rather, the screens just divide up the text into amounts that you can scan easily.

Removing White Space

TIP

In Print Layout view, you can hide the white space. Point to the lower edge of the horizontal ruler, and click the **Hide White Space** ScreenTip is visible. To return the white space to view, click the same place again.

Magnifying a Document

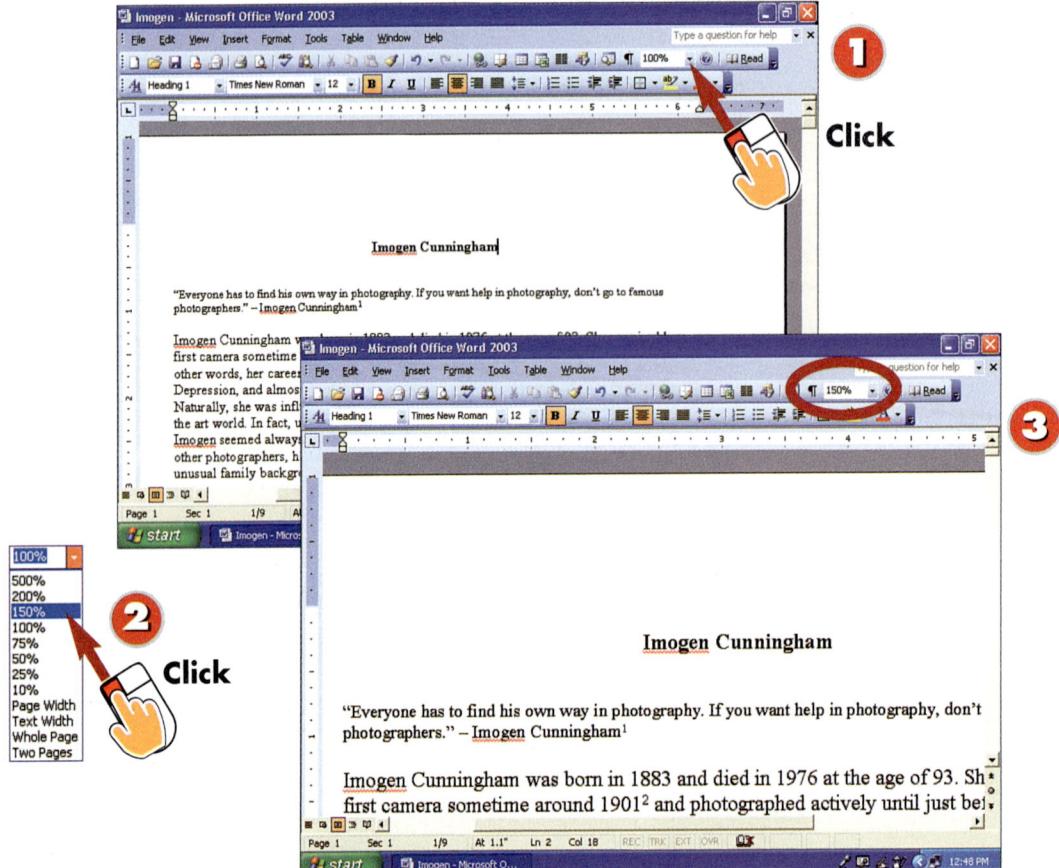

1 Note the **Zoom** box at the right end of the Standard toolbar. By default, Word displays documents at 100% magnification. Click the **down arrow** to the right of the Zoom box.

2 Click the magnification percentage that you want to use.

3 Word applies the setting you chose.

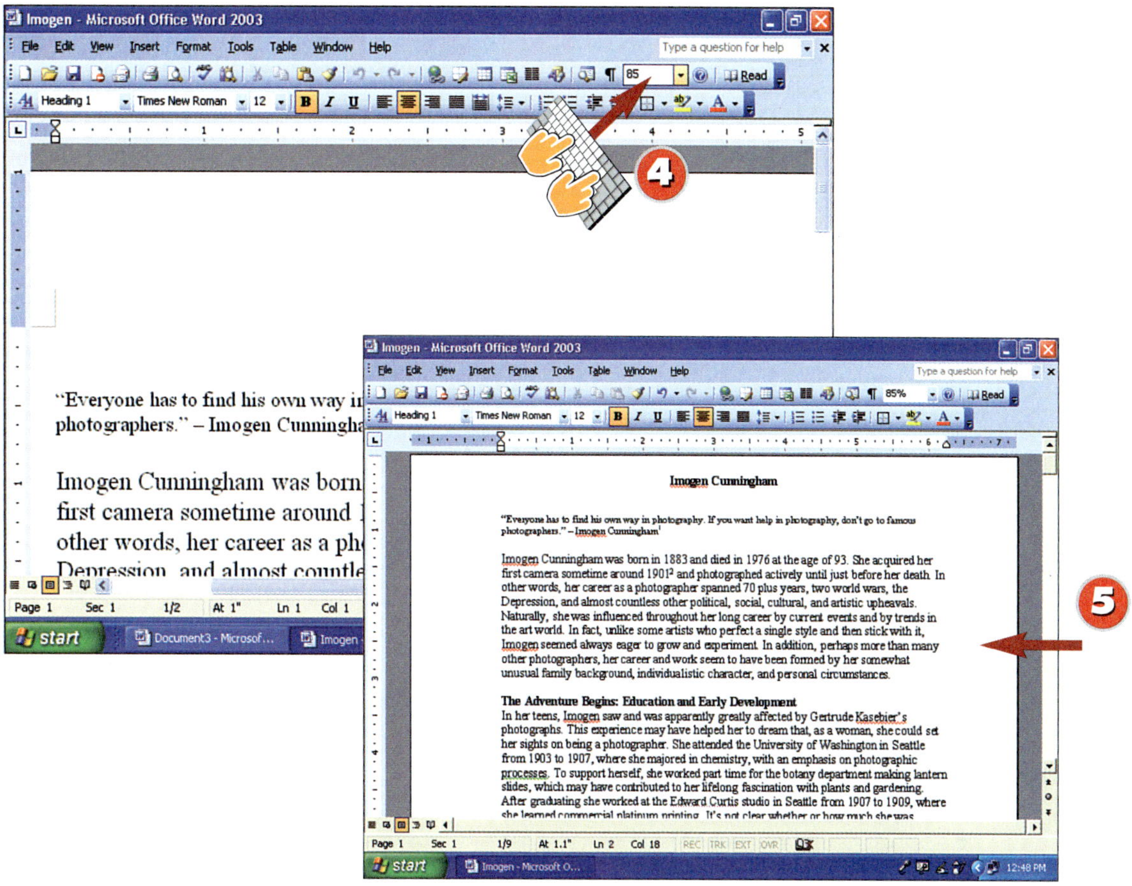

4. To use a setting that isn't one of the options in the Zoom list, click the current entry in the **Zoom** box, type a new number (you need not type the percent sign), and press **Enter**.

5. Word applies the setting you typed.

End

TIP

Using Other Zoom Settings

When you are using Print Layout view, the end of the Zoom list contains four handy options for zooming to the width of your page, the width of your text, the entire page, and two pages. Feel free to experiment with these settings.

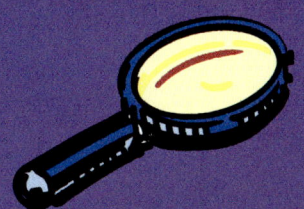

Comparing Two Documents Side By Side

Start

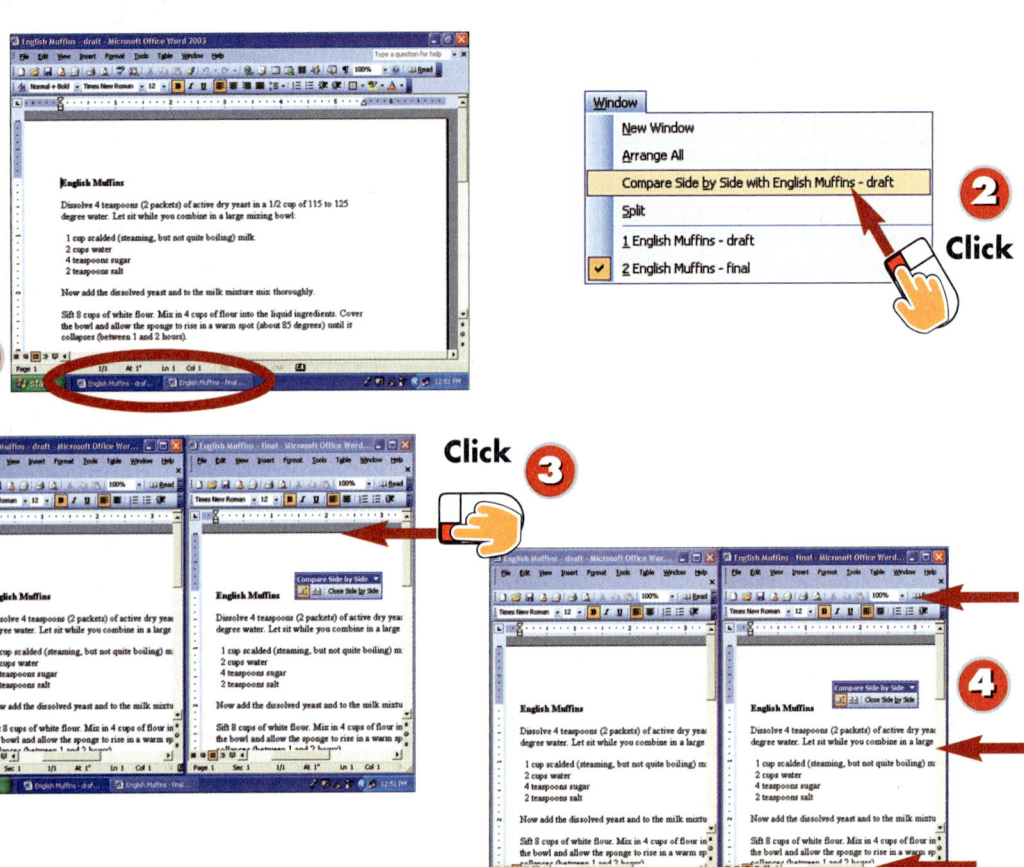

Click

Click

1. Open the two documents that you want to display side by side. (For now, open only these two documents.)

2. Open the **Window** menu and choose **Compare Side by Side with** *document name*.

3. The documents are arranged side by side and the title bar of the active document is dark. To activate the other document, click anywhere in its window.

4. Try using the scroll bars and changing the zoom setting on one document to control both documents at the same time.

INTRODUCTION

When you have two versions of a document and want to compare them side by side, you can easily arrange your Word window to do so with a click of the mouse. Once the two documents are aligned side by side, scrolling or zooming one of them scrolls or zooms them both, making it easy to scan both documents at the same time.

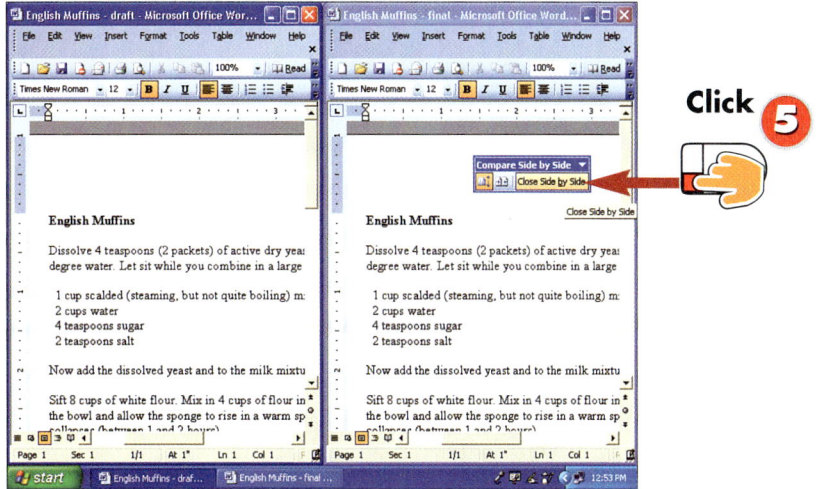

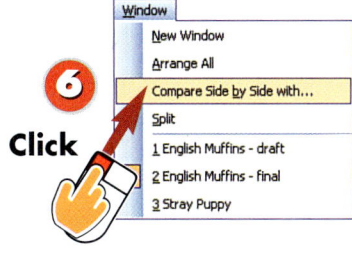

5 To break the side by side arrangement, click the **Close Side by Side** button on the Compare Side by Side toolbar.

6 Open a third document, switch to one that you want to compare, and open the **Window** menu. No document name is appended to the Compare Side by Side with command.

7 Choose **Compare Side by Side with**. In the dialog box that opens, click the document that you want to compare with the one that's currently displayed, and click **OK**.

8 Word displays those documents side by side. Click the **Close Side by Side** button in the Compare Side by Side toolbar to restore each to its previous size and position.

Seeing More of Both Documents

HINT

If you can't see the entire width of both documents when they are set up side by side, you might want to experiment with increasing the resolution of your Windows XP display. To do so, right-click a blank part of your desktop and choose **Properties** in the menu that appears. In the Display Properties dialog box, click the **Settings** tab, and drag the **Screen resolution** slider to the right to increase the resolution. Click **OK**, and then click **Yes** when Windows asks if you want to keep the changed settings.

Previewing a Document

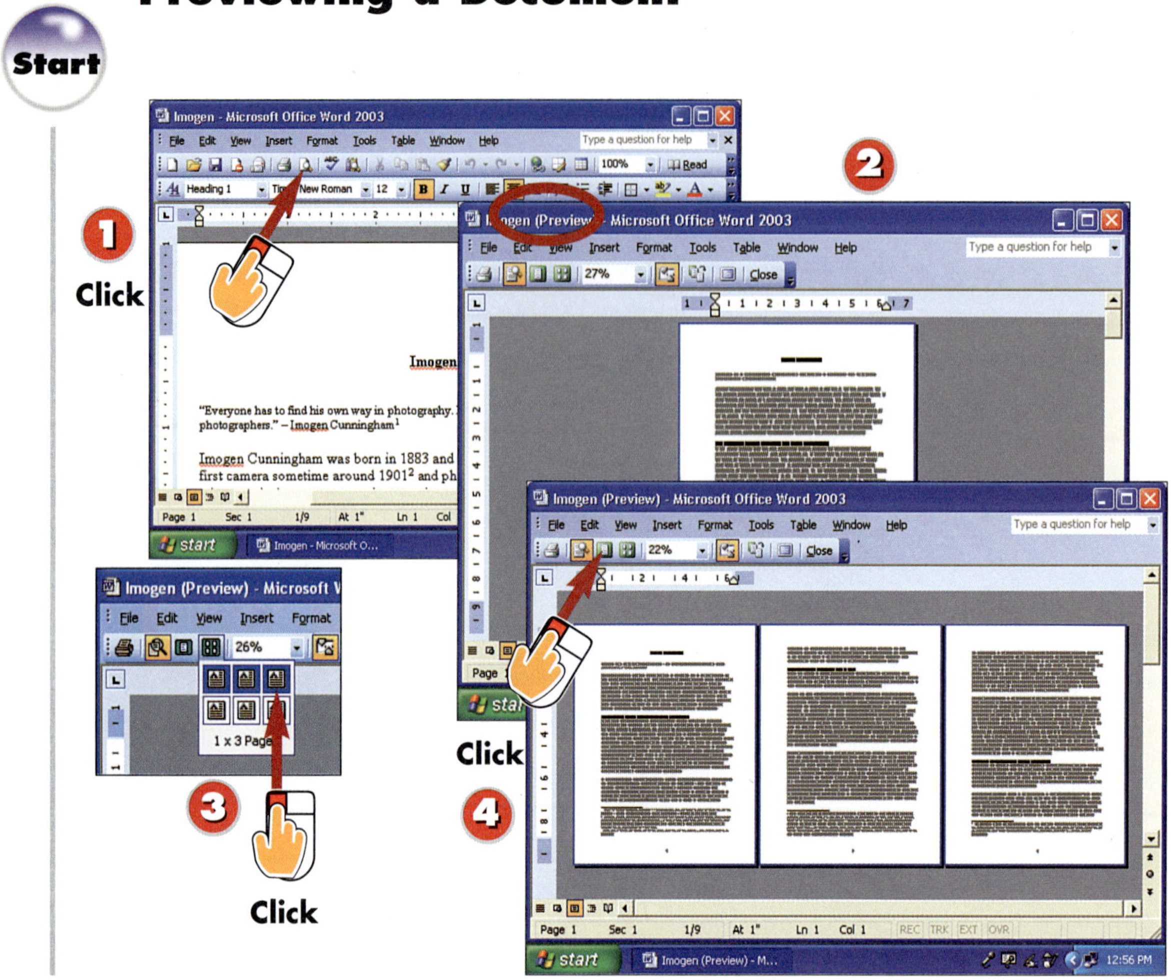

Start

1 **Click**

2

3 **Click**

4 **Click**

1 With the document that you want to print displayed in the Word window, click the **Print Preview** button on the Standard toolbar.

2 Word switches to Print Preview mode. Press the **Page Up** and **Page Down** keys on your keyboard to bring different parts of the document into view.

3 To view several pages at the same time, click the **Multiple Pages** button on the Print Preview toolbar and drag to select the number of pages you want to view.

4 Word displays the number of pages you selected. Click the **One Page** button to return to viewing a single page.

Word enables you to see what a printed document will look like before you actually send it to the printer. Using Print Preview is a great way to avoid wasting paper, because you can spot problems in your document before you print.

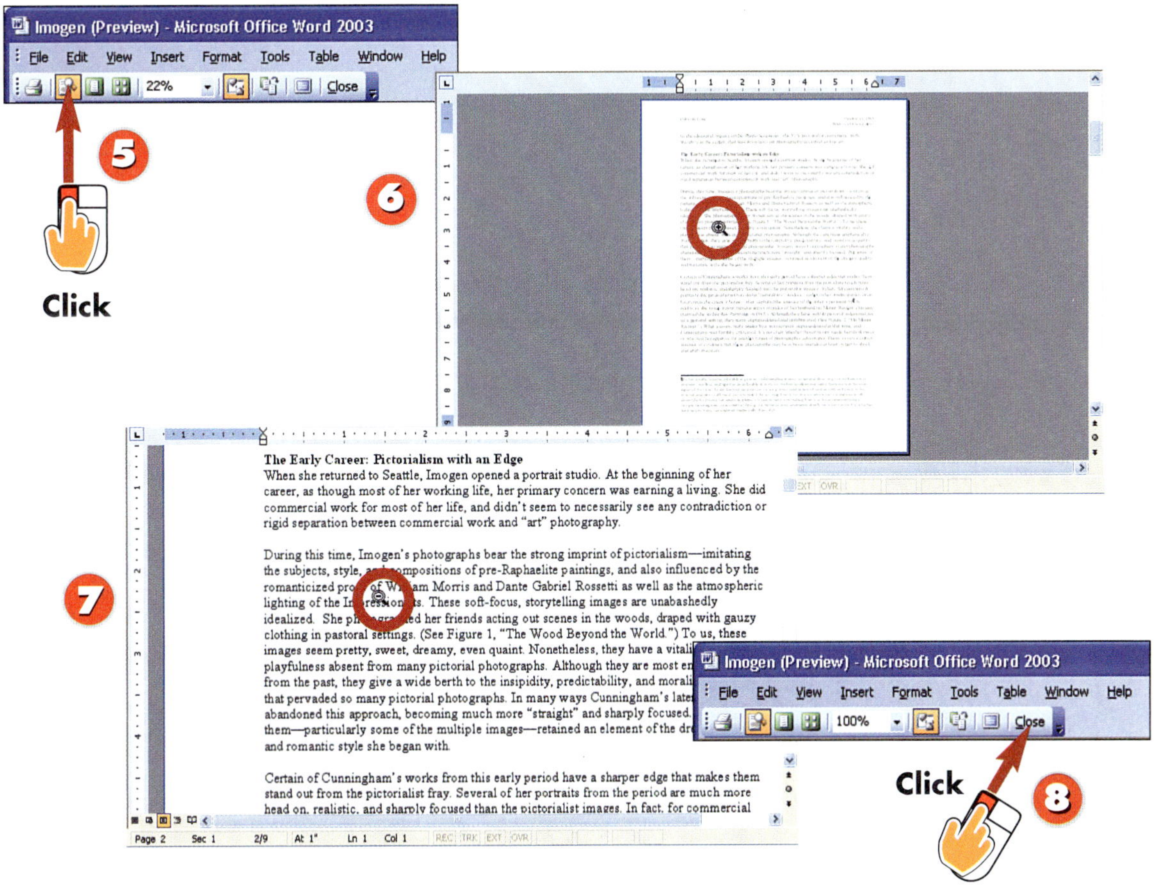

Click

Click

5. Click the **Magnifier** toolbar button if it isn't already selected. (If you are displaying multiple pages, click the page you want to magnify as well.)

6. The mouse pointer changes to a magnifying glass with a plus sign. Click on the area of the page you want to magnify.

7. The document is magnified, and the plus sign in the magnifying glass changes to a minus sign. Click again to zoom back out.

8. To close Print Preview, click the **Close** button in the Print Preview toolbar.

End

HINT

Fit Your Document on One Page
If your document is spilling over onto two pages and you'd like to get it to fit on one page, you can click the **Shrink to Fit** button on the Print Preview toolbar (the third button from the right) to make the text fit on a single page.

Printing a Document

Start

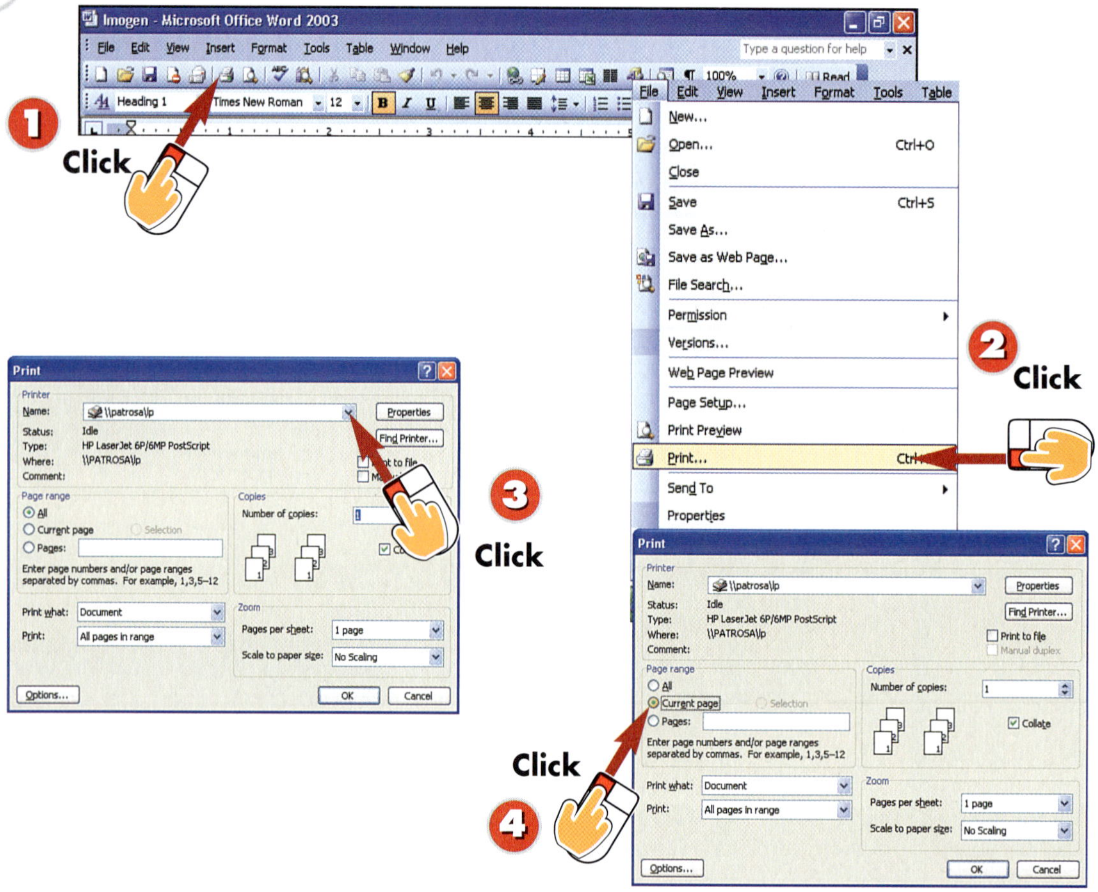

1 Click

2 Click

3 Click

4 Click

---

1 To print one copy of your document, click the **Print** button on the Standard toolbar.

2 For other printing options, such as printing multiple copies of a document or a portion of a document, open the **File** menu and choose **Print** to open the Print dialog box.

3 If you have more than one printer, select the one you want to use in the **Name** drop-down list.

4 To print only the page on which the insertion point appears, click the **Current page** option button.

Word assumes that you will frequently want to print one complete copy of your document, so it provides a toolbar button to let you do just that. If you need to customize your print job, however, you'll find all the options you need in the Print dialog box, which you open by issuing the **File**, **Print** command. Before you follow these steps, make sure that your printer is turned on.

TIP

Printing Multiple Pages on One Sheet of Paper Word can scale your document pages. To print more than one document page on a sheet of paper, choose the number of pages in the **Pages per sheet** drop-down list in the Print dialog box.

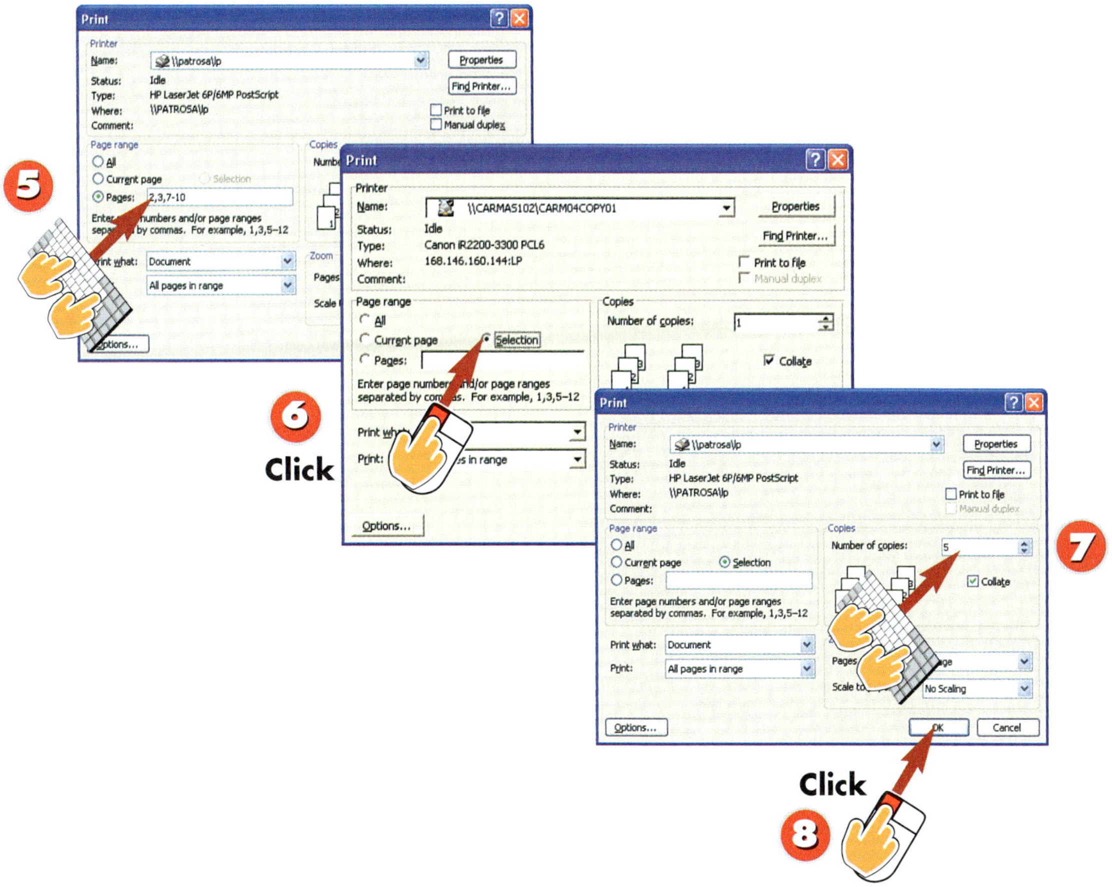

Click

Click

5 To print a range of pages, type the desired page numbers in the **Pages** text box.

6 To print only a block of text, select the text you want to print before displaying the Print dialog box, and then mark the **Selection** option button.

7 To print multiple copies, type the number of copies you want in the **Number of copies** text box.

8 When you've made your choices, click the **OK** button.

End

HINT

Closing the Print Dialog Box
If you display the Print dialog box but then decide you're not ready to print yet, click the **Cancel** button instead of the **OK** button to close the dialog box without printing.

Printing an Envelope

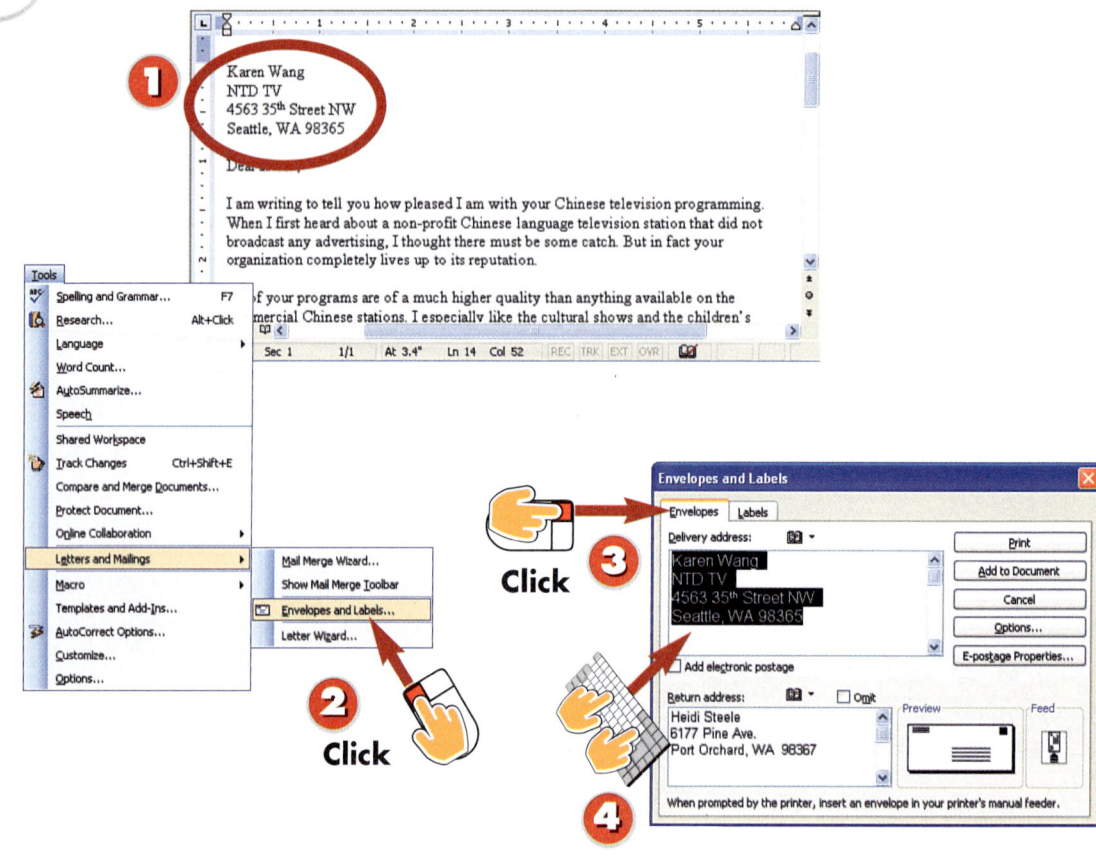

Click

Click

Click

1. If you used Word to type a letter, and that letter features the recipient's mailing address, open the letter now.

2. Open the **Tools** menu, choose **Letters and Mailings**, and choose **Envelopes and Labels**.

3. The Envelopes and Labels dialog box opens. Click the **Envelopes** tab.

4. Word finds the address in the document you have open. Edit it in the **Delivery address** box if needed.

Printing an envelope in Word is simple. You check to make sure that the address is right, put the envelope in the printer, and issue the command to print. Word assumes that you want to print on a standard business-size envelope, but you can choose a different envelope size if necessary.

HINT

Choosing a Different Envelope Size

To print on a different size envelope, click the **Options** button in the Envelopes tab of the Envelopes and Labels dialog box. Display the **Envelope Size** drop-down list and select the desired size. (If you don't see the size you want, click **Custom Size** at the bottom of the list, and click **OK**.) Then click **OK** to close the Envelope Options dialog box.

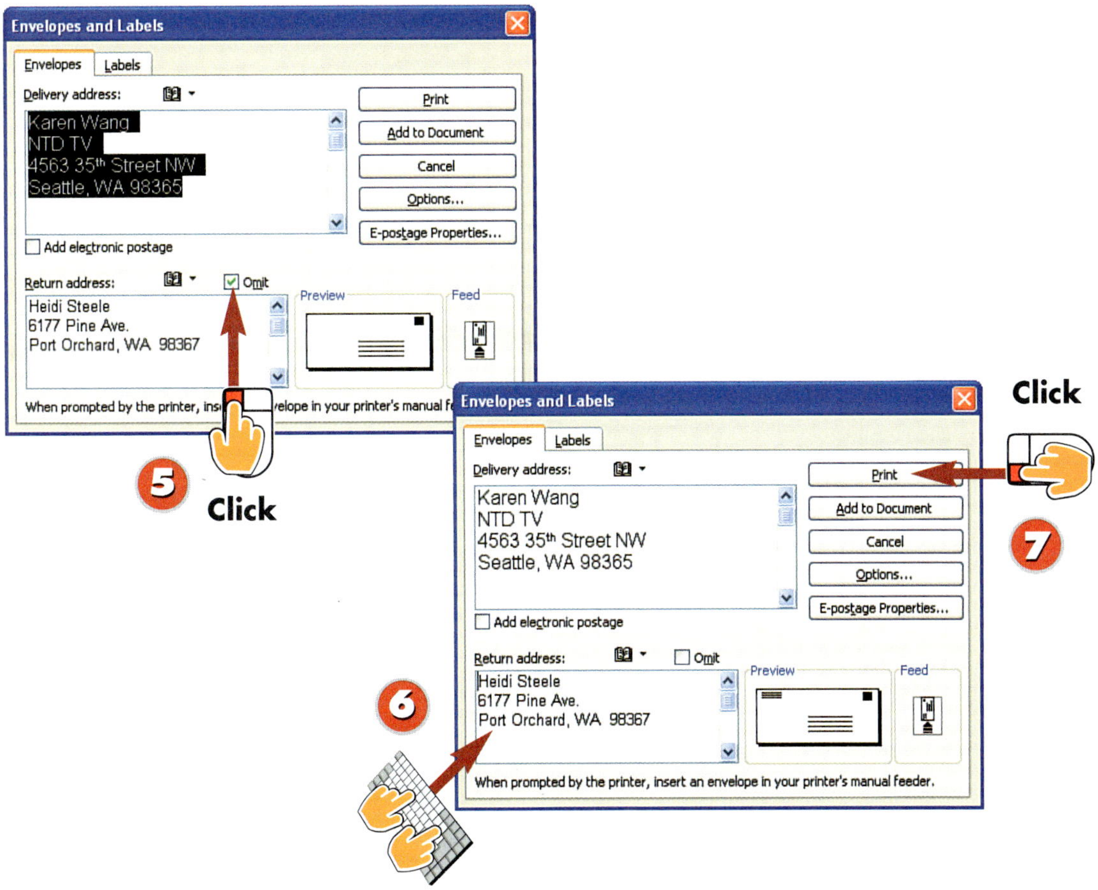

Envelopes and Labels

Envelopes | Labels

Delivery address:

Karen Wang
NTD TV
4563 35th Street NW
Seattle, WA 98365

☐ Add electronic postage

Return address: ☑ Omit

Heidi Steele
6177 Pine Ave.
Port Orchard, WA 98367

Preview | Feed

When prompted by the printer, ins... ...relope in your printer's manual f...

Print
Add to Document
Cancel
Options...
E-postage Properties...

⑤ Click

Envelopes and Labels

Envelopes | Labels

Delivery address:

Karen Wang
NTD TV
4563 35th Street NW
Seattle, WA 98365

☐ Add electronic postage

Return address: ☐ Omit

Heidi Steele
6177 Pine Ave.
Port Orchard, WA 98367

Preview | Feed

When prompted by the printer, insert an envelope in your printer's manual feeder.

Print
Add to Document
Cancel
Options...
E-postage Properties...

Click

⑦

⑥

⑤ Word automatically includes your return address on the envelope. If you have envelopes with a preprinted return address, mark the **Omit** check box.

⑥ If you do want to print a return address, make sure the **Omit** check box is cleared, and that the address in the **Return address** box is correct (editing it if necessary).

⑦ Put the envelope in your printer and click the **Print** button.

End

HINT

Feeding the Envelope
If you aren't sure how to insert your envelope into your printer, look at the Feed area in the Envelopes and Labels dialog box. It shows the orientation for your envelope in your printer.

TIP

Setting Your Return Address
Word stores your return address in the User Information tab of the Options dialog box (to view this dialog box, open the **Tools** menu and choose **Options**), and uses it in several ways. You can change it here anytime.

TIP

No Delivery Address?
You can follow the steps here even if you don't have a document that contains the recipient's address onscreen. You just have to take the extra step of typing the delivery address in step 4.

Printing Labels

Start

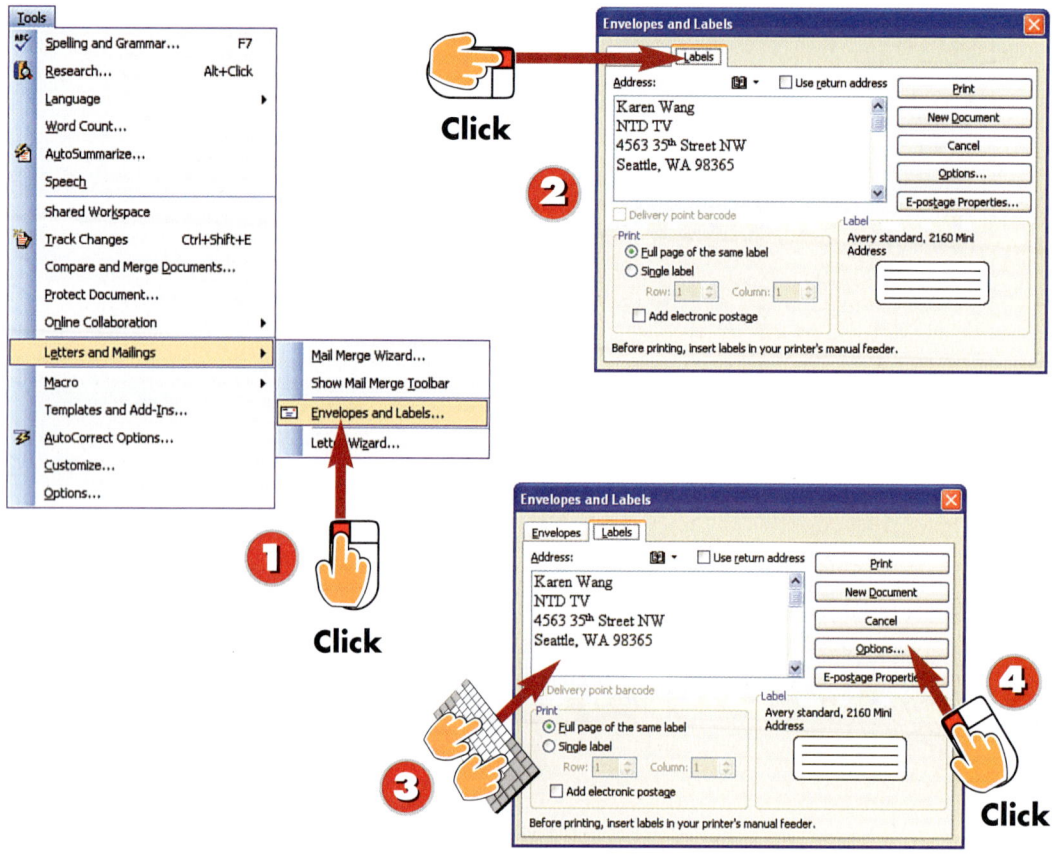

Click

1 **Click**

3

Click

4

1 Open the **Tools** menu, choose **Letters and Mailings**, and choose **Envelopes and Labels**.

2 The Envelopes and Labels dialog box opens. Click the **Labels** tab.

3 Type (or edit) the address you want to appear on the label in the **Address** box. To print your return address, mark the **Use return address** check box.

4 Click the **Options** button to display the Label Options dialog box.

INTRODUCTION

The steps for printing labels are very similar to those described in the previous task for printing envelopes. The one difference is that you'll probably need to choose a label type other than the default because labels come in such a wide variety of sizes.

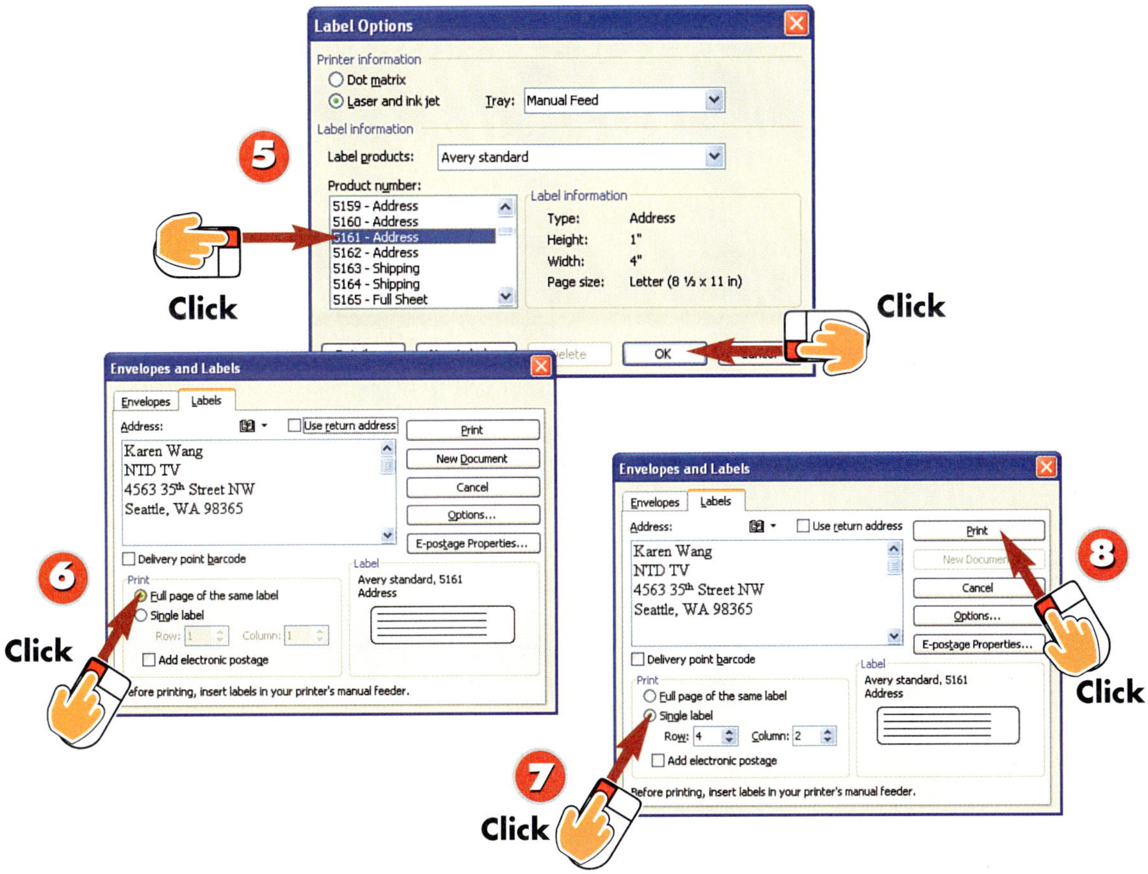

Label Options

Printer information
- ○ Dot matrix
- ⦿ Laser and ink jet   Tray: Manual Feed

Label information

Label products: Avery standard

Product number:
- 5159 - Address
- 5160 - Address
- **5161 - Address**
- 5162 - Address
- 5163 - Shipping
- 5164 - Shipping
- 5165 - Full Sheet

Label information
Type:	Address
Height:	1"
Width:	4"
Page size:	Letter (8 ½ x 11 in)

Click

Click

OK ... Delete

Envelopes and Labels

Envelopes | Labels

Address: ☐ Use return address

Karen Wang
NTD TV
4563 35th Street NW
Seattle, WA 98365

Print
New Document
Cancel
Options...
E-postage Properties...

☐ Delivery point barcode

Print
- ⦿ Full page of the same label
- ○ Single label
  - Row: 1   Column: 1
- ☐ Add electronic postage

Label
Avery standard, 5161
Address

Before printing, insert labels in your printer's manual feeder.

Click

Envelopes and Labels

Envelopes | Labels

Address: ☐ Use return address

Karen Wang
NTD TV
4563 35th Street NW
Seattle, WA 98365

Print
New Document
Cancel
Options...
E-postage Properties...

☐ Delivery point barcode

Print
- ○ Full page of the same label
- ⦿ Single label
  - Row: 4   Column: 2
- ☐ Add electronic postage

Label
Avery standard, 5161
Address

Before printing, insert labels in your printer's manual feeder.

Click

Click

5 Click your labels' product number in the **Product number** list, and click **OK**. (If you don't have Avery labels, choose a different brand from the **Label products** list.)

6 Mark the **Full page of the same label** option button if you want a whole page of labels with the same address on each one.

7 If you want a single label, mark the **Single label** option button, and then enter the label's row and column number.

8 Put the sheet of labels in your printer, and click the **Print** button.

End

Formatting Characters and Paragraphs

Formatting a document (improving its appearance) can be a lot of fun, but it can also leave you rather befuddled if you don't understand how the formatting commands work. This part gives you an organized introduction to the techniques you'll use every day to format characters and paragraphs. You start with changing the fonts and font size, applying bold, italic, underline, and so on. You also learn formatting that affects paragraphs, such as setting alignment, adding indents, creating bulleted and numbered lists, and working with custom tabs.

Formatting Tools

The Font Size list

The Italic button

The Numbering button

The Font list

The Bold button

Paragraph Alignment buttons

The Bullets button

The Highlight button

The Tab Stop Indicator button

The Formatting toolbar

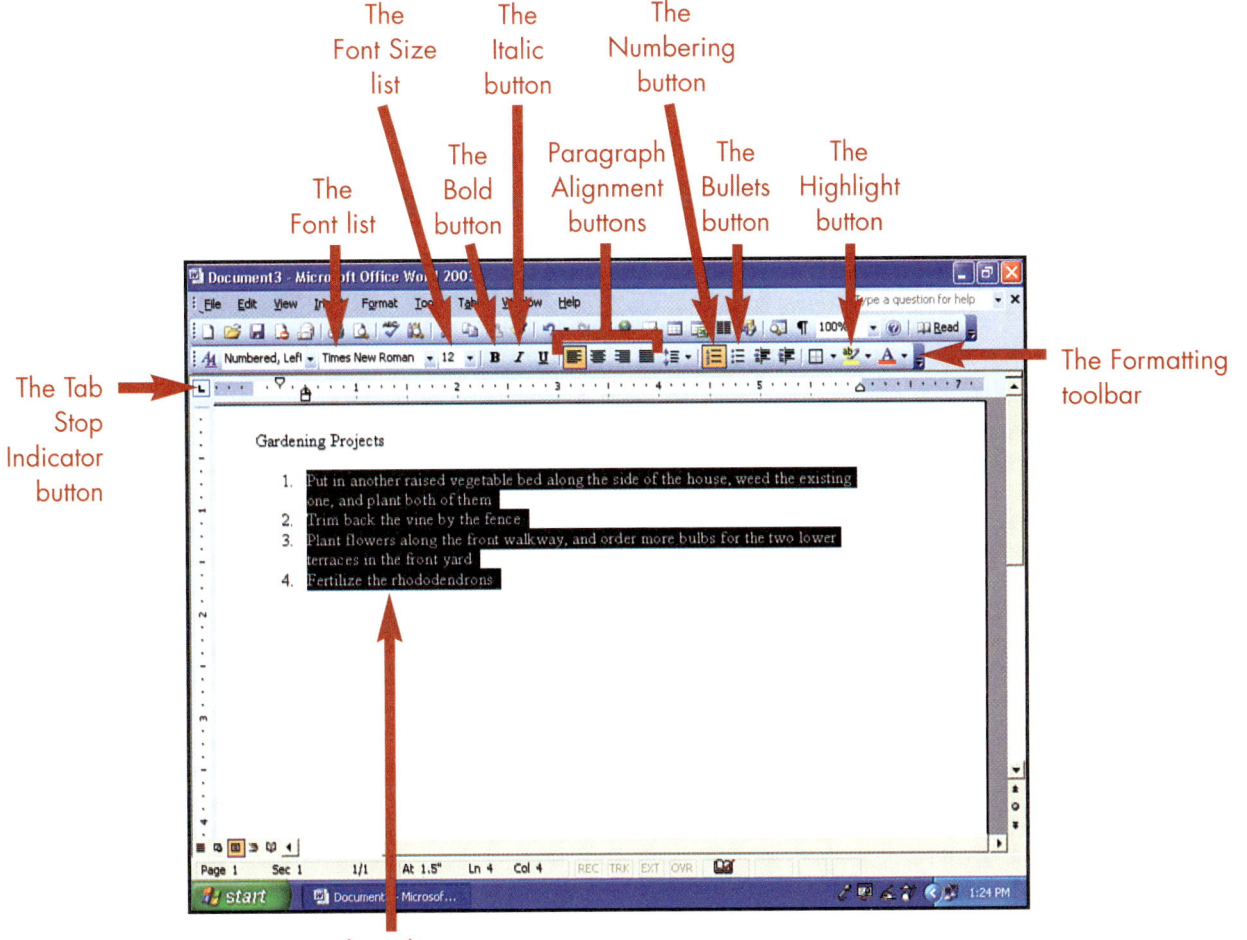

Selected text

Making Text Bold, Italic, and Underlined

Start

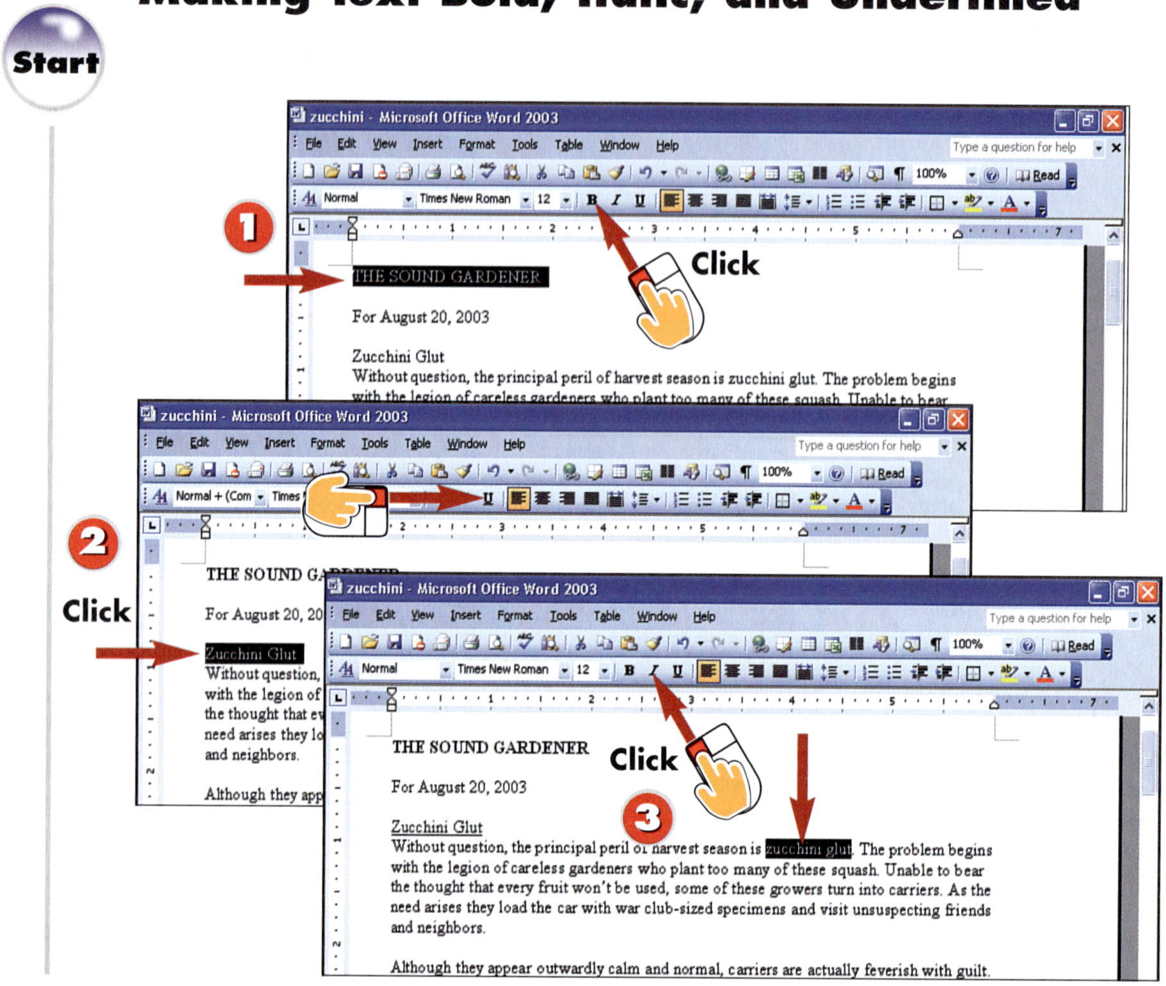

Click

Click

Click

1. To make text bold, select the text and click the **Bold** button on the Formatting toolbar.

2. Bold formatting is applied (to better see the effect, click anywhere in the document to deselect the text). To underline text, select the desired text and click the **Underline** button.

3. Underline formatting is applied (again, click anywhere in the document to better see the effect). To italicize text, select the desired text and click the **Italic** button.

Applying a little **bold**, *italics*, or underlining here and there can add just the right emphasis to your text. You can also apply more than one of these three formats to the same text. A word that has all three formats applied looks like **_this_**.

TIP

Using Shortcut Keys
Instead of clicking the Bold, Italic, and Underline toolbar buttons, you can press **Ctrl+B** for bold, **Ctrl+I** for italic, or **Ctrl+U** for underlining.

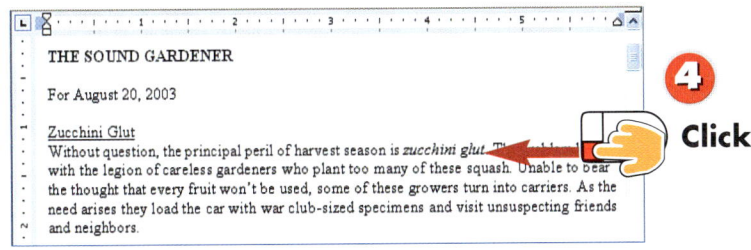

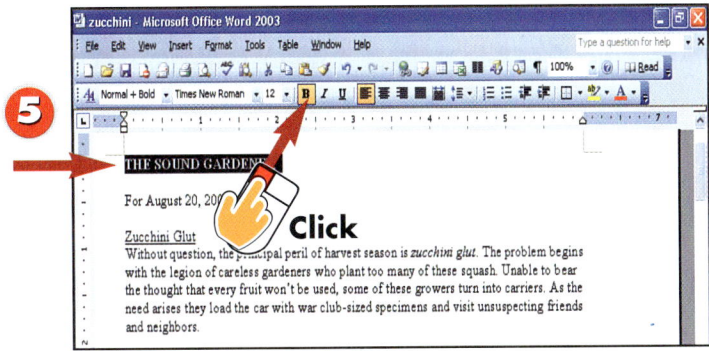

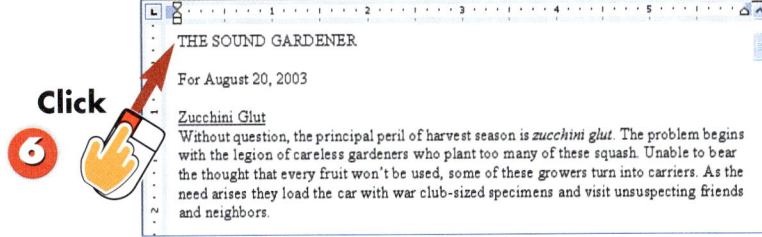

4 Click anywhere in the document to deselect the text so that you can better view the italicized characters.

5 To turn off bold, italic, or underlining, select the text first, and then click the **Bold**, **Italic**, or **Underline** button. (In this example, the text is bold, so the **Bold** button is selected.)

6 Click anywhere in the document to deselect the text; the formatting has been removed.

End

Changing the Font and Font Size

Start

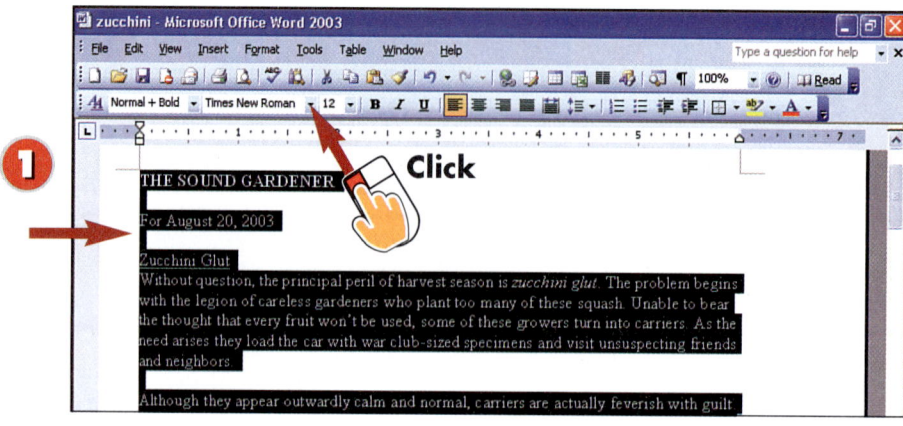

1

Click

2 **Click**

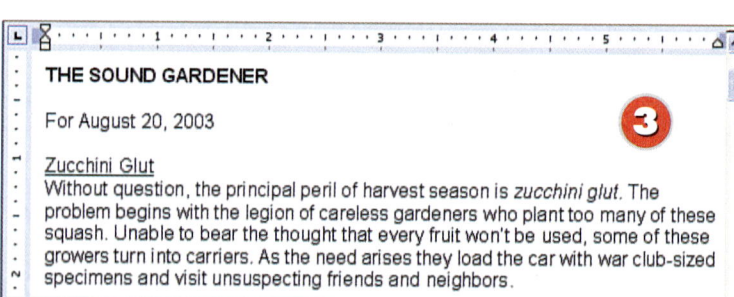

3

1 After you've selected the text whose font you want to change, click the **down arrow** to right of the **Font** list on the Formatting toolbar.

2 A list of available fonts appears. Drag the scroll bar on the right edge of the list to move through the list, and click the font that you want to use.

3 Click anywhere in the document to deselect the text so that you can see the new font more clearly.

INTRODUCTION

One of the things that people like most about word processing is that you can quickly change the font (typeface) and font size of your text. Font size is measured in points. (A 10-point to 12-point font is commonly used for body text.) Word assumes that you want to use a Times New Roman, 12-point font, but as you'll see here, you can change these settings with just a few mouse clicks.

TIP

Frequently Used Fonts
The fonts that you use most frequently appear above the double line in the Font list so that you can access them easily. Below the double line is an alphabetical list of all the fonts installed on your computer.

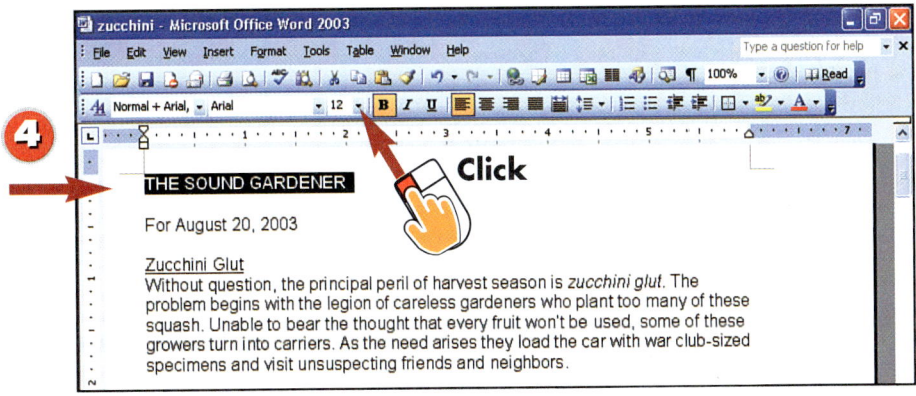

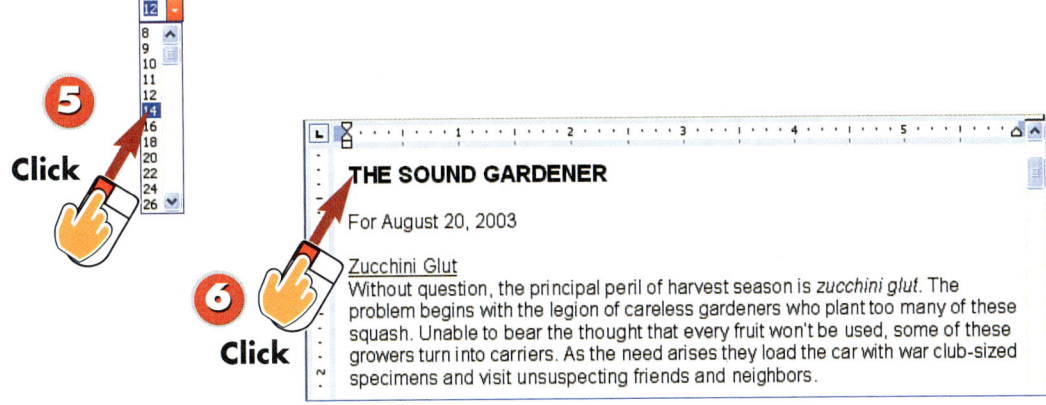

4 Select the text whose font size you want to change and click the **down arrow** to the right of the **Font Size** list on the Formatting toolbar.

5 A list of available font sizes appears. Drag the scroll bar on the right edge of the list to move through the list, and click the font size that you want to use.

6 Click anywhere to deselect the text so that you can more easily see the new size.

End

Adding Highlighting and Color to Your Text

Start

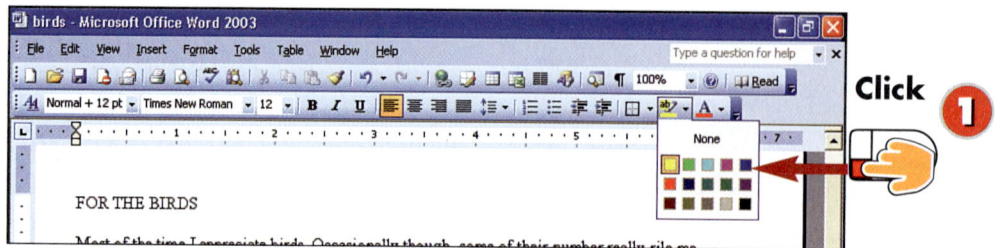

Click ①

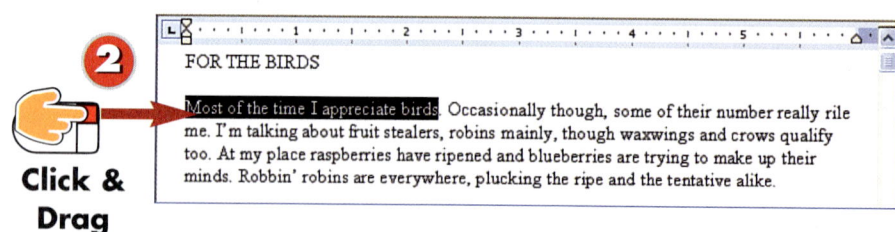

② **Click & Drag**

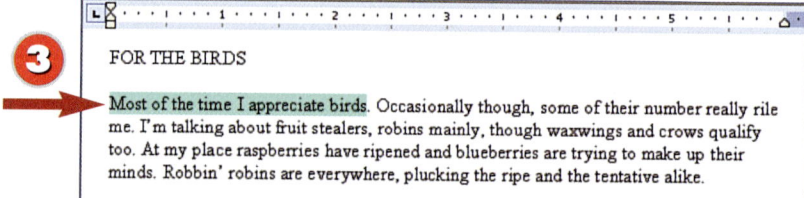

③

① To select the highlight color, click the **down arrow** to the right of the **Highlight** button on the Formatting toolbar and click the color that you want to use in the palette that appears.

② The mouse pointer takes on the shape of a highlighter pen. Drag across the text you want to highlight, and then release the mouse button.

③ The text is now highlighted with the color you chose.

INTRODUCTION

Word offers a highlight feature you can use just as you would a highlighter pen. This tool comes in handy when you're editing text onscreen—it lets you call attention to blocks of text that you want to comment on, that need further revision, and so on. Word also lets you change the color of characters themselves (as opposed to the background behind the characters) by applying a font color. Although highlighting is useful regardless of whether you have a color printer (if you don't have a color printer, the highlighting will print in a shade of gray), you're not as likely to use font colors unless you can print in color.

TIP

Highlighting Text
Here is another method for highlighting text: Select the desired text, and then click the **Highlight** button. If the color you want is not showing on the button, click the **down arrow** and click the desired color in the palette.

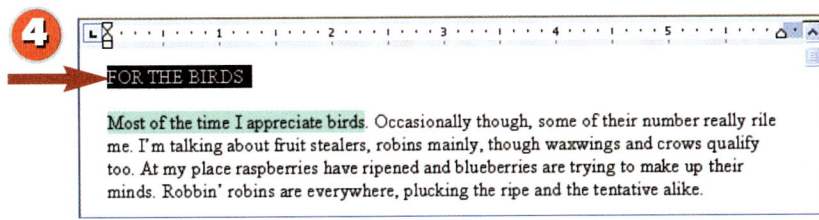

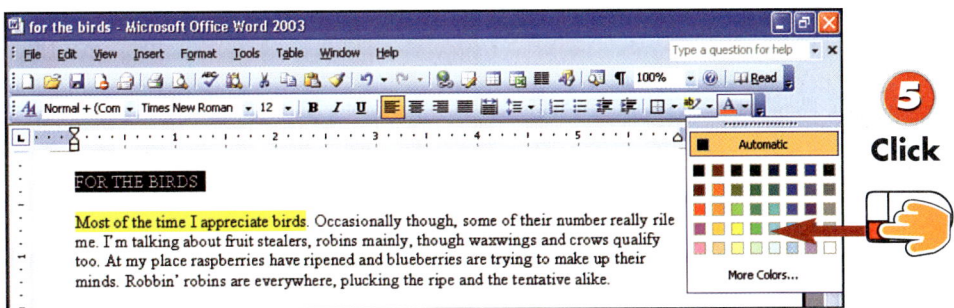

Click

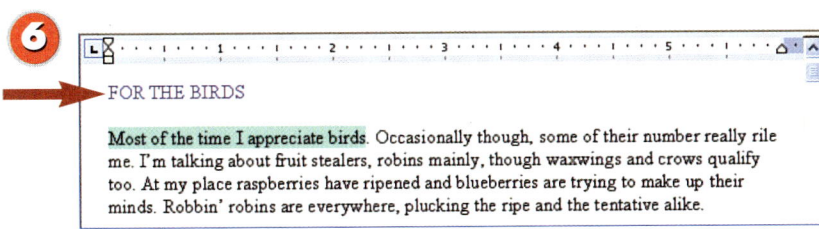

4 To change your font color, start by selecting the text.

5 Click the **down arrow** to the right of the **Font Color** button on the Formatting toolbar and click the desired color in the palette that appears.

6 Click anywhere in the document to deselect your text and see the font color that you applied.

End

Changing Paragraph Alignment

Start

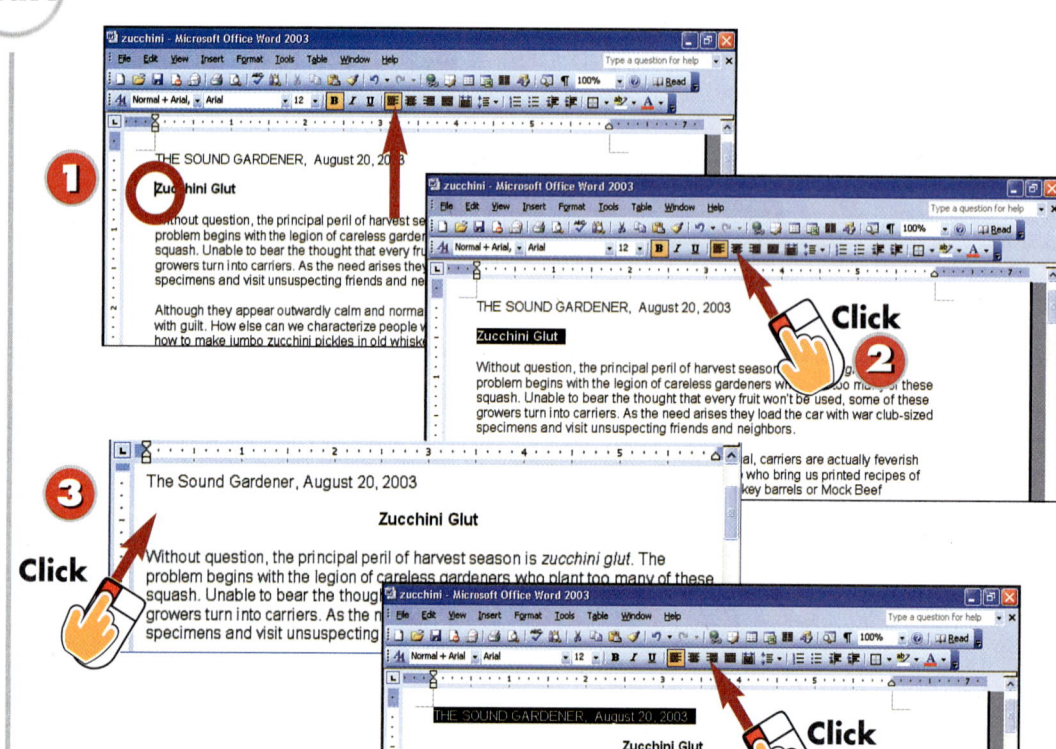

1. The paragraph that contains the insertion point is left-aligned, so the Align Left button is selected.

2. To center a paragraph, select it and click the **Center** button.

3. The paragraph is centered; click anywhere in the document to deselect the paragraph.

4. To right-align a paragraph, select it and click the **Align Right** button.

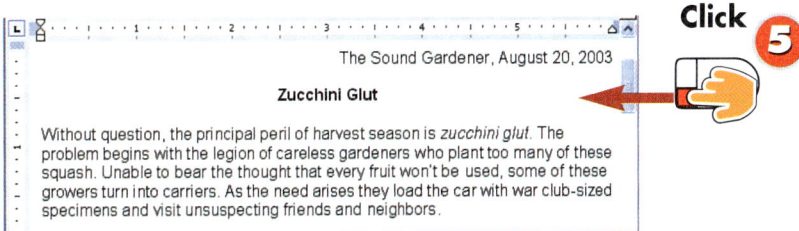

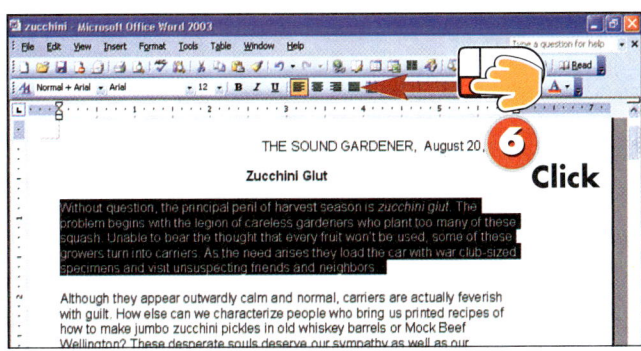

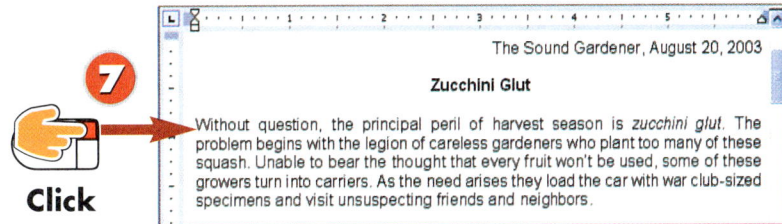

5 The paragraph is right-aligned; click anywhere in the document to deselect the paragraph.

6 To justify a paragraph, select it and click the **Justify** button.

7 The paragraph is justified; click anywhere in the document to deselect the paragraph.

Aligning Paragraphs

If you are changing the alignment of a single paragraph, you don't actually need to select it first. You can just place the insertion point anywhere in the paragraph, and then click the desired alignment button. If you want to align several paragraphs at once, however, you do need to select all of them first.

Changing Line Spacing

Start

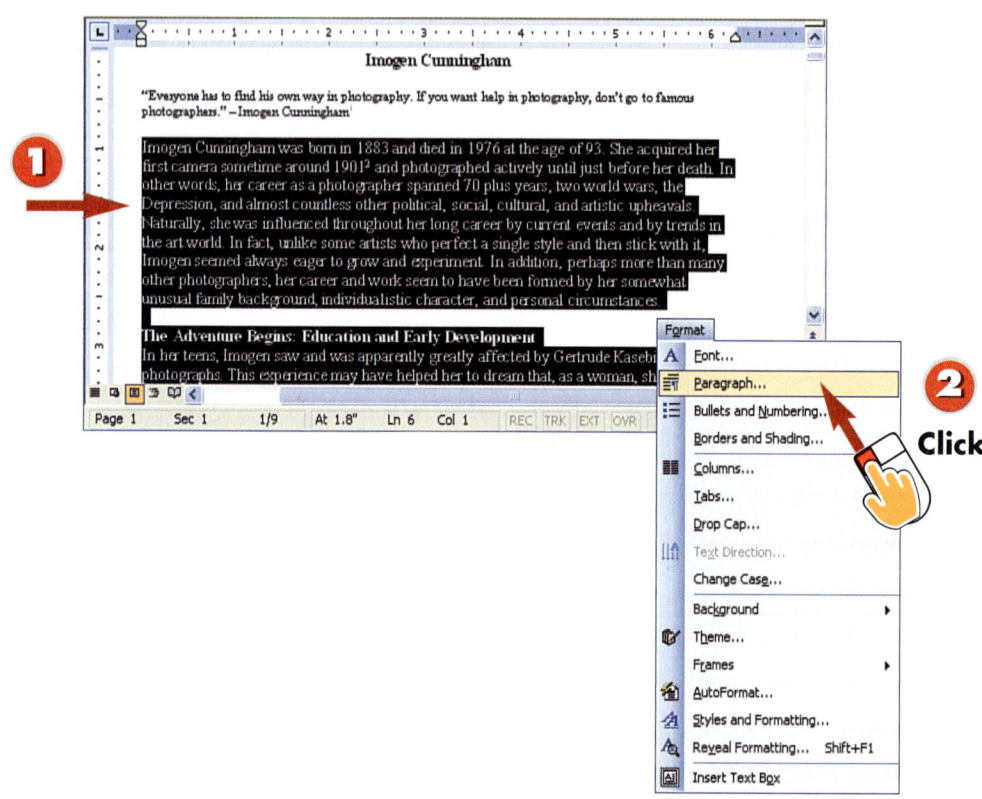

1. Select the paragraphs you want to change.

2. Open the **Format** menu and choose **Paragraph** to display the Paragraph dialog box.

Line spacing is the amount of space between lines within a paragraph. Word uses single spacing by default, but you can change this setting to double spacing, which is great for rough drafts (you have room to write your edits between the lines), or one-and-a-half line spacing, which can make your text easier to read.

TIP

Using the Keyboard to Change Line Spacing

If you don't like the hassle of displaying the Paragraph dialog box, you can change line spacing with the keyboard instead. Select the paragraphs whose spacing you want to change and then press **Ctrl+2** for double spacing, **Ctrl+5** for one-and-a-half line spacing, or **Ctrl+1** for single spacing.

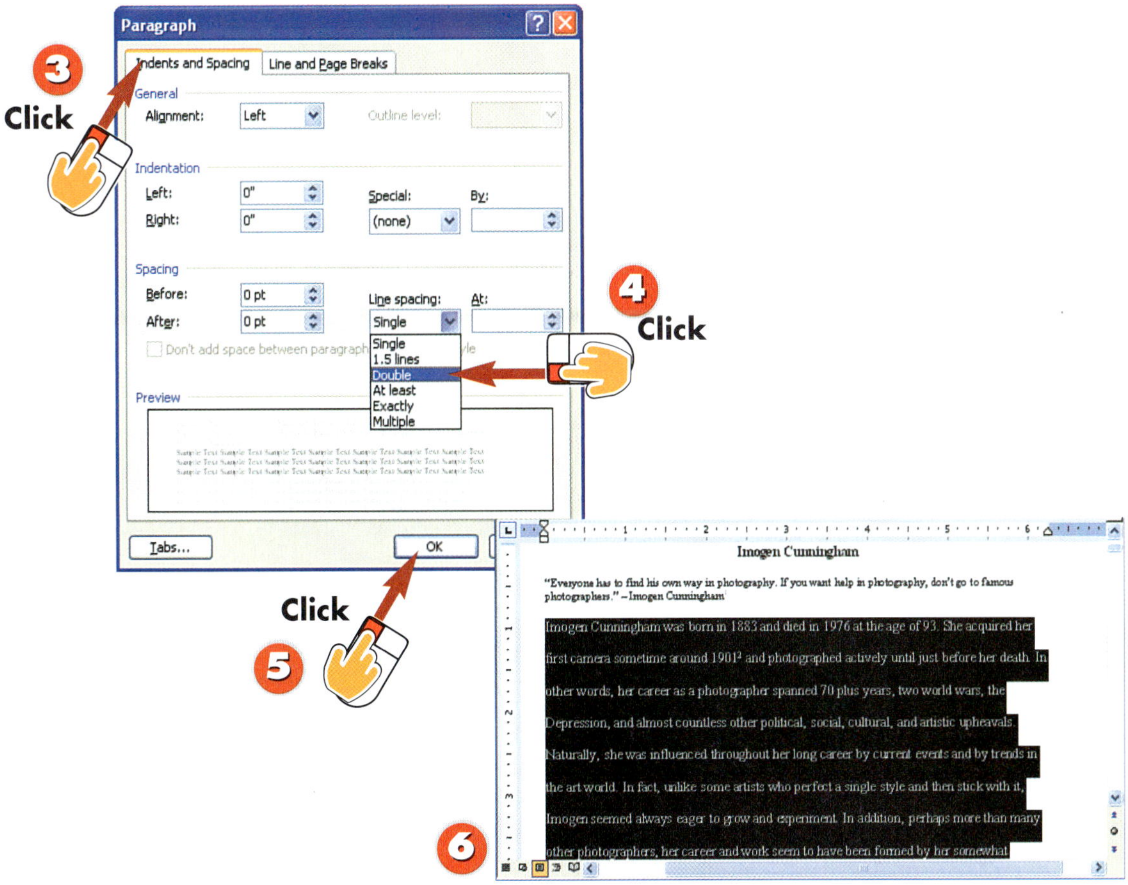

Click ③

Paragraph

Indents and Spacing | Line and Page Breaks

General
Alignment: Left | Outline level:

Indentation
Left: 0" | Special: | By:
Right: 0" | (none)

Spacing
Before: 0 pt | Line spacing: | At:
After: 0 pt | Single
Don't add space between paragraphs

Single
1.5 lines
Double
At least
Exactly
Multiple

④ **Click**

Preview

Sample Text Sample Text Sample Text Sample Text Sample Text Sample Text Sample Text Sample Text Sample Text Sample Text Sample Text Sample Text Sample Text Sample Text Sample Text Sample Text Sample Text Sample Text Sample Text Sample Text

Tabs... | OK

Click ⑤

Imogen Cunningham

"Everyone has to find his own way in photography. If you want help in photography, don't go to famous photographers." — Imogen Cunningham

Imogen Cunningham was born in 1883 and died in 1976 at the age of 93. She acquired her first camera sometime around 1901[2] and photographed actively until just before her death. In other words, her career as a photographer spanned 70 plus years, two world wars, the Depression, and almost countless other political, social, cultural, and artistic upheavals. Naturally, she was influenced throughout her long career by current events and by trends in the art world. In fact, unlike some artists who perfect a single style and then stick with it, Imogen seemed always eager to grow and experiment. In addition, perhaps more than many other photographers, her career and work seem to have been formed by her somewhat

⑥

③ Click the **Indents and Spacing** tab if it isn't already in front.

④ Click the **down arrow** button to the right of the **Line spacing** list and click the desired spacing in the list.

⑤ Click the **OK** button.

⑥ Word applies the line spacing you chose to the selected paragraphs; click anywhere in the document to deselect the text.

End

Repeating Your Last Action
You can press F4 to repeat most actions, a shortcut that is especially useful for formatting. If you have just applied formatting that required going into a dialog box and now want to apply the same formatting elsewhere, just select the desired block of text and press **F4**.

TIP

Adding Indents

Start

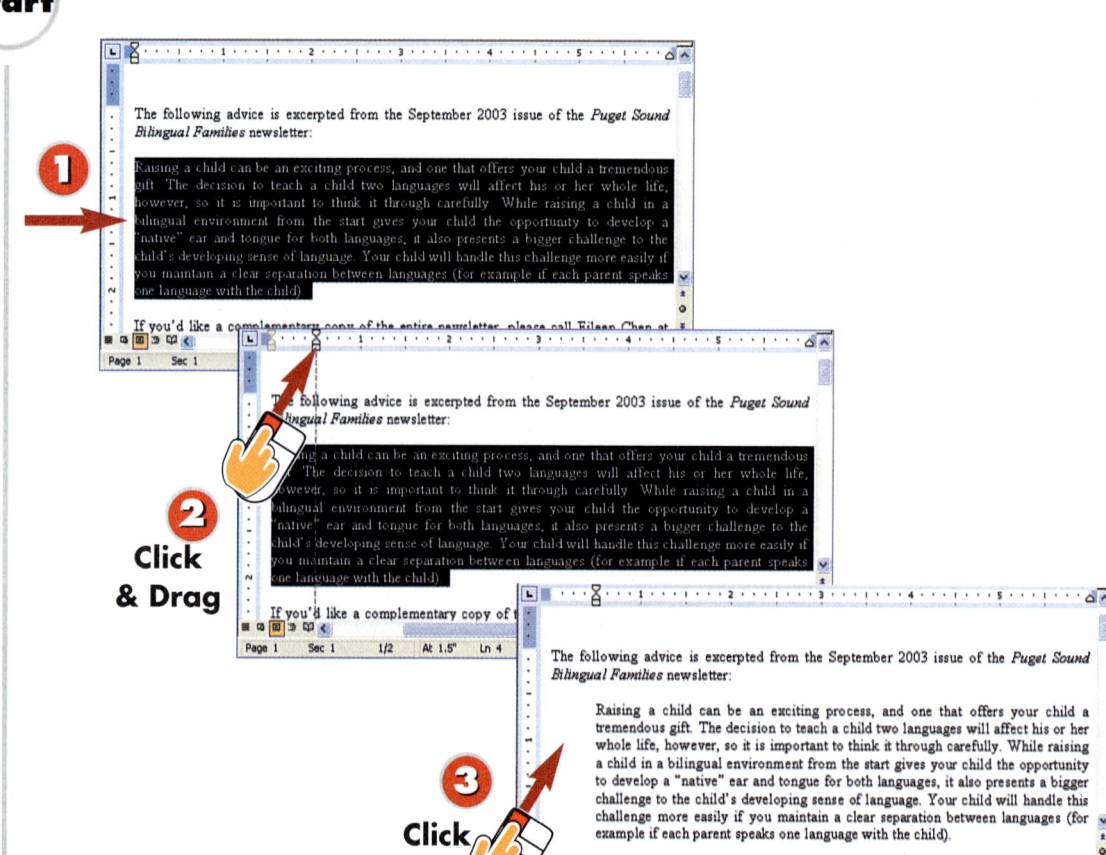

1

2
Click
& Drag

3
Click

1 To set a left indent, first select the paragraphs you want to indent.

2 Drag the **Left Indent** marker to the desired position on the ruler. As you drag, the text is indented. When it's in the right place, release the mouse button.

3 Click anywhere in the document to deselect the text.

Word enables you to indent paragraphs from the left margin, the right margin, or both. You can also create a first-line indent, which indents only the first line of a paragraph, or a hanging indent, which indents all of the lines except the first. Word provides several ways to set indents. Here, you learn to add indents by dragging the indent markers on the ruler. To undo any indent you set, select the indented paragraphs and then drag the appropriate marker back to its original position on the ruler.

Why Is My Marker Gray?
If you select multiple paragraphs, any indent markers that apply to some—but not all—of the selected paragraphs will appear light gray on the ruler. If you move a light gray indent marker, it will apply that indent to *all* the selected paragraphs.

Click & Drag

Click

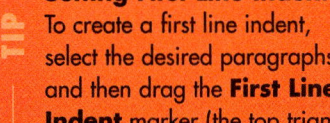

End

---

4 To set a right indent, first select the paragraphs that you want to indent.

5 Drag the **Right Indent** marker to the desired position on the ruler. As you drag, the text is indented. When it's in the right spot, release the mouse button.

6 Click anywhere to deselect the text.

TIP

Setting First Line Indents
To create a first line indent, select the desired paragraphs and then drag the **First Line Indent** marker (the top triangle above the Left Indent marker).

TIP

Setting Hanging Indents
To create a hanging indent, select the desired paragraphs and then drag the **Hanging Indent** marker (the bottom triangle directly above the Left Indent marker).

TIP

Locating the Correct Indent Marker
If you're not sure which indent marker is which, try pointing to one. A ScreenTip will appear to tell you which marker you're pointing to.

Creating Bulleted and Numbered Lists

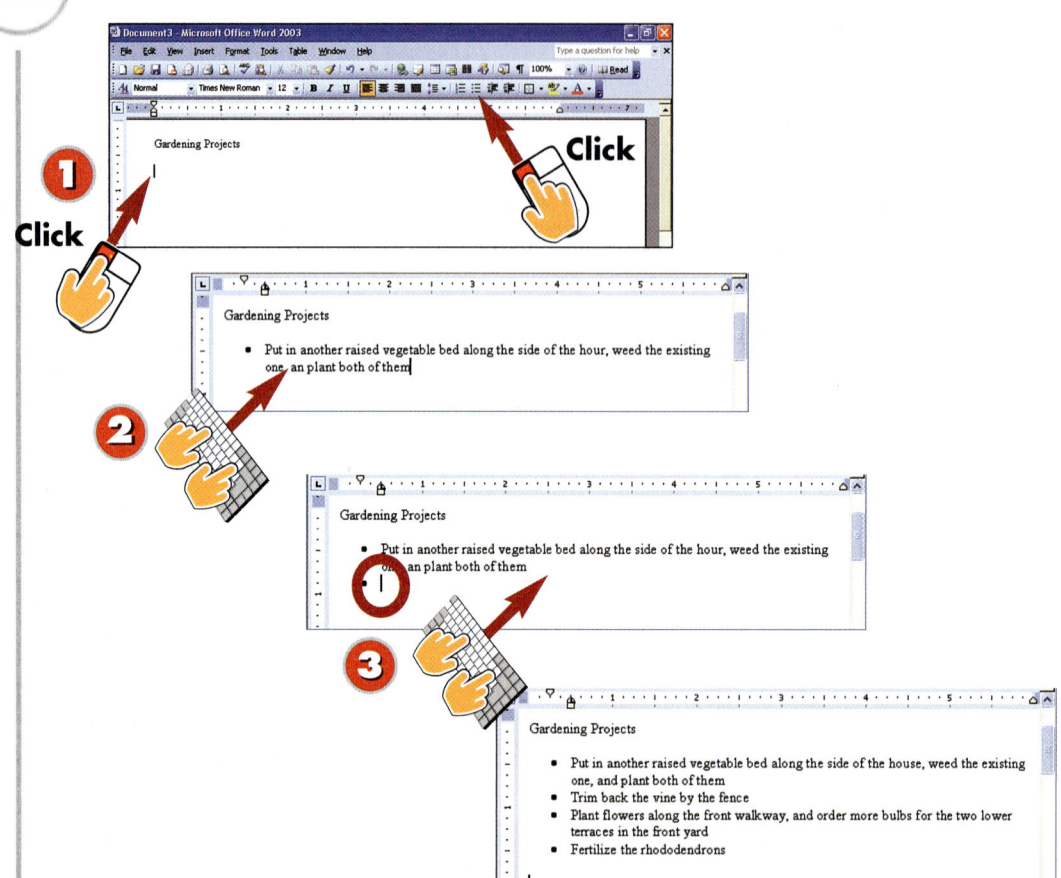

Start

Click

Click

1

2

3

4

① Click where you want the list to start, and then click the **Bullets** button on the Formatting toolbar.

② Word inserts a bullet. Type the first item in the list.

③ Press **Enter**. Word inserts a bullet on the next line for you.

④ Continue typing items in your list. After the last item, press **Enter** twice to turn off the bullets.

INTRODUCTION

Setting off items in a list with numbers or bullets is a great way to present information clearly. Word's bulleted and numbered list features add the bullets or numbers for you, and they create hanging indents so that when text in an item wraps to the next line, it doesn't wrap underneath the number or bullet.

TIP

Creating Blank Lines Between Items
If you want a blank line between items in a bulleted or numbered list, press **Shift+Enter** and then **Enter** at the end of each item (instead of just pressing **Enter**).

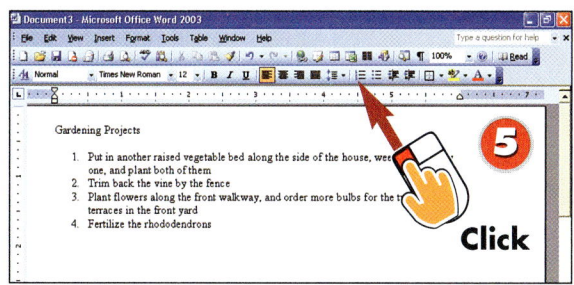

Click

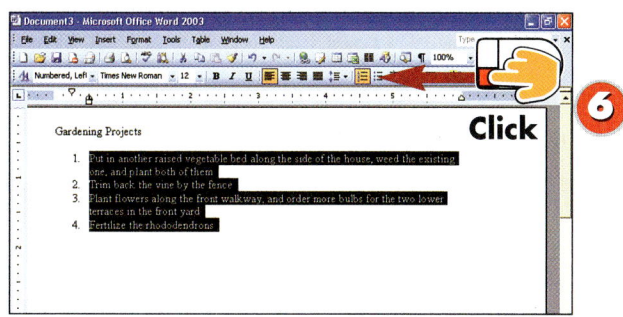

Click

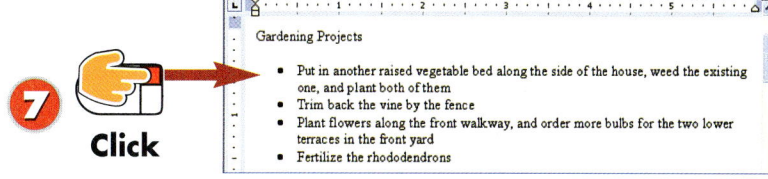

Click

5 To create a numbered list, follow steps 1 through 4, but click the **Numbering** button on the Formatting toolbar.

6 To change a numbered list to a bulleted list (or vice versa), select the list, and then click the **Bullets** or **Numbering** button.

7 Word makes the change for you. Click anywhere to deselect the text.

End

Setting a Custom Left or Right Tab

Start

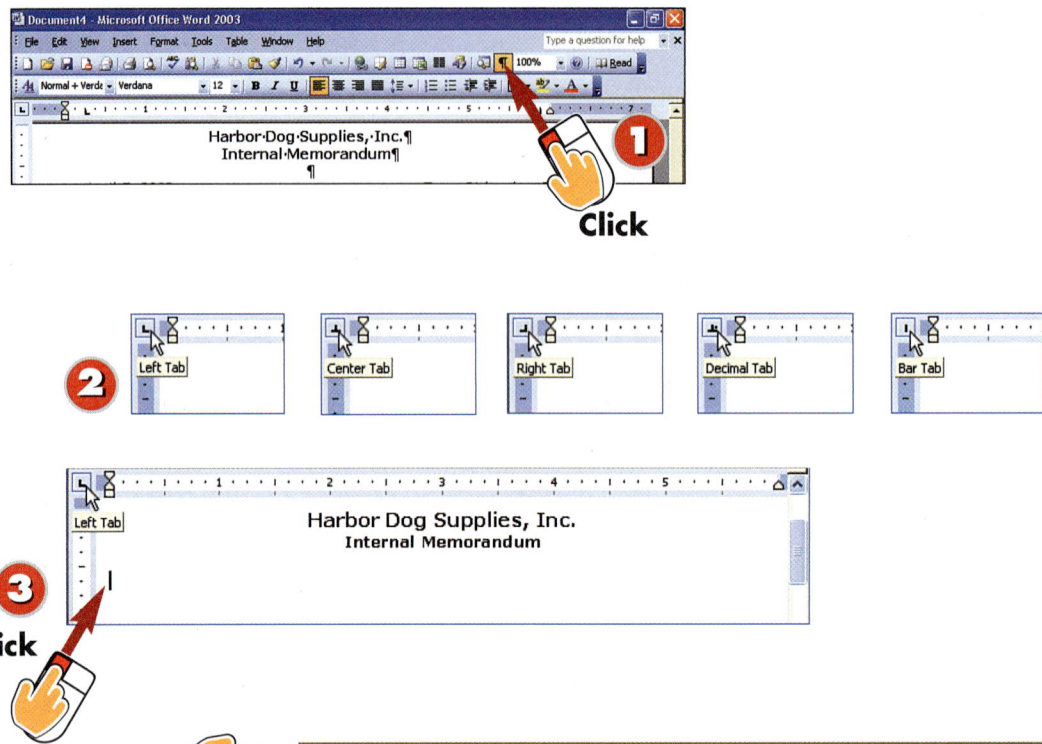

1 Click the **Show/Hide** button. (Although this step is not required, it can make working with custom tabs a little easier.)

2 Before you insert any type of custom tab, first click the **Tab Stop Indicator** button until you see the symbol for the tab you want.

3 To insert a left tab, display the left-tab symbol on the **Tab Stop Indicator** button, and click in the paragraph where you want to use the tab.

4 Click at the desired location on the ruler to insert the tab.

TIP

Moving and Deleting Custom Tabs
To move a custom tab, first click the **Show/Hide** button to better see where the tabs are placed. Then, select the paragraphs that contain the tab, and drag the tab marker on the ruler to the desired position. To delete a custom tab, select the paragraphs that contain the tab, and then drag the tab marker downward, off the ruler.

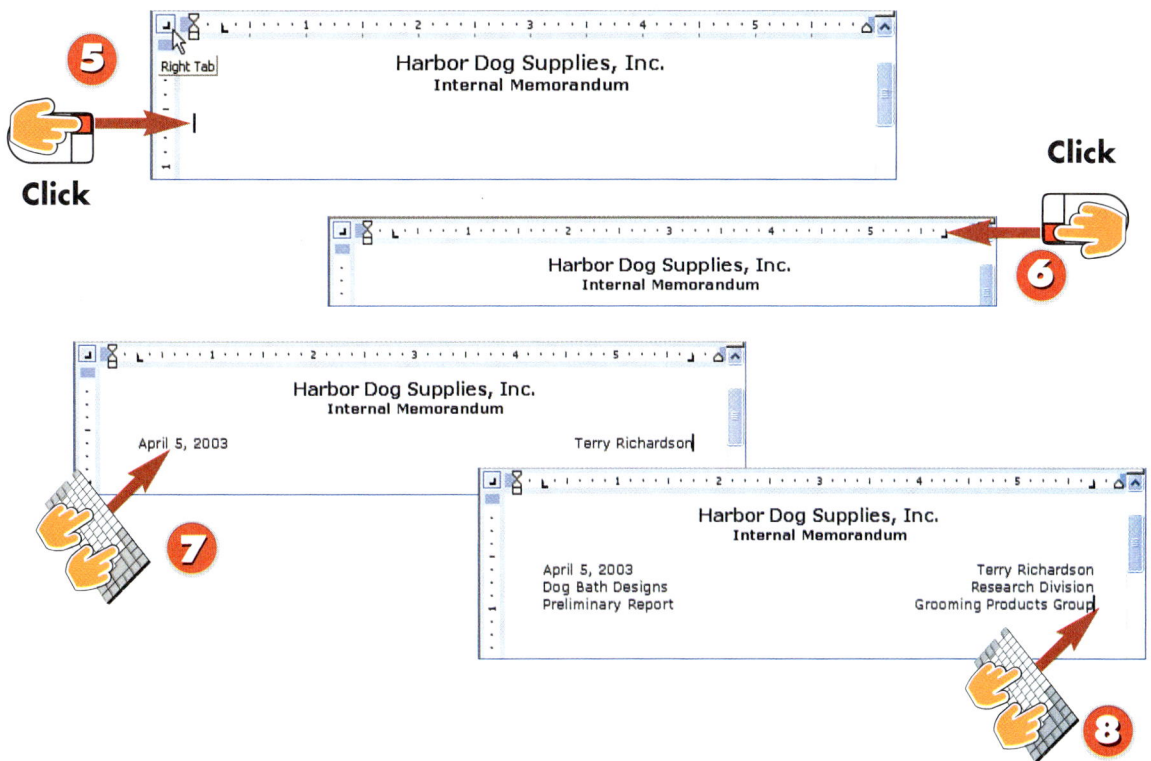

Click

Click

5. To insert a right tab, display the right-tab symbol on the **Tab Stop Indicator** button, and click in the paragraph where you want to use the tab.

6. Click at the desired location on the ruler to insert the tab.

7. Press **Tab** to move to the first tab stop, and type your text. Then press **Tab** to get to next tab stop (if any) and type your text.

8. Press **Enter** after typing the last block of text on the line, and type the remaining paragraphs that use the custom tabs.

End

TIP

Viewing Tab Settings
To see what custom tabs are in effect for any paragraph, click anywhere in the paragraph, and then look at the ruler.

TIP

The Tab Stop Indicator Button
The Tab Stop Indicator button also displays symbols for first-line and hanging indents, but it's probably easier to create these indents using the indent markers (refer to "Adding Indents" earlier in this part).

TIP

Restoring Default Tabs
To restore the default tabs below a paragraph that contains custom tabs, click in the paragraph where you'd like the default tabs to begin, and delete the custom tabs. The default tabs will automatically reappear.

Setting a Custom Center or Decimal Tab

Start

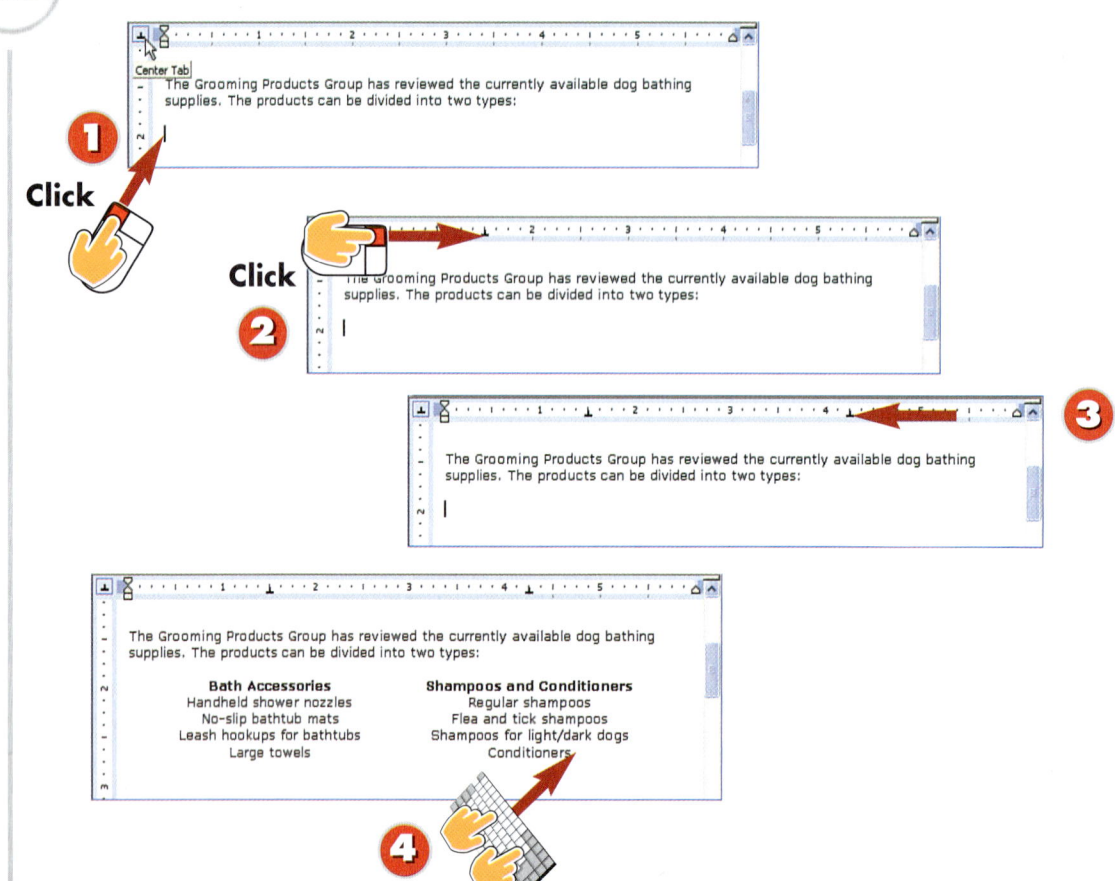

Click

Click

To insert a center tab, display the center-tab symbol on the **Tab Stop Indicator** button, and click in the paragraph where you want to use the tab.

Click at the desired location on the ruler to insert the tab.

Insert any additional tabs in the paragraph. In this example, a second center tab was added to the right.

Type your text using the custom tabs (see steps 7 and 8 in the preceding task).

Center tabs let you center text over the tab stop, and decimal tabs align text along the decimal point. (Decimal tabs are most useful for typing columns of numbers.) Setting custom center and decimal tabs is exactly the same as setting left and right tabs. If you haven't done so, look over the preceding task to get an overview of working with custom tabs before continuing with these steps.

TIP

Clicking the Show/Hide Button

Click the **Show/Hide** button on the Formatting toolbar to be able to see where tabs have been inserted in your document.

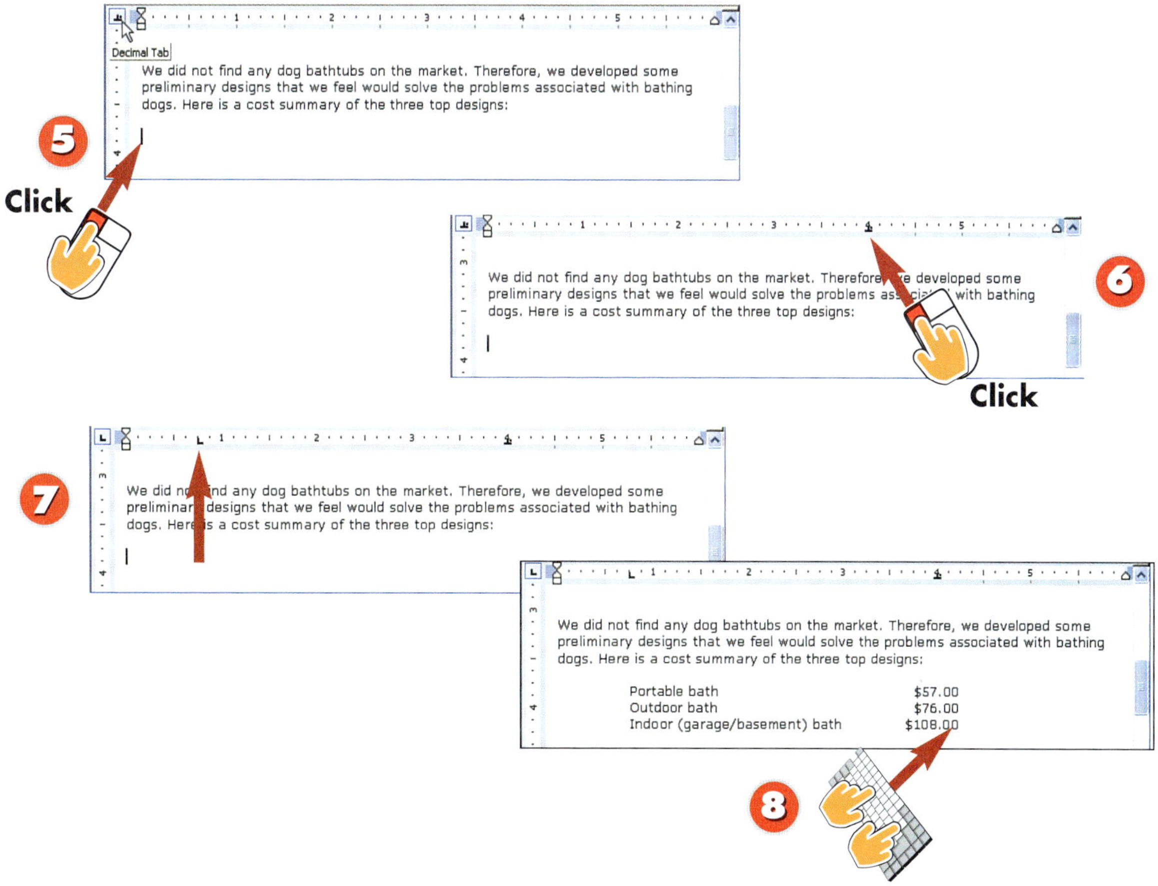

Decimal Tab

We did not find any dog bathtubs on the market. Therefore, we developed some preliminary designs that we feel would solve the problems associated with bathing dogs. Here is a cost summary of the three top designs:

5 **Click**

We did not find any dog bathtubs on the market. Therefore, we developed some preliminary designs that we feel would solve the problems associated with bathing dogs. Here is a cost summary of the three top designs:

6

Click

7

We did not find any dog bathtubs on the market. Therefore, we developed some preliminary designs that we feel would solve the problems associated with bathing dogs. Here is a cost summary of the three top designs:

We did not find any dog bathtubs on the market. Therefore, we developed some preliminary designs that we feel would solve the problems associated with bathing dogs. Here is a cost summary of the three top designs:

Portable bath	$57.00
Outdoor bath	$76.00
Indoor (garage/basement) bath	$108.00

8

5 To insert a decimal tab, display the decimal-tab symbol on the **Tab Stop Indicator** button, and click in the paragraph where you want to use the tab.

6 Click at the desired location on the ruler to insert the tab.

7 Insert any additional tabs in the paragraph. In this example, a left tab was added to the left of the decimal tab.

8 Again, type your text using the custom tabs as described in steps 7 and 8 in the preceding task.

End

TIP

Using Bar Tabs

A *bar tab* creates a vertical line at the tab stop. You can use it to add vertical lines to divide columns of text on your page. In general, however, it's easier to create vertical lines with the Tables feature.

TIP

Why Is My Custom Tab Gray?

If you select multiple paragraphs, any custom tabs that are in some—but not all—of the selected paragraphs will appear gray on the ruler. If you move a gray tab, it will apply to *all* the selected paragraphs when you release the mouse button (and it will turn black). If you delete a gray tab, it will be removed from the paragraphs that contained it.

Adding a Border to a Paragraph

Start

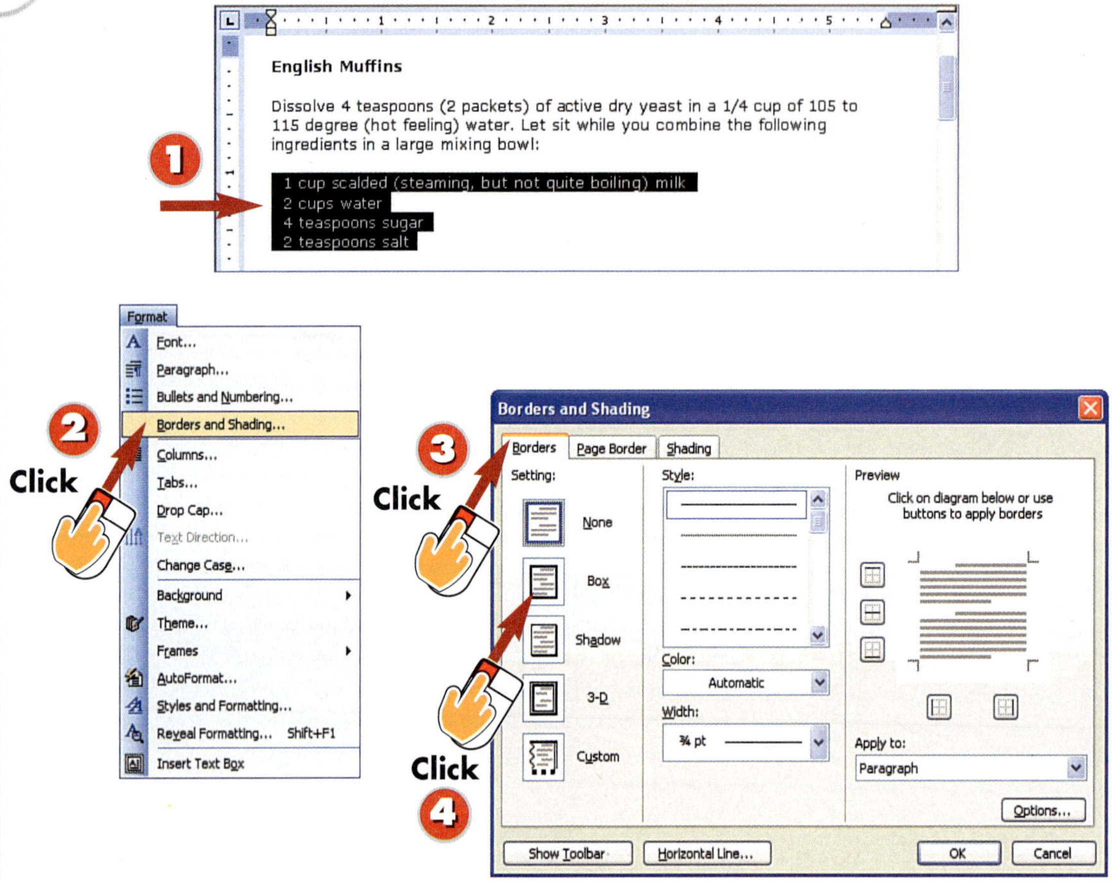

English Muffins

Dissolve 4 teaspoons (2 packets) of active dry yeast in a 1/4 cup of 105 to 115 degree (hot feeling) water. Let sit while you combine the following ingredients in a large mixing bowl:

1

1 cup scalded (steaming, but not quite boiling) milk
2 cups water
4 teaspoons sugar
2 teaspoons salt

Format

A Font...
   Paragraph...
   Bullets and Numbering...
   Borders and Shading...
   Columns...
   Tabs...
   Drop Cap...
   Text Direction...
   Change Case...
   Background
   Theme...
   Frames
   AutoFormat...
   Styles and Formatting...
   Reveal Formatting...   Shift+F1
   Insert Text Box

2 Click

3 Click

Borders and Shading

Borders | Page Border | Shading

Setting:
None
Box
Shadow
3-D
Custom

Style:

Color:
Automatic

Width:
¾ pt

Preview
Click on diagram below or use buttons to apply borders

Apply to:
Paragraph

Options...

Show Toolbar   Horizontal Line...   OK   Cancel

4 Click

1 Select the paragraphs to which you want to add the border.

2 Open the **Format** menu and choose **Borders and Shading** to display the Borders and Shading dialog box.

3 Click the **Borders** tab if it isn't already in front.

4 Click the option that most closely matches what you want under **Setting**.

You don't have to know anything about graphics to set off paragraphs with attractive borders, and you can even add a decorative border around the whole page. In this task, you learn how to add a border. In the next task, you learn how to further enhance the appearance of a paragraph with shading, which adds background color to the paragraph.

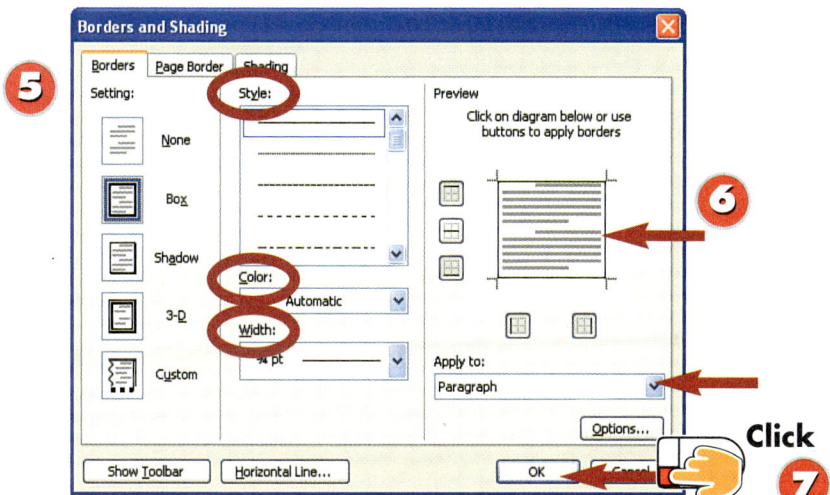

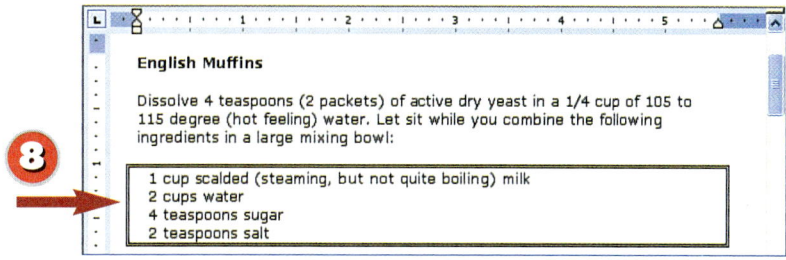

5   Choose the options you like in the **Style**, **Color**, and **Width** lists.

6   The **Preview** area shows the options you've chosen.

7   Make sure that it says **Paragraph** in the **Apply to** list, and then click **OK**.

8   Word applies the border to the selected paragraphs.

End

Indenting the Left and Right Borders

If you don't want the right and left borders on a paragraph to extend all the way to the margins, set left and right indents (refer to "Adding Indents" earlier in this part).

Removing Borders from a Paragraph

To remove borders from a paragraph, select the paragraph, choose **Format, Borders and Shading**, click the **Borders** tab, click **None** under **Setting**, and click **OK**.

Adding a Border Around the Entire Page

To add a border around your entire page, click the **Page Border** tab in the Borders and Shading dialog box, and then select from the same set of options as those in the **Borders** tab.

Shading a Paragraph

Start

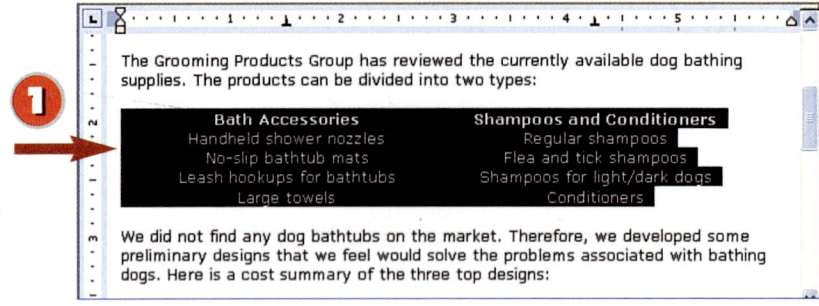

The Grooming Products Group has reviewed the currently available dog bathing supplies. The products can be divided into two types:

Bath Accessories	Shampoos and Conditioners
Handheld shower nozzles	Regular shampoos
No-slip bathtub mats	Flea and tick shampoos
Leash hookups for bathtubs	Shampoos for light/dark dogs
Large towels	Conditioners

We did not find any dog bathtubs on the market. Therefore, we developed some preliminary designs that we feel would solve the problems associated with bathing dogs. Here is a cost summary of the three top designs:

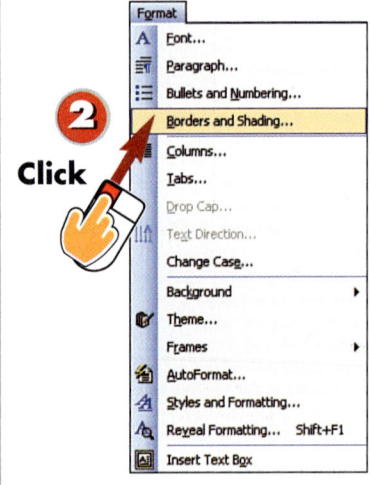

Click

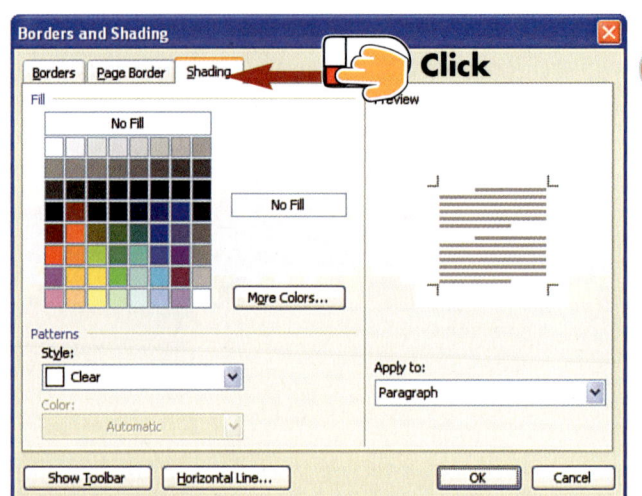

Click

1 Select the paragraphs to which you want to add shading.

2 Open the **Format** menu and choose **Borders and Shading** to display the Borders and Shading dialog box.

3 The Borders and Shading dialog box opens. Click the **Shading** tab.

INTRODUCTION

If you want to set a paragraph or two off from the rest of your text, adding shading might do the trick. For additional emphasis, you can also add borders, as described in the preceding task.

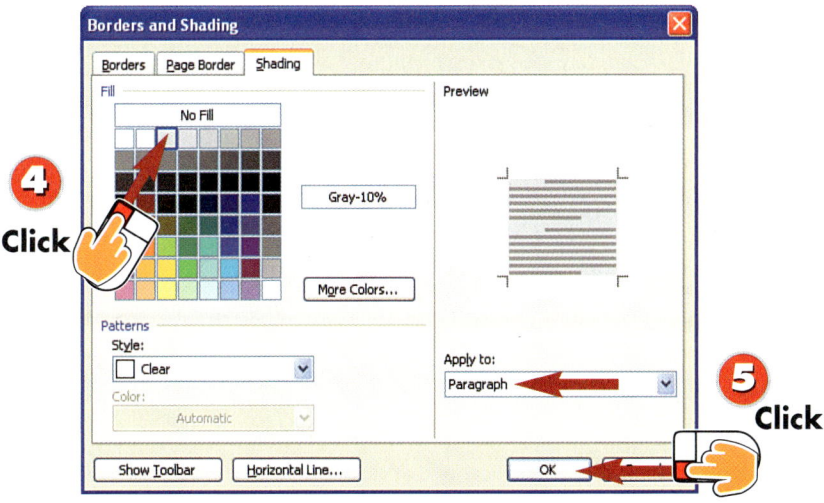

Click

Click

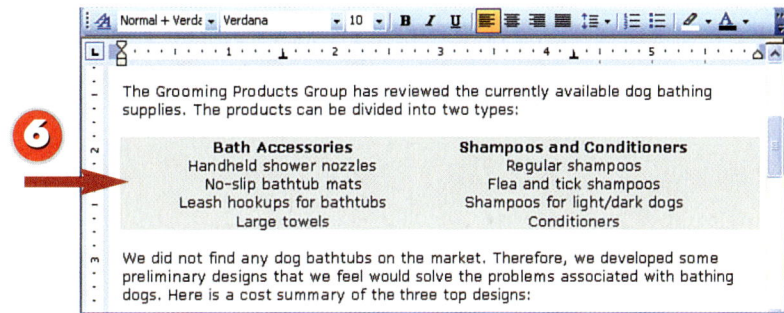

4. Click the color you want to use under **Fill**.

5. Make sure that it says **Paragraph** in the **Apply to** list, and then click **OK**.

6. The shading is applied to the selected paragraphs.

End

Removing Shading from a Paragraph

To remove shading from a paragraph, select the paragraph, choose **Format, Borders and Shading**, click the **Shading** tab, click **No Fill** under **Fill**, and click **OK**.

Copying Font and Paragraph Formatting

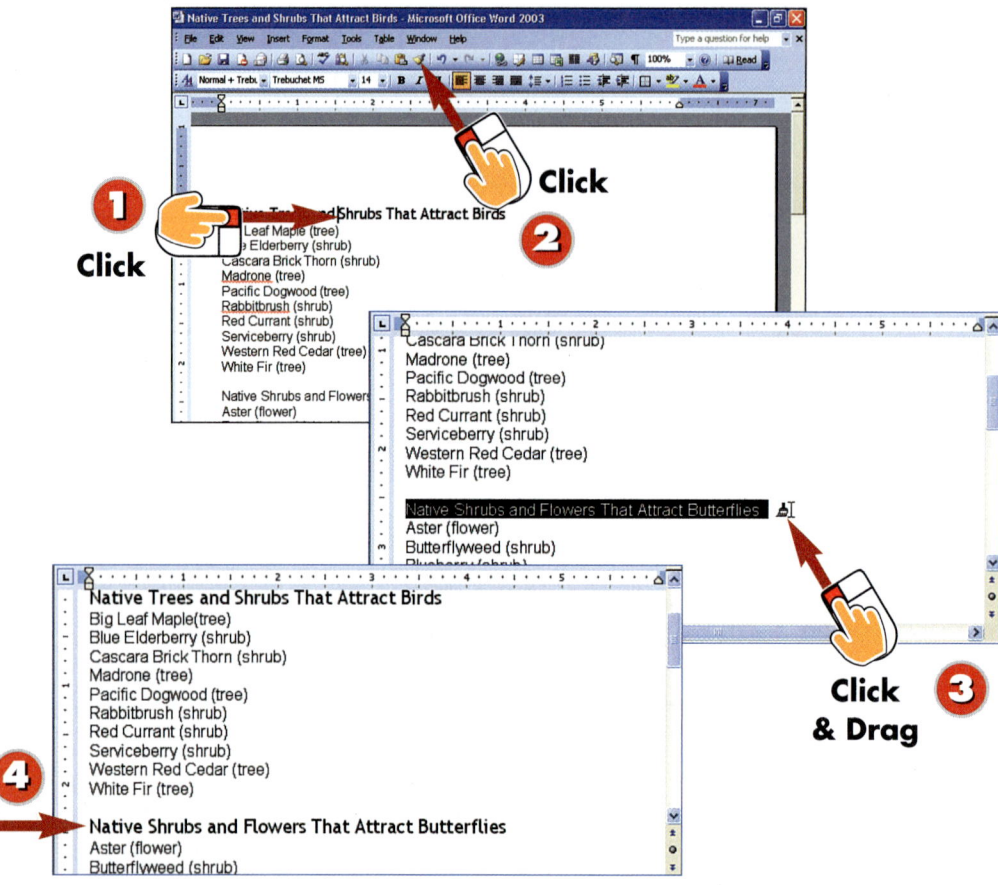

1 To copy just the font formatting, click anywhere in the text that has the formatting you want to copy.

2 Click the **Format Painter** button on the Formatting toolbar.

3 The mouse pointer becomes an I-beam with a paintbrush attached to it. Drag over the text where you want to apply the formatting.

4 Release the mouse button. Word applies the formatting to the selected text.

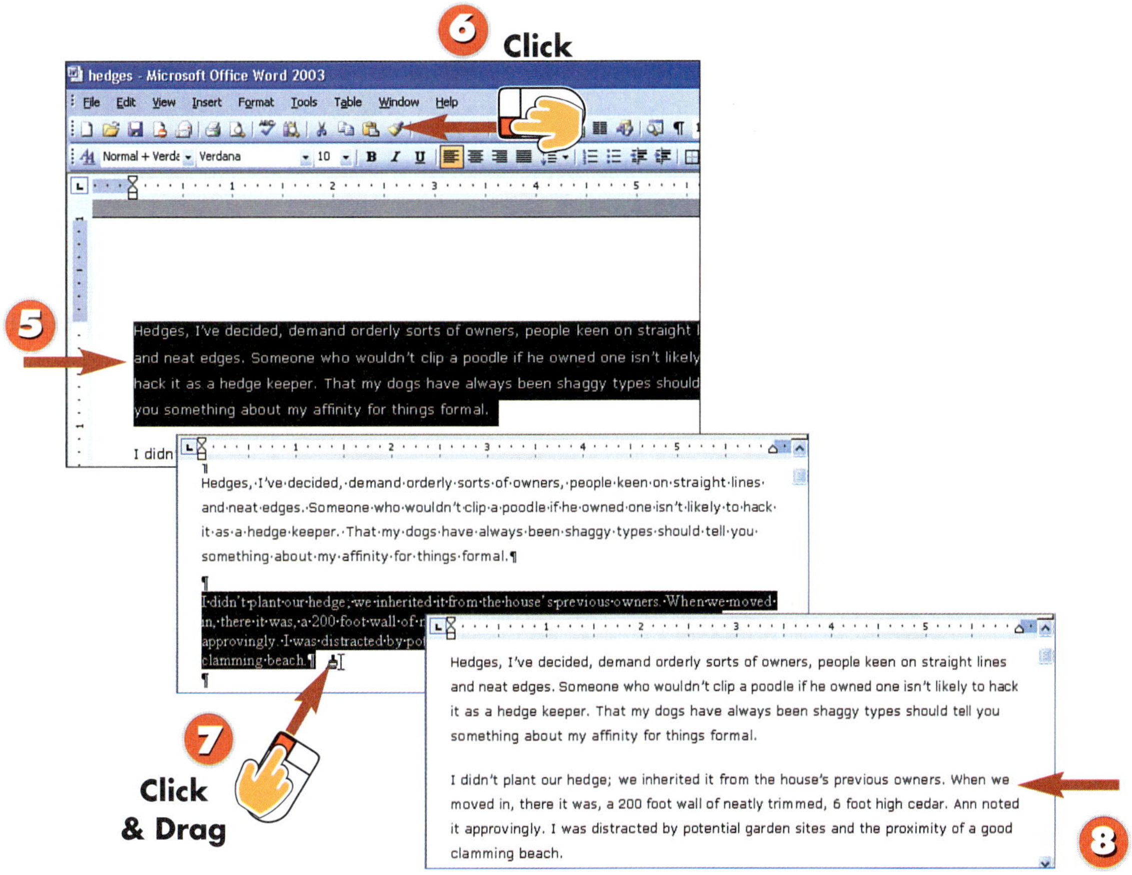

6 **Click**

5

7 **Click & Drag**

8

5 To copy paragraph and font formatting, select the entire paragraph that contains the formatting, including the paragraph mark.

6 Click the **Format Painter** button on the Formatting toolbar.

7 The mouse pointer becomes an I-beam with a paintbrush attached to it. Drag over the paragraph to which you want to apply the formatting.

8 Release the mouse button. Word applies the formatting to the selected text.

End

Copying Formatting to Multiple Places
TIP
To apply the same formatting to several blocks of text, double-click the **Format Painter** button. The Format Painter will stay turned on while you drag over multiple blocks of text. Click the button again to turn it off.

Using the Show/Hide Button
TIP
To see where the paragraph mark is in order to select it in step 5, you may need to click the Show/Hide toolbar button.

Checking the Formatting of Your Text

Start

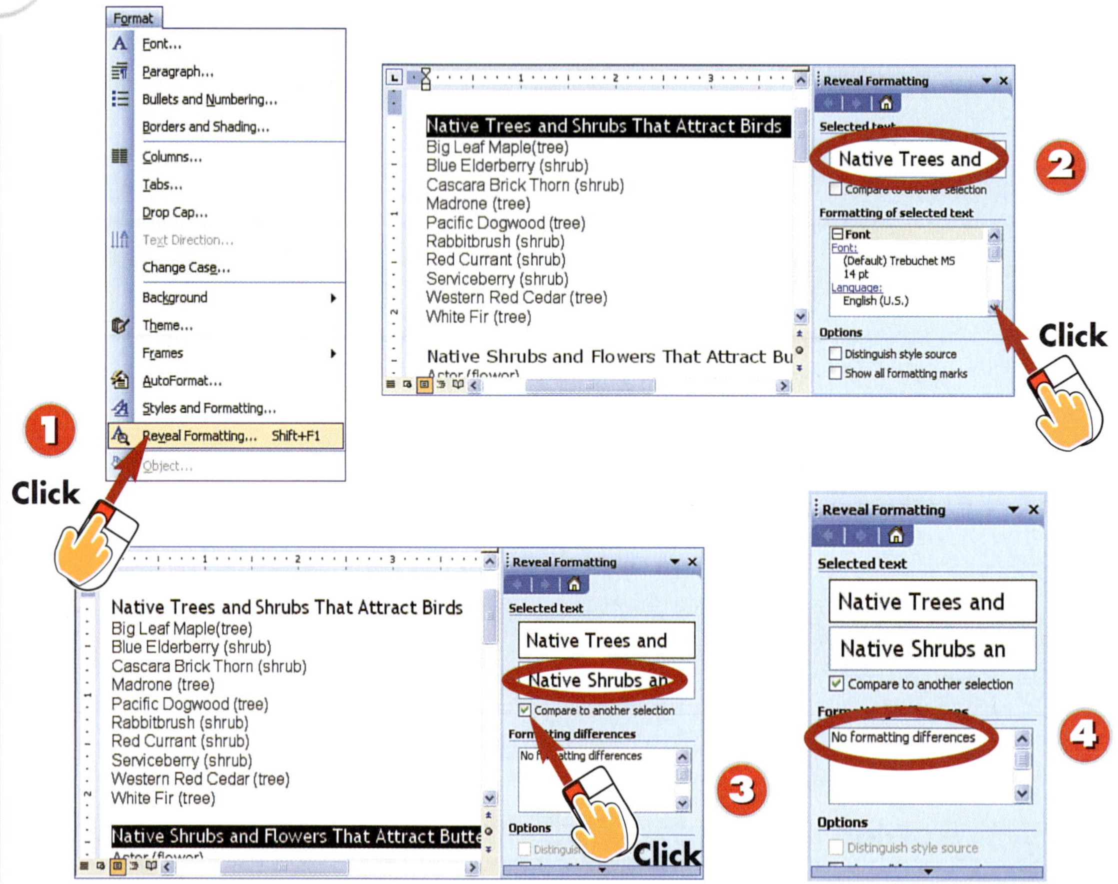

Format
- A̲ Font...
- 三̲ Paragraph...
- ≣ Bullets and Numbering...
-    Borders and Shading...
- ▦ Columns...
-    Tabs...
-    Drop Cap...
- ⏧ Text Direction...
-    Change Case...
-    Background   ▶
- 🎨 Theme...
-    Frames   ▶
- 🗎 AutoFormat...
- 🅰️ Styles and Formatting...
- ✍ Reveal Formatting...   Shift+F1
-    Object...

1 **Click**

Native Trees and Shrubs That Attract Birds
Big Leaf Maple(tree)
Blue Elderberry (shrub)
Cascara Brick Thorn (shrub)
Madrone (tree)
Pacific Dogwood (tree)
Rabbitbrush (shrub)
Red Currant (shrub)
Serviceberry (shrub)
Western Red Cedar (tree)
White Fir (tree)

Native Shrubs and Flowers That Attract Bu...
Actor (flower)

Reveal Formatting
Selected text
Native Trees and
☐ Compare to another selection
Formatting of selected text
⊟ Font
Font:
(Default) Trebuchet MS
14 pt
Language:
English (U.S.)
Options
☐ Distinguish style source
☐ Show all formatting marks

2 **Click**

Native Trees and Shrubs That Attract Birds
Big Leaf Maple(tree)
Blue Elderberry (shrub)
Cascara Brick Thorn (shrub)
Madrone (tree)
Pacific Dogwood (tree)
Rabbitbrush (shrub)
Red Currant (shrub)
Serviceberry (shrub)
Western Red Cedar (tree)
White Fir (tree)

Native Shrubs and Flowers That Attract Butte...
Actor (flower)

Reveal Formatting
Selected text
Native Trees and
Native Shrubs an
☑ Compare to another selection
Formatting differences
No formatting differences
Options
☐ Distingui...

3 **Click**

Reveal Formatting
Selected text
Native Trees and
Native Shrubs an
☑ Compare to another selection
Form...
No formatting differences
Options
☐ Distinguish style source

4

1 Open the **Format** menu and choose **Reveal Formatting** to display the Reveal Formatting task pane.

2 Select the text that you want to examine. A sample of the text appears. Under **Formatting of selected text**, scroll down the list and review the formatting.

3 To compare the formatting, mark the **Compare to another selection** check box and select the second block of text. A sample appears in a second box under **Selected text**.

4 Review the differences under **Formatting differences**. If there are no differences, **No formatting differences** appears in this list.

Suppose you are finishing a document that was started by someone else and you want to see what formatting has already been applied. Or maybe you have been inconsistent in your formatting and now want to clean it up and finalize your document. Word's Reveal Formatting feature enables you to both examine the formatting of a single selected block of text and to compare the formatting of selections. Furthermore, Word can adjust the formatting of the second selection to match the first.

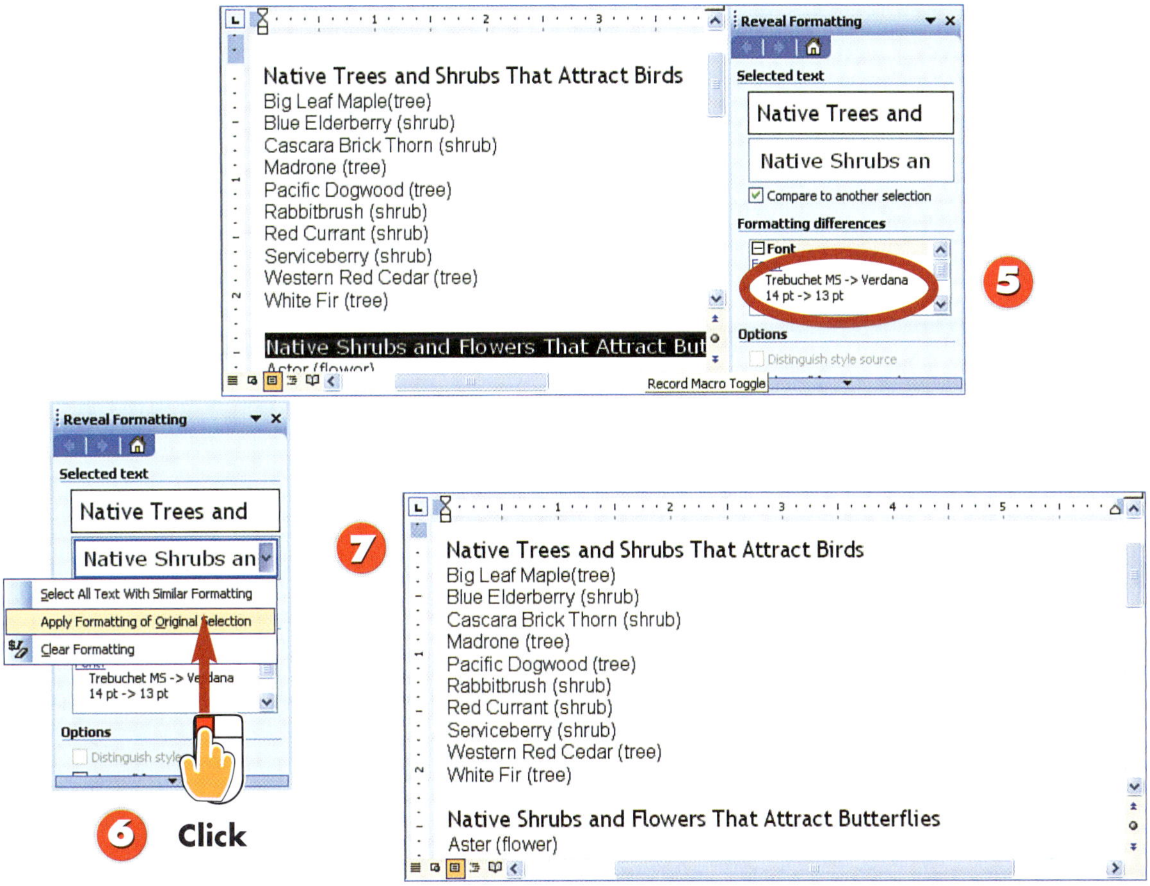

Reveal Formatting

Selected text

Native Trees and

Native Shrubs an

☑ Compare to another selection

Formatting differences

⊟ Font

Trebuchet MS -> Verdana
14 pt -> 13 pt

5

Options

☐ Distinguish style source

Native Trees and Shrubs That Attract Birds
Big Leaf Maple(tree)
Blue Elderberry (shrub)
Cascara Brick Thorn (shrub)
Madrone (tree)
Pacific Dogwood (tree)
Rabbitbrush (shrub)
Red Currant (shrub)
Serviceberry (shrub)
Western Red Cedar (tree)
White Fir (tree)
Native Shrubs and Flowers That Attract But
Aster (flower)

Record Macro Toggle

Reveal Formatting

Selected text

Native Trees and

Native Shrubs an

Select All Text With Similar Formatting
Apply Formatting of Original Selection
Clear Formatting

Trebuchet MS -> Verdana
14 pt -> 13 pt

Options

☐ Distinguish style

6 **Click**

7

Native Trees and Shrubs That Attract Birds
Big Leaf Maple(tree)
Blue Elderberry (shrub)
Cascara Brick Thorn (shrub)
Madrone (tree)
Pacific Dogwood (tree)
Rabbitbrush (shrub)
Red Currant (shrub)
Serviceberry (shrub)
Western Red Cedar (tree)
White Fir (tree)

Native Shrubs and Flowers That Attract Butterflies
Aster (flower)

---

5 If there are differences, they will be listed. The formatting to the left of each arrow (**->**) is from the first selection; the formatting to the right is from the second.

6 To format the second selection to match the first, point to the second sample box and click the **down arrow** on its right, then choose **Apply Formatting of Original Selection**.

7 Close the **Reveal Formatting** task pane, and click to deselect the text. The second selection is now formatted to match the first.

End

Formatting Pages

In the preceding part, you learned how to format characters and paragraphs. In this part, you learn how to apply formatting that affects entire pages. You'll start with changing margins, and then go on to inserting page breaks, centering a page vertically, and numbering pages. Finally, you learn how to create headers and footers—in other words, text that appears at the top or bottom of every page in your document.

Formatting Options

Insert page numbers

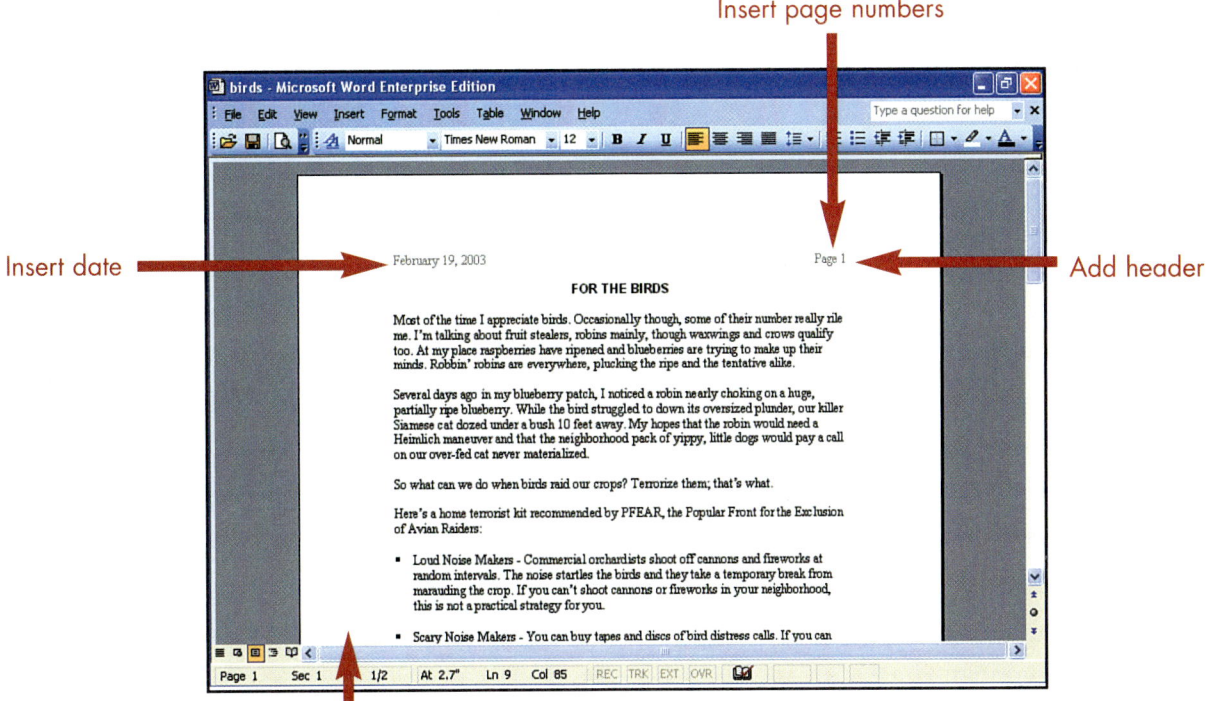

Insert date

Add header

Change margins

Changing Margins

Start

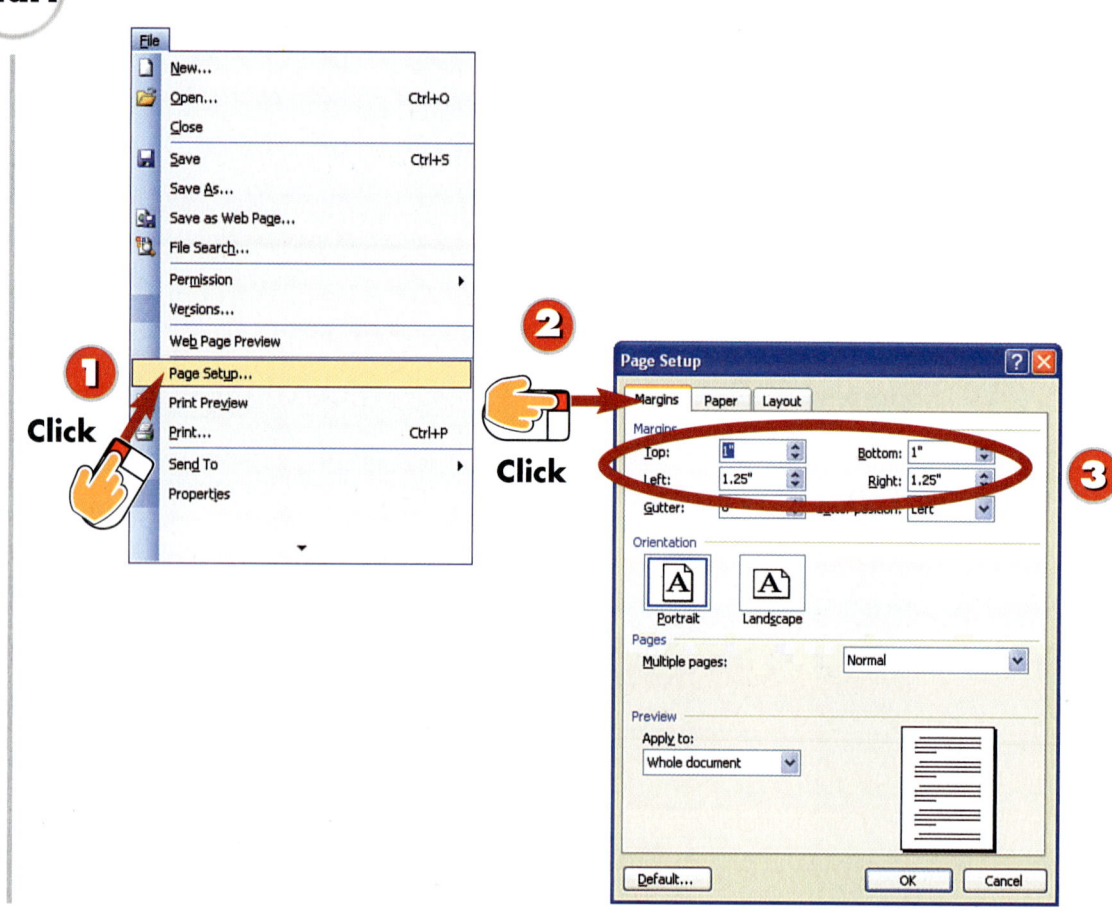

Click

Click

1. Open the **File** menu and choose **Page Setup**. (It doesn't matter where your insertion point is.)

2. In the Page Setup dialog box, click the **Margins** tab if it isn't already in front.

3. The **Top**, **Bottom**, **Left**, and **Right** text boxes let you change the width of all four margins.

Word's default margins are 1 inch on the top and bottom of the page and 1¼ inches on the left and right. You can decrease the margins if you need to squeeze a bit more text onto the page, or increase them to give your document a more spacious feel. When you change the margins, Word applies the new setting to all the pages in your document.

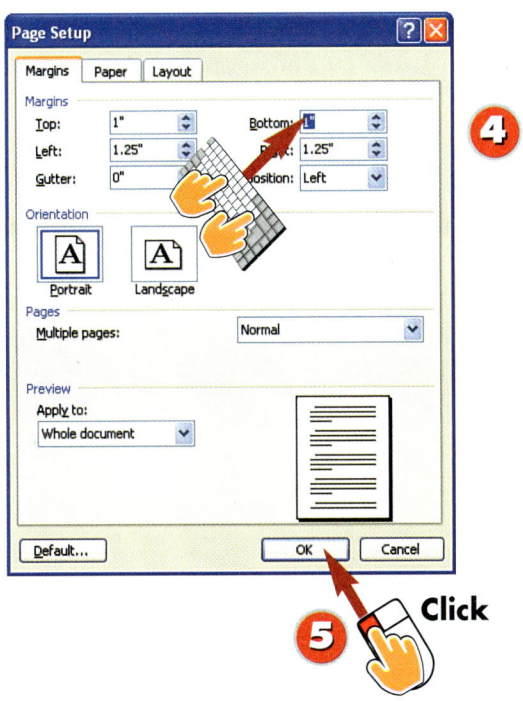

Click

④ Select the number in the text box for the margin you want to change. Type over the number with a new number in inches. (You don't have to type the '' symbol.)

⑤ Repeat step 4 to change any other margins, and then click the **OK** button.

End

Previewing New Margins Before Printing
If you want to see what your margins will look like before you print, use Print Preview or change the Zoom setting to Whole Page (see "Previewing a Document" and "Magnifying a Document" in Part 5).

Changing Paper Orientation
You can change the orientation of your document from *portrait* to *landscape*. Landscape orientation prints your document "sideways" across the paper, so that the long edge of the paper is the top of the page. To do so, click the **Paper Size** tab in the Page Setup dialog box, mark the **Landscape** option button, and click **OK**.

Inserting a Page Break

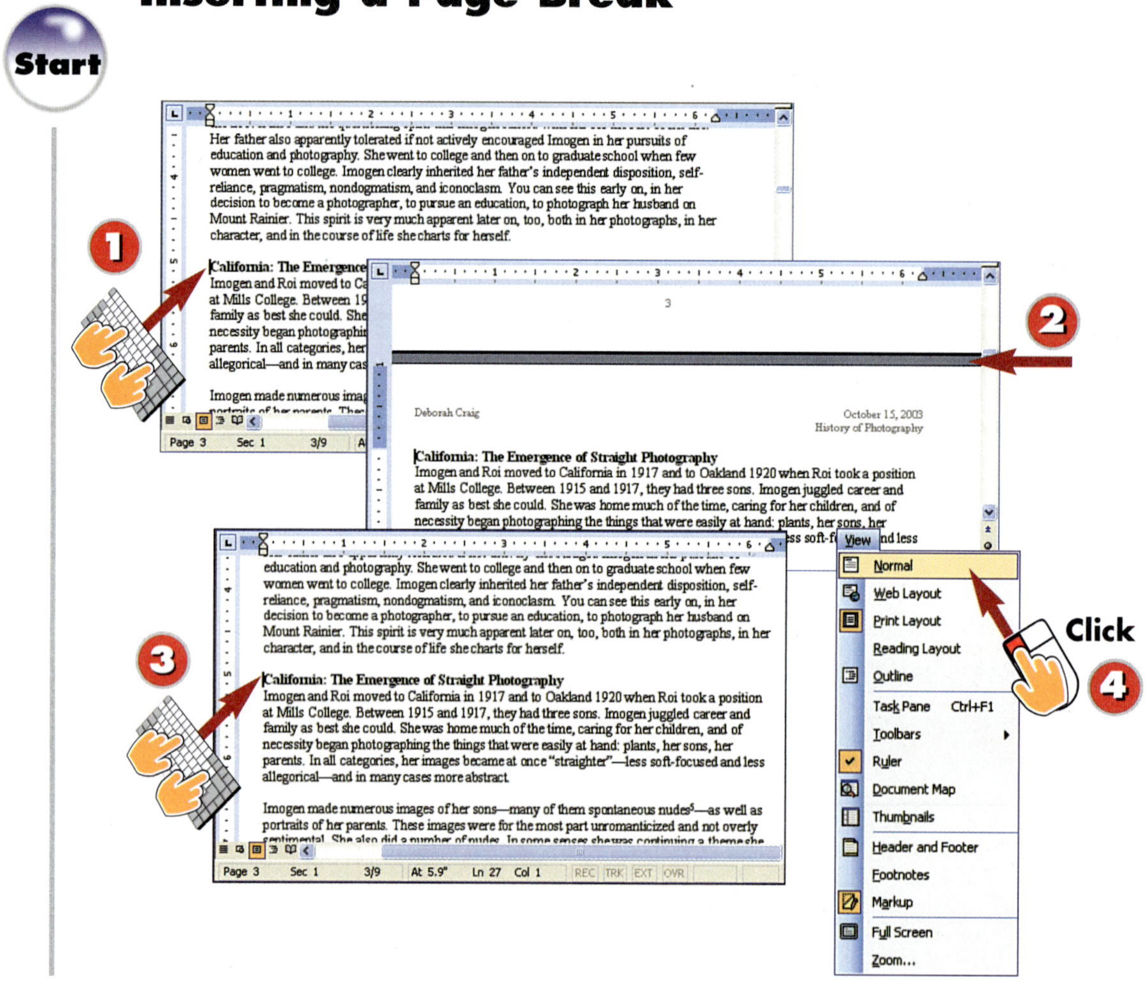

Start

3

Deborah Craig   October 15, 2003
                                History of Photography

California: The Emergence of Straight Photography
Imogen and Roi moved to California in 1917 and to Oakland 1920 when Roi took a position
at Mills College. Between 1915 and 1917, they had three sons. Imogen juggled career and
family as best she could. She was home much of the time, caring for her children, and of
necessity began photographing the things that were easily at hand: plants, her sons, her

education and photography. She went to college and then on to graduate school when few
women went to college. Imogen clearly inherited her father's independent disposition, self-
reliance, pragmatism, nondogmatism, and iconoclasm. You can see this early on, in her
decision to become a photographer, to pursue an education, to photograph her husband on
Mount Rainier. This spirit is very much apparent later on, too, both in her photographs, in her
character, and in the course of life she charts for herself.

California: The Emergence of Straight Photography
Imogen and Roi moved to California in 1917 and to Oakland 1920 when Roi took a position
at Mills College. Between 1915 and 1917, they had three sons. Imogen juggled career and
family as best she could. She was home much of the time, caring for her children, and of
necessity began photographing the things that were easily at hand: plants, her sons, her
parents. In all categories, her images became at once "straighter"—less soft-focused and less
allegorical—and in many cases more abstract.

Imogen made numerous images of her sons—many of them spontaneous nudes[5]—as well as
portraits of her parents. These images were for the most part unromanticized and not overly

Page 3   Sec 1   3/9   At 5.9"   Ln 27   Col 1   REC TRK EXT OVR

View
Normal
Web Layout
Print Layout
Reading Layout
Outline
Task Pane   Ctrl+F1
Toolbars
Ruler
Document Map
Thumbnails
Header and Footer
Footnotes
Markup
Full Screen
Zoom...

Click

1. To insert a hard page break, click where you want to break the page and press **Ctrl+Enter**.

2. Word inserts a hard page break at the insertion point, and moves the text below the break onto the next page.

3. To remove a hard page break, click at the beginning of the first line underneath the break, and press the **Backspace** key. The page break disappears.

4. Page breaks look different in Normal view. To see how they appear, choose **View, Normal**.

When you fill up a page with text, Word inserts a *soft page break* to end the page and wrap text to the next page. There are times, however, when you need to end a page before it's filled with text. To do so, you insert a *hard page break*. For example, you can use a hard page break to separate a title page from the text that follows, or to start a new section of a report at the top of the next page.

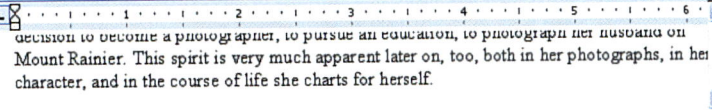

5 In Normal view, a soft page break appears as a horizontal dotted line running across your document.

6 A hard page break appears as a horizontal dotted line with the words *Page Break* in the middle of it.

7 To remove a hard page break while in Normal view, click on the dotted line and press **Delete**.

End

Previewing Page Breaks

You can see the results of inserting a hard page break most clearly by switching to Print Preview or by changing the Zoom setting in Print Layout view to Whole Page. (See "Previewing a Document" and "Magnifying a Document" in Part 5.)

Centering a Page Vertically

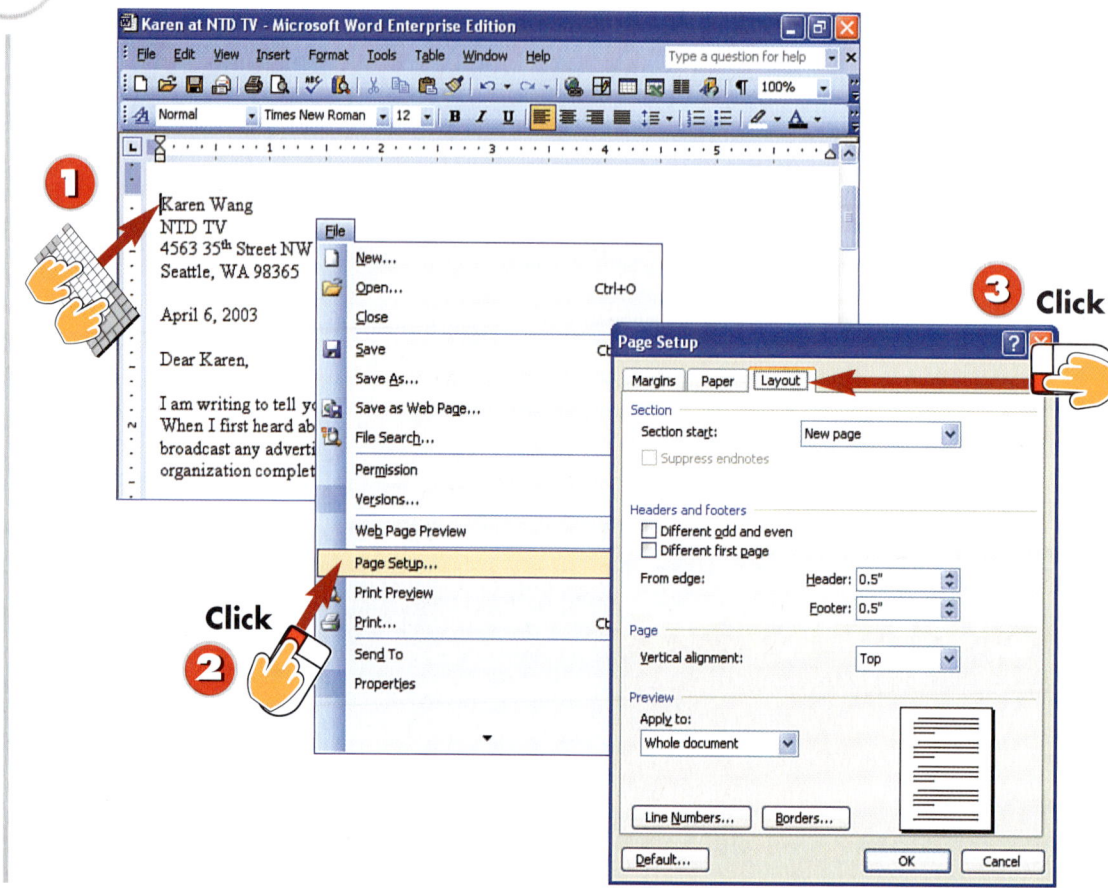

Start

Click

Click

1. Press the **Backspace** or **Delete** key to remove any blank lines from above and below the text you want to center vertically.

2. Open the **File** menu and choose **Page Setup** to open the Page Setup dialog box.

3. Click the **Layout** tab if it isn't already in front.

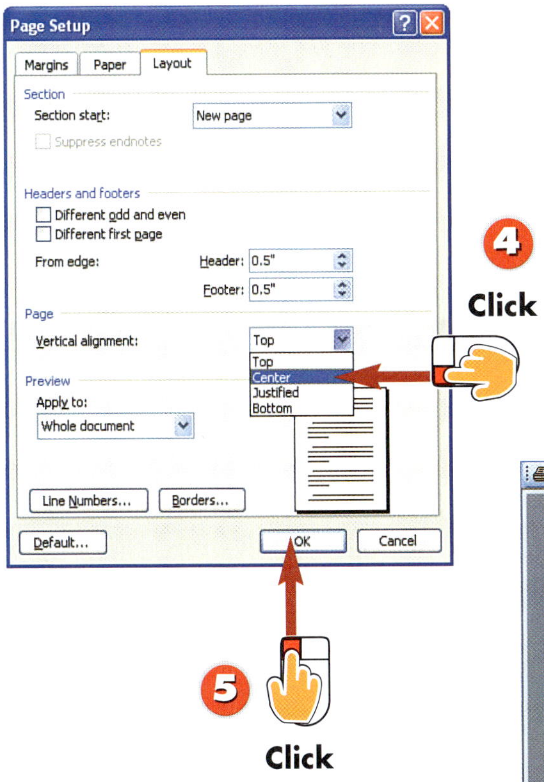

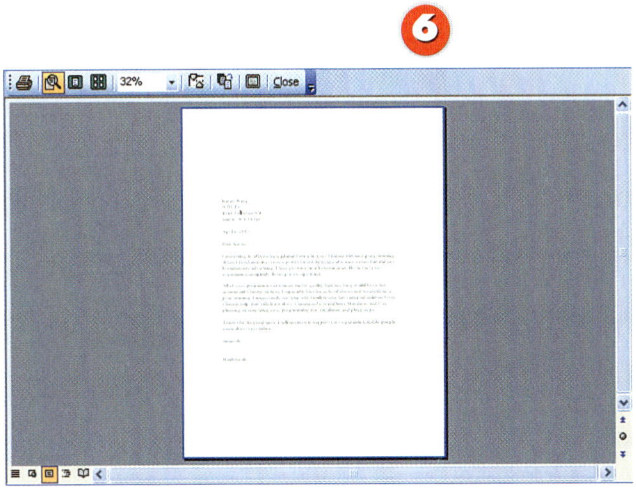

Page Setup

Margins | Paper | Layout

Section
Section start: New page

☐ Suppress endnotes

Headers and footers
☐ Different odd and even
☐ Different first page
From edge: Header: 0.5"
           Footer: 0.5"

Page
Vertical alignment: Top
  Top
  Center
  Justified
  Bottom

Preview
Apply to:
Whole document

Line Numbers... | Borders...

Default... | OK | Cancel

Click ④

Click ⑤

⑥

Print Preview toolbar: 32% Close

④ Click the **down arrow** to the right of the **Vertical alignment** drop-down list, and click **Center**.

⑤ Click the **OK** button.

⑥ If you like, preview the document in Print Preview before printing.

End

Numbering Pages

Start

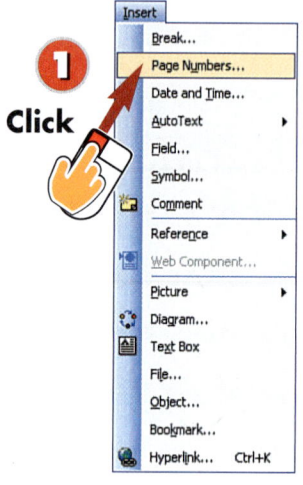

Click

1

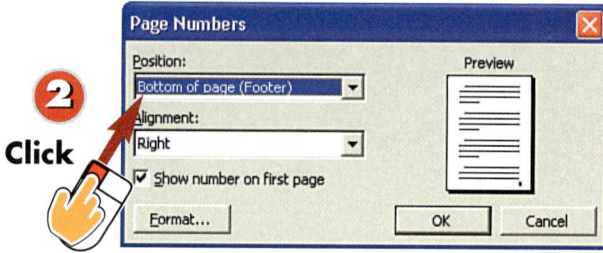

Click

2

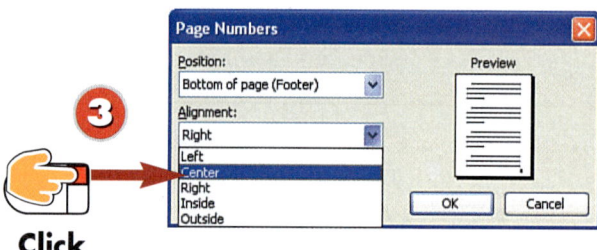

3

Click

1 Open the **Insert** menu and choose **Page Numbers**. (It doesn't matter where your insertion point is in the document when you issue the command.)

2 If you want the number at the bottom of the page, skip to step 4. To place the number at the top, click the **down arrow** next to the **Position** list and choose **Bottom of page (Footer)**.

3 Click the **down arrow** to the right of the **Alignment** list and choose the alignment you prefer for your page numbers.

INTRODUCTION

Word offers two methods for adding page numbers to your document. First, you can use the **Insert**, **Page Numbers** command, as described in this task, to tell Word what type of page number you want and where it should appear. Word then adds the page number *field* to the header or footer for you. Second, you can enter the page number field by inserting it directly into the header or footer (see the next two tasks). This second method gives you more control over the appearance of your page numbers.

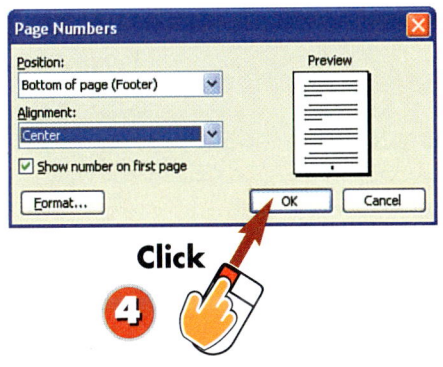

Click

4

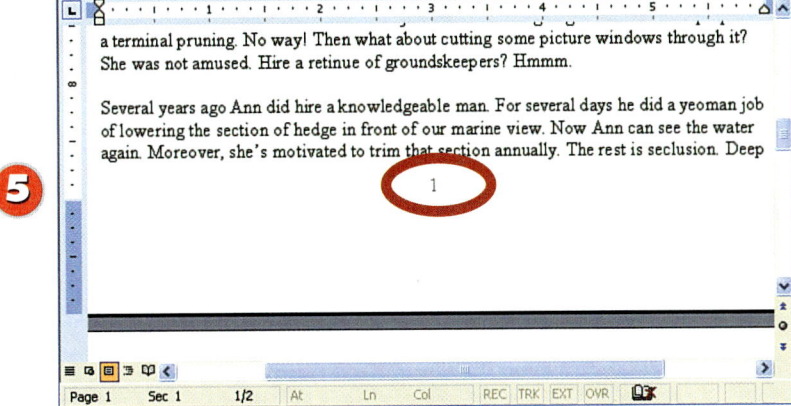

5

a terminal pruning. No way! Then what about cutting some picture windows through it? She was not amused. Hire a retinue of groundskeepers? Hmmm.

Several years ago Ann did hire a knowledgeable man. For several days he did a yeoman job of lowering the section of hedge in front of our marine view. Now Ann can see the water again. Moreover, she's motivated to trim that section annually. The rest is seclusion. Deep

1

Page 1   Sec 1   1/2   At   Ln   Col   REC TRK EXT OVR

4 Click the **OK** button.

5 Word inserts page numbers in the location you specified.

End

Viewing Page Numbers
Page numbers are visible in Print Layout view and Print Preview. They aren't, however, in Normal view.

Deleting Page Numbers
To delete a page number, follow steps 1 and 2 in the next task to activate the header or footer area (depending on where you inserted the page number field). Then click the page number field once (it will turn gray), and then click it again to select the field (it will be surrounded with small black squares). Now press **Delete**.

Creating Headers and Footers

Start

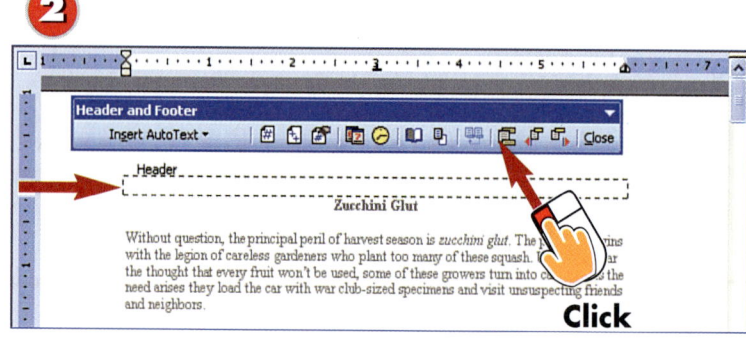

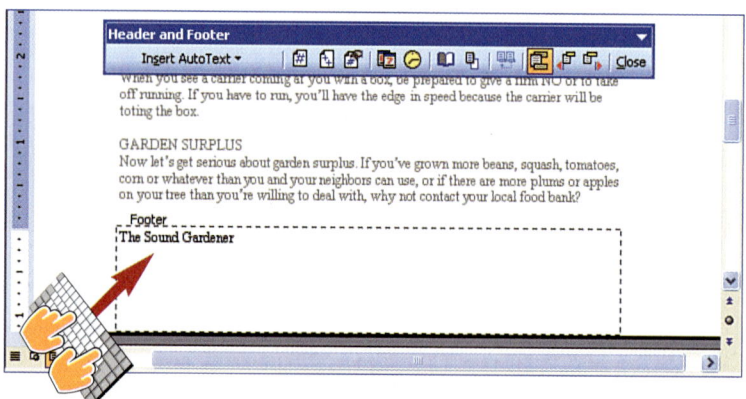

---

1 Open the **View** menu and choose **Header and Footer**. (It doesn't matter where your insertion point is when you issue the command.)

2 Word activates the header area and displays the Header and Footer toolbar. Click the **Switch Between Header and Footer** button.

3 Word activates the footer area. (Click the **Switch Between Header and Footer** button again when you want to switch back to the header area.) Type any text that you want to appear at the left margin.

INTRODUCTION

A *header* appears at the top of every page, and a *footer* appears at the bottom of every page. You can use headers and footers to display the document title, your name, the name of your organization, and so on. In this task, you learn how to type standard text in your headers and footers. In the next task, you use the Header and Footer toolbar to insert fields that display information such as the page number and the current date.

TIP

Activating the Header and Footer Areas
Another way to activate the header and footer areas is to double-click the header or footer area while in Print Layout view. (This only works if you have already entered text in the header or footer area.)

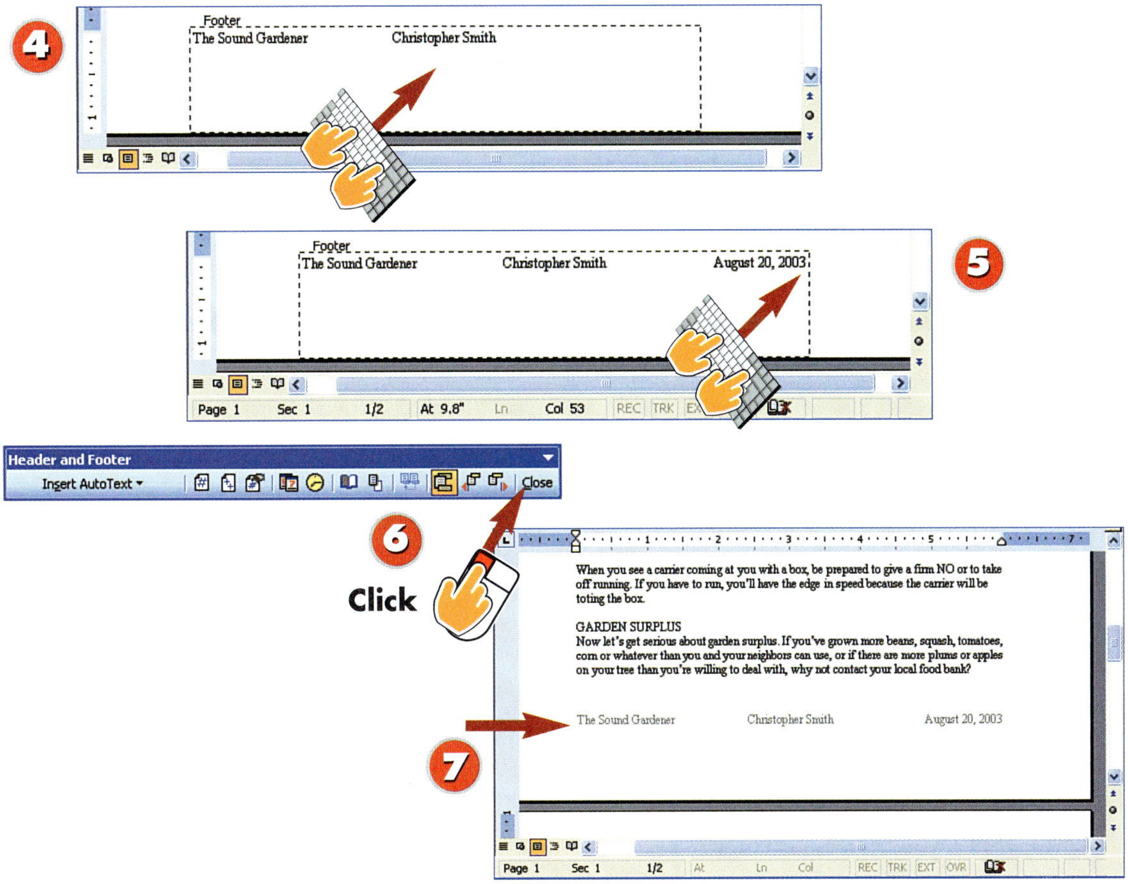

Click

When you see a carrier coming at you with a box, be prepared to give a firm NO or to take off running. If you have to run, you'll have the edge in speed because the carrier will be toting the box.

GARDEN SURPLUS
Now let's get serious about garden surplus. If you've grown more beans, squash, tomatoes, corn or whatever than you and your neighbors can use, or if there are more plums or apples on your tree than you're willing to deal with, why not contact your local food bank?

The Sound Gardener   Christopher Smith   August 20, 2003

4 Press the **Tab** key to jump to a center tab in the center of the footer. Type any text that you want centered here.

5 Press the **Tab** key again to move to a right tab at the right edge of the footer. Type any text that you want flush right here.

6 Click the **Close** button in the Header and Footer toolbar to return to viewing your document text.

7 View your header and footer in Print Layout view or Print Preview.

End

Changing the Font in Your Headers and Footers
You can format the font and font size of your header and footer text just as you do standard text. Select the text and choose the formatting you want from the Font and Font Size lists in the Formatting toolbar. (See "Changing the Font and Font Size" in Part 6.)

Viewing Headers and Footers
You can see your headers and footers in Print Layout view (**View, Print Layout**) and Print Preview (**File, Print Preview**). They are not visible in Normal view.

Inserting Dates and Page Numbers in Headers and Footers

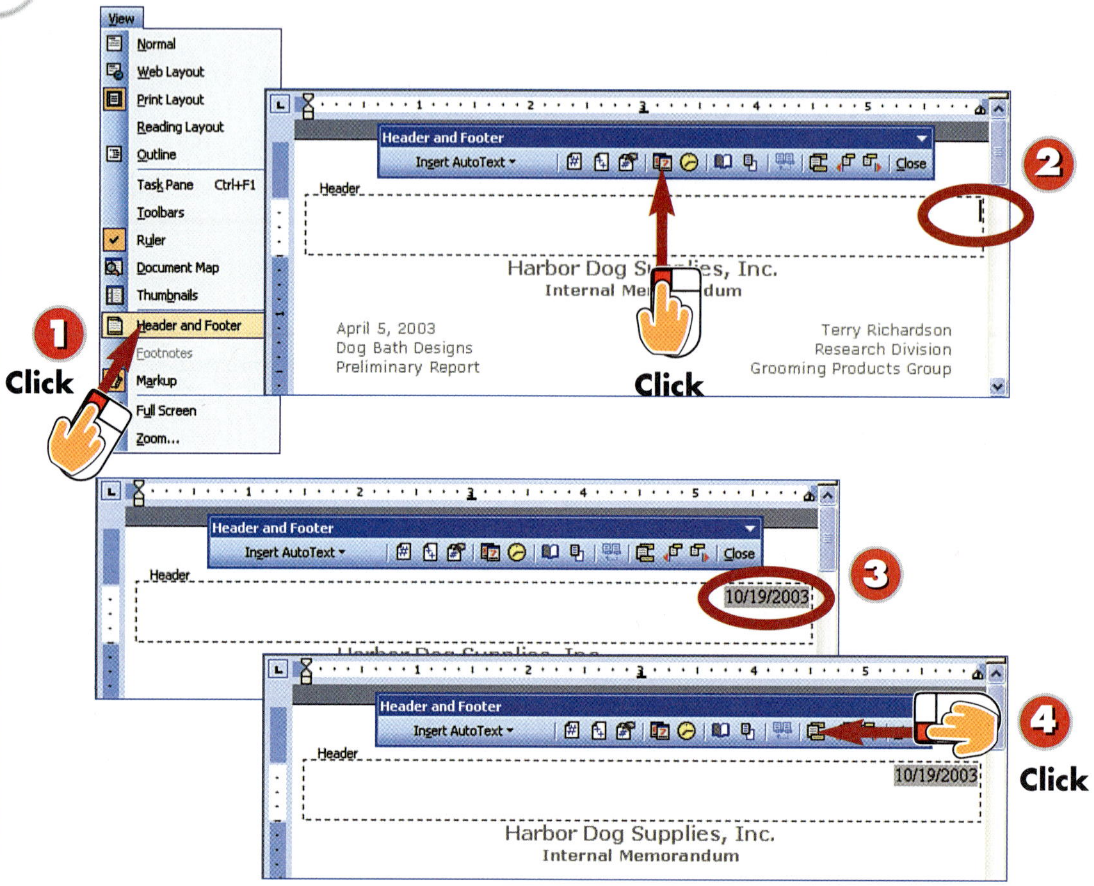

Start

View
- Normal
- Web Layout
- Print Layout
- Reading Layout
- Outline
- Task Pane   Ctrl+F1
- Toolbars
- ✔ Ruler
- Document Map
- Thumbnails
- Header and Footer
- Footnotes
- Markup
- Full Screen
- Zoom...

Click ①

②

Header and Footer
Insert AutoText ▾   Close

Header

Harbor Dog Supplies, Inc.
Internal Memorandum

April 5, 2003
Dog Bath Designs
Preliminary Report

Terry Richardson
Research Division
Grooming Products Group

Click

Header and Footer
Insert AutoText ▾   Close

Header   10/19/2003

③

Harbor Dog Supplies, Inc.

Header and Footer
Insert AutoText ▾

Header

10/19/2003

Harbor Dog Supplies, Inc.
Internal Memorandum

④

Click

① Open the **View** menu and choose **Header and Footer**.

② Press **Tab** twice to move to the right edge of the header area, and click the **Insert Date** button.

③ Word inserts the current date. (To insert the current time, click the **Insert Time** button to the right of the **Insert Date** button.)

④ Click the **Switch Between Header and Footer** button to move to the footer area.

The Header and Footer toolbar makes it easy to insert commonly used blocks of text into a header or footer, as well as fields for the date, the page number, the time, and so on. Here, you take a quick tour of some of the options available on the toolbar. Feel free to experiment on your own.

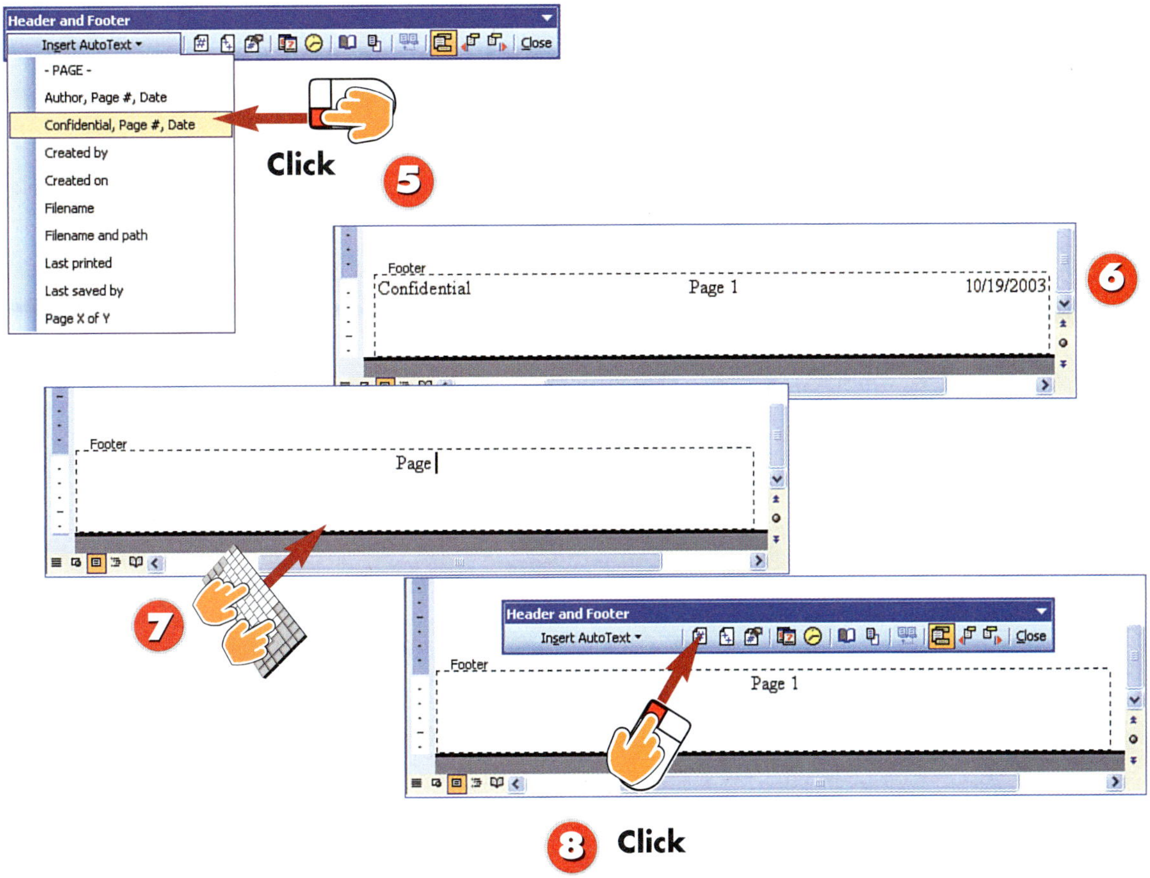

Header and Footer

Insert AutoText ▾

- PAGE -
Author, Page #, Date
Confidential, Page #, Date
Created by
Created on
Filename
Filename and path
Last printed
Last saved by
Page X of Y

Click ❺

Footer
Confidential   Page 1   10/19/2003 ❻

Footer
Page |

❼

Header and Footer

Insert AutoText ▾

Footer
Page 1

❽ **Click**

❺ Click the **Insert AutoText** button, and then choose one of the AutoText entries you'd like to see.

❻ Word inserts the AutoText entry in the footer. Select and delete this entry. Try a few other AutoText entries, and delete the last one.

❼ Press the **Tab** key, type **Page**, and then press the **Spacebar**.

❽ Click the **Insert Page Number** button, and then click **Close** in the Header and Footer toolbar.

 **End**

Deleting Fields
To delete a field, select it by double-clicking it or dragging over it with the mouse and then press the **Delete** key.

Changing the Date Format
To change the date format that Word uses when you click the Insert Date button, open the **Insert** menu and choose **Date and Time**. In the Date and Time dialog box, select the desired date format, click the **Default** button, click **Yes** in the message box that appears, and then click **OK**.

PART 8

Handy Editing Techniques

The features presented in this part are all designed to save you editing time and increase your efficiency. You don't *have* to use any of them, but they sure will help. You learn how to ask Word to search a document for a particular word or phrase and replace it with something else, how to check your spelling and grammar and fix spelling errors automatically, how to insert the date automatically, and much more.

Advanced Editing Tools

The Find and Replace dialog box

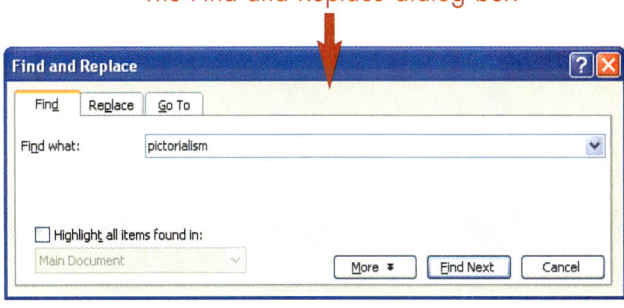

The Spelling and Grammar dialog box

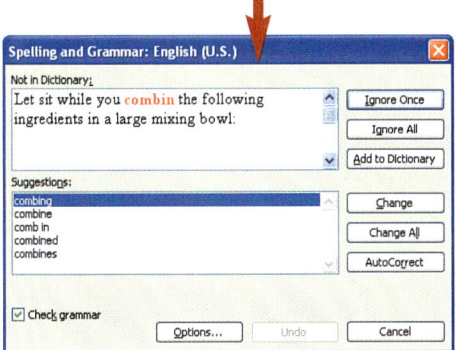

The AutoCorrect dialog box

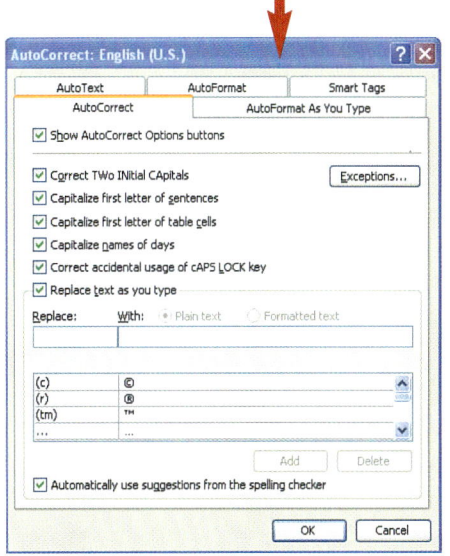

Searching for Text

Start

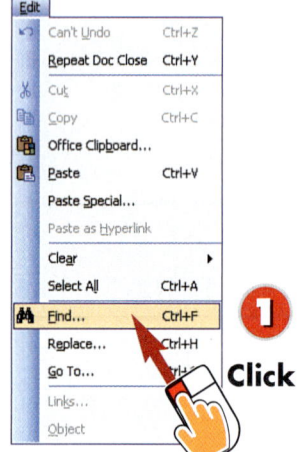

Click

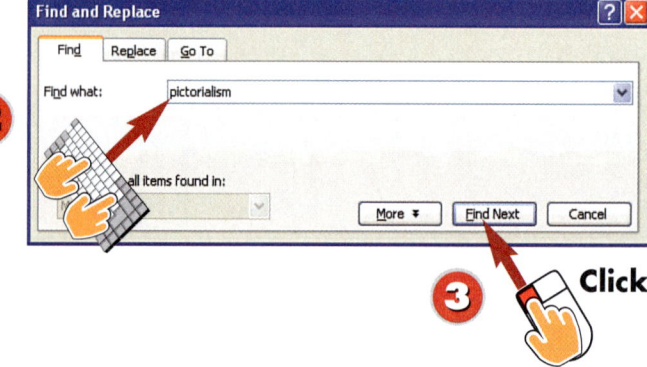

Click

1 Open the **Edit** menu and choose **Find** to open the Find and Replace dialog box with the **Find** tab displayed.

2 Type the text that you want to find in the **Find what** text box.

3 Click the **Find Next** button.

INTRODUCTION

If you frequently type long documents, you have probably had the experience of scrolling through each page trying to find all the places where you used a particular word or phrase. Word can help you with this process, searching for text quickly and accurately.

TIP

Using More Options in Your Search

If you want to be more specific about what text you're looking for, click the **More** button at the bottom of the Find and Replace dialog box to display more options. Two options you may use frequently are **Match case**, which tells Word to only find text that matches the uppercase and lowercase you have used in the **Find what** text box, and **Find whole words only**, which tells Word to only find your text if is *not* part of another word. (So if you are searching for *bench*, it would not find the word *benchmark*.) To hide the options again, click the **Less** button.

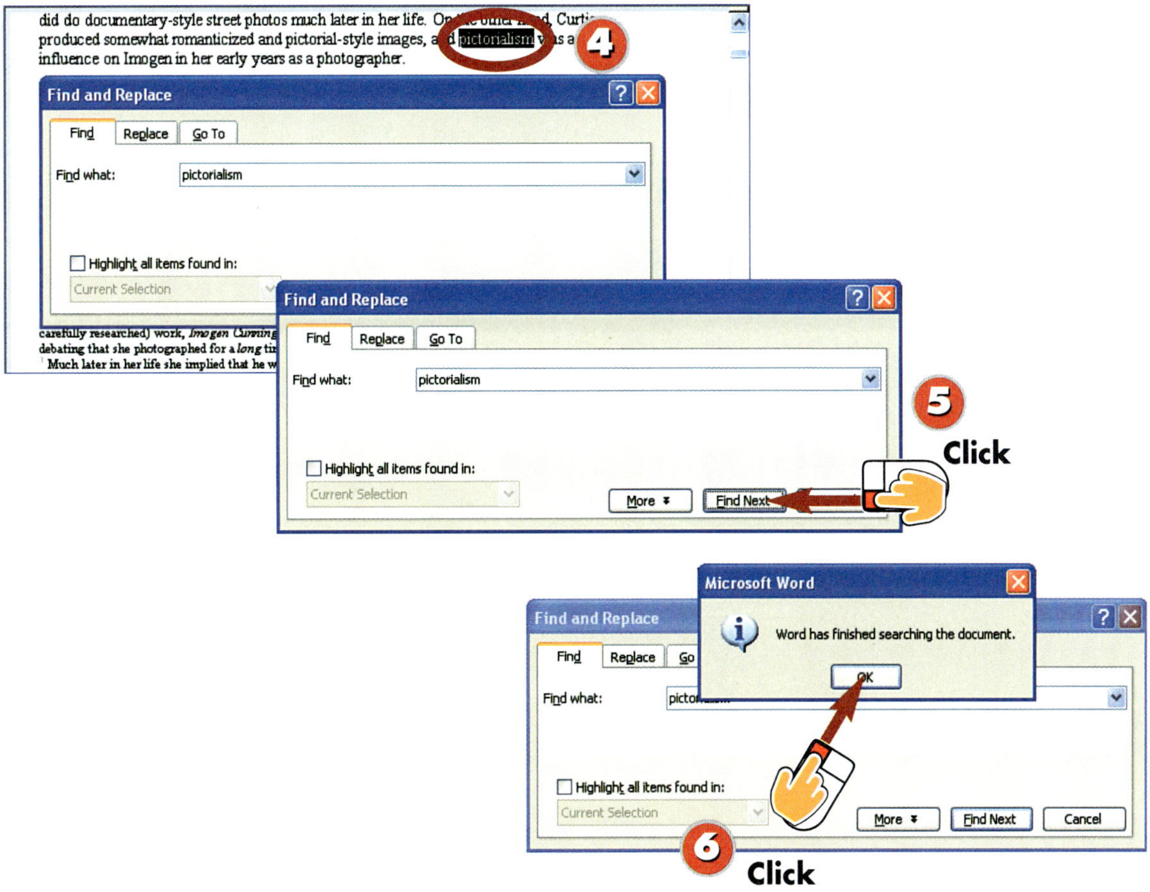

did do documentary-style street photos much later in her life. On the other hand, Curtis produced somewhat romanticized and pictorial-style images, and (pictorialism) was a influence on Imogen in her early years as a photographer.

Find and Replace

Find | Replace | Go To

Find what: pictorialism

☐ Highlight all items found in:
Current Selection

carefully researched) work, *Imogen Cunning* debating that she photographed for a *long* tir Much later in her life she implied that he w

Find and Replace

Find | Replace | Go To

Find what: pictorialism

☐ Highlight all items found in:
Current Selection

More ☷ | Find Next

5 Click

Microsoft Word

ⓘ Word has finished searching the document.

OK

Find and Replace

Find | Replace | Go

Find what: pictor...

☐ Highlight all items found in:
Current Selection

More ☷ | Find Next | Cancel

6 Click

4 Word highlights the first occurrence of the text you typed.

5 Continue clicking the **Find Next** button to look for more matches.

6 Click **OK** when Word informs you that it has finished searching the document, and then click the **Cancel** button in the Find and Replace dialog box to close it.

End

Searching Up or Down
By default, Word begins your search at the insertion point and proceeds down to the end of the document, then from the top of the document back down to the insertion point. You can also choose to search only up or down from the insertion point rather than searching the entire document. To make this change, choose the desired option in the **Search** list (available when you click the **More** button—see the other tip in this task).

Finding and Replacing Text

Start

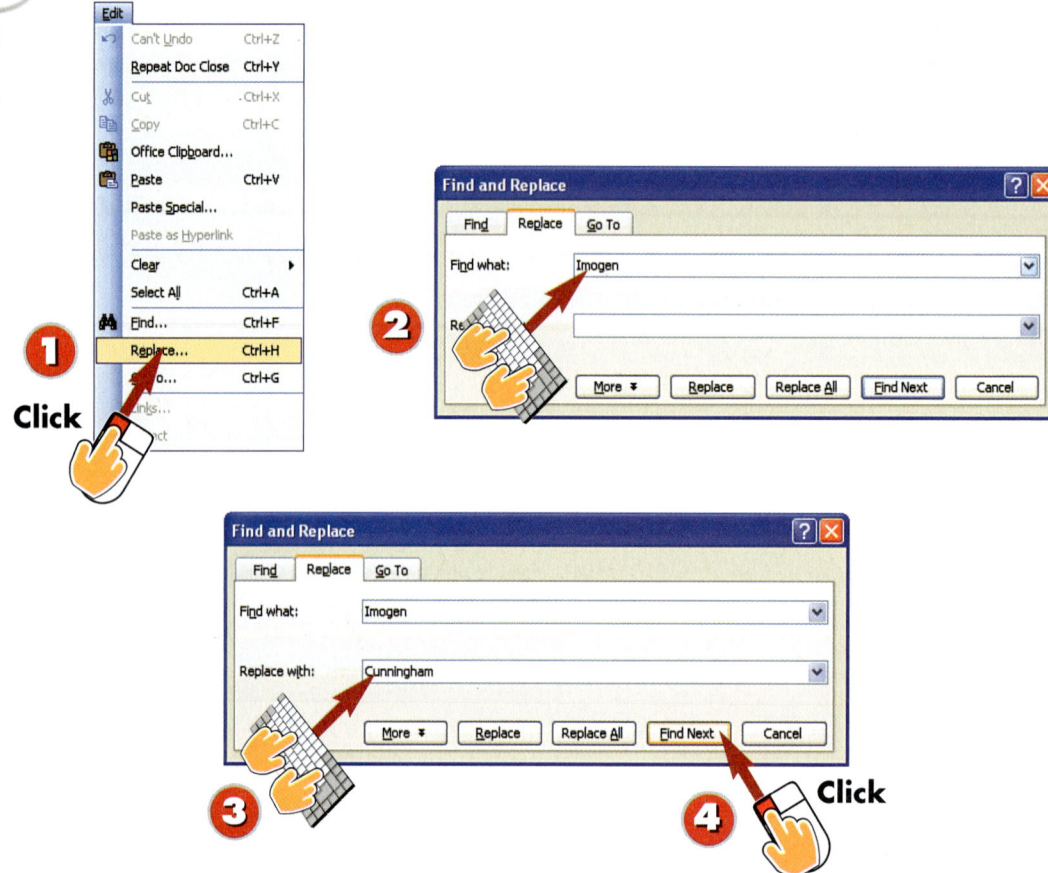

Click

Click

① Open the **Edit** menu and choose **Replace** to open the Find and Replace dialog box with the **Replace** tab displayed.

② Type the text that you want to find in the **Find what** text box.

③ In the **Replace with** text box, type the text that you want to replace the **Find what** text.

④ Click the **Find Next** button.

Sometimes you not only need to find text, you also have to replace it with something else. Word's Replace feature takes the tedium out of making the same change in several places. Whenever you find yourself about to change something by hand throughout your entire document, stop and see whether Word's Replace feature could do the work for you.

TIP

Using More Options to Replace Text
If you want to be more specific about what text you're looking for, click the **More** button at the bottom of the Find and Replace dialog box. To hide the options again, click the **Less** button.

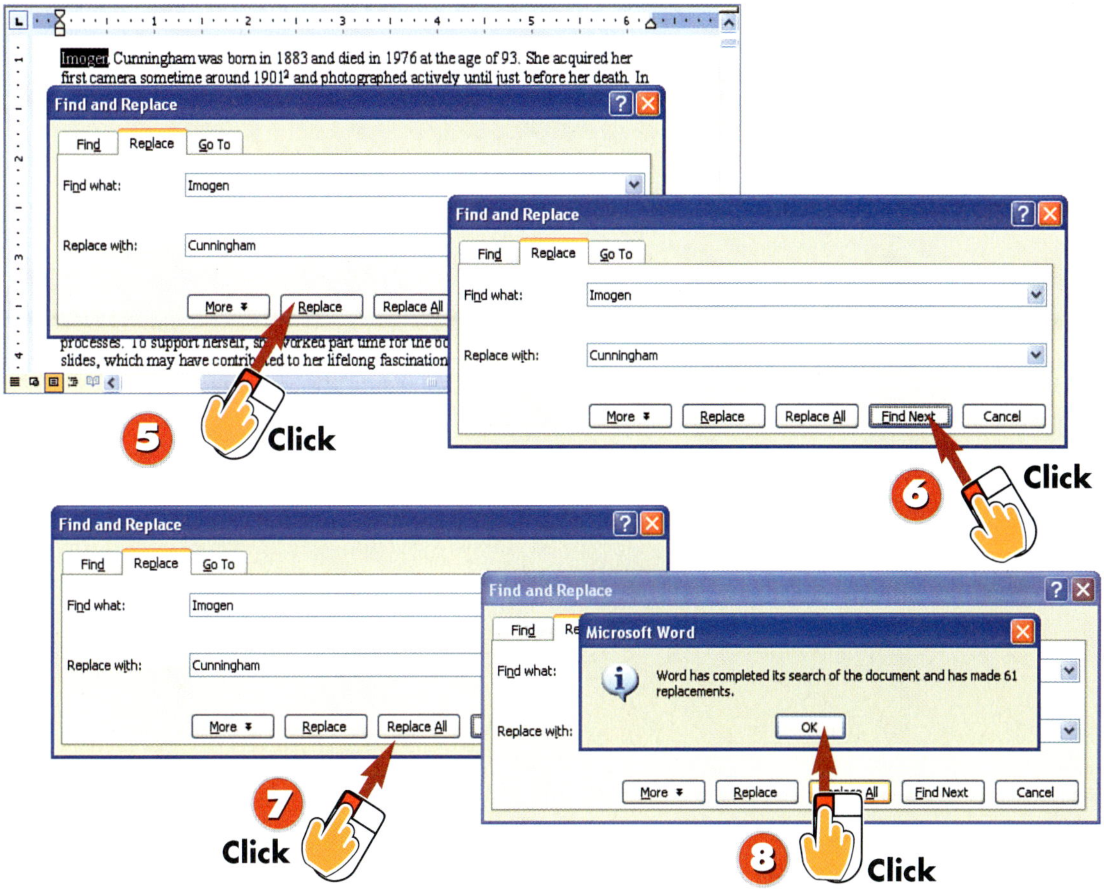

Find and Replace

Find | Replace | Go To

Find what: Imogen

Replace with: Cunningham

More ⌄ | Replace | Replace All

Imogen Cunningham was born in 1883 and died in 1976 at the age of 93. She acquired her first camera sometime around 1901[2] and photographed actively until just before her death. In

processes. To support herself, she worked part time for the bo slides, which may have contributed to her lifelong fascination

5 **Click**

Find and Replace

Find | Replace | Go To

Find what: Imogen

Replace with: Cunningham

More ⌄ | Replace | Replace All | Find Next | Cancel

6 **Click**

Find and Replace

Find | Replace | Go To

Find what: Imogen

Replace with: Cunningham

More ⌄ | Replace | Replace All

7 **Click**

Find and Replace

Find | Re | Microsoft Word

Find what:

Word has completed its search of the document and has made 61 replacements.

OK

Replace with:

More ⌄ | Replace | Replace All | Find Next | Cancel

8 **Click**

5 Word highlights the first occurrence of the word. To replace it, click the **Replace** button.

6 To skip this instance without making the change, click the **Find Next** button.

7 To replace all instances of the text in one fell swoop, click the **Replace All** button.

8 Click **OK** when Word informs you that it has finished searching the document, and then click the **Cancel** button in the Find and Replace dialog box to close it.

End

Using the Thesaurus

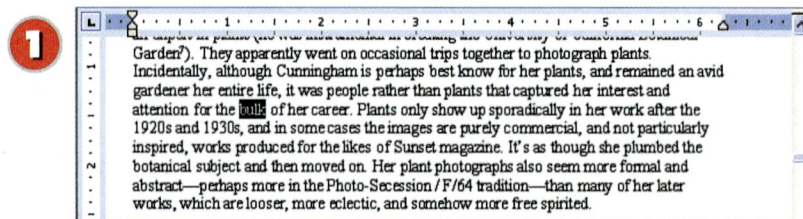

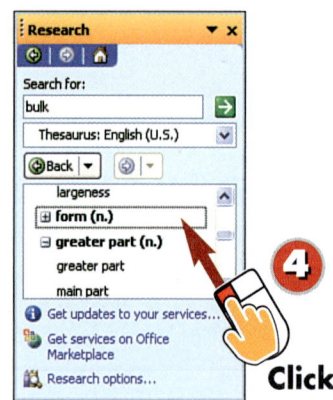

Click

Click

1. Select the word for which you want to find a synonym, and press **Shift+F7** (or open the **Tools** menu, choose **Language**, and select **Thesaurus**).

2. Word displays the Research task pane, with the word you selected in the **Search for** text box and suggested meanings and synonyms in the results list (meanings are in boldface).

3. If the meaning at the top of the results list is not the one you need, scroll down the list to look for other meanings.

4. If you see a **plus sign** next to a meaning, click the meaning to display its synonyms. To hide the synonyms, click the meaning again.

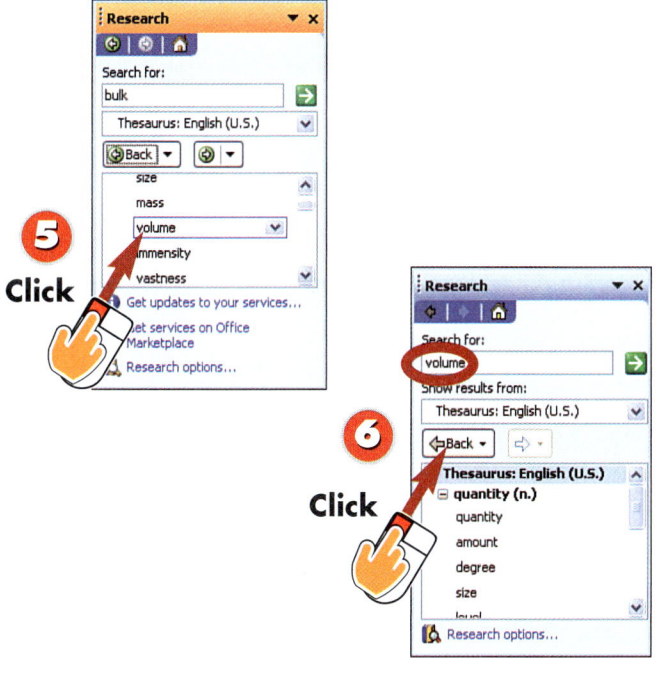

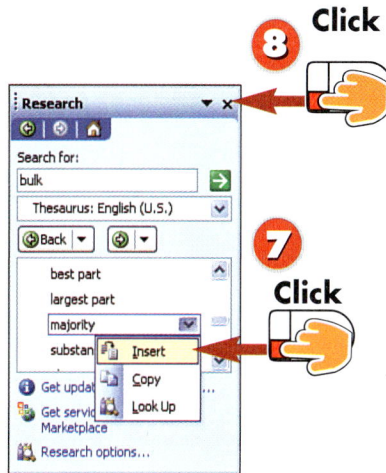

Click

Click

Click

Click

Click

⑤ If you want to see the synonyms of a word in the results list, click the word.

⑥ Word places the word in the **Search for** list and displays its synonyms in the results list. To go back to the previous contents of the results list, click the **Back** button.

⑦ When you see the word that you want to use to replace the word you chose in step 1, click it, and click **Insert** in the list that appears.

⑧ Word replaces the selected word with the one you chose. When you are finished, click the **Close** button in the Research task pane to close it.

End

Looking Up Other Words
If you want to look up synonyms for a word that isn't in the results list, select the current entry in the **Search for** text box, type over it with the word whose synonyms you want to find, and click the **Start searching** button (the green arrow) .

Using Automatic Spell Checking

Start

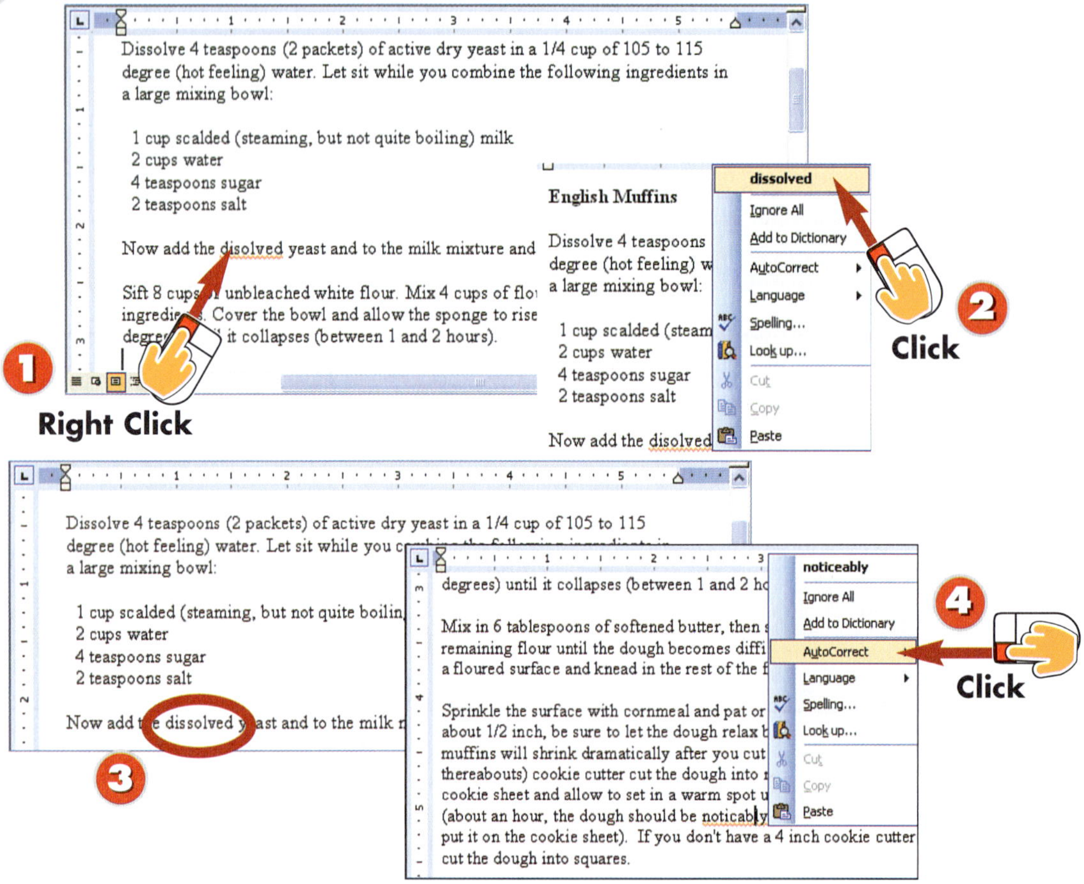

Right Click

Click

Click

---

1 To correct the spelling of a word marked with a red wavy line, right-click the word.

2 A context menu appears with a list of possible spellings. If you see the one you want, click it.

3 Word makes the correction for you.

4 If the mistake is one that you make frequently, right-click the word and point to the **AutoCorrect** option in the context menu that appears.

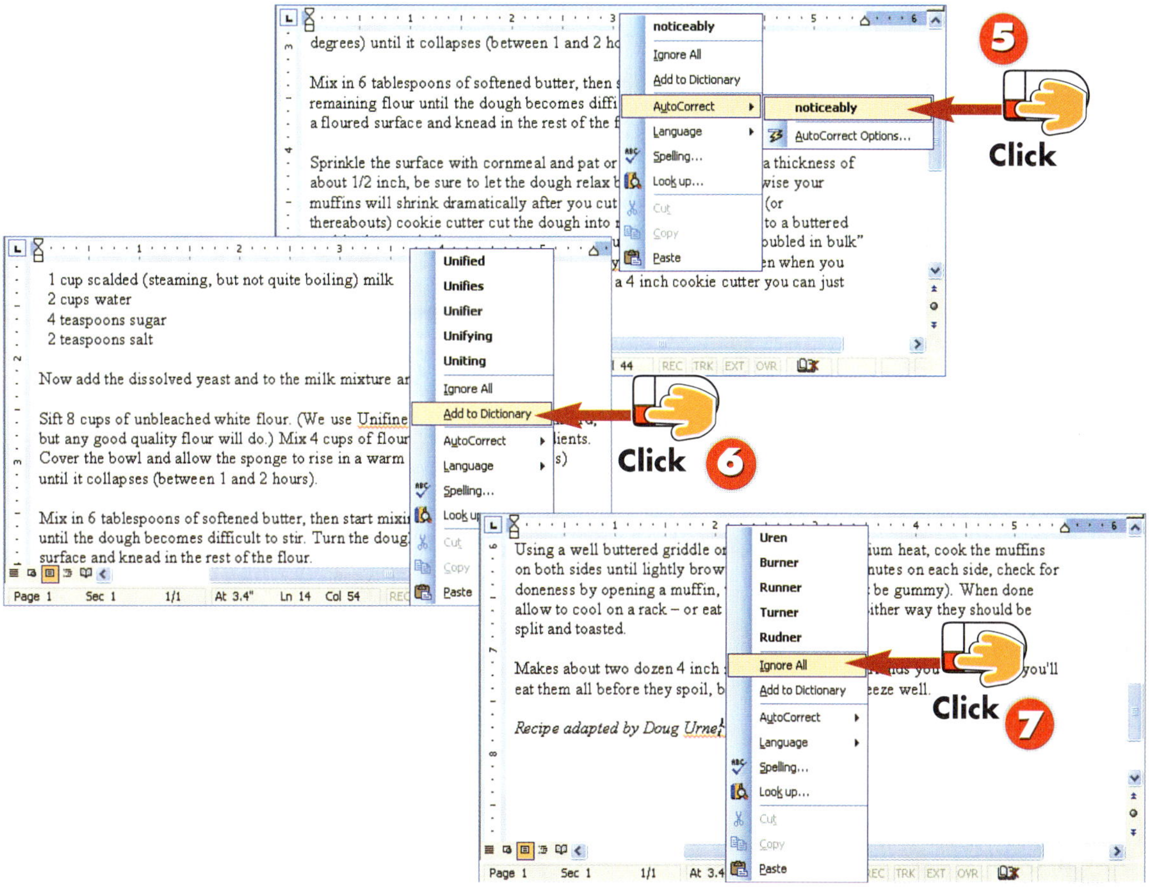

noticeably

Ignore All

Add to Dictionary

AutoCorrect ▶ noticeably

Language ▶ 🔏 AutoCorrect Options...

Spelling...

Look up...

Click

degrees) until it collapses (between 1 and 2 ho

Mix in 6 tablespoons of softened butter, then s
remaining flour until the dough becomes diffi
a floured surface and knead in the rest of the f

Sprinkle the surface with cornmeal and pat or   a thickness of
about 1/2 inch, be sure to let the dough relax b   wise your
muffins will shrink dramatically after you cut   (or
thereabouts) cookie cutter cut the dough into   to a buttered
                                                        ubled in bulk"
                                                        en when you
                                                 a 4 inch cookie cutter you can just

Unified

Unifies

Unifier

Unifying

Uniting

Ignore All

Add to Dictionary

AutoCorrect ▶
Language ▶
Spelling...
Look up

Click ⑥

1 cup scalded (steaming, but not quite boiling) milk
2 cups water
4 teaspoons sugar
2 teaspoons salt

Now add the dissolved yeast and to the milk mixture a

Sift 8 cups of unbleached white flour. (We use Unifine
but any good quality flour will do.) Mix 4 cups of flour
Cover the bowl and allow the sponge to rise in a warm
until it collapses (between 1 and 2 hours).

Mix in 6 tablespoons of softened butter, then start mixi
until the dough becomes difficult to stir. Turn the doug
surface and knead in the rest of the flour.

Page 1   Sec 1   1/1   At 3.4"   Ln 14 Col 54

Uren
Burner
Runner
Turner
Rudner

Ignore All

Add to Dictionary

AutoCorrect ▶
Language ▶
Spelling...
Look up...
Cut
Copy
Paste

Click ⑦

Using a well buttered griddle o   ium heat, cook the muffins
on both sides until lightly brow   nutes on each side, check for
doneness by opening a muffin,   be gummy). When done
allow to cool on a rack – or eat   ither way they should be
split and toasted.

Makes about two dozen 4 inch   ds you   you'll
eat them all before they spoil, b   eze well.

Recipe adapted by Doug Urne

Page 1   Sec 1   1/1   At 3.4

⑤ Click the correct spelling in the submenu to create an AutoCorrect entry (see "Correcting Text Automatically" later in this part for more information about Word's AutoCorrect feature).

⑥ If Word incorrectly flags a word as a misspelling, and it's one you use frequently, right-click it and choose **Add to Dictionary** to add it to the dictionary that Word uses to check your spelling.

⑦ If Word incorrectly flags a word as a misspelling, but it's one you don't use often, right-click the word and choose **Ignore All** to prevent Word from flagging it in this document.

End

Turning Off Automatic Grammar Checking

To turn off the automatic grammar checking, open the **Tools** menu and choose **Options**. In the dialog box that appears, click the **Spelling & Grammar** tab. Clear the **Check grammar as you type** check box, and click **OK**. (If you want to turn off automatic spell-checking, clear the **Check spelling as you type** check box.)

Checking Your Spelling with the Spell Checker

Start

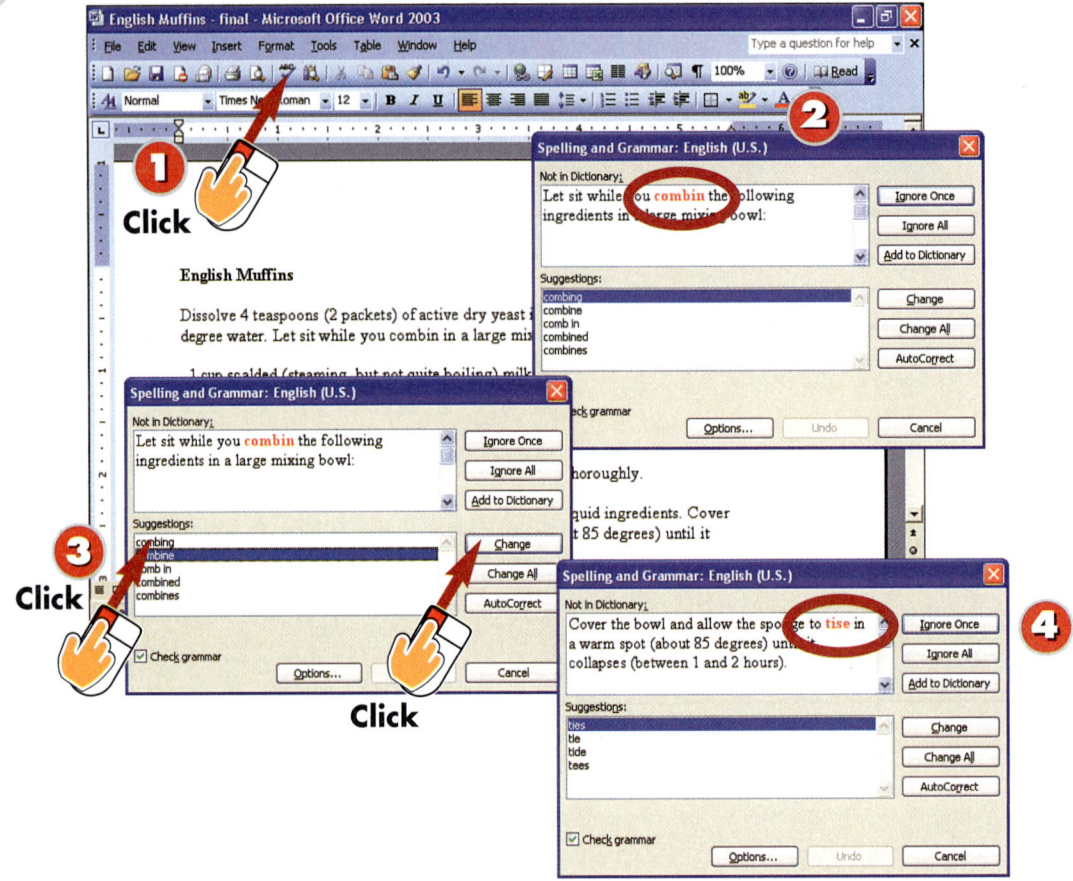

Click

Click

Click

1. Click the **Spelling and Grammar** button on the Standard toolbar to start checking your document.

2. The Spelling and Grammar dialog box opens, and Word begins searching for errors. When Word finds a spelling error, it highlights it in red.

3. If the correct spelling is listed under **Suggestions**, click it and click **Change** to change this instance of the word, or **Change All** to change all instances.

4. Sometimes, the correct spelling for a misspelled word does not appear in the Suggestions area.

The spell checker enables you to check the spelling (and grammar) of an entire document all at once. You won't really need to use it if you use automatic spelling checking to fix your spelling on-the-fly (see the preceding task). However, if you've disabled automatic spell checking, or if you're working on a rather large document, the spell checker will come in handy.

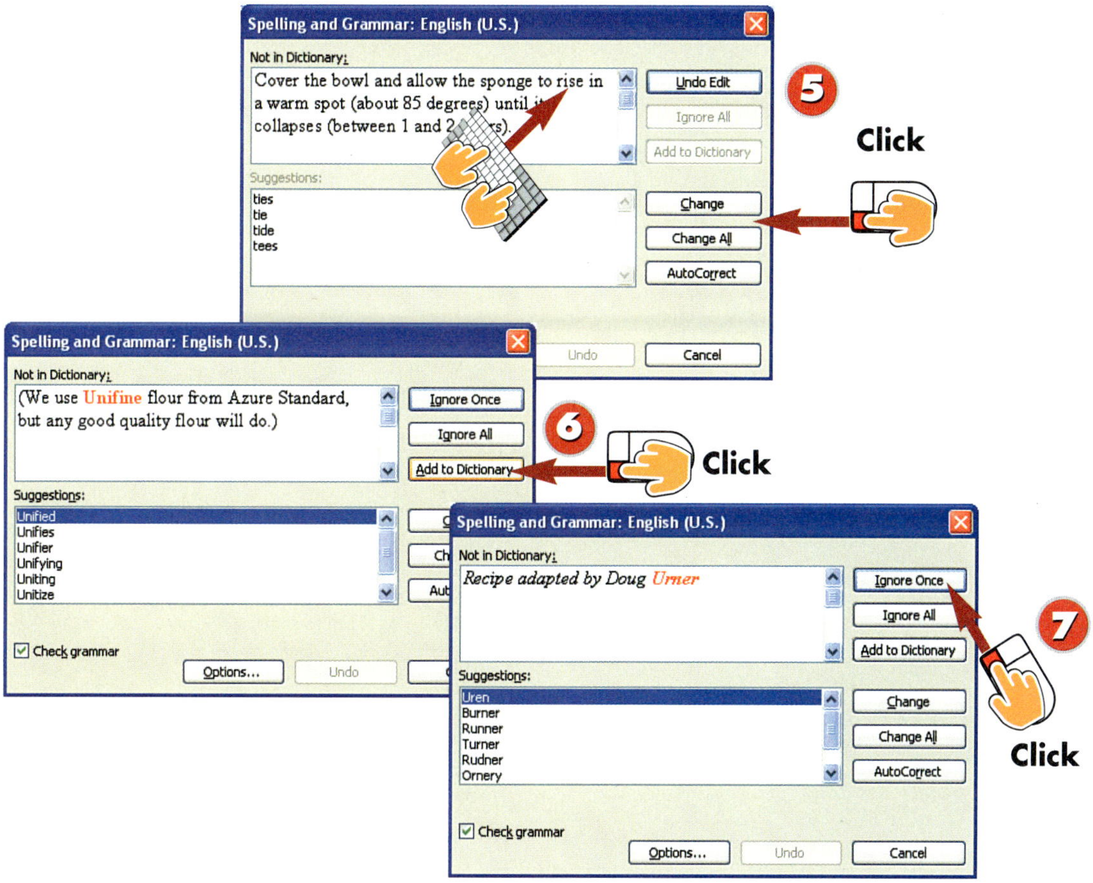

Spelling and Grammar: English (U.S.)

Not in Dictionary:

Cover the bowl and allow the sponge to rise in a warm spot (about 85 degrees) until it collapses (between 1 and 2 ... rs).

Suggestions:
ties
tie
tide
tees

Undo Edit
Ignore All
Add to Dictionary
Change
Change All
AutoCorrect
Undo
Cancel

5 **Click**

Spelling and Grammar: English (U.S.)

Not in Dictionary:

(We use Unifine flour from Azure Standard, but any good quality flour will do.)

Suggestions:
Unified
Unifies
Unifier
Unifying
Uniting
Unitize

Ignore Once
Ignore All
Add to Dictionary

☑ Check grammar
Options...   Undo

6 **Click**

Spelling and Grammar: English (U.S.)

Not in Dictionary:

Recipe adapted by Doug Urner

Suggestions:
Uren
Burner
Runner
Turner
Rudner
Ornery

Ignore Once
Ignore All
Add to Dictionary
Change
Change All
AutoCorrect

☑ Check grammar
Options...   Undo   Cancel

7 **Click**

5 If this happens, select the word in the Spelling and Grammar dialog box, type over it with the correct spelling, and click the **Change** or **Change All** button.

6 If Word incorrectly flags a word you use frequently as a misspelling, click **Add to Dictionary** to add it to the dictionary that Word uses to check your spelling.

7 If Word incorrectly flags a word as a misspelling, but it's one you don't use often, click **Ignore Once** to ignore it once or **Ignore All** to ignore it throughout the document.

8 When Word tells you that it has finished the spell check, click **OK**.

End

Turning Off Grammar Checking
If you don't want Word to look for grammatical problems during the spell check, clear the **Check grammar** check box in the lower-left corner of the Spelling and Grammar dialog box.

Checking Your Grammar

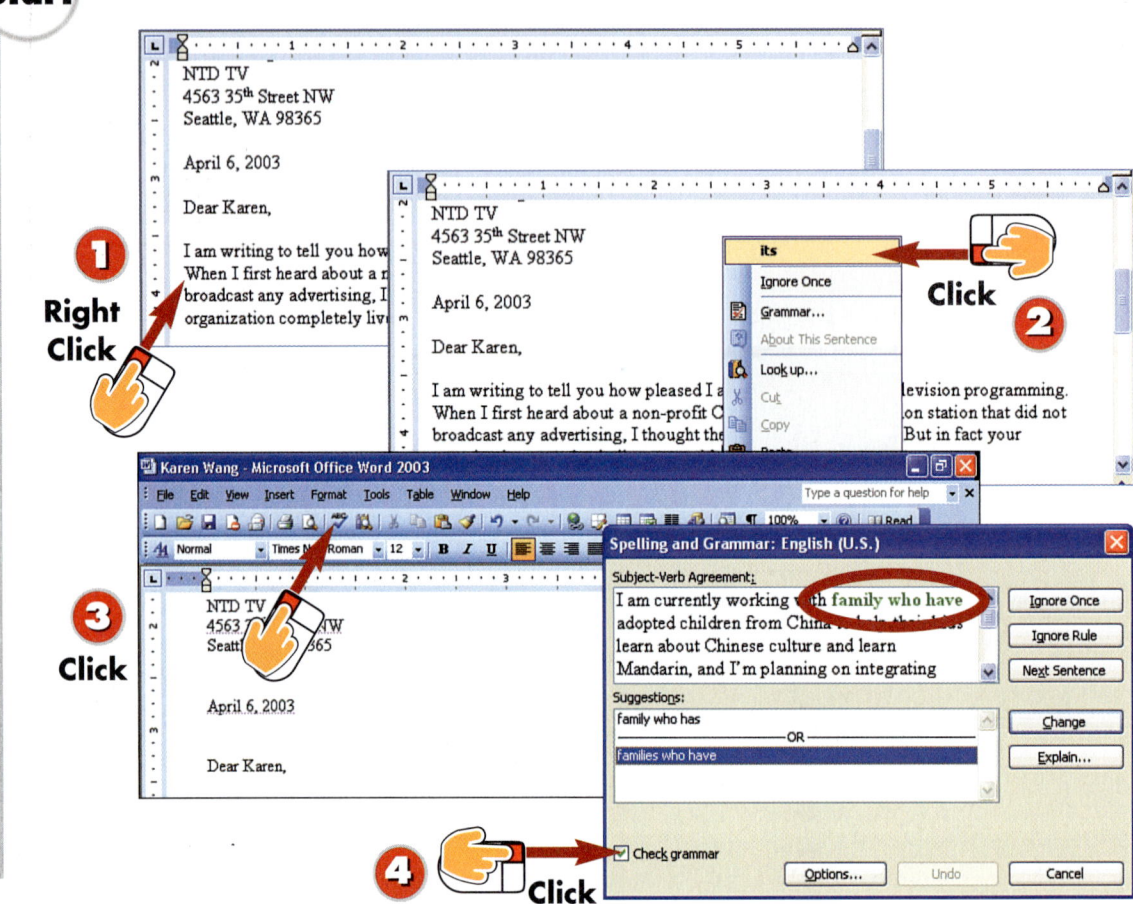

Start

1 **Right Click**

2 **Click**

3 **Click**

4 **Click**

1 To check the grammar of text marked with a green wavy line, right-click the text.

2 If the context menu that appears contains a suggested fix that you like, click it to make the change. (If you don't see a fix you like, click **Ignore Once**.)

3 To use the spell checker to check your grammar, click the **Spelling and Grammar** button on the Standard toolbar.

4 In the Spelling and Grammar dialog box, make sure the **Check grammar** check box is marked.

INTRODUCTION

Just as Word keeps an eye out for possible spelling errors as you type, it also watches for potential grammar problems. When it finds one, it marks the text with a green wavy underline. You can right-click the underlined text to check your grammar on-the-fly or wait until you are finished typing the document and then run a spell check, which by default includes a grammar check. This task describes how to do both.

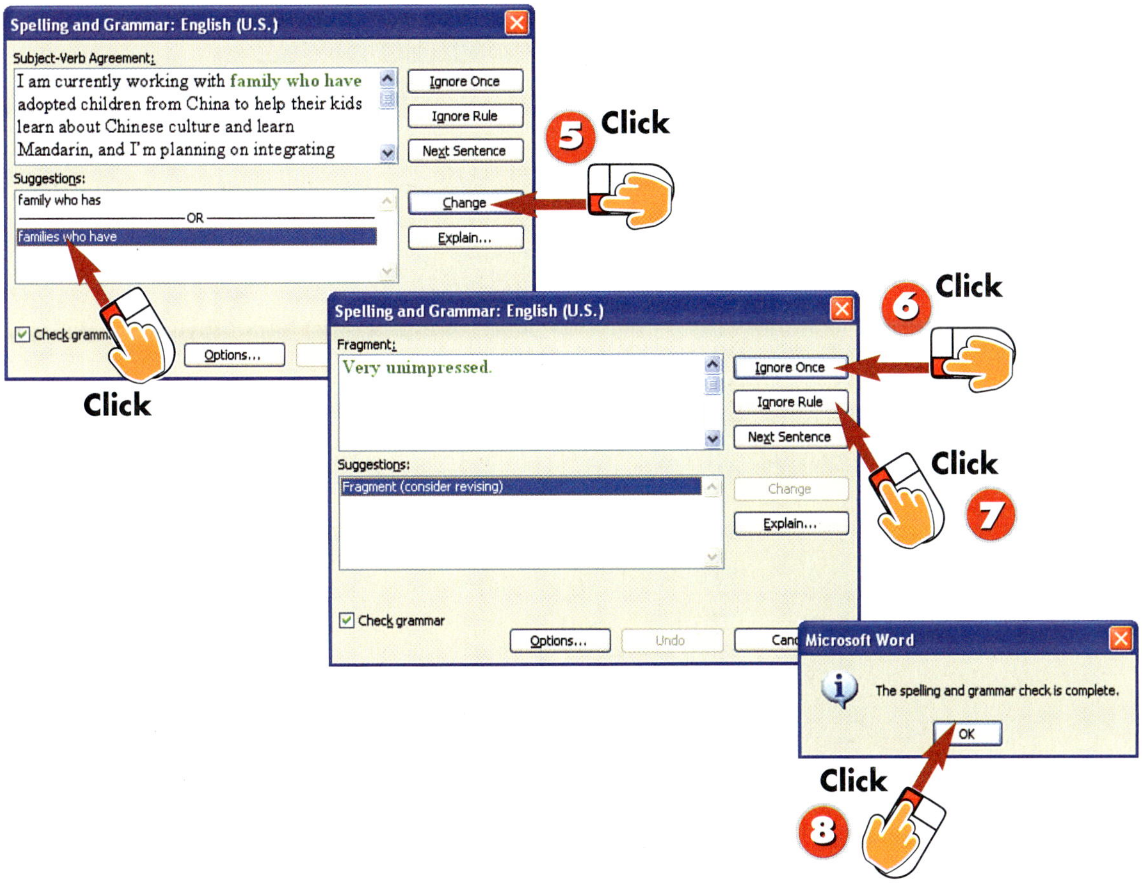

Spelling and Grammar: English (U.S.)

Subject-Verb Agreement:

I am currently working with family who have adopted children from China to help their kids learn about Chinese culture and learn Mandarin, and I'm planning on integrating

Ignore Once
Ignore Rule
Next Sentence

5 Click

Suggestions:

family who has
—— OR ——
families who have

Change
Explain...

☑ Check gramm

Options...

Click

Spelling and Grammar: English (U.S.)

Fragment:

Very unimpressed.

Ignore Once
Ignore Rule
Next Sentence

6 Click

Suggestions:

Fragment (consider revising)

Change
Explain...

Click 7

☑ Check grammar

Options... | Undo | Canc

Microsoft Word

ⓘ The spelling and grammar check is complete.

OK

Click 8

5 When Word finds a possible grammatical error, it highlights it in green. If the correct fix is listed in the **Suggestions** area, click it and click the **Change** button.

6 If you want Word to ignore the flagged text, click the **Ignore Once** button.

7 If you don't want Word to suggest fixes like this one in the rest of the document, click **Ignore Rule**. (Click **Explain** to learn more about the rule Word is using.)

8 When Word tells you that it has finished the spelling and grammar check, click **OK**.

End

TIP

Word Does Some Things Better Than Others
Although Word makes a valiant attempt to catch grammatical problems, it frequently flags text that is perfectly fine, misses mistakes, or worse yet, suggests them. If you aren't finding the grammar checker helpful, see the tips in the two preceding tasks to learn how to turn off the automatic grammar checking and disable the grammar checker during a spell check.

Correcting Text Automatically

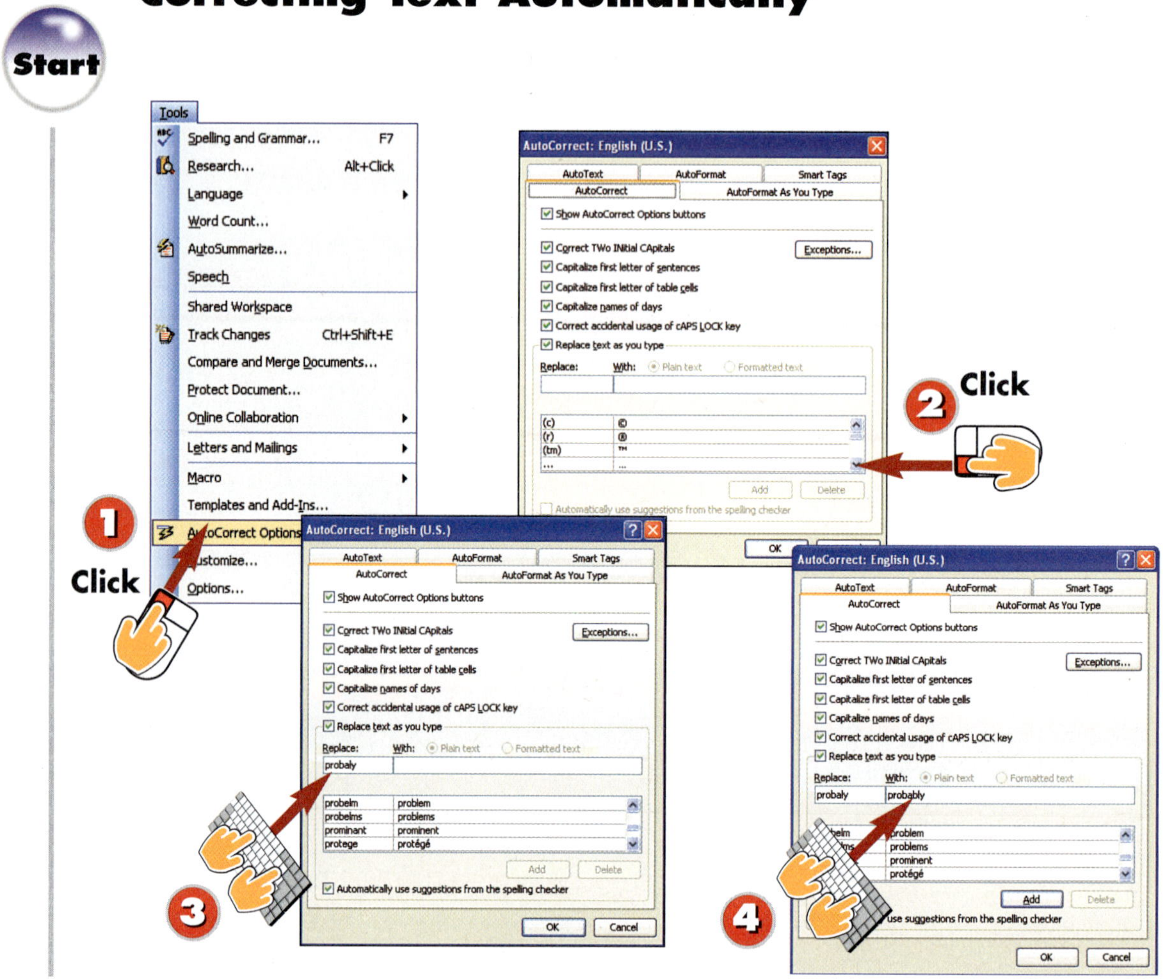

Start

Click ①

Click ② 2

③

④

① Open the **Tools** menu and choose **AutoCorrect Options** to open the AutoCorrect dialog box with the AutoCorrect tab displayed.

② Scroll through the list at the bottom of the dialog box to see what errors AutoCorrect knows how to fix. Word replaces the items in the left column with the ones in the right.

③ Click in the **Replace** text box and type an incorrect spelling for a word you commonly misspell (in this example, **probaly**).

④ Click in the **With** text box and type the correct spelling for the word (here, **probably**).

Word's AutoCorrect feature fixes spelling errors for you automatically. By default, AutoCorrect makes corrections based on suggestions from the spell checker. It also has its own list of many commonly misspelled words, and you can add your own favorite typos to the list. In addition, you can use AutoCorrect to automatically enter special symbols, long names, or phrases that you have to type frequently.

Using AutoCorrect to Insert Repetitive Text

If you want to use AutoCorrect to insert a long name or phrase, type an abbreviation for the phrase in the **Replace** box (see step 3), and type the full spelling in the **With** box (see step 4).

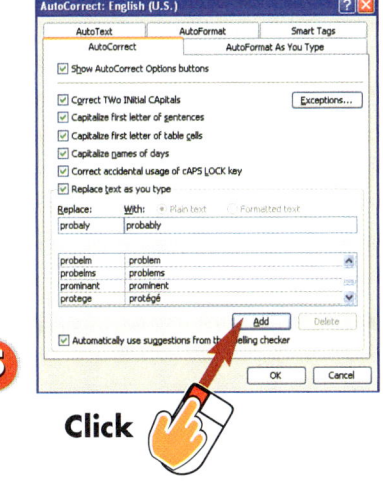

Click

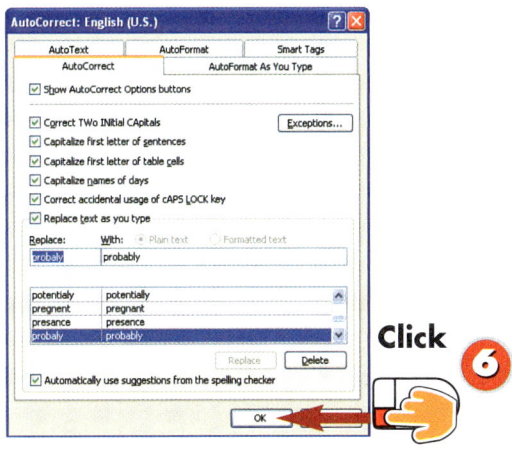

Click

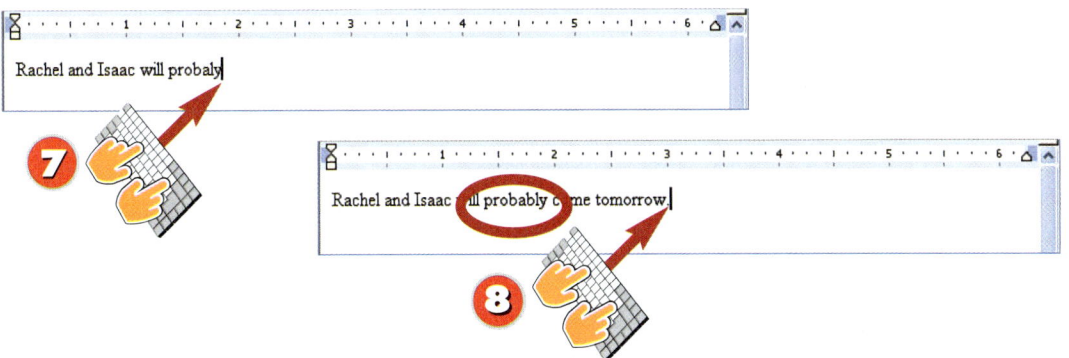

Rachel and Isaac will probaly

Rachel and Isaac will probably come tomorrow.

5 Click the **Add** button.

6 The entry is added to the list. Click **OK**.

7 Type some text that contains the incorrectly spelled word you entered in step 4 (in this example, **Rachel and Isaac will probaly**).

8 Press the **Spacebar**. Word automatically replaces **probaly** with **probably**. Finish the sentence.

End

TIP

Removing AutoCorrect Entries
If you add an AutoCorrect entry and later decide to delete it, open the **Tools** menu and choose **AutoCorrect Options** to open the AutoCorrect dialog box with the AutoCorrect tab displayed. Click the entry in the list in the AutoCorrect tab, click the **Delete** button, and click **OK**.

CAUTION
If you enter an abbreviation for a long name or phrase in the Replace box, choose one that you don't ever want to leave as is in your document. Otherwise, Word will change it to the full "correct" spelling every time you type it.

Inserting a Special Character

Start

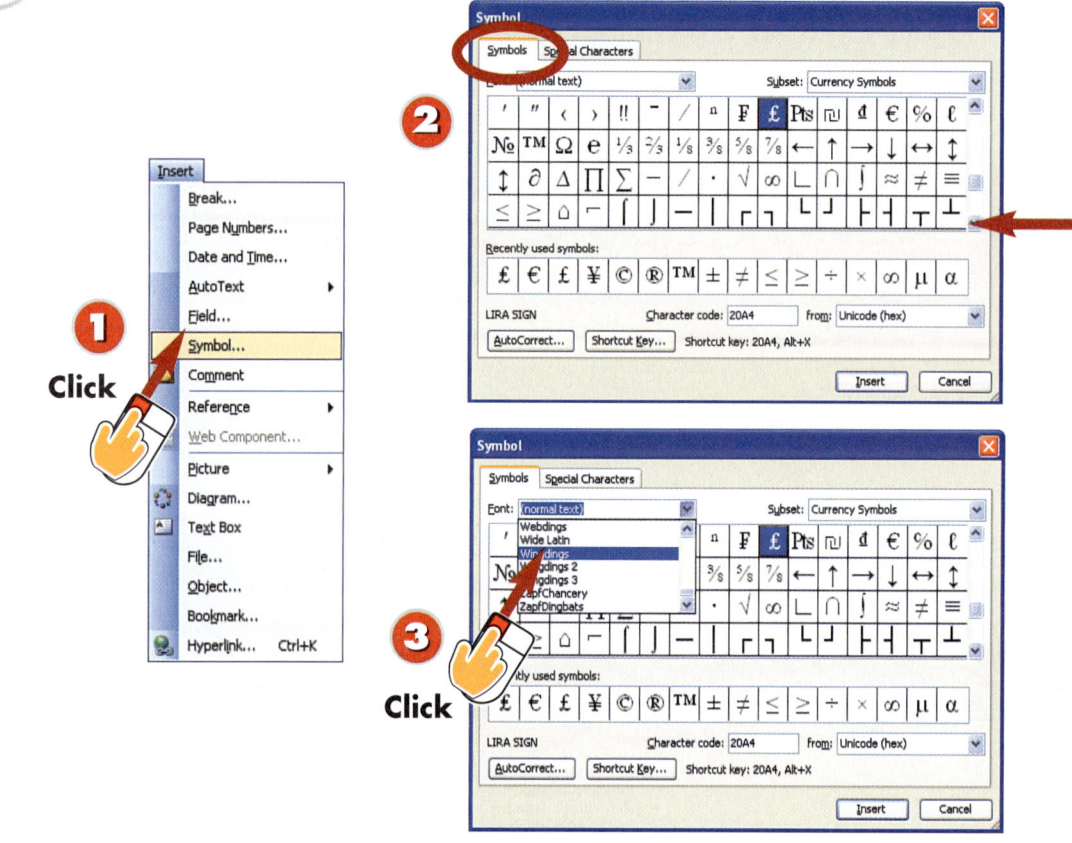

Click

Click

① To insert a symbol, click in the document in the spot where you want the symbol to go, open the **Insert** menu, and choose **Symbol**.

② The Symbol dialog box opens. In the **Symbols** tab, look through the available symbols to find the one you want.

③ If you don't see the symbol you want, click the **down arrow** next to the **Font** field and choose a different font set from the list that appears.

INTRODUCTION

Many everyday documents, such as letters and memos, require special characters here and there. For example, you might need to use the trademark symbol (™), a long dash (—), or an ellipsis (…). Word inserts many of these symbols for you automatically as you type (refer to the preceding task, "Correcting Text Automatically," for more information). If it doesn't insert the one you need, however, you can likely find it in the Symbol dialog box.

TIP

Using AutoCorrect
To see which symbols Word adds automatically, choose **Tools, AutoCorrect Options**, in the AutoCorrect tab. To see additional symbols, view the **Replace as you type** options in the AutoFormat As You Type tab.

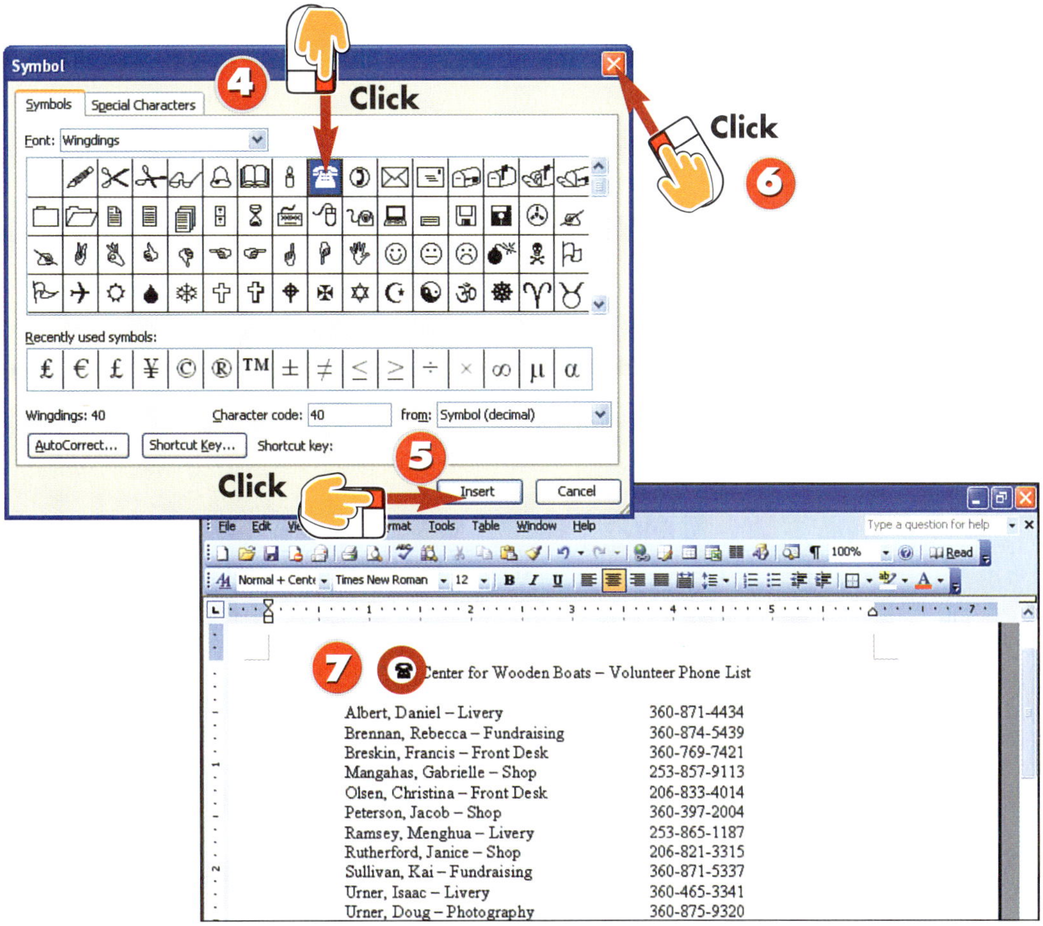

Symbol

Symbols | Special Characters

Font: Wingdings

Click

Click

Recently used symbols:

£ € £ ¥ © ® ™ ± ≠ ≤ ≥ ÷ × ∞ μ α

Wingdings: 40   Character code: 40   from: Symbol (decimal)

AutoCorrect...   Shortcut Key...   Shortcut key:

Click   Insert   Cancel

File   Edit   Vi   rmat   Tools   Table   Window   Help   Type a question for help

Normal + Cente ▼ Times New Roman ▼ 12 ▼ B I U

☎ Center for Wooden Boats – Volunteer Phone List

Albert, Daniel – Livery	360-871-4434
Brennan, Rebecca – Fundraising	360-874-5439
Breskin, Francis – Front Desk	360-769-7421
Mangahas, Gabrielle – Shop	253-857-9113
Olsen, Christina – Front Desk	206-833-4014
Peterson, Jacob – Shop	360-397-2004
Ramsey, Menghua – Livery	253-865-1187
Rutherford, Janice – Shop	206-821-3315
Sullivan, Kai – Fundraising	360-871-5337
Urner, Isaac – Livery	360-465-3341
Urner, Doug – Photography	360-875-9320

4 To insert a symbol, first click it.

5 Click the **Insert** button.

6 Click the **Close** button in the upper-right corner of the Symbol dialog box.

7 Word inserts the symbol in your document.

End

Changing the Size of Symbols

TIP

You can enlarge symbols that you've inserted in your document just like regular text. Drag over a symbol to select it, and then choose a larger point size from the **Font Size** list in the Formatting toolbar. (See "Changing the Font and Font Size" in Part 6.)

Inserting the Date

Start

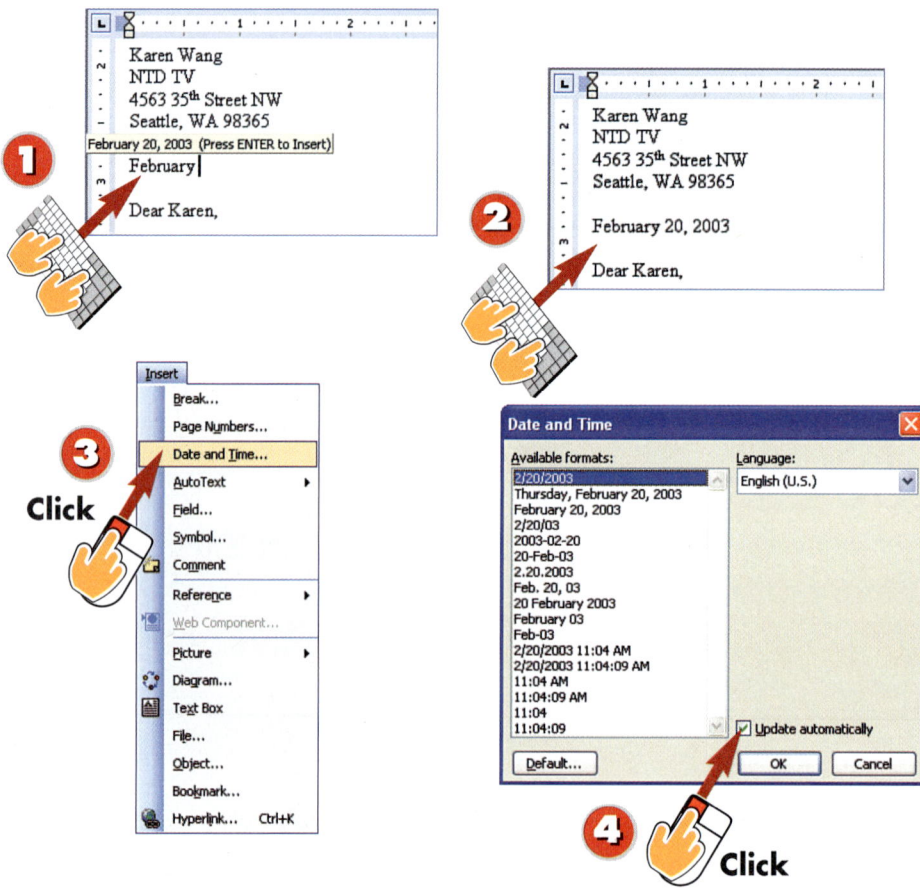

Click

Click

1. Begin typing today's date. After you type a portion of the date, a yellow box containing the completed date appears.

2. Press **Enter** to let Word fill in the rest of the date for you.

3. If you want to insert the date as a field, open the **Insert** menu and choose **Date and Time**.

4. The Date and Time dialog box opens. Click the **Update automatically** check box to select it.

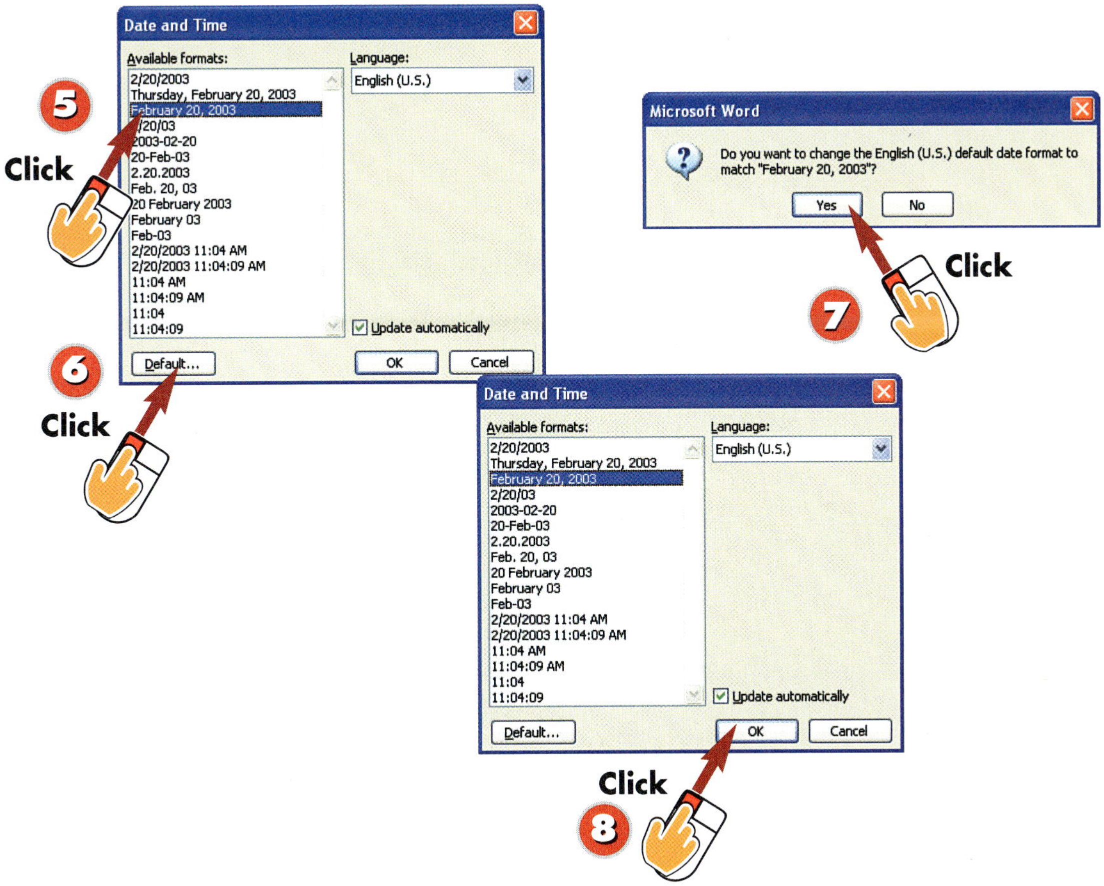

Date and Time

Available formats:

2/20/2003
Thursday, February 20, 2003
February 20, 2003
2/20/03
2003-02-20
20-Feb-03
2.20.2003
Feb. 20, 03
20 February 2003
February 03
Feb-03
2/20/2003 11:04 AM
2/20/2003 11:04:09 AM
11:04 AM
11:04:09 AM
11:04
11:04:09

Language:
English (U.S.)

☑ Update automatically

Click **5**

6 **Click**

Default...   OK   Cancel

Microsoft Word

? Do you want to change the English (U.S.) default date format to match "February 20, 2003"?

Yes   No

7 **Click**

Date and Time

Available formats:

2/20/2003
Thursday, February 20, 2003
February 20, 2003
2/20/03
2003-02-20
20-Feb-03
2.20.2003
Feb. 20, 03
20 February 2003
February 03
Feb-03
2/20/2003 11:04 AM
2/20/2003 11:04:09 AM
11:04 AM
11:04:09 AM
11:04
11:04:09

Language:
English (U.S.)

☑ Update automatically

Default...   OK   Cancel

Click
8

5 Click the date format that you want to use.

6 If you want to use this format all the time, click the **Default** button.

7 Click **Yes** in the message box that appears.

8 Click **OK** in the Date and Time dialog box. Word inserts the date in your document.

End

Inserting Standard Blocks of Text

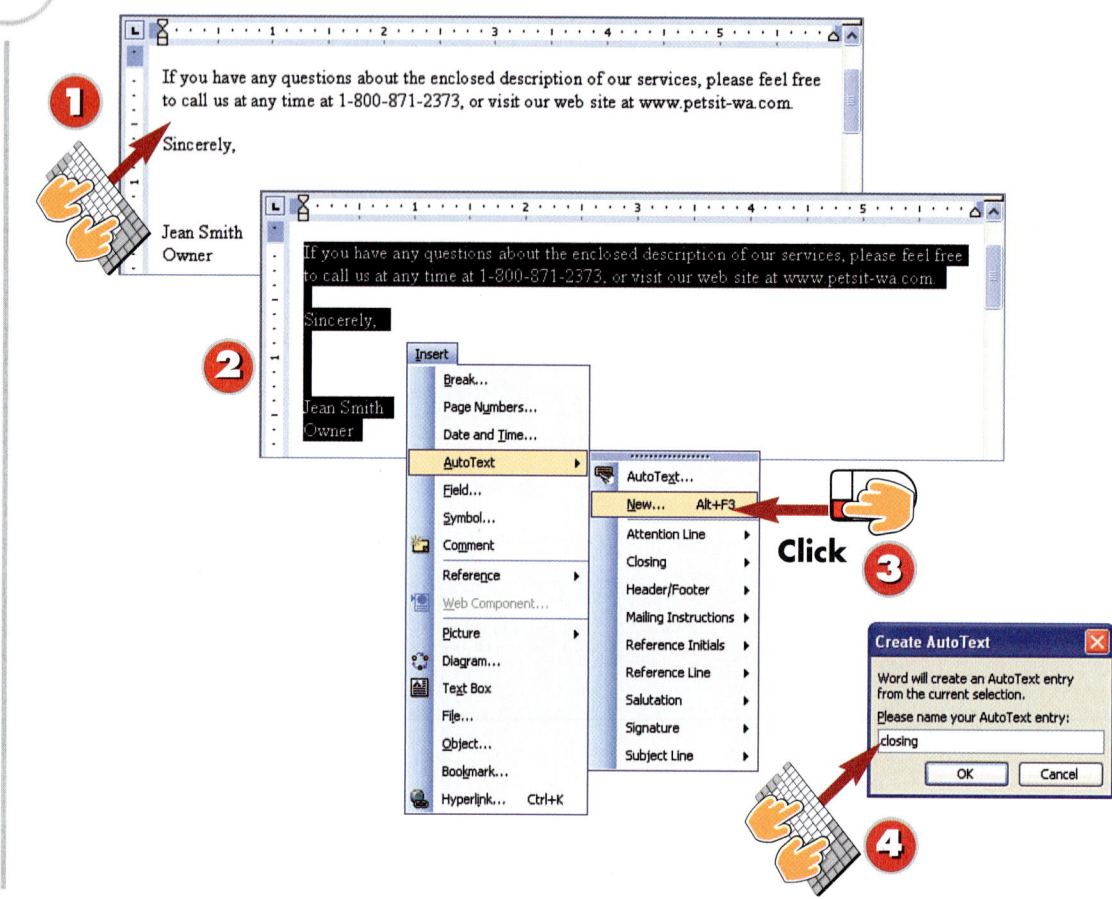

1. Type the text that you want Word to "memorize."

2. Select the text.

3. Open the **Insert** menu, choose **AutoText,** and select **New** (or press **Alt+F3**).

4. Type a name for the entry in the Create AutoText dialog box. (Choose a name that is at least four characters long.)

INTRODUCTION

AutoText is an extremely handy feature that lets Word "memorize" large blocks of text. Once you've created an AutoText entry, you can insert it in your text by simply beginning to type the name of the entry. As soon as you've typed the first few characters, Word's AutoComplete feature takes over and inserts the entire block of text for you.

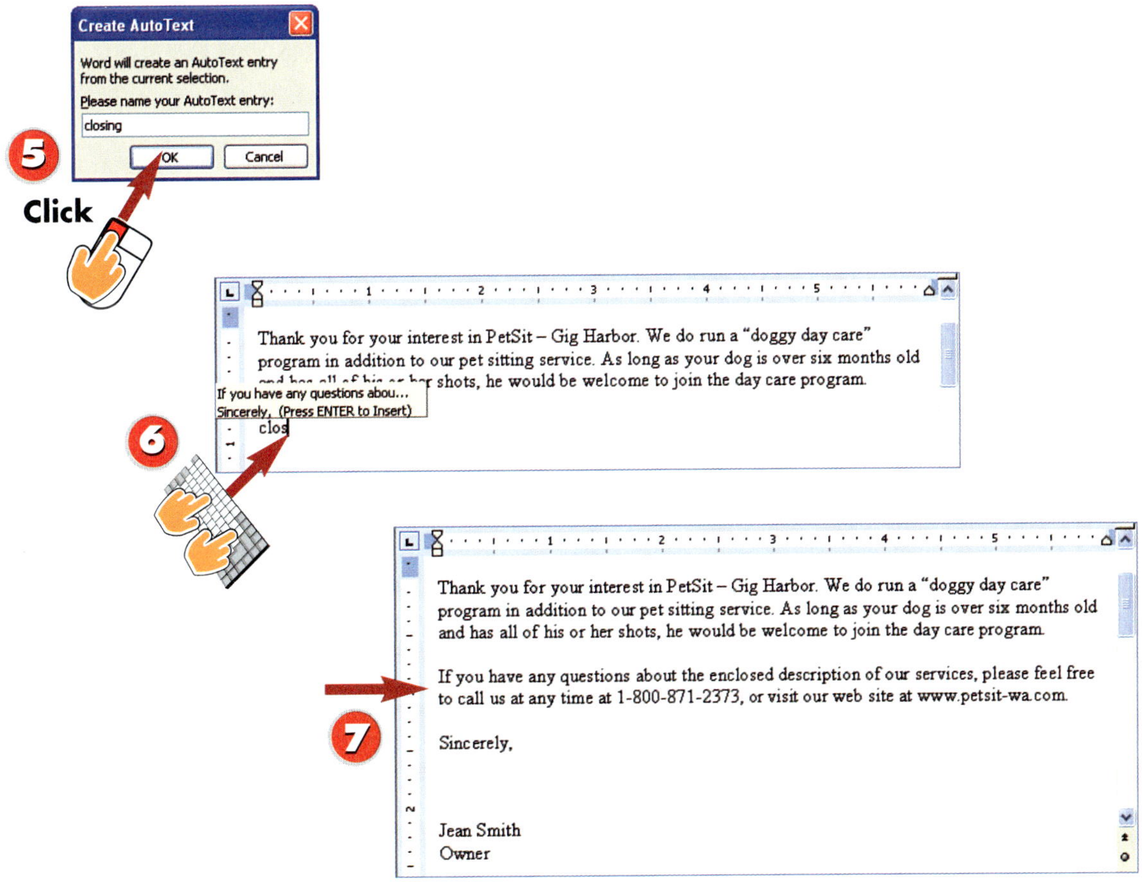

Create AutoText

Word will create an AutoText entry from the current selection.

Please name your AutoText entry:

closing

OK   Cancel

5

Click

Thank you for your interest in PetSit – Gig Harbor. We do run a "doggy day care" program in addition to our pet sitting service. As long as your dog is over six months old and has all of his or her shots, he would be welcome to join the day care program.

If you have any questions abou...
Sincerely, (Press ENTER to Insert)

clos

6

Thank you for your interest in PetSit – Gig Harbor. We do run a "doggy day care" program in addition to our pet sitting service. As long as your dog is over six months old and has all of his or her shots, he would be welcome to join the day care program.

If you have any questions about the enclosed description of our services, please feel free to call us at any time at 1-800-871-2373, or visit our web site at www.petsit-wa.com.

Sincerely,

Jean Smith
Owner

7

5 Click **OK**.

6 Click in a document in the spot where you want to insert the text, and type the first few letters of the name you typed in step 4. As soon as you see the yellow box, press **Enter**.

7 Word inserts the AutoText entry in your document.

End

AutoText Reduces Errors

One of the advantages of using AutoText is that you only have to proof-read the block of text once, before you create the AutoText entry. From then on, each time you insert the entry in a document, you can rest assured that it is error free.

Using Columns and Tables

In this part, you learn two different ways of arranging columns of text on the page. Word's Columns feature lets you create "newspaper-style" columns, in which the text wraps from one column to the next. You might use columns for your office newsletter or a brochure. The Tables feature, in contrast, is great for creating columns of text that do not wrap. Tables are useful for creating everything from simple charts to resumes and invoices.

A Word Table

Column

Shading

Border

Row

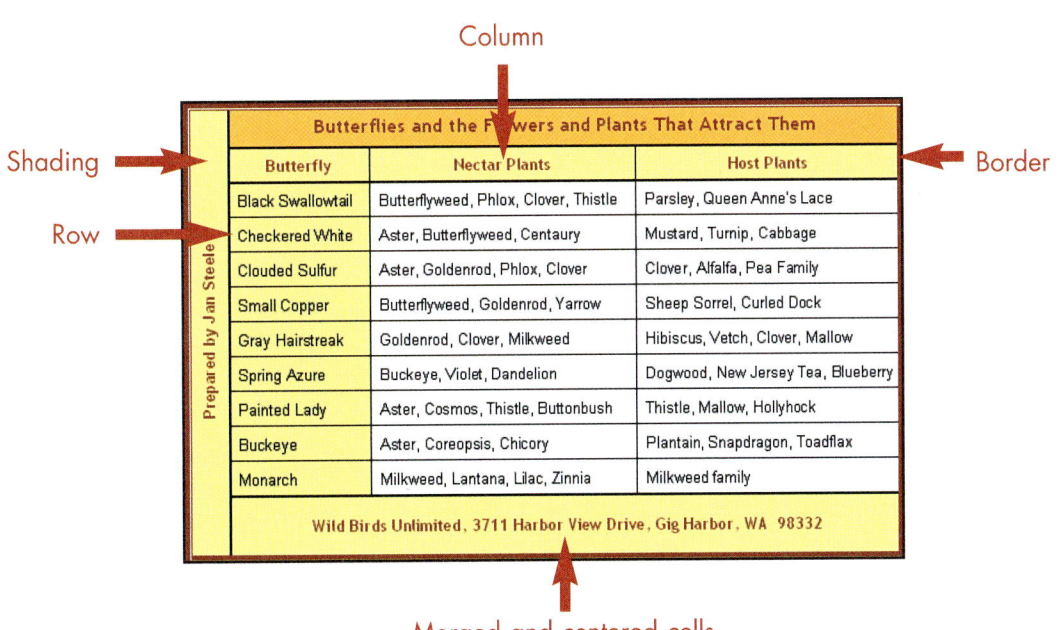

Butterflies and the Flowers and Plants That Attract Them		
Butterfly	**Nectar Plants**	**Host Plants**
Black Swallowtail	Butterflyweed, Phlox, Clover, Thistle	Parsley, Queen Anne's Lace
Checkered White	Aster, Butterflyweed, Centaury	Mustard, Turnip, Cabbage
Clouded Sulfur	Aster, Goldenrod, Phlox, Clover	Clover, Alfalfa, Pea Family
Small Copper	Butterflyweed, Goldenrod, Yarrow	Sheep Sorrel, Curled Dock
Gray Hairstreak	Goldenrod, Clover, Milkweed	Hibiscus, Vetch, Clover, Mallow
Spring Azure	Buckeye, Violet, Dandelion	Dogwood, New Jersey Tea, Blueberry
Painted Lady	Aster, Cosmos, Thistle, Buttonbush	Thistle, Mallow, Hollyhock
Buckeye	Aster, Coreopsis, Chicory	Plantain, Snapdragon, Toadflax
Monarch	Milkweed, Lantana, Lilac, Zinnia	Milkweed family
Wild Birds Unlimited, 3711 Harbor View Drive, Gig Harbor, WA 98332		

Prepared by Jan Steele

Merged and centered cells

Creating Columns

Start

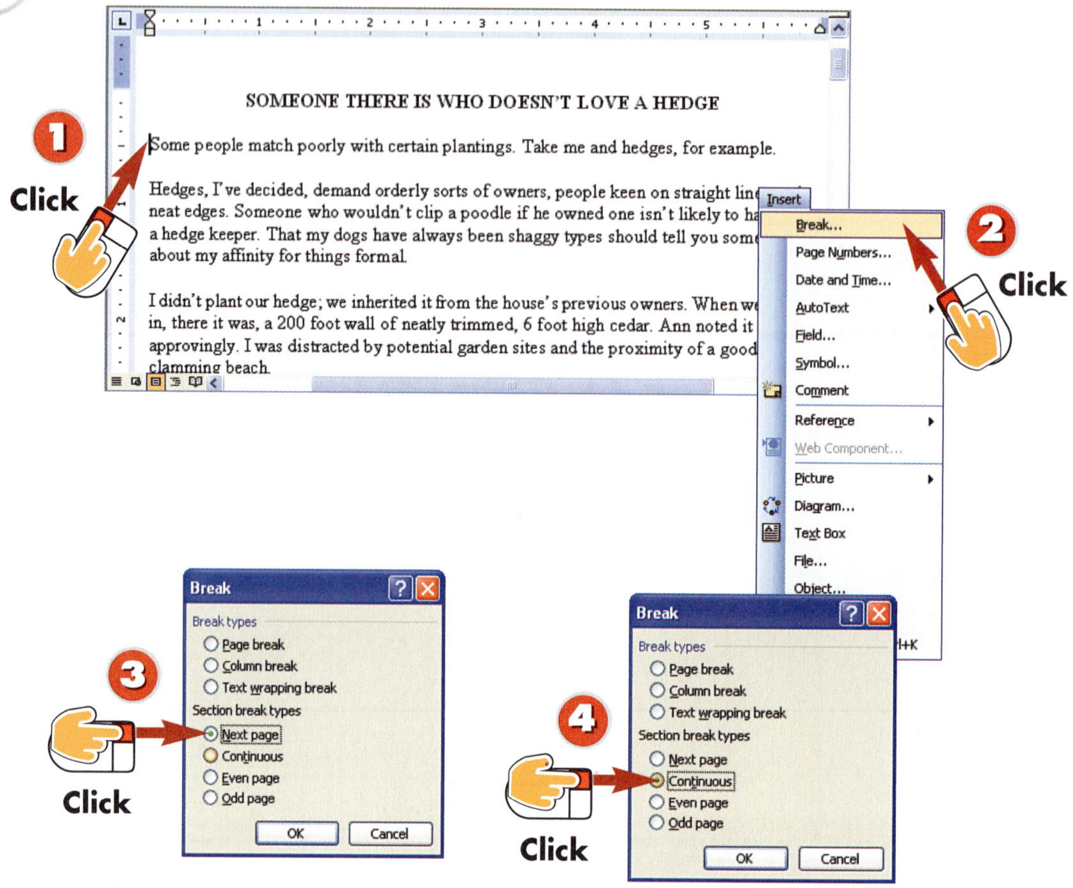

SOMEONE THERE IS WHO DOESN'T LOVE A HEDGE

① Some people match poorly with certain plantings. Take me and hedges, for example.

Click

Hedges, I've decided, demand orderly sorts of owners, people keen on straight lines and neat edges. Someone who wouldn't clip a poodle if he owned one isn't likely to hate a hedge keeper. That my dogs have always been shaggy types should tell you something about my affinity for things formal.

I didn't plant our hedge; we inherited it from the house's previous owners. When we in, there it was, a 200 foot wall of neatly trimmed, 6 foot high cedar. Ann noted it approvingly. I was distracted by potential garden sites and the proximity of a good clamming beach.

Insert
- Break...
- Page Numbers...
- Date and Time...
- AutoText
- Field...
- Symbol...
- Comment
- Reference
- Web Component...
- Picture
- Diagram...
- Text Box
- File...
- Object...

② Click

Break
Break types
- ○ Page break
- ○ Column break
- ○ Text wrapping break

Section break types
- ◉ Next page
- ○ Continuous
- ○ Even page
- ○ Odd page

OK   Cancel

③ Click

Break
Break types
- ○ Page break
- ○ Column break
- ○ Text wrapping break

Section break types
- ○ Next page
- ◉ Continuous
- ○ Even page
- ○ Odd page

OK   Cancel

④ Click

① Make sure that you're using Print Layout view (open the **View** menu and choose **Print Layout**), and move the insertion point to where you want the columns to begin.

② Open the **Insert** menu and choose **Break** to open the Break dialog box.

③ To make the columns begin at the top of a new page, choose **Next page**.

④ To keep the columns on the same page as the text above them, choose **Continuous**.

If you would like to produce newsletters, bulletins, journal articles, and so on, you'll appreciate Word's ability to format text in multiple columns. When you use this feature, the text snakes from column to column. If you want to create columns of text that *do not* wrap from one column to the next, use either custom tabs (see Part 6) or a table (see the last four tasks in this part). If you don't want columns in part of your document, follow steps 1 through 5 to insert a *section break*. Otherwise, begin with step 6.

TIP

Inserting a Column Break
To force text to the next column, move the insertion point to the place where you want the text to break, and choose **Insert**, **Break**. In the **Break** dialog box, click the **Column Break** option button, and click **OK**.

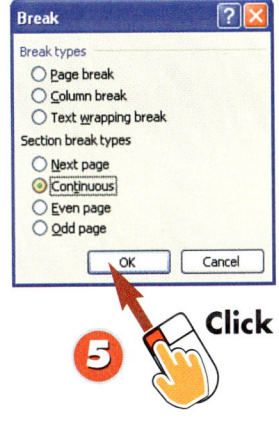

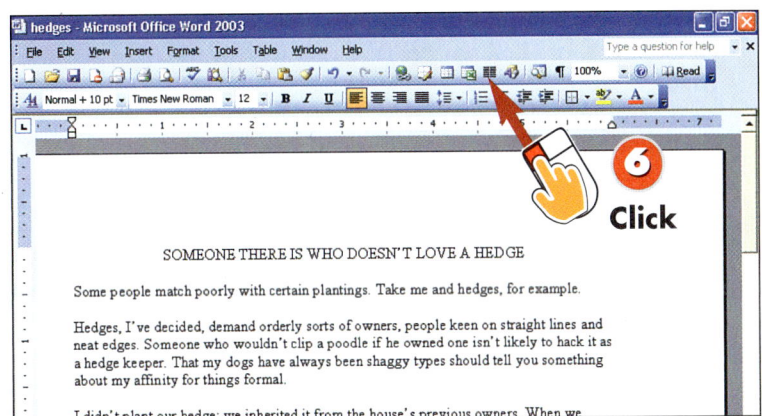

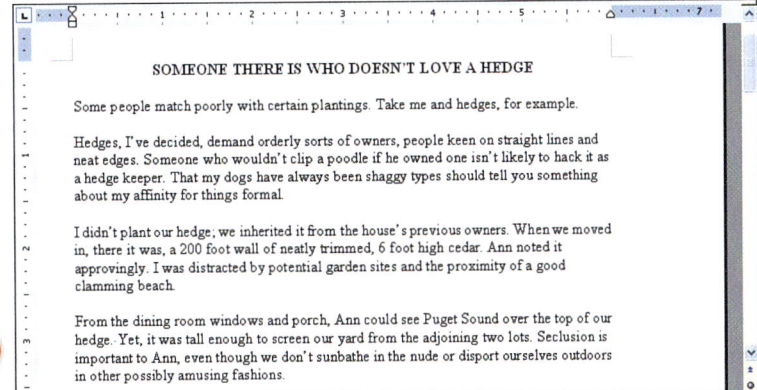

5 Click **OK**, and then double-check to make sure that your insertion point is in the section where you want the columns to begin.

6 Click the **Columns** button on the Formatting toolbar.

7 In the grid that appears, click the desired number of columns.

8 Word creates the number of columns that you specified.

TIP

What If I Have Text at the End of the Document That I Don't Want in Columns?

If you have text at the end of your document that you do not want in columns, select the text that you want in step 1 (instead of placing your insertion point where you want the columns to begin). Word will only format the selected text in columns, leaving the text outside of the selection as is.

TIP

Changing the Number of Columns

If you decide to change the number of columns in your document, simply repeat steps 6–8. If you want no columns, click the leftmost column in the grid in step 7.

Formatting Columns

Start

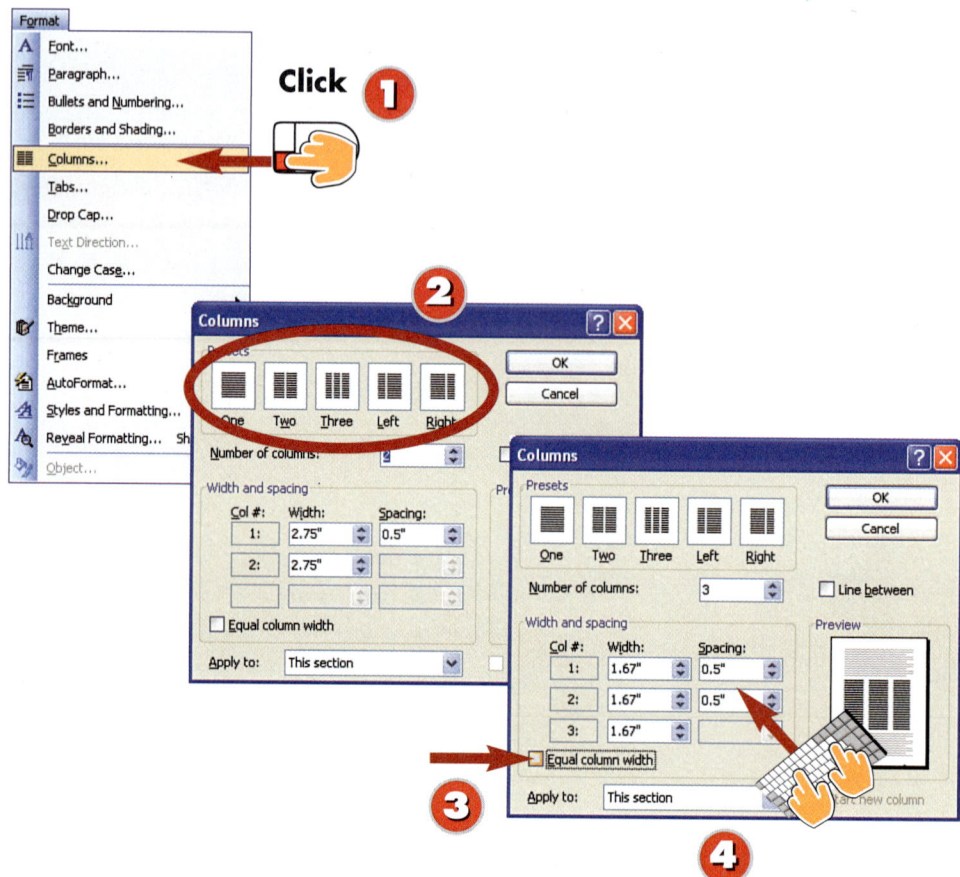

Click ❶

1. Click anywhere in the multiple-column text, open the **Format** menu, and choose **Columns** to open the Columns dialog box.

2. If you like, click a preset format under **Presets** at the top of the dialog box.

3. If you have specific requirements for column widths, first make sure that the **Equal column width** check box is not marked.

4. Then enter the desired settings for each column under **Width and spacing**.

TIP

Balancing Lengths
To balance the length of your columns on the last page of a document, press **Ctrl+End** to move to the end of the document, and then open the **Insert** menu and choose **Break**. Click the **Continuous** option button, and click **OK**.

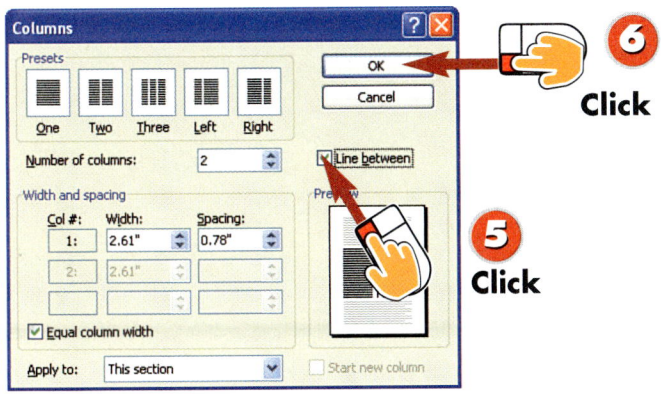

Click

Click

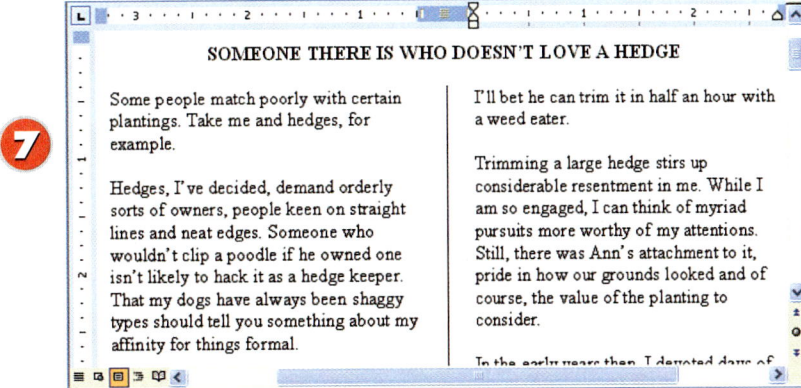

SOMEONE THERE IS WHO DOESN'T LOVE A HEDGE

Some people match poorly with certain plantings. Take me and hedges, for example.

Hedges, I've decided, demand orderly sorts of owners, people keen on straight lines and neat edges. Someone who wouldn't clip a poodle if he owned one isn't likely to hack it as a hedge keeper. That my dogs have always been shaggy types should tell you something about my affinity for things formal.

I'll bet he can trim it in half an hour with a weed eater.

Trimming a large hedge stirs up considerable resentment in me. While I am so engaged, I can think of myriad pursuits more worthy of my attentions. Still, there was Ann's attachment to it, pride in how our grounds looked and of course, the value of the planting to consider.

In the early years then, I devoted days of

5 To add vertical lines between your columns, click the **Line between** check box to mark it.

6 When you have made all of your selections, click **OK**.

7 Word applies the settings you chose to your text.

End

Creating a Table

Start

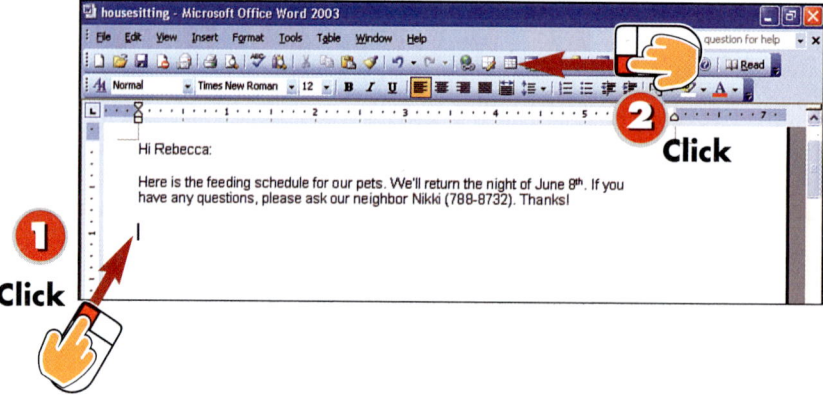

① Click

② Click

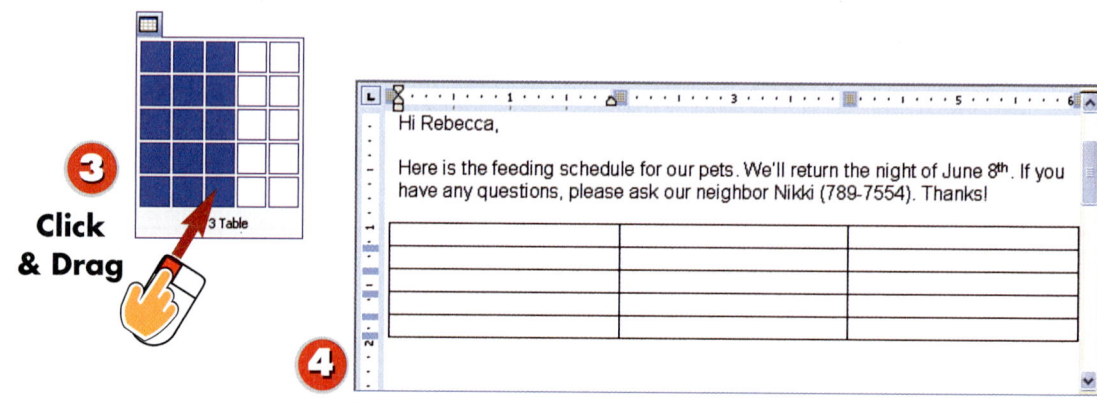

③ Click & Drag

④

① Move the insertion point to the place where you want to insert the table.

② Click the **Insert Table** button on the Standard toolbar.

③ The squares in the grid that appears represent cells. Drag through the approximate number of rows and columns that you want, and then release the mouse button.

④ A table with the number of rows and columns you specified appears in the document.

End

TIP

Drawing a Table
You can also draw a table "by hand" by using the **Draw Table** button on the Tables and Borders toolbar. See "Drawing a Table" and "Adjusting the Appearance of Your Table" later in this part to learn more about this method.

Deleting a Table

Start

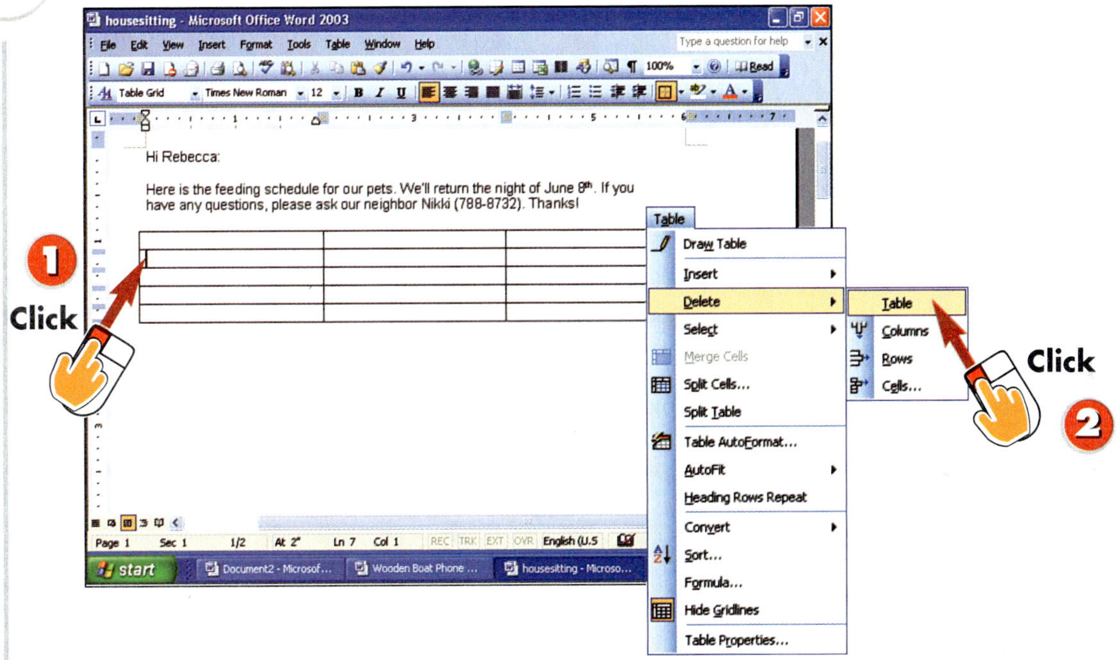

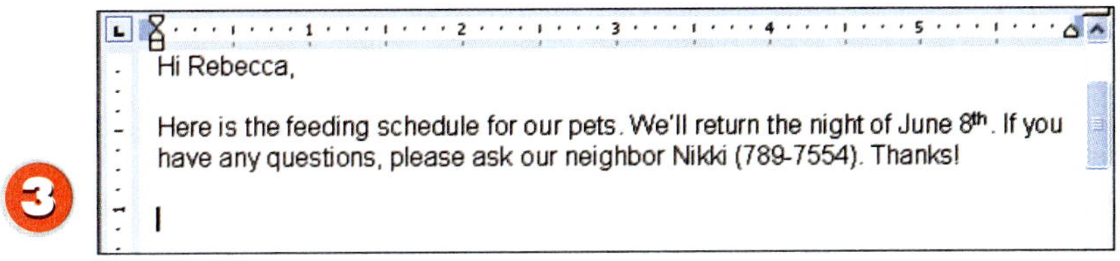

Click

Click

1 Place the insertion point in the table.

2 Open the **Table** menu, choose **Delete**, and select **Table**.

3 The table is deleted from your document.

End

Navigating a Table

Start

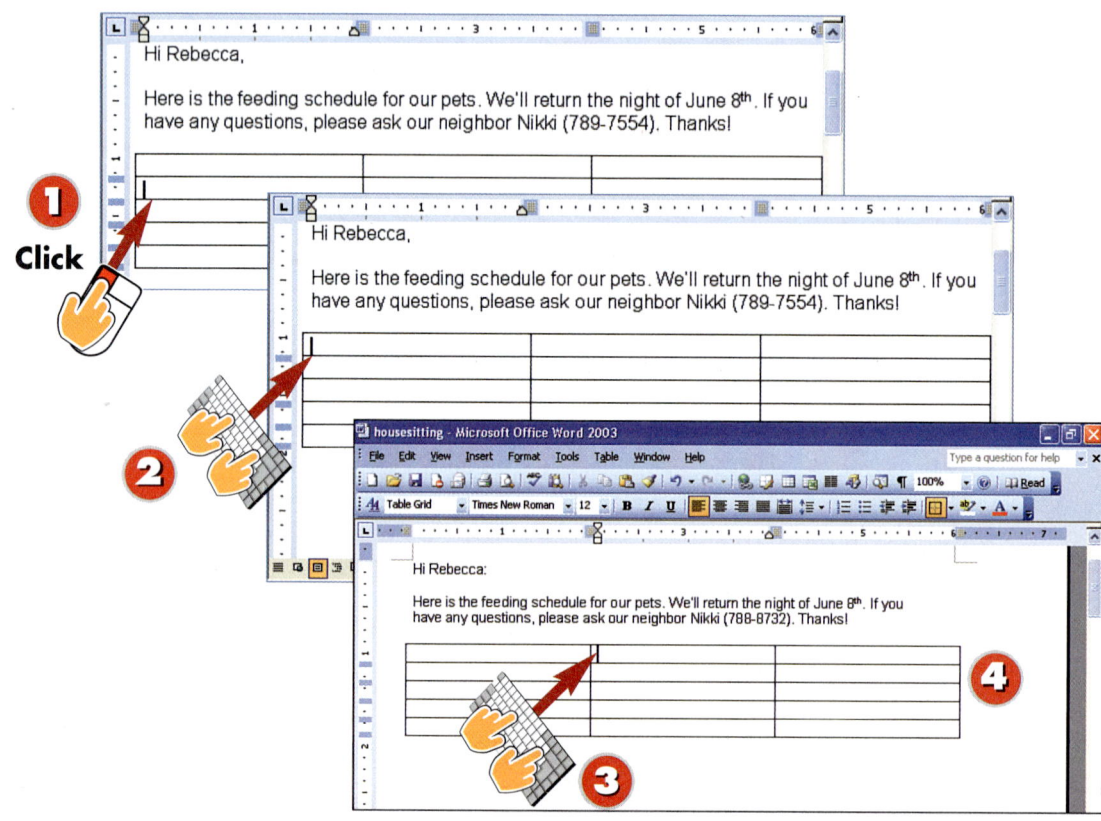

1 Click

① To use the mouse to move to a particular cell, just click in the cell.

② To move to the row above or below, press the **up-** or **down-arrow** key on your keyboard.

③ To move to the cell to the right or left, press the **right-** or **left-arrow** key on your keyboard. (If there is text in a cell, these arrow keys move the insertion point through the text.)

④ You can also press the **Tab** key to move into the cell to the right, or press **Shift+Tab** to move to the left. (If the destination cell contains text, it will be selected.)

INTRODUCTION

Typing text in a table is much like typing in a regular document, but navigating within a table is somewhat different. In this task, you first learn how to move the insertion point from cell to cell within a table, and then you get a few pointers about entering text.

TIP

Adding Text Above a Table
If you start a table at the very top of a document and then decide that you want to insert text above the table, click the far left edge of the upper-left cell in the table and press **Enter**. Word inserts a blank line above the table, and you can now click in the blank line and type your text.

5

	Morning	Evening
Joss (black male Standard Poodle)	1 ½ cups of adult Innova	1 ½ cups of adult Innova
Sneaker (white male Standard Poodle)	1 ½ cups of adult Innova	1 ½ cups of adult Innova
Sapphire (white and gray cat)	Bowl full of senior cat Innova	A few scratches under the chin
Trouper (tabby cat)	¼ cup of adult cat Innova	¼ cup of adult cat Innova

6

	Morning	Evening
Joss (black male Standard Poodle)	1 ½ cups of adult Innova	1 ½ cups of adult Innova
Sneaker (white male Standard Poodle)	1 ½ cups of adult Innova	1 ½ cups of adult Innova
Sapphire (white and gray cat)	Bowl full of senior cat Innova	A few scratches under the chin
Trouper (tabby cat)	¼ cup of adult cat Innova	¼ cup of adult cat Innova

7

	Morning	Evening
Joss (black male Standard Poodle)	1 ½ cups of adult Innova	1 ½ cups of adult Innova
Sneaker (white male Standard Poodle)	1 ½ cups of adult Innova	1 ½ cups of adult Innova
Sapphire (white and gray cat)	Bowl full of senior cat Innova	A few scratches under the chin
Trouper (tabby cat)	¼ cup of adult cat Innova	¼ cup of adult cat Innova

5 When you type text in a cell, if the entry is too wide to fit in the cell, Word automatically wraps the text to the next line and increases the row height.

6 Press **Enter** in a cell to end the paragraph and add a blank line to that row.

7 If you accidentally press Enter in a cell and want to remove the blank line, just press the **Backspace** key.

End

TIP

Inserting a Tab Within a Cell
If you want to insert a tab within a cell, press **Ctrl+Tab** instead of **Tab**. (Pressing the **Tab** key by itself just selects the contents of the cell to the right.)

Adding, Deleting, and Resizing Rows and Columns

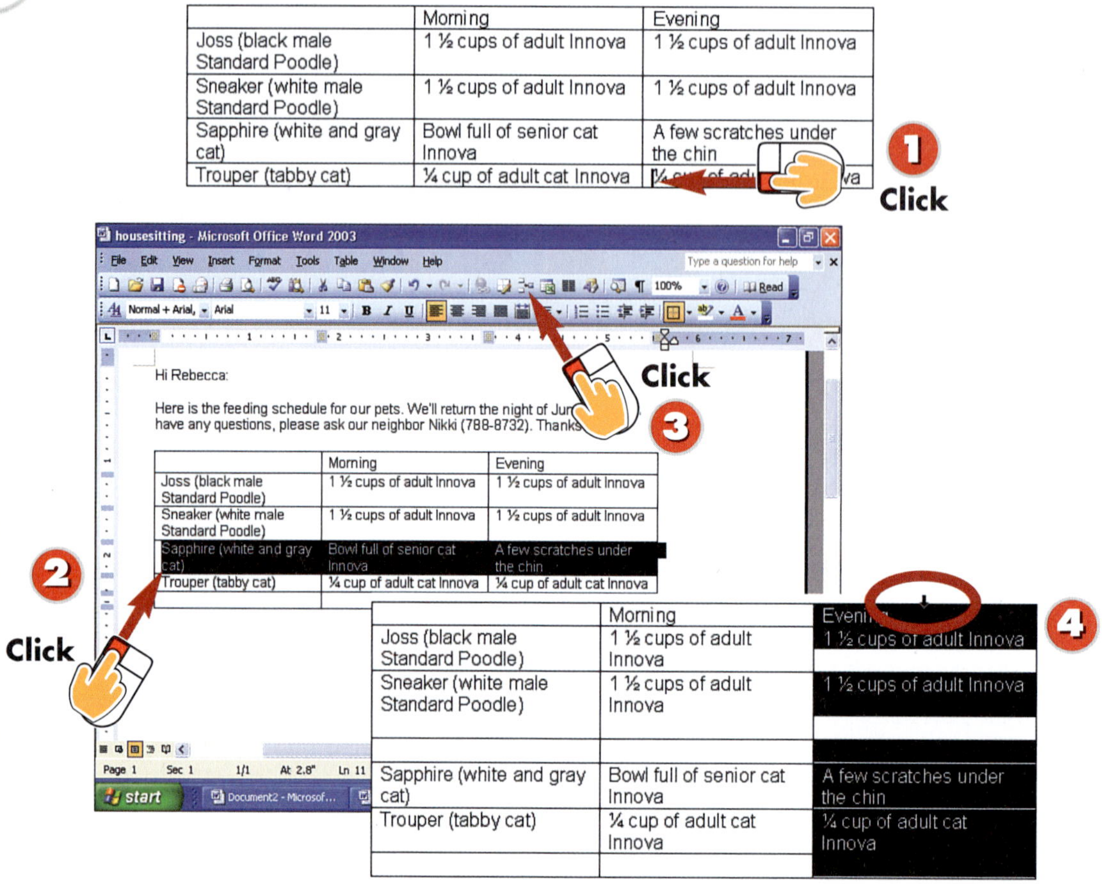

Start

	Morning	Evening
Joss (black male Standard Poodle)	1 ½ cups of adult Innova	1 ½ cups of adult Innova
Sneaker (white male Standard Poodle)	1 ½ cups of adult Innova	1 ½ cups of adult Innova
Sapphire (white and gray cat)	Bowl full of senior cat Innova	A few scratches under the chin
Trouper (tabby cat)	¼ cup of adult cat Innova	¼ cup of adult cat Innova

1 Click

Click 3

Hi Rebecca:

Here is the feeding schedule for our pets. We'll return the night of Jur have any questions, please ask our neighbor Nikki (788-8732). Thanks

	Morning	Evening
Joss (black male Standard Poodle)	1 ½ cups of adult Innova	1 ½ cups of adult Innova
Sneaker (white male Standard Poodle)	1 ½ cups of adult Innova	1 ½ cups of adult Innova
Sapphire (white and gray cat)	Bowl full of senior cat Innova	A few scratches under the chin
Trouper (tabby cat)	¼ cup of adult cat Innova	¼ cup of adult cat Innova

2 Click

4

	Morning	Evening
Joss (black male Standard Poodle)	1 ½ cups of adult Innova	1 ½ cups of adult Innova
Sneaker (white male Standard Poodle)	1 ½ cups of adult Innova	1 ½ cups of adult Innova
Sapphire (white and gray cat)	Bowl full of senior cat Innova	A few scratches under the chin
Trouper (tabby cat)	¼ cup of adult cat Innova	¼ cup of adult cat Innova

1. To add a row at the end of the table, click anywhere in the lower-right cell in the table, and press the **Tab** key.

2. To add a row in the middle of the table, first select the row below the location of the new one by clicking to its left.

3. Click the **Insert Rows** button on the Standard toolbar to insert the row. (The Insert Table button turns into Insert Rows when a row is selected.)

4. To insert a column, first select the column to the right of where the new one will go by clicking at the top of the column when the mouse pointer changes to a black arrow.

INTRODUCTION

As you enter text in a table, you will almost certainly need to change its structure. This task describes the most common adjustments you'll need to make. As you experiment with these techniques, keep in mind that Word does not prevent you from making a table too wide to fit on the page. If you're adding columns and increasing column widths, check Print Preview periodically to make sure that the table isn't running off the page.

TIP

Table Off the Page? If you have widened your table too much, open the **Table** menu, choose **AutoFit**, and select **AutoFit to Window**.

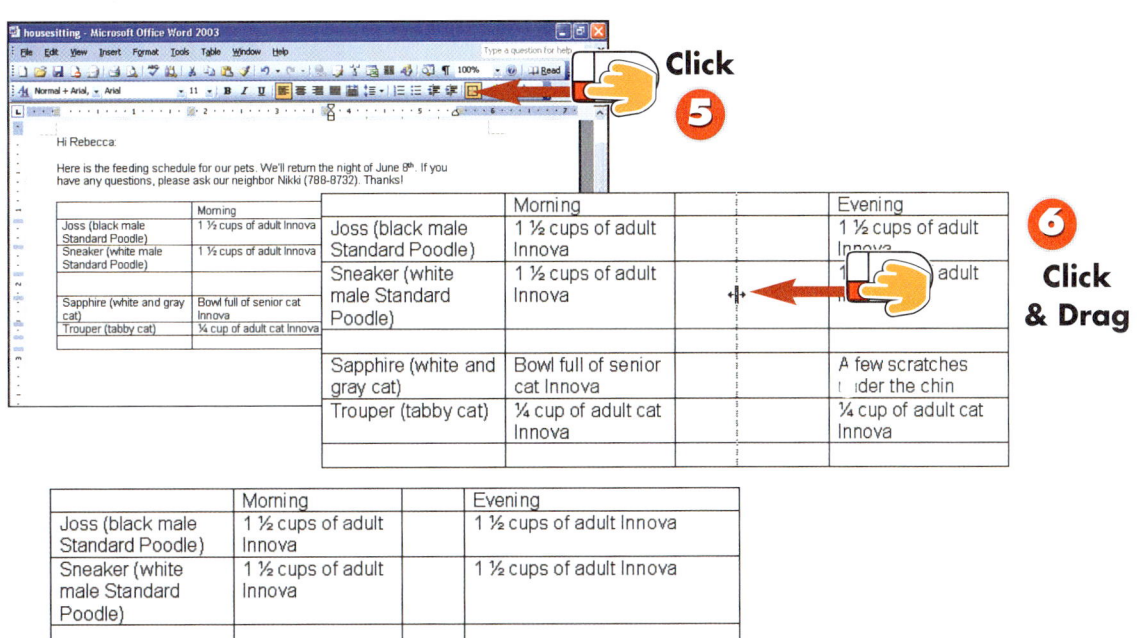

Click ⑤

Click & Drag ⑥

Click & Drag ⑦

⑤ Click the **Insert Columns** button on the Standard toolbar. (The Insert Table button turns into Insert Columns when a column is selected.)

⑥ To adjust a column's width, point to its right border and drag it to the desired location.

⑦ To resize a row, point to its bottom border and drag it to the desired location.

End

Why Are All the Table Menu Commands Dim?
Most of the commands in the Table menu are active only when the insertion point is in a table. If you notice that the commands are dim, it's a sign that you accidentally clicked outside the table. Simply click inside the table and then display the Table menu again.

Deleting a Row or Column
To delete a row or column, select it first (see steps 2 and 4), and then open the **Table** menu, choose **Delete**, and choose **Rows** or **Columns**.

Formatting a Table

Start

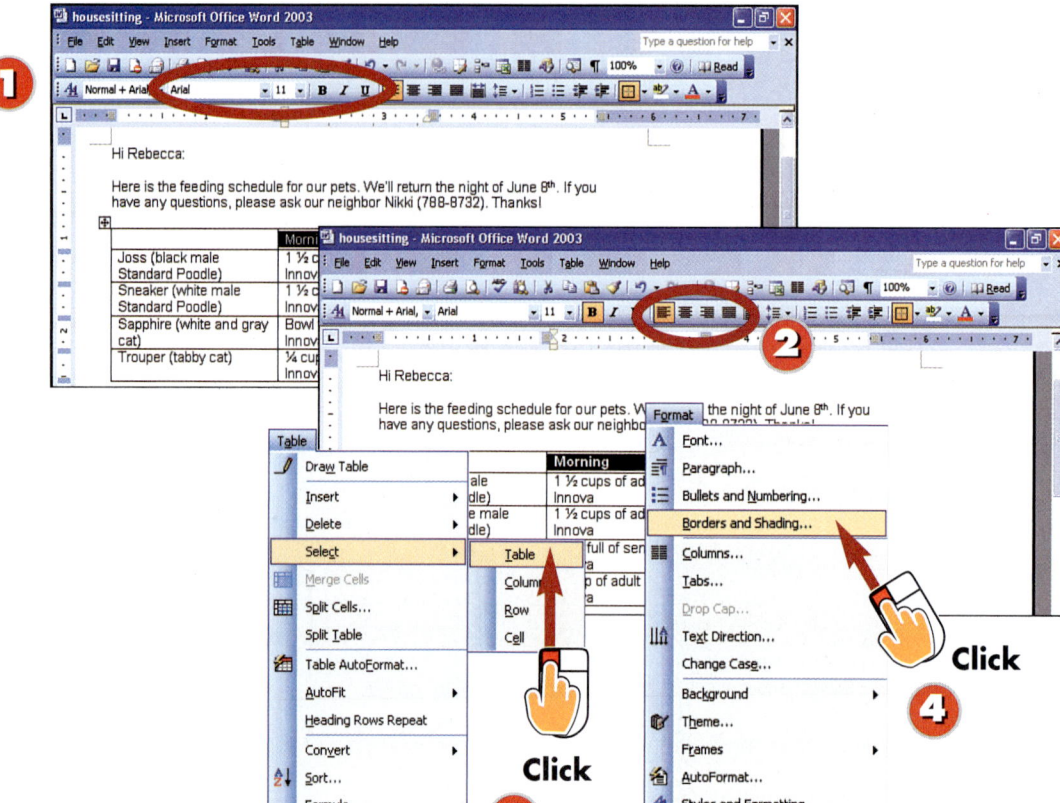

1 To change text formatting, select the cells you want to change (or some text within a single cell) and then use the various familiar buttons on the Formatting toolbar.

2 To change the horizontal alignment of text within cells, select the cells and then click the desired alignment button on the Formatting toolbar.

3 To change the border around the outside of the table, first select the entire table by opening the **Table** menu, choosing **Select**, and choosing **Table**.

4 Next, open the **Format** menu and choose **Borders and Shading**.

Formatting a table involves changing the appearance of the text and adding borders and shading. Be careful to select the exact cells that you want to format before using the commands described in this task, and remember that you can always click the Undo button in the Standard toolbar if you make a change you don't like. To learn more ways to format a table, see "Adjusting the Appearance of Your Table" later in this part.

TIP

Adding Shading to Cells
If you want to add shading to some of the cells in your table, select the cells, and then open the **Format** menu and choose **Borders and Shading**. Click the **Shading** tab, click the color you'd like to use, and click **OK**.

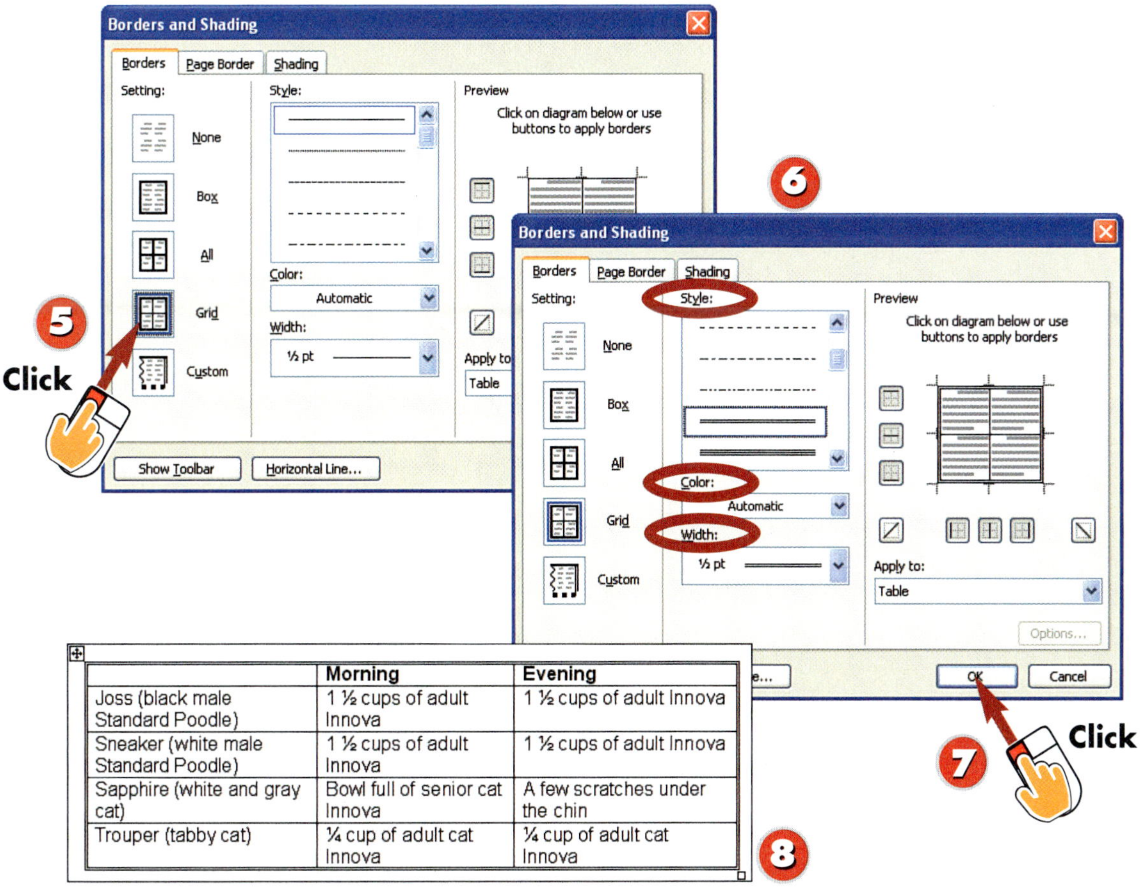

Borders and Shading

Borders | Page Border | Shading

Setting:
- None
- Box
- All
- Grid
- Custom

Style:

Color: Automatic

Width: ½ pt

Preview
Click on diagram below or use buttons to apply borders

Apply to: Table

Show Toolbar | Horizontal Line...

5 **Click**

6

Borders and Shading

Borders | Page Border | Shading

Setting:
- None
- Box
- All
- Grid
- Custom

Style:

Color: Automatic

Width: ½ pt

Preview
Click on diagram below or use buttons to apply borders

Apply to: Table

Options...

OK | Cancel

7 **Click**

	Morning	Evening
Joss (black male Standard Poodle)	1 ½ cups of adult Innova	1 ½ cups of adult Innova
Sneaker (white male Standard Poodle)	1 ½ cups of adult Innova	1 ½ cups of adult Innova
Sapphire (white and gray cat)	Bowl full of senior cat Innova	A few scratches under the chin
Trouper (tabby cat)	¼ cup of adult cat Innova	¼ cup of adult cat Innova

8

5 Click the **Grid** option in the **Setting** area to change only the outside border, or **All** to change all of the borders in the table.

6 Choose the desired options from the **Style**, **Color**, and **Width** lists.

7 Click the **OK** button, and then click to deselect the table.

8 Word applies the border options you chose.

End

Moving and Resizing a Table

TIP

To move your table around on the page, use the small square that contains a four-headed arrow, located just outside the upper-left corner of the table (see the figure for step 1). Click on this square and drag the table to the desired location. To resize your table, point to the small square just outside the lower-right corner, and drag diagonally up and to the left to shrink the table, or down and to the right to enlarge it.

Drawing a Table

Start

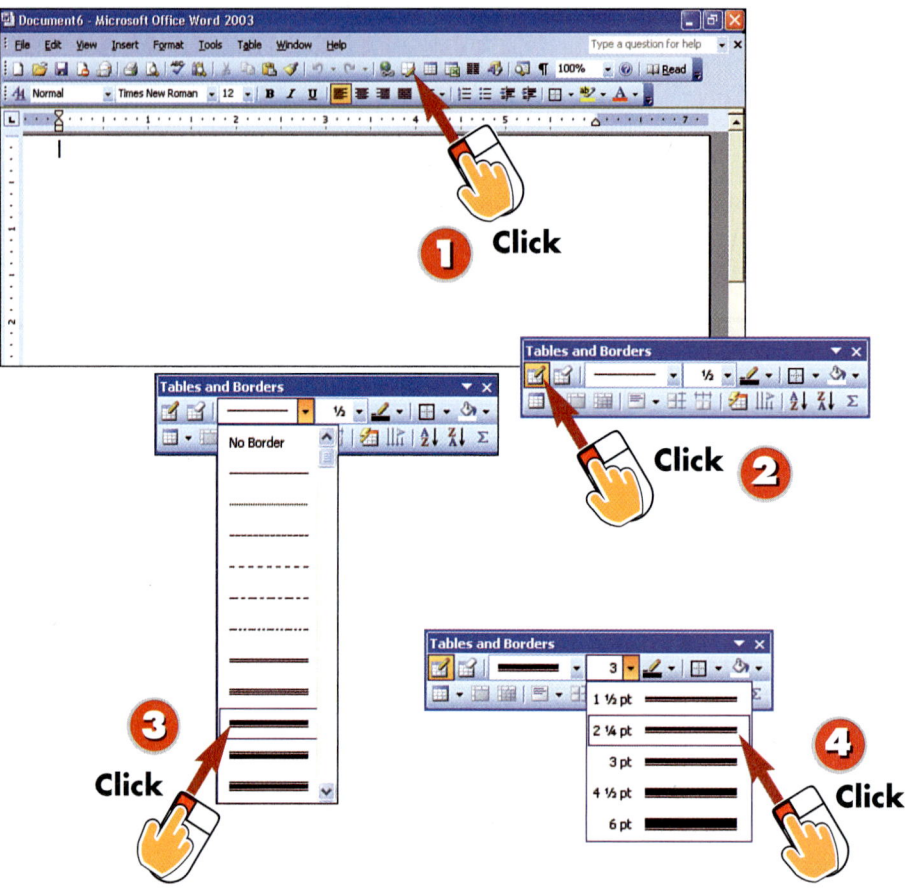

1 Click

2 Click

3 Click

4 Click

1 Click the **Tables and Borders** button on the Standard toolbar to display the Tables and Borders toolbar.

2 Click the **Draw Table** button if it isn't already selected (pushed in). Your mouse pointer will now look like a small pencil when it's over your document.

3 Click the **down arrow** next to the **Line Style** field and choose a line style for the outside border of your table.

4 Click the **down arrow** next to the **Line Weight** field and choose a line weight for the outside border of your table.

INTRODUCTION

If you want to make a complex table, you'll probably find it easier to "draw" the table with your mouse than to use the Insert Table toolbar button. In this task, you use the **Draw Table** button in the Tables and Borders toolbar to draw the outline of a table and then fill in the rows and columns. This method of creating a table is extremely flexible: If you can envision a design for your table, you can almost certainly create it.

TIP

Changing Line Appearance To change the appearance of a line after you've already drawn it, select the desired options in the **Line Style**, **Line Weight**, and **Border Color** lists in the Tables and Borders toolbar, and draw the line again with the Draw Table tool.

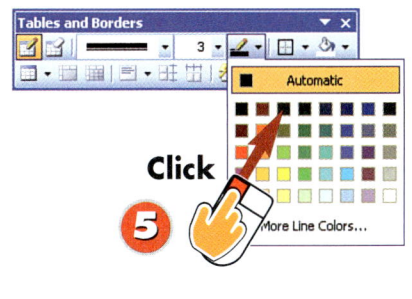

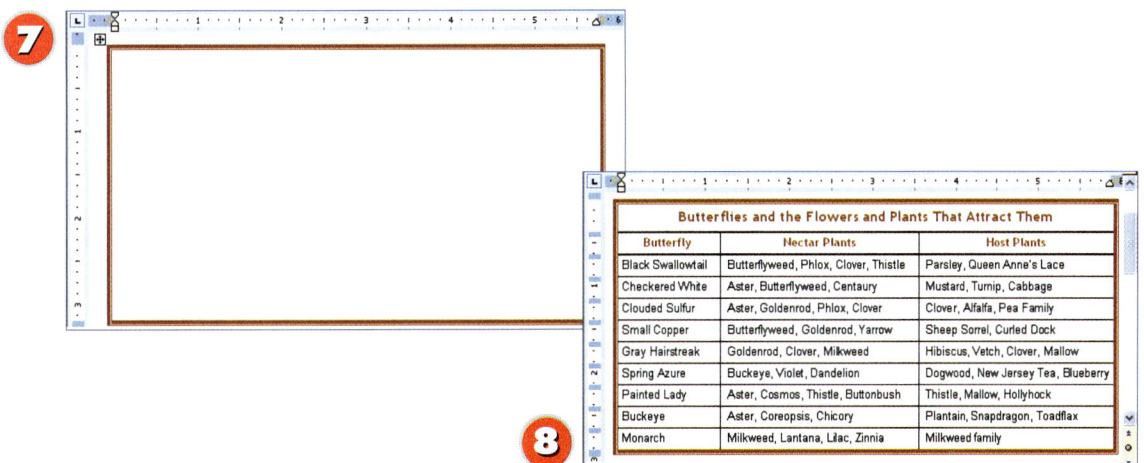

Butterflies and the Flowers and Plants That Attract Them		
Butterfly	**Nectar Plants**	**Host Plants**
Black Swallowtail	Butterflyweed, Phlox, Clover, Thistle	Parsley, Queen Anne's Lace
Checkered White	Aster, Butterflyweed, Centaury	Mustard, Turnip, Cabbage
Clouded Sulfur	Aster, Goldenrod, Phlox, Clover	Clover, Alfalfa, Pea Family
Small Copper	Butterflyweed, Goldenrod, Yarrow	Sheep Sorrel, Curled Dock
Gray Hairstreak	Goldenrod, Clover, Milkweed	Hibiscus, Vetch, Clover, Mallow
Spring Azure	Buckeye, Violet, Dandelion	Dogwood, New Jersey Tea, Blueberry
Painted Lady	Aster, Cosmos, Thistle, Buttonbush	Thistle, Mallow, Hollyhock
Buckeye	Aster, Coreopsis, Chicory	Plantain, Snapdragon, Toadflax
Monarch	Milkweed, Lantana, Lilac, Zinnia	Milkweed family

5 Click the **down arrow** next to the **Border Color** button and click a color for the outside border of your table.

6 Starting in the upper-left corner, drag diagonally down and to the right; release when the outline is the right size.

7 Word creates the outline of your table. Repeat steps 3–5 to choose what kind of lines you want, and draw the internal lines in the table.

8 Click the **Draw Table** button to turn it off, and enter the text in the table. For tips on improving the appearance of the text in your table, see the next task.

End

Hiding Lines
To hide a line in a table, first display the Line Style list and choose the **No Border** option. Then click the **Draw Table** button and drag over the line. If you want to actually *remove* a line, merging the cells that were on either side of it, see the next task.

Adjusting the Appearance of Your Table

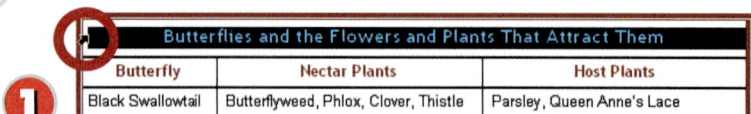

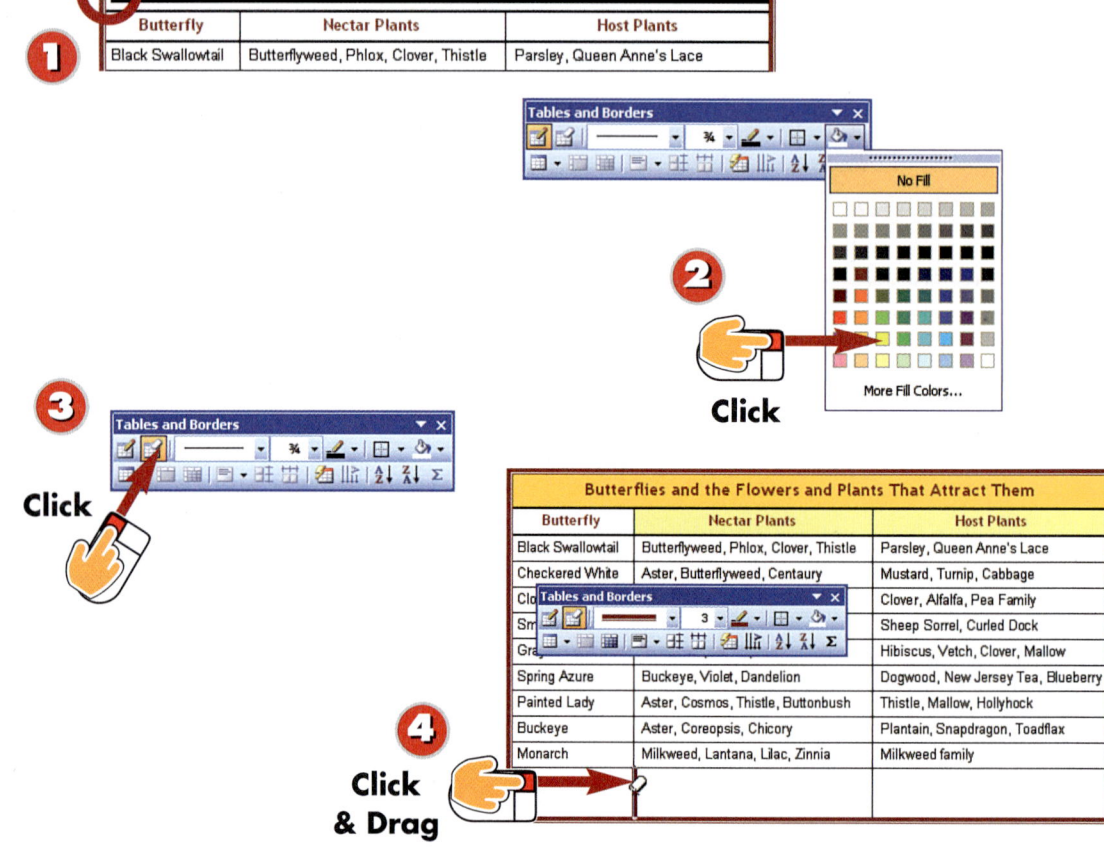

Start

1 To select a cell, point just inside the left edge of the cell. When the mouse pointer becomes a black arrow, click once (or drag to select multiple cells).

2 To add shading to a cell, select the cell, click the **down arrow** to the right of the **Shading Color** button on the Tables and Borders toolbar, and click the desired color.

3 To remove a line in a table and merge the cells on either side of the line, first click the **Eraser** button in the Tables and Borders toolbar.

4 The mouse pointer becomes an eraser. Drag over the line to highlight it, and then release the mouse button.

INTRODUCTION

Regardless of whether you create your table with the **Insert Table** button or you draw it with the **Draw Table** button, you can easily adjust the table and the text it contains with tools in the Tables and Borders toolbar. In this task, you first learn how to select a single cell or group of cells—an essential part of formatting cells in your table—and then you practice using some of the most useful tools in the Tables and Borders toolbar.

TIP

No Tables and Borders Toolbar?
Remember that you can display the Tables and Borders toolbar at any time by clicking the **Tables and Borders** button in the Standard toolbar.

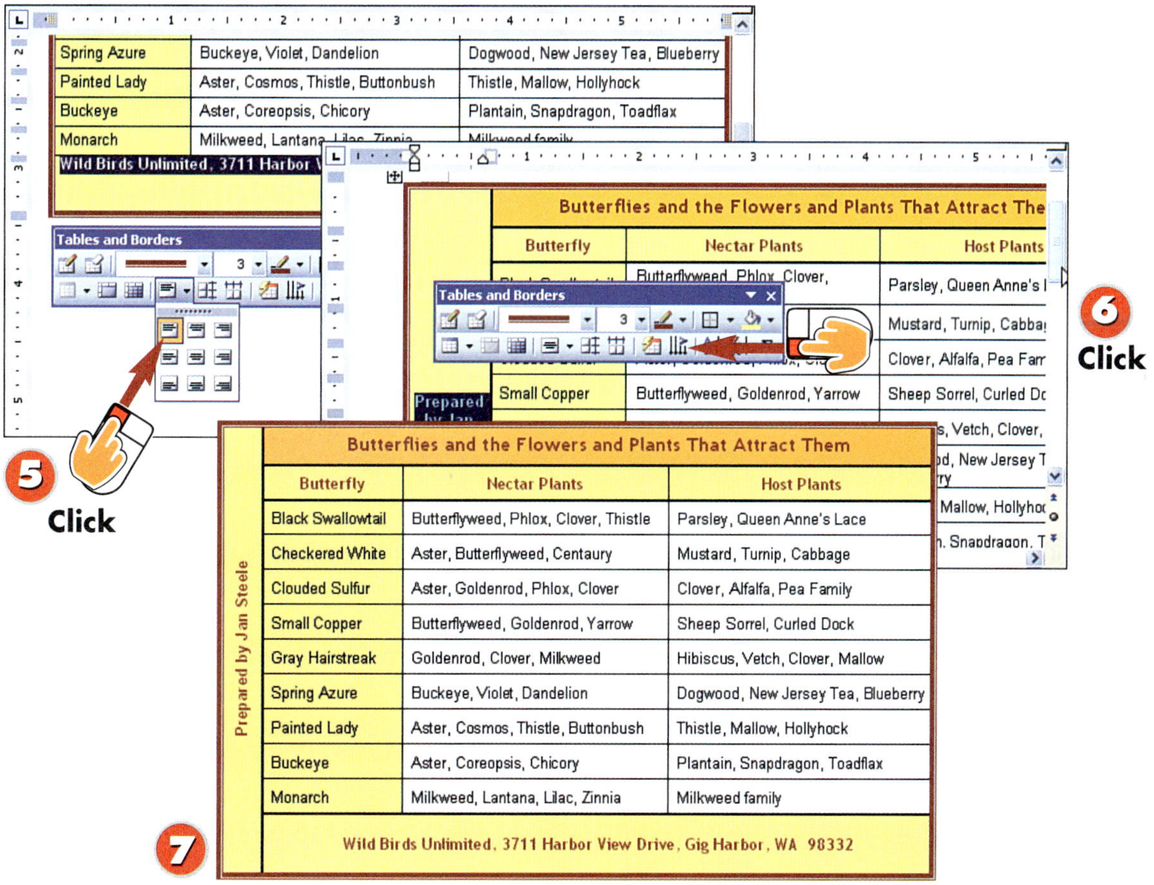

Table: Spring Azure group (top screenshot)

Spring Azure	Buckeye, Violet, Dandelion	Dogwood, New Jersey Tea, Blueberry
Painted Lady	Aster, Cosmos, Thistle, Buttonbush	Thistle, Mallow, Hollyhock
Buckeye	Aster, Coreopsis, Chicory	Plantain, Snapdragon, Toadflax
Monarch	Milkweed, Lantana, Lilac, Zinnia	Milkweed family
Wild Birds Unlimited, 3711 Harbor V		

Tables and Borders

Click — 5

Butterflies and the Flowers and Plants That Attract Them (middle screenshot)

Butterfly	Nectar Plants	Host Plants
	Butterflyweed, Phlox, Clover,	Parsley, Queen Anne's L
		Mustard, Turnip, Cabba
		Clover, Alfalfa, Pea Fam
Small Copper	Butterflyweed, Goldenrod, Yarrow	Sheep Sorrel, Curled Do

Tables and Borders

Prepared by Jan

Click — 6

Butterflies and the Flowers and Plants That Attract Them (bottom table)

Prepared by Jan Steele

Butterfly	Nectar Plants	Host Plants
Black Swallowtail	Butterflyweed, Phlox, Clover, Thistle	Parsley, Queen Anne's Lace
Checkered White	Aster, Butterflyweed, Centaury	Mustard, Turnip, Cabbage
Clouded Sulfur	Aster, Goldenrod, Phlox, Clover	Clover, Alfalfa, Pea Family
Small Copper	Butterflyweed, Goldenrod, Yarrow	Sheep Sorrel, Curled Dock
Gray Hairstreak	Goldenrod, Clover, Milkweed	Hibiscus, Vetch, Clover, Mallow
Spring Azure	Buckeye, Violet, Dandelion	Dogwood, New Jersey Tea, Blueberry
Painted Lady	Aster, Cosmos, Thistle, Buttonbush	Thistle, Mallow, Hollyhock
Buckeye	Aster, Coreopsis, Chicory	Plantain, Snapdragon, Toadflax
Monarch	Milkweed, Lantana, Lilac, Zinnia	Milkweed family

Wild Birds Unlimited, 3711 Harbor View Drive, Gig Harbor, WA 98332

Click — 5

5. To change the vertical/horizontal alignment of text in your table, select the cell, click the **down arrow** to the right of the **Align** button, and click the desired option.

6. To change the direction of text from left-to-right to either bottom-to-top or top-to-bottom, select the cell and then click the **Change Text Direction** button one or more times.

7. Word applies the changes you've made. Make any further adjustments to your table until you're satisfied with its appearance.

End

TIP

Making Rows the Same Height or Columns the Same Width

If you want to make multiple rows the same height or multiple columns the same width, select the rows or columns (see steps 2 and 4 of "Adding, Deleting, and Resizing Rows and Columns" earlier in this part), and then click the **Distribute Rows Evenly** or **Distribute Columns Evenly** button on the Tables and Borders toolbar.

Adding Images to Your Document

Working with images used to be out of reach for almost everyone but professional graphic designers. These days, however, it takes only a click or two to spice up a document with a splashy image or colorful title. In this part, you learn how to insert, manipulate, and format images; how to adjust the way text flows around an image; and how to use WordArt, a wonderful tool that lets you create special effects for text.

An Image in Word

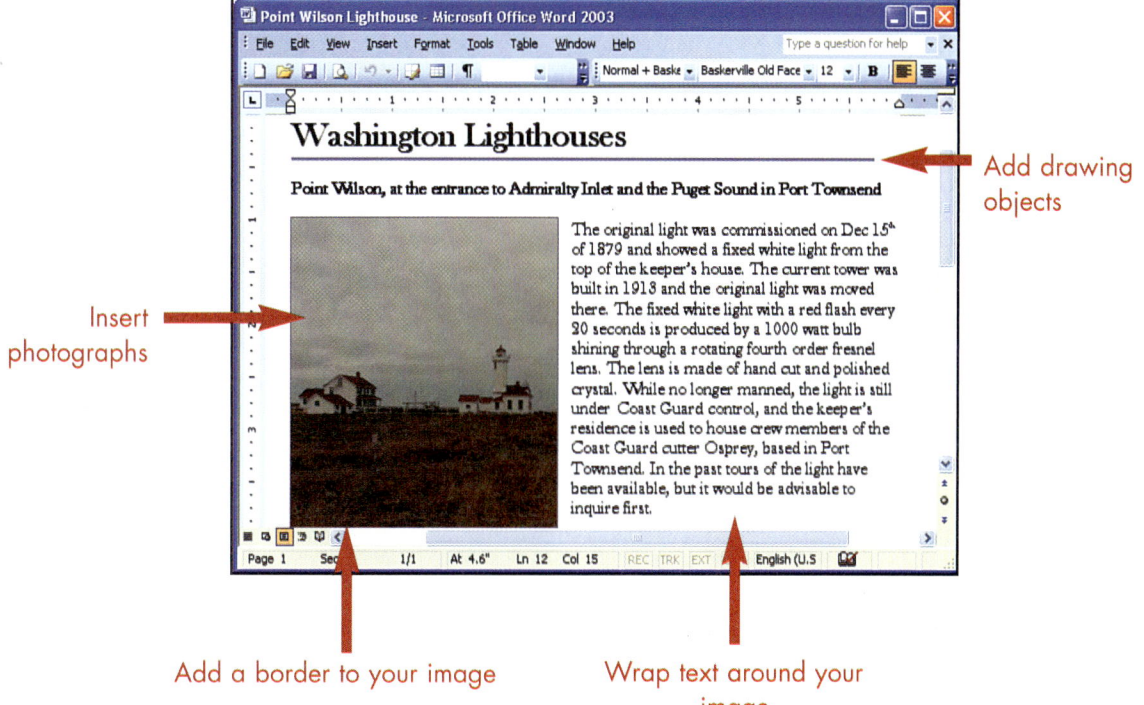

Add drawing objects

Insert photographs

Add a border to your image

Wrap text around your image

Inserting an Image in Your Document

Start

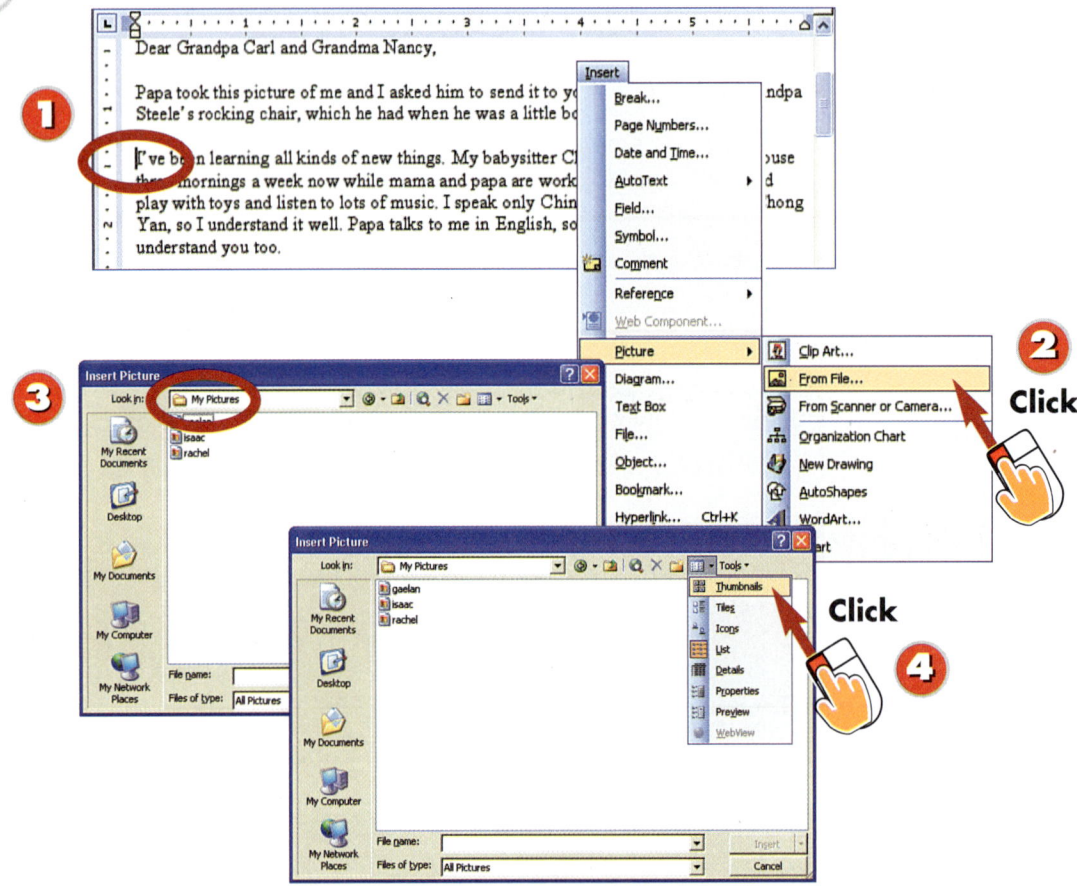

1 Move the insertion point to the spot in your document where you want to insert the image.

2 Open the **Insert** menu, choose **Picture**, and select **From File** to open the Insert Picture dialog box.

3 Navigate to the folder that contains the image you want to insert. (Use the same methods as those described in "Opening a Document" in Part 4.)

4 To display your image files as thumbnails, making it easier to browse through them, click the **down arrow** to the right of the **Views** button, and select **Thumbnails**.

INTRODUCTION

Adding an image to your document is not as hard as you might think. In fact, it only takes a click or two. This task describes how to insert a digital photograph, although you can use any type of image you like, and the image file can be located in any folder on your computer system. In addition, you can use clip art that comes on the Microsoft Office (or Word) CD. After you've added an image to your document, you'll want to look over the next three tasks to learn how to adjust its location and appearance, among other things.

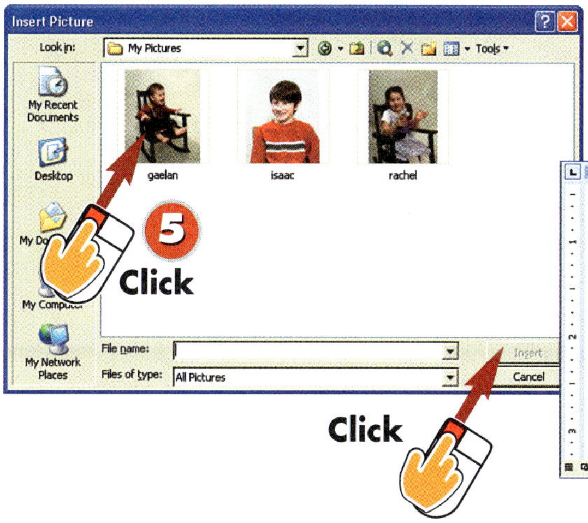

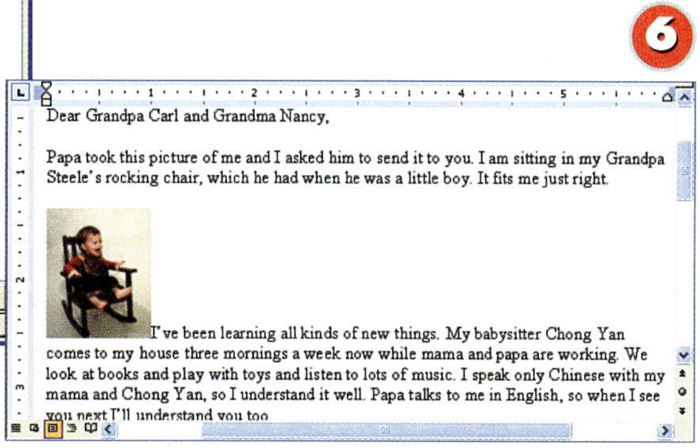

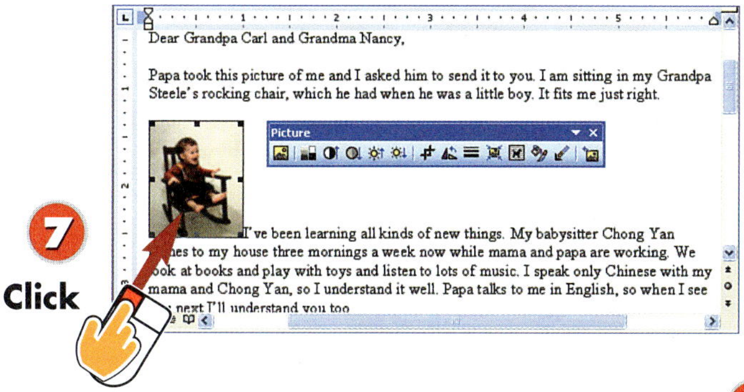

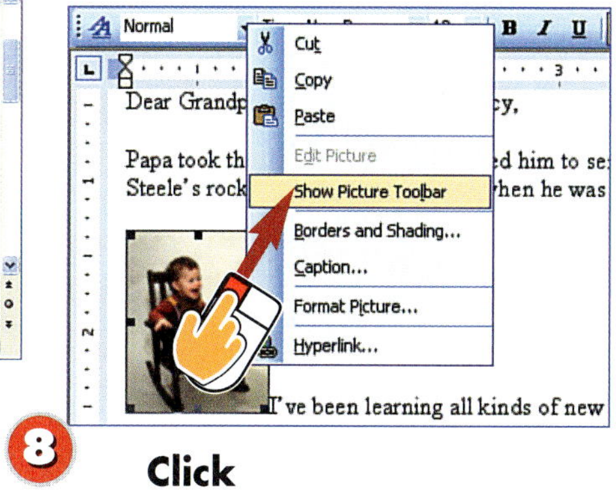

Click

Click

Click

Click

Click

5 Click the image you want to insert, and then click the **Insert** button.

6 The image is inserted in your document. (Don't worry if it is not the right size or in the right place. You'll learn how to make these changes in the next task.)

7 Click the image. The **Picture** toolbar may appear automatically.

8 If it doesn't, right-click the image and choose **Show Picture Toolbar**. You will use this toolbar in the next three tasks.

End

Inserting Images

To insert an image from your digital camera or scanner, first install the software that came with the device, and connect the device to your computer. Choose **Insert**, **Picture**, **From Scanner or Camera**. Select the device, click the **Custom Insert** button, and then follow the directions onscreen (these will vary with the device).

Using Clip Art

To use a clip-art image, choose **Insert**, **Picture**, **Clip Art**. In the Clip Art task pane, enter the type of image you want to search for, and click **Go**. Thumbnails of the image will appear in the results list; click an image you like to insert it.

Moving and Sizing an Image

Start

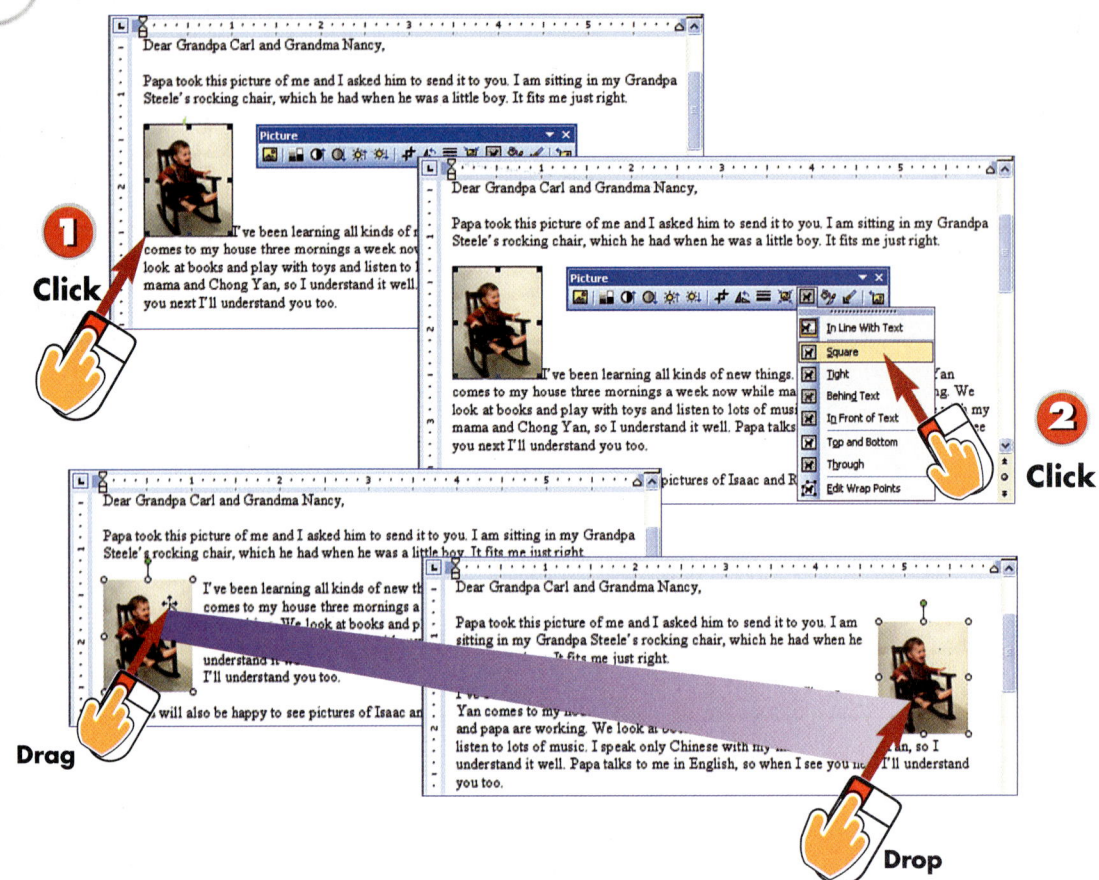

Click

Drag

Click

Drop

1. Click the image to select it. When a image is selected, small squares (called *selection handles*) appear around the image. When the image is in-line, the squares are black.

2. To move the selected image, click the **Text Wrapping** button in the Picture toolbar, and click **Square**. (You can always choose a different option later.)

3. The selection handles become white circles. Point to middle of the image (the mouse pointer changes to a four-headed arrow) and drag the image to the desired location.

4. Release the mouse button when the image is in the desired place.

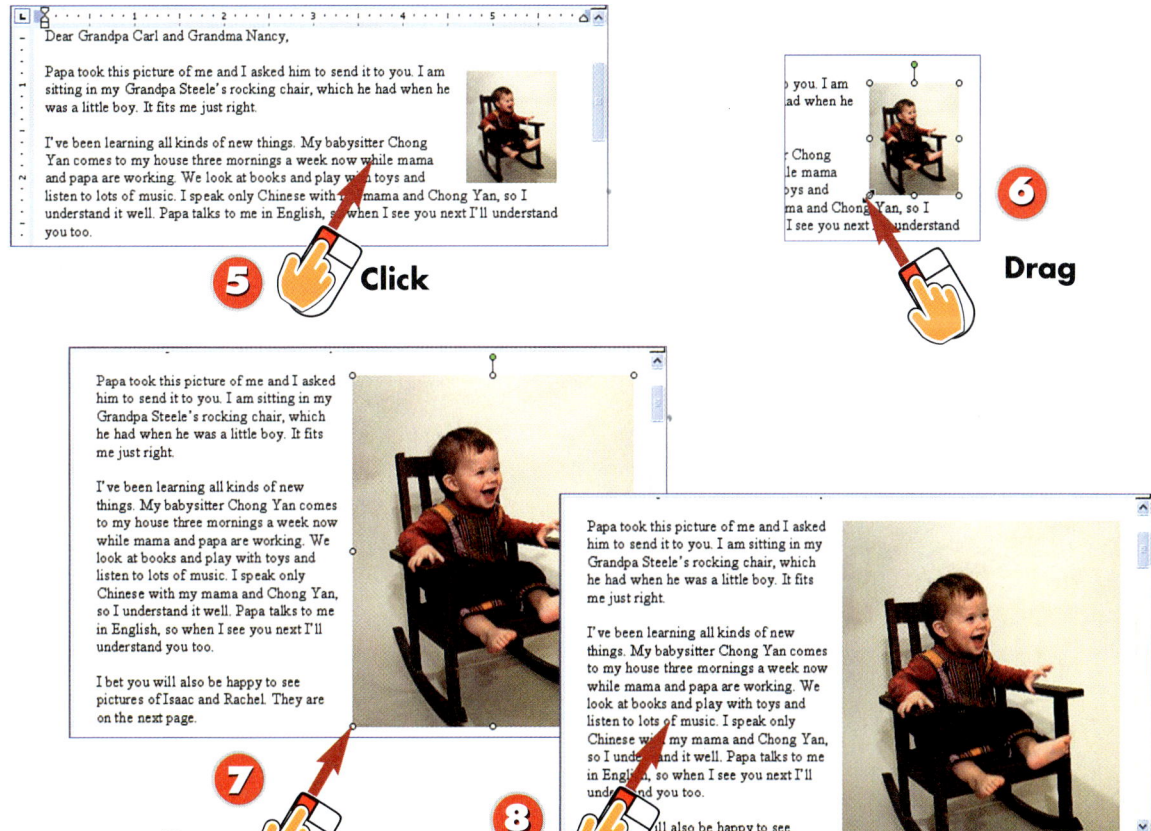

5 Click

Drag

7 **Drag**

8 **Click**

5 Click outside of the image to deselect it. This makes it easier to see how the image looks in its new location.

6 To resize the image, select it, and then point to a corner selection handle (the mouse pointer becomes a diagonal double-headed arrow).

7 Drag to enlarge or shrink the image, and release the mouse button when the image is the correct size. (You can use the same method when an image is in-line.)

8 Click outside of the image to deselect it so you can see whether the image is the size you want.

End

Positioning the Image

TIP

To position an image precisely, select the image (after you've set a text wrapping option) and then double-click it to display the Format Picture dialog box. Click the **Layout** tab, mark the **Left**, **Center**, or **Right** option button, and click **OK**.

Sizing Your Image More Precisely

TIP

If you need to make your image a precise size, double-click it to display the Format Picture dialog box. Click the **Size** tab, enter the desired height and width in the **Height** and **Width** text boxes, and click **OK**. (If you need to measure the image in pixels instead of inches, first open the **Tools** menu and choose **Options**, click the **General** tab, mark the **Show pixels for HTML features** check box, and click **OK**.)

Cropping an Image and Adding Borders

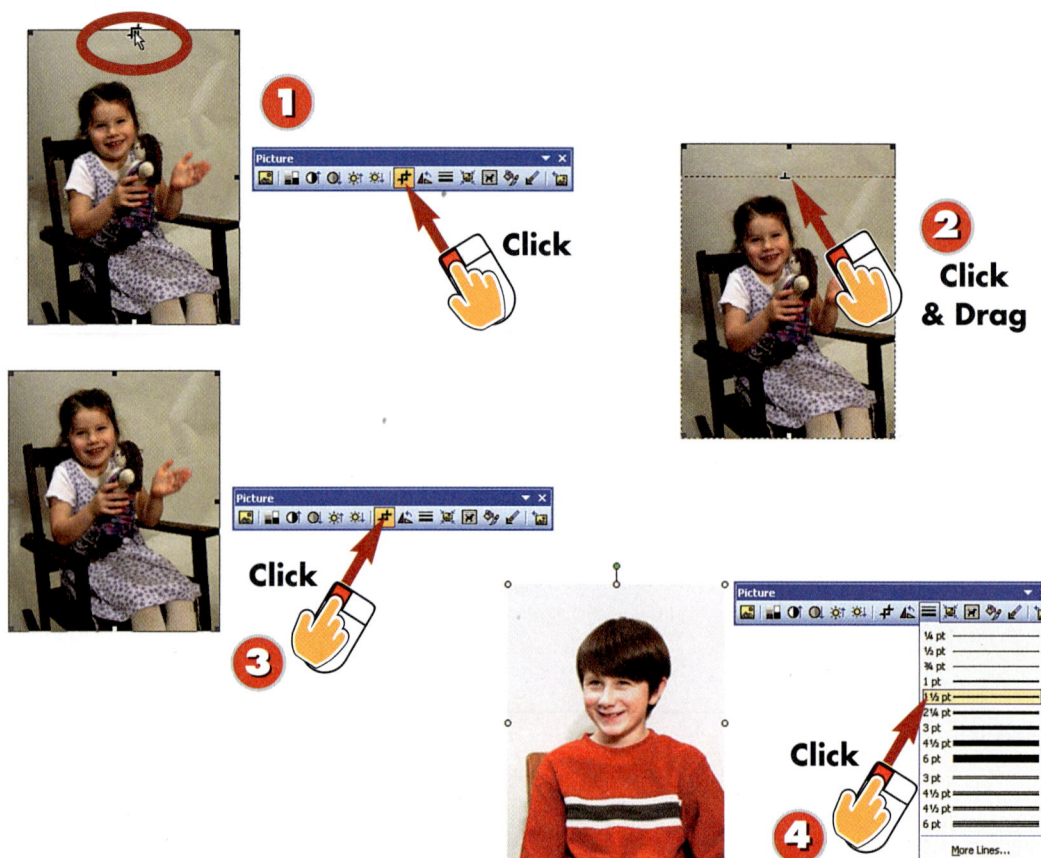

1. To crop an image, select it and click the **Crop** button on the Picture toolbar. A special cropping pointer appears.

2. Drag a selection handle and release the mouse button when the desired portion is cropped out.

3. In this example, the upper part of the image is cropped out. Click the **Crop** button again to turn it off.

4. To add a border to an image, make sure the image is no longer in-line, select it, click the **Line Style** button on the Picture toolbar, and choose a line style from the list that appears.

INTRODUCTION

Word enables you to alter images in a wide variety of ways. In this task, you learn two techniques that will get you started: cropping and adding or removing borders. You crop an image to remove a portion of it. Adding borders around an image gives it definition, while removing borders makes it blend into the surrounding text. You can crop an image regardless of whether it is in-line, but you cannot add a border to an in-line image. (To take your image "out of line," click it and choose a text wrapping option; see steps 1–3 in the preceding task for help.)

TIP

Displaying the Picture Toolbar
If you don't see the Picture toolbar, Open the **View** menu, choose **Toolbars**, and select **Picture**.

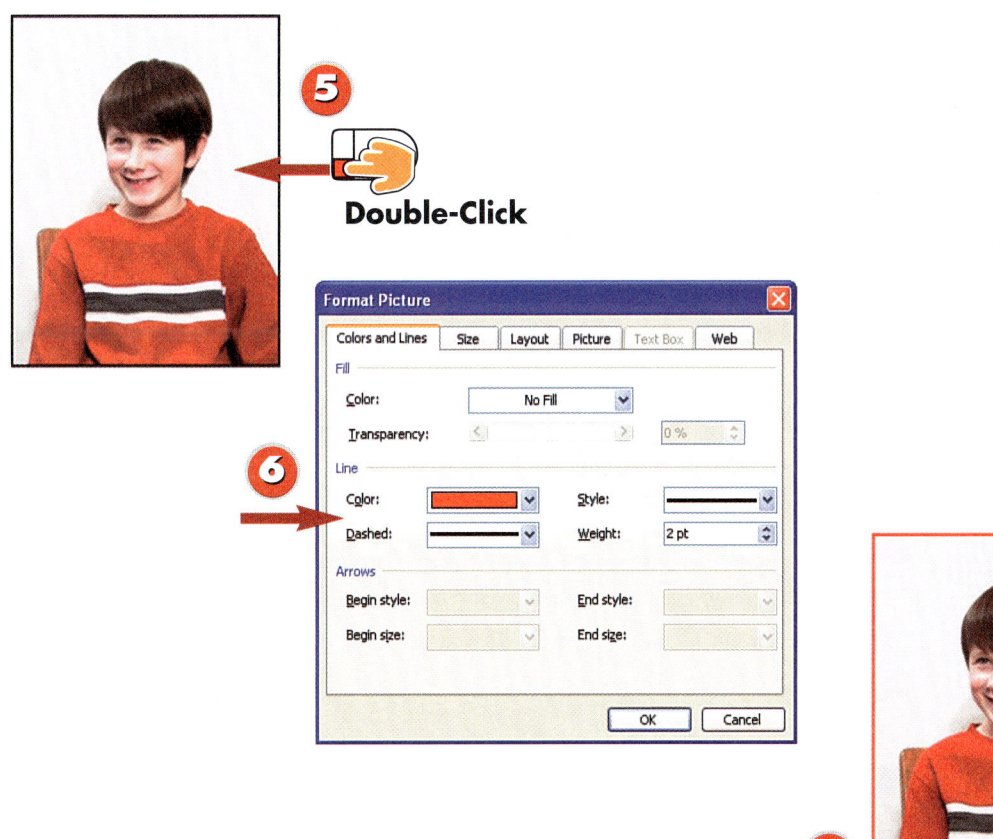

Double-Click

5 Word adds a border to the image. (You may want to deselect the image so that you can see the border more clearly.) To adjust the border's appearance, first double-click the image.

6 The **Format Picture** dialog box opens. Click the **Colors and Lines** tab, choose the desired settings in the **Line** area, and click **OK**.

7 Word modifies the border. (Again, you may want to deselect the image to see the border more clearly.)

End

Removing a Border
To remove a border, double-click the image to display the Format Picture dialog box, click the **Colors and Lines** tab, display the **Color** drop-down list under **Line**, choose **No Line**, and then click **OK**.

Controlling Text Flow Around an Image

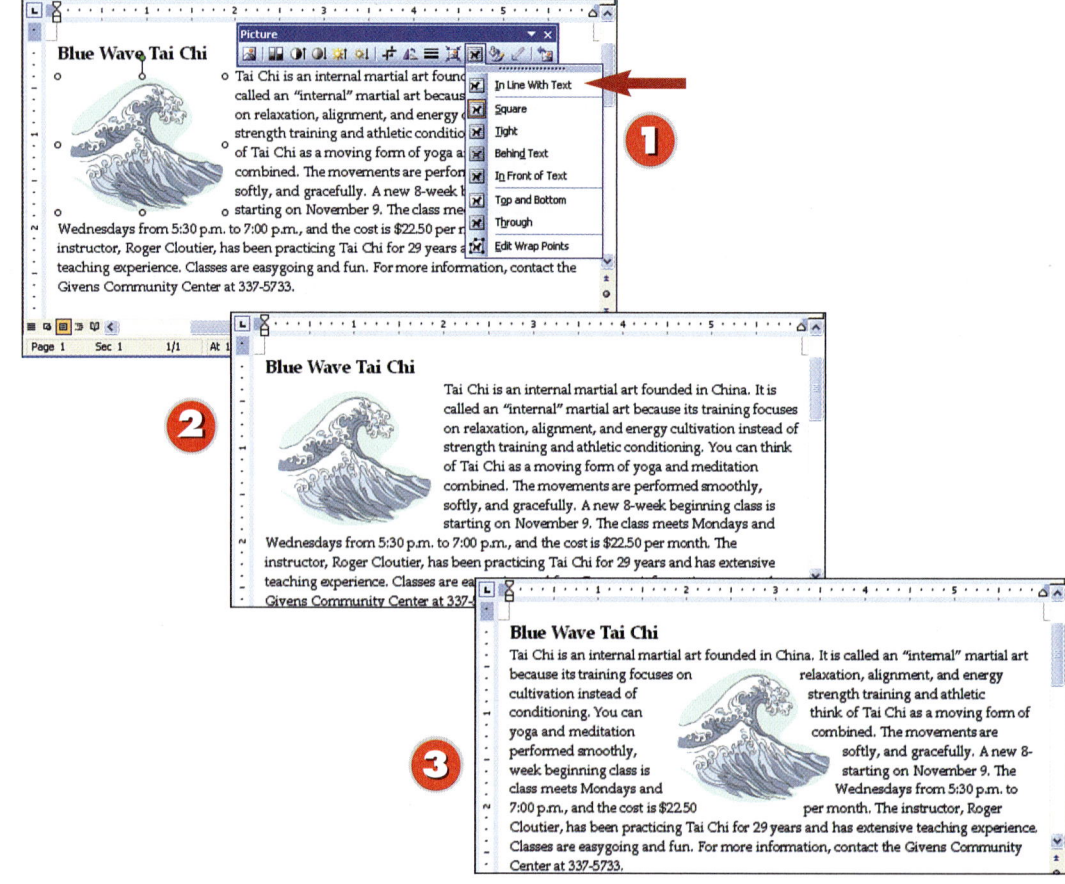

1. To change the way text wraps around your image, select the image, click the **Text Wrapping** button on the Picture toolbar, and click one of the options in the list that appears.

2. The **Square** option wraps the text in a square shape around the image.

3. The **Tight** option wraps the text right up to the outside edges of the image. This option only works with images that have irregular boundaries, such as the clip art image shown here.

INTRODUCTION

Word gives you several options for controlling how text flows around your image. In this task, you see examples of the five most common text-wrapping options. Keep in mind, however, that you can always drag an image around your document regardless of the text wrapping option you choose (refer to "Moving and Sizing an Image" earlier in this part).

 The **Behind Text** option doesn't wrap the text at all; the image is sent behind the text so that the text flows over the image.

 The **In Front of Text** option also doesn't wrap the text; the image appears in front of the text so that the text is not visible behind it.

The **Top and Bottom** option wraps the text above and below the image, but not along its sides.

End

Adding Shapes to Your Document

Start

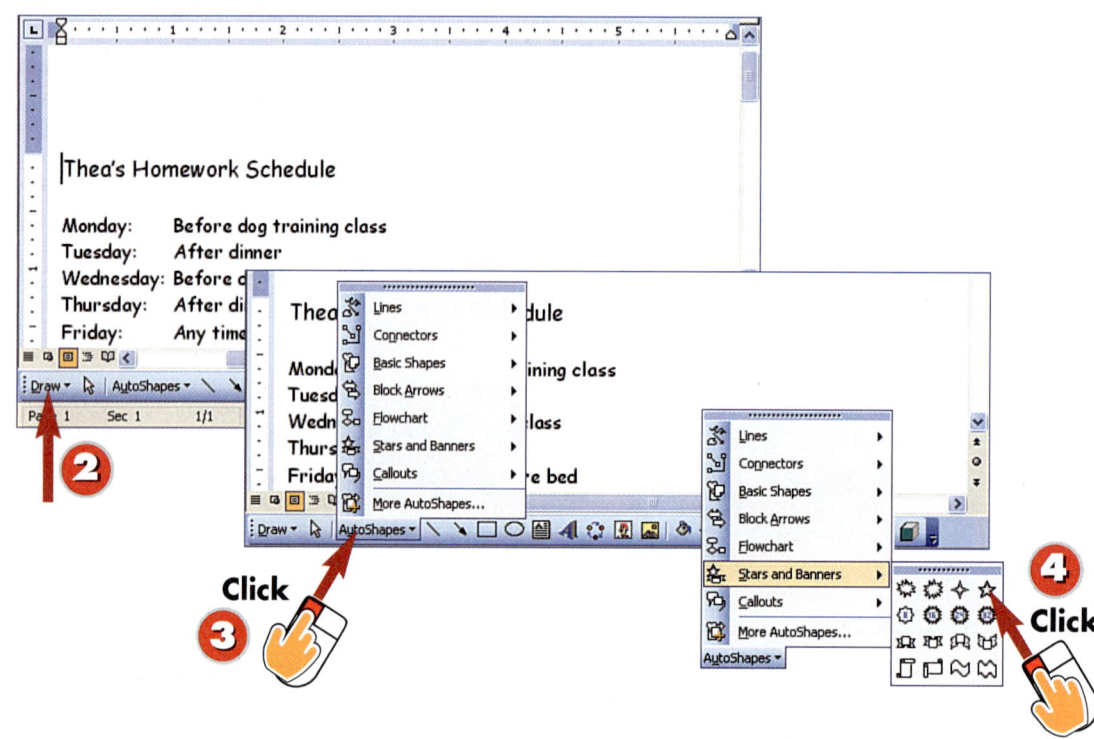

1. Click the **Drawing** button on the Standard toolbar.

2. The Drawing toolbar appears at the bottom of the Word window by default.

3. Click the **AutoShapes** button to display a menu with categories of AutoShapes.

4. Point to a category, and then click the desired shape in the submenu that appears.

INTRODUCTION

Sometimes you don't need a complex image in your document—just something simple, such as an arrow or a box. Word's AutoShapes feature enables you to quickly draw all manner of arrows, rectangles, ovals, and so on. After you have inserted a shape, you can use the methods described in these last two tasks to move and resize it, crop it, and modify its borders. In this task, you add a shape to a document and then change its fill color.

Creating a Perfect Shape
TIP
If you are using the rectangle shape and want to draw a perfect square, hold down the **Shift** key as you drag. This also works with the oval shape to get a perfect circle, the star shape to get a perfectly proportioned star, and so on.

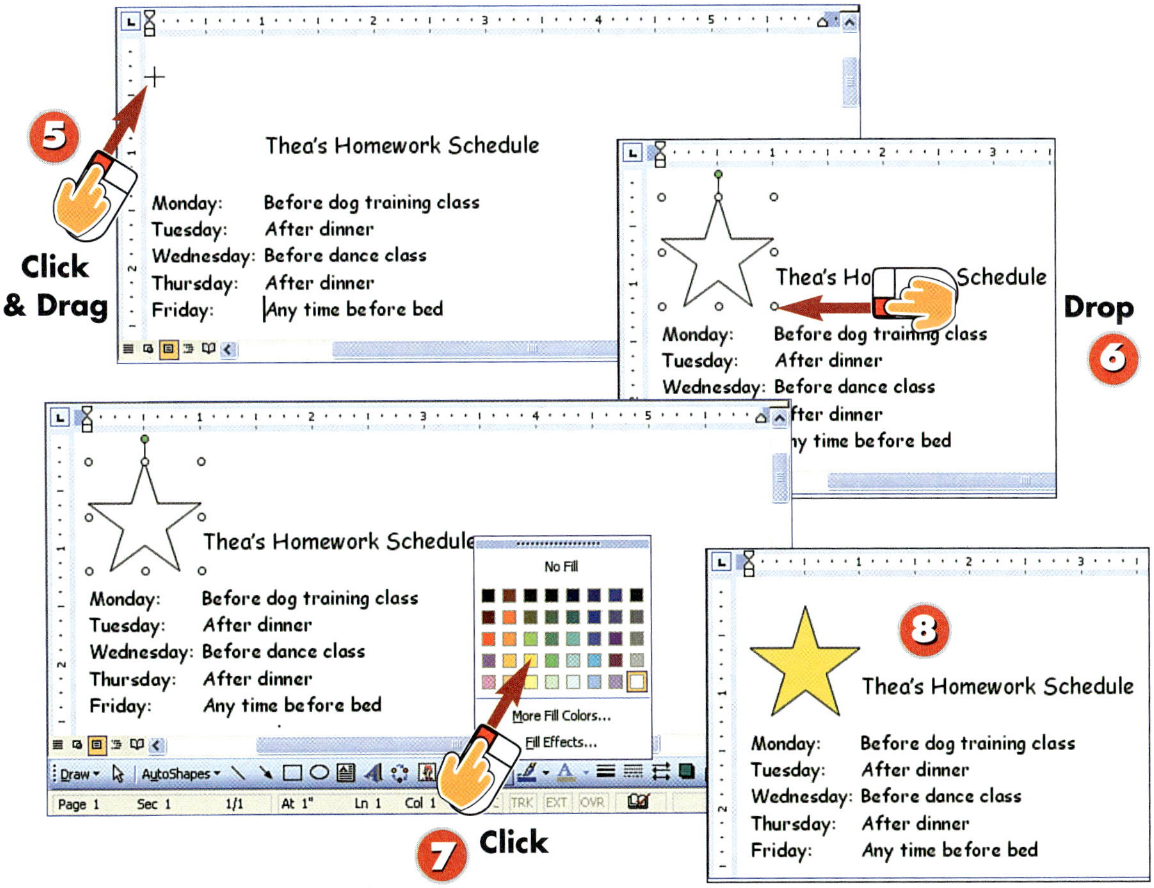

5
Click & Drag
Thea's Homework Schedule
Monday: Before dog training class
Tuesday: After dinner
Wednesday: Before dance class
Thursday: After dinner
Friday: Any time before bed
Drop
6
No Fill
More Fill Colors...
Fill Effects...
7
Click
8

5. Point with the crosshair mouse pointer to the upper-left corner of the area where you want to draw the shape, and drag diagonally down and to the right.
6. Release the mouse button to finish drawing the shape.
7. Keeping the shape selected, click the **down arrow** to the right of the **Fill Color** button in the Drawing toolbar, and click a color.
8. The shape takes on the fill color you chose. (Deselect the shape to see it more clearly.)

End

TIP

Turning Off the Drawing Canvas

By default, Word inserts a *drawing canvas* for drawing shapes. This is not necessary, however, for simple drawings such as the ones described here. To turn the drawing canvas off, open the **Tools** menu and choose **Options**, click the **General** tab, clear the **Automatically create drawing canvas when inserting AutoShapes** check box, and click **OK**. This task assumes that the drawing canvas is turned off.

TIP

Deleting a Shape

If you don't like a shape that you drew, just click it to select it and press the **Delete** key on your keyboard.

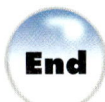

Creating WordArt

Start

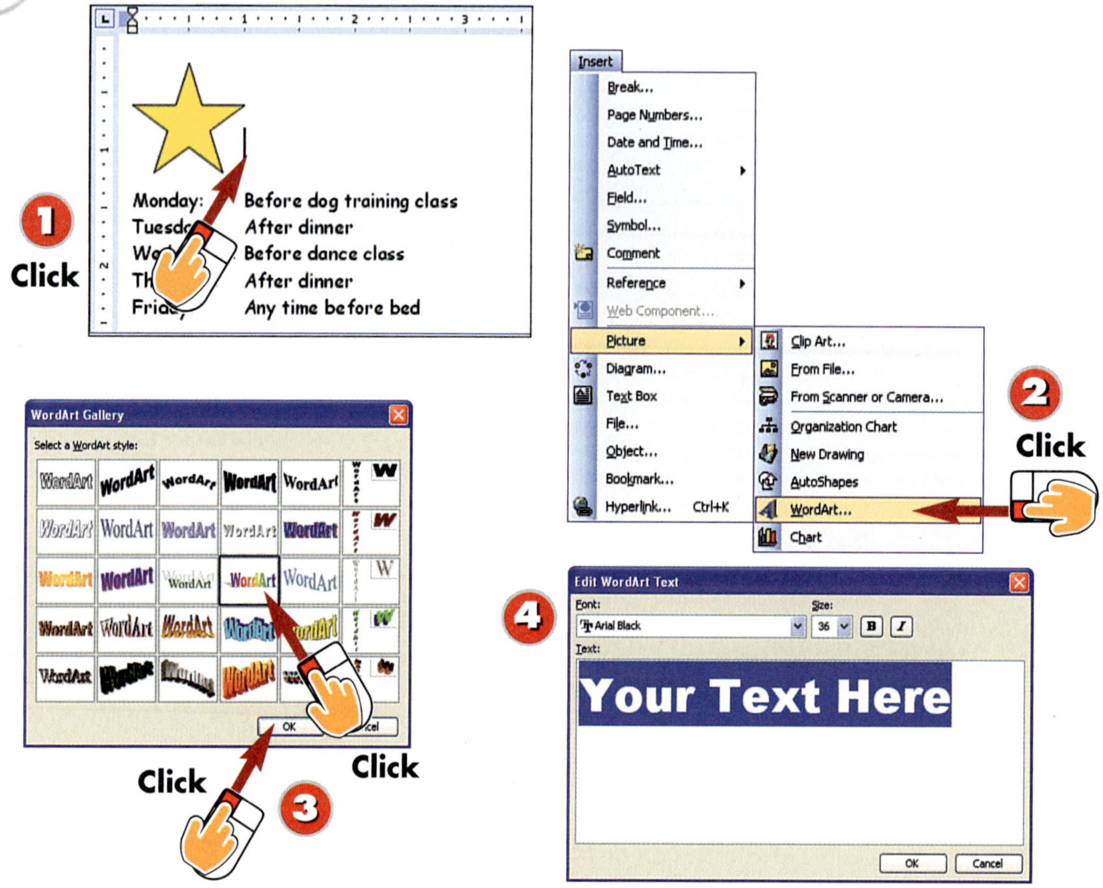

1 **Click**

Monday: Before dog training class
Tuesd...   After dinner
W...   Before dance class
Th...   After dinner
Fri...   Any time before bed

Insert

Break...
Page Numbers...
Date and Time...
AutoText
Field...
Symbol...
Comment
Reference
Web Component...
Picture →   Clip Art...
Diagram...   From File...
Text Box   From Scanner or Camera...
File...   Organization Chart
Object...   New Drawing
Bookmark...   AutoShapes
Hyperlink...   Ctrl+K   WordArt...
    Chart

2 **Click**

WordArt Gallery

Select a WordArt style:

3 **Click**   **Click**

OK

4

Edit WordArt Text

Font: Size:
Arial Black   36   **B** *I*

Text:

Your Text Here

OK   Cancel

1 Click where you want the WordArt image to go.

2 Open the **Insert** menu, choose **Picture**, and select **WordArt**. (If your Drawing toolbar is displayed, you can also click the **Insert WordArt** button on this toolbar.)

3 The WordArt Gallery dialog box opens. Click the look that you want to start with, and click the **OK** button.

4 The Edit WordArt Text window appears.

INTRODUCTION

When you add images to a document, you aren't limited to working with images separate from your text. *WordArt* lets you add flair to your text itself. It's perfect for creating splashy headings and titles. You start with a basic "look" for your word or phrase, and then tweak it to get the exact effect you want. Once you've created a WordArt image, you can use the techniques described earlier in this part to move or resize it, or to add borders.

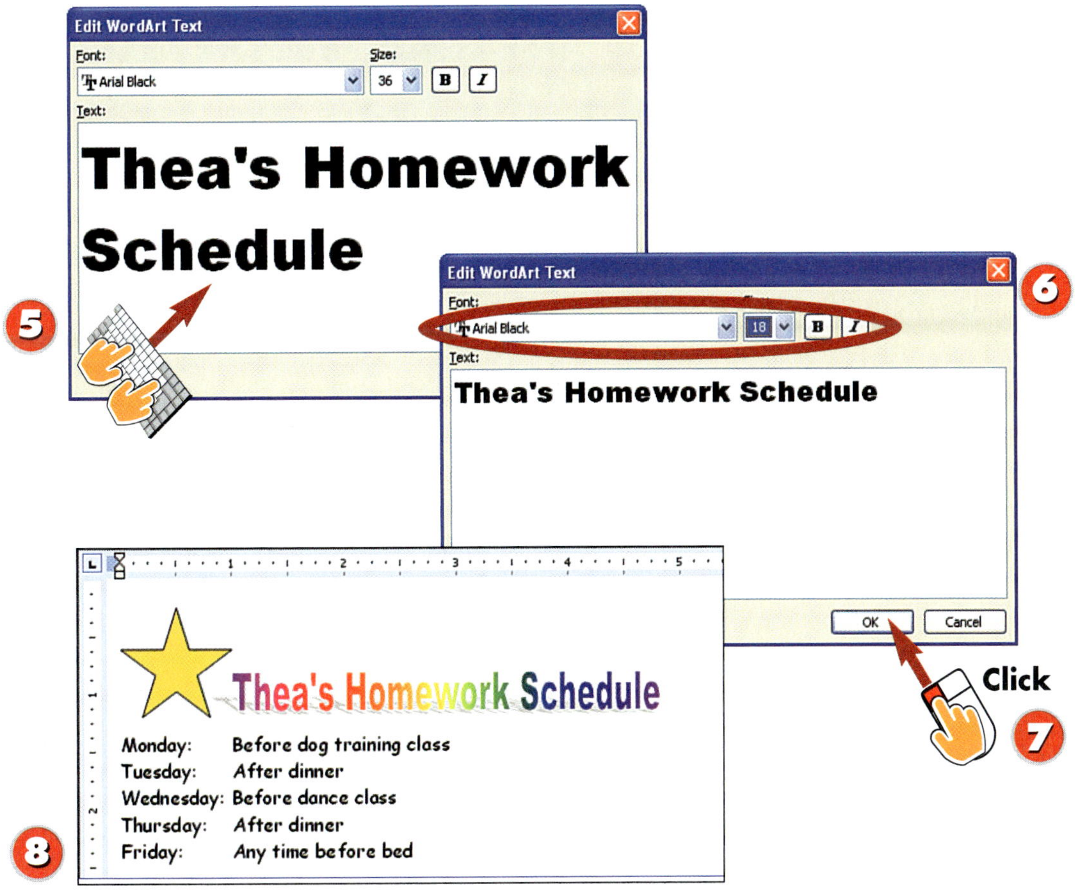

Edit WordArt Text

Font: Arial Black   Size: 36   **B** *I*

Text:

Thea's Homework Schedule

Edit WordArt Text

Font: Arial Black   18   **B** *I*

Text:

Thea's Homework Schedule

OK   Cancel

Click

⭐ **Thea's Homework Schedule**

Monday:	Before dog training class
Tuesday:	After dinner
Wednesday:	Before dance class
Thursday:	After dinner
Friday:	Any time before bed

5 Type the text for your WordArt image, replacing the *Your Text Here* dummy text. (The text won't take on the look you chose in step 3 until it's inserted in your document.)

6 Use the **Font** and **Size** drop-down lists and the **Bold** and **Italic** buttons to make additional adjustments to the text.

7 Click the **OK** button.

8 The WordArt image is inserted in your document.

End

Modifying a WordArt Image
To revise WordArt text or change its appearance after you've created the image, use the WordArt toolbar. This toolbar appears as soon as you insert a WordArt image. If you don't see it, open the **View** menu, choose **Toolbars**, and select **WordArt**.

Performing Mass Mailings

Word's mail-merge feature automates the process of inserting personal information, such as names and addresses, into a document that you want to use in a mass mailing. You can use it to create such documents as personalized form letters for a fundraising campaign, cover letters for a batch of resumes, or marketing letters for publicity packages. Not only that, you can also use mail merge to print envelopes or labels to go with your letters. You should follow the steps in the first seven tasks in this part (from "Starting the Main Document" to "Merging the Documents") in sequence. Each task picks up where the previous one left off. Once you've run through these seven tasks a time or two, you'll have no problem following the instructions in the last four tasks to merge your envelopes or labels.

A Mail-Merge Main Document

Mail Merge toolbar

Merge field

Merge field

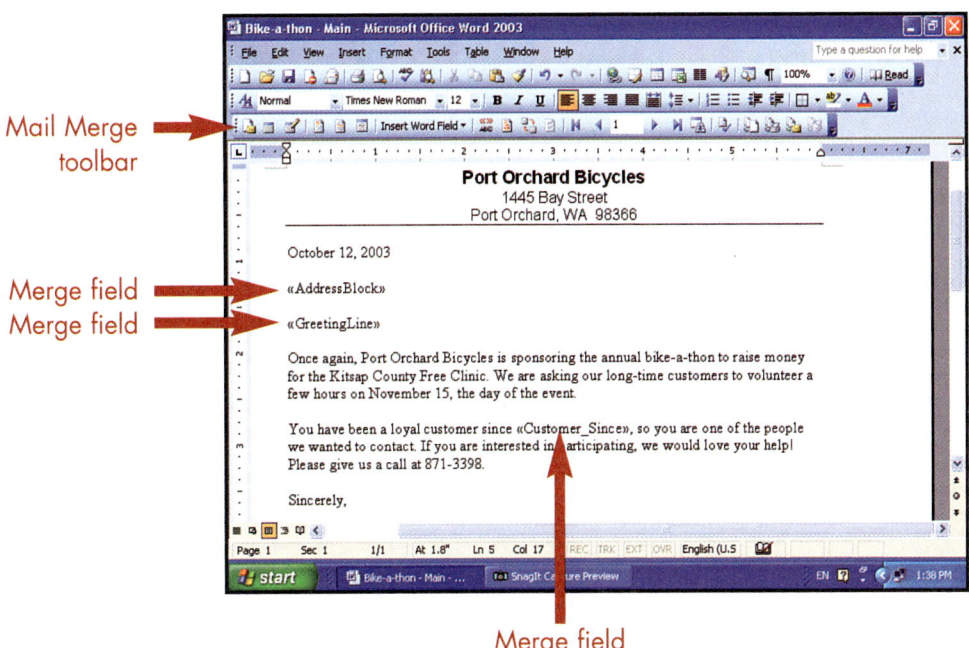

Merge field

Starting the Main Document

Start

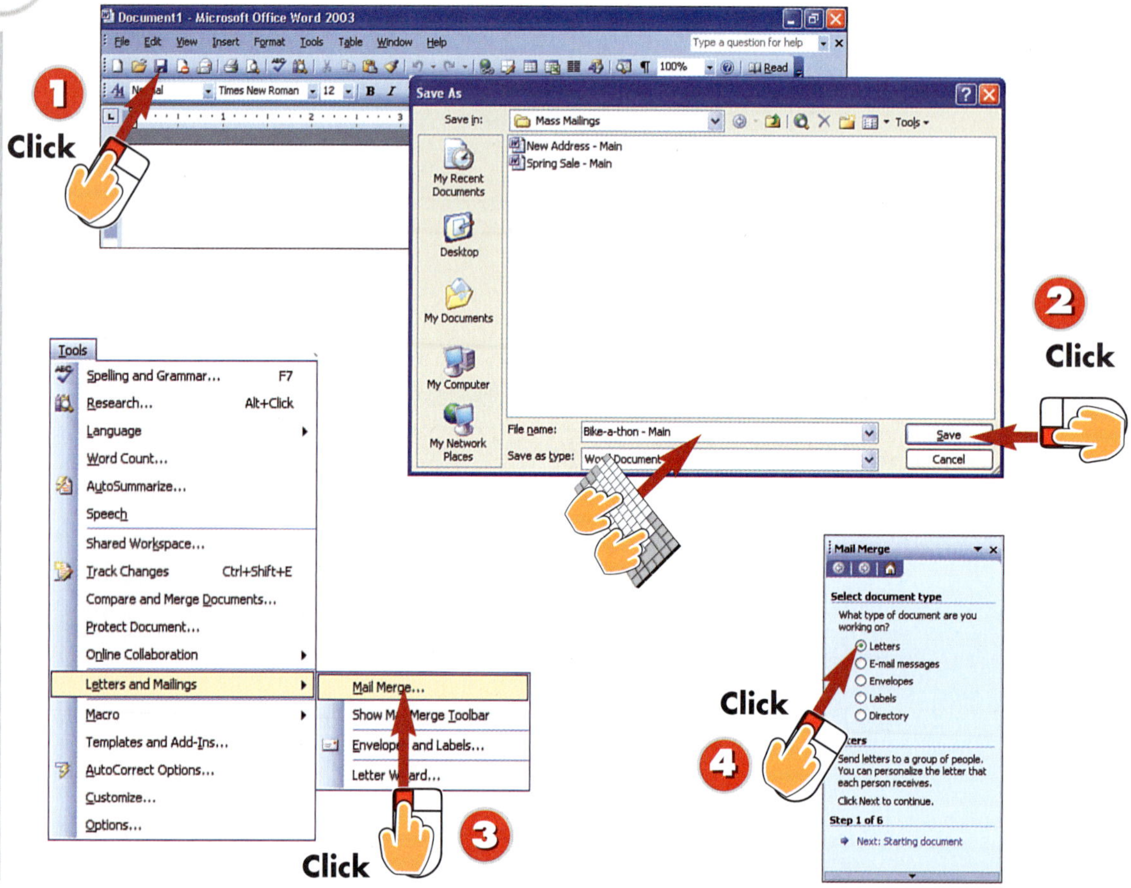

1 **Click**

2 **Click**

3 **Click**

4 **Click**

Click

1. After you start a new, blank document, click the **Save** button on the Standard toolbar.

2. Locate the folder where you want to save the document, give the document a name that ends with **Main**, and click **Save**.

3. Open the **Tools** menu, choose **Letters and Mailings**, and select **Mail Merge** to display the Mail Merge task pane.

4. Click the **Letters** option button in the Mail Merge task pane to select it.

In this phase of the mail-merge process, you simply tell Word which document you want to use as the *main document*. You can either open an existing main document or start a new one. If you start a new one, as described in these steps, you don't have to type any of the document now; you simply save a blank document. In "Completing the Main Document" later in this part, you come back to the main document and enter both regular text and special *merge fields*, telling Word where to insert each piece of information from the data source.

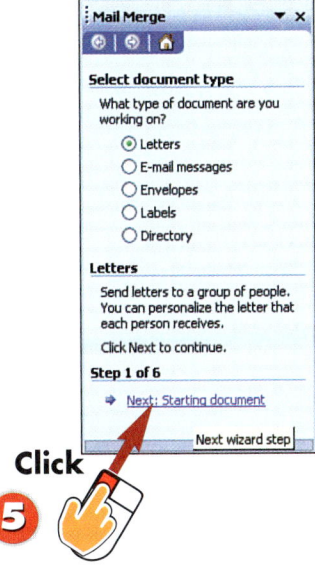

Click

5

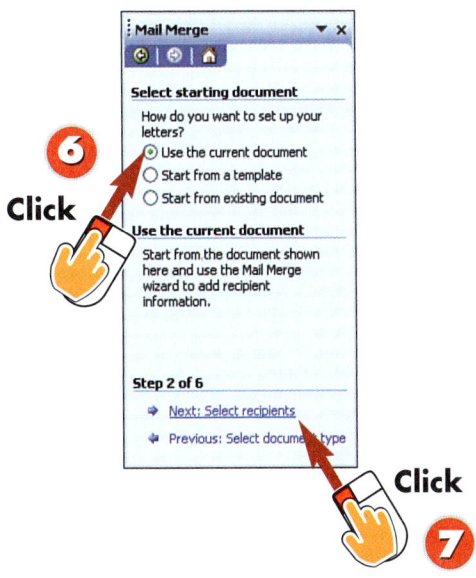

6

Click

Click

7

5 Scroll down if necessary to display the bottom of the task pane, and click **Next: Starting document**.

6 Click the **Use the current document** option button to select it.

7 Scroll down if necessary to display the bottom of the task pane, and click **Next: Select recipients**. Continue to the next task.

End

Repeating Wizard Steps

TIP

As you are working your way through the Mail Merge wizard, at any point you can click the **Previous** link at the bottom of the task pane to return to a previous step. When you are finished redoing a particular step, click the **Next** link to return to where you were.

Choosing the Fields for Your Data Source

Start

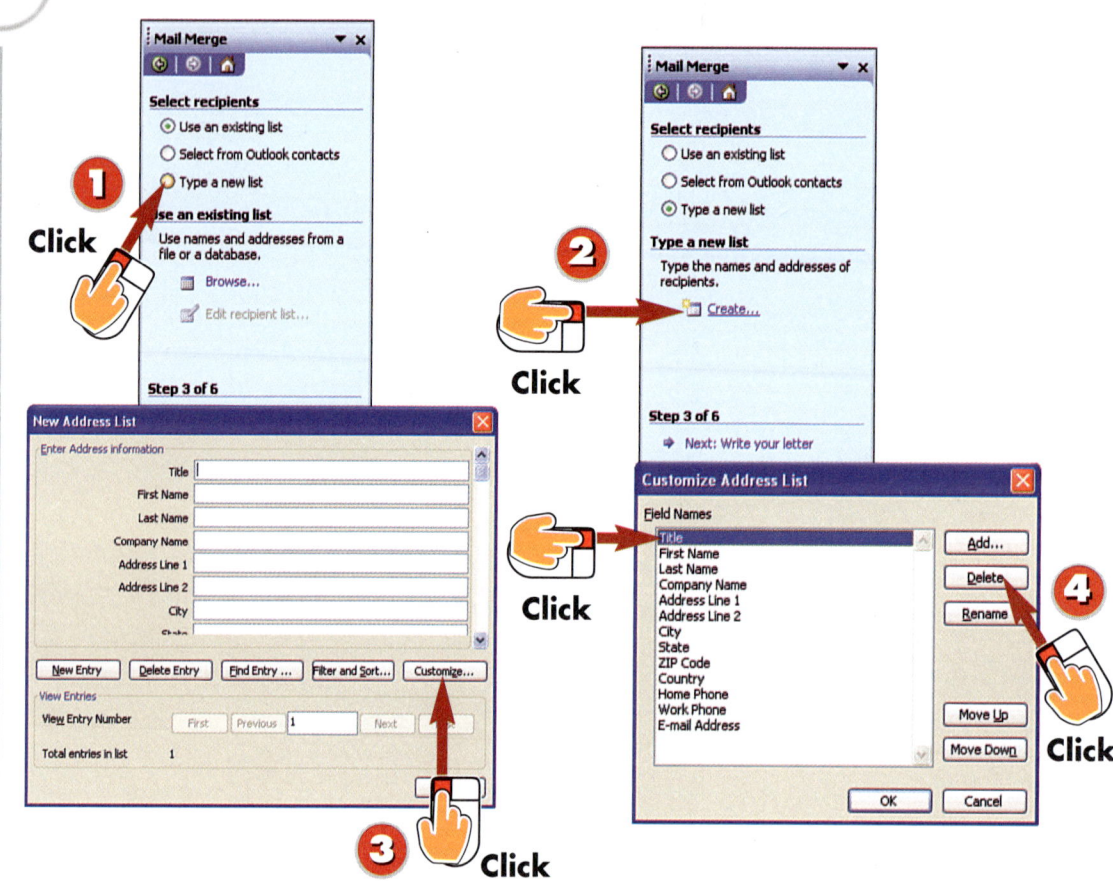

1. Click the **Type a new list** option button in the Mail Merge task pane to select it.

2. Click **Create** to open the New Address List dialog box.

3. Each line in the New Address List dialog box represents a field. Click the **Customize** button to add or remove fields.

4. In the Customize Address List dialog box, delete any fields you won't use by selecting them one by one, clicking the **Delete** button, and clicking **Yes** to confirm the deletion.

In this phase of the mail-merge process, you tell Word which document you want to use as your *data source*. You can create a new one or open an existing one. You learn how to create a new one here. In "Beginning an Envelope Mail Merge" and "Beginning a Label Mail Merge" later in this part, you learn how to open an existing data source. The key step in creating a data source is telling Word which *fields*, or pieces of information, you want to store. Typical fields are title, first name, last name, company, address, city, state, zip code, and so on.

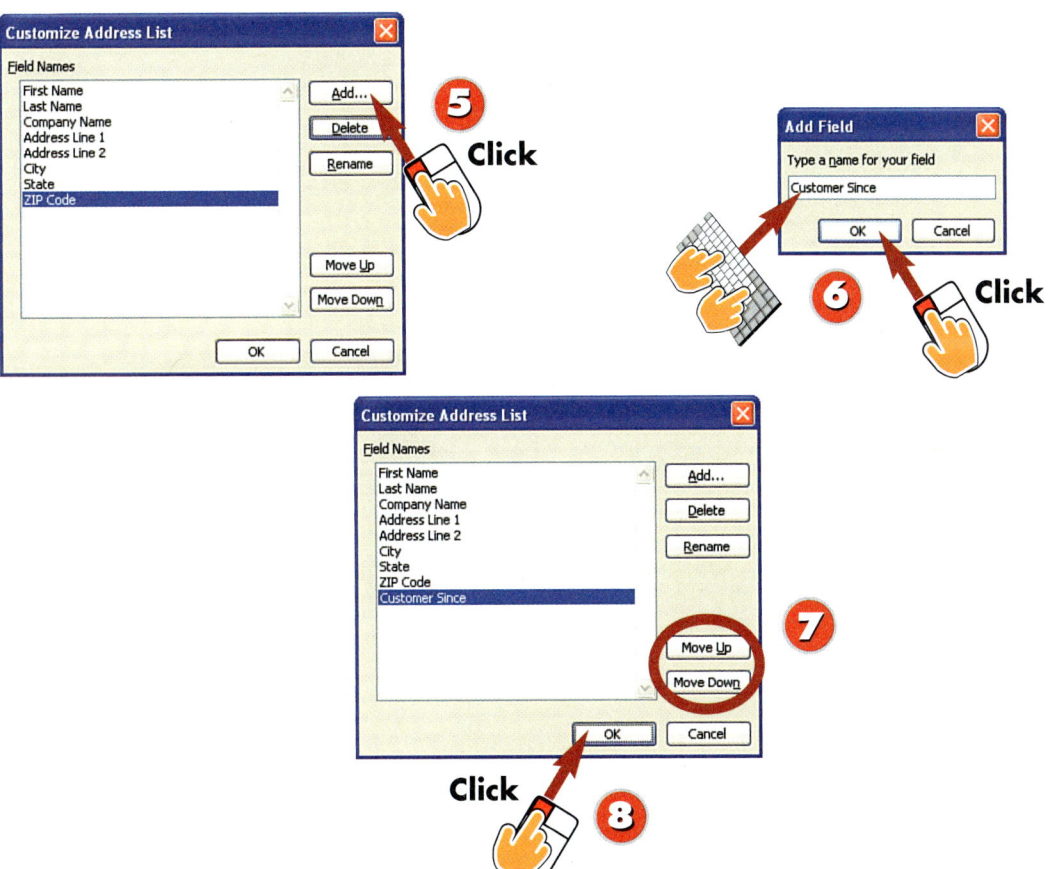

5 To add a field you'd like to use, click the **Add** button.

6 In the Add Field dialog box, type a name for your field and click the **OK** button.

7 To change the order of the fields as they appear in the New Address List dialog box, click the field you want to move and then click the **Move Up** or **Move Down** button.

8 When you are finished customizing your fields, click **OK**, and then continue to the next task.

Using Other Types of Fields

You can store other types of information in your data source besides people's names and addresses. In this task, for example, a field called Customer Since is created to store the year that the customer first did business with the store. You can use merge fields anywhere you like in your main document. The Customer Since field will be used in the body of the letter to personalize it (see "Completing the Main Document" later in this part).

Create Your Data Source

By default, Word stores your data source in an Access database. If Access isn't installed on your computer, Word still saves your data source in Access database format and can still read the file.

Entering Records into the Data Source

Start

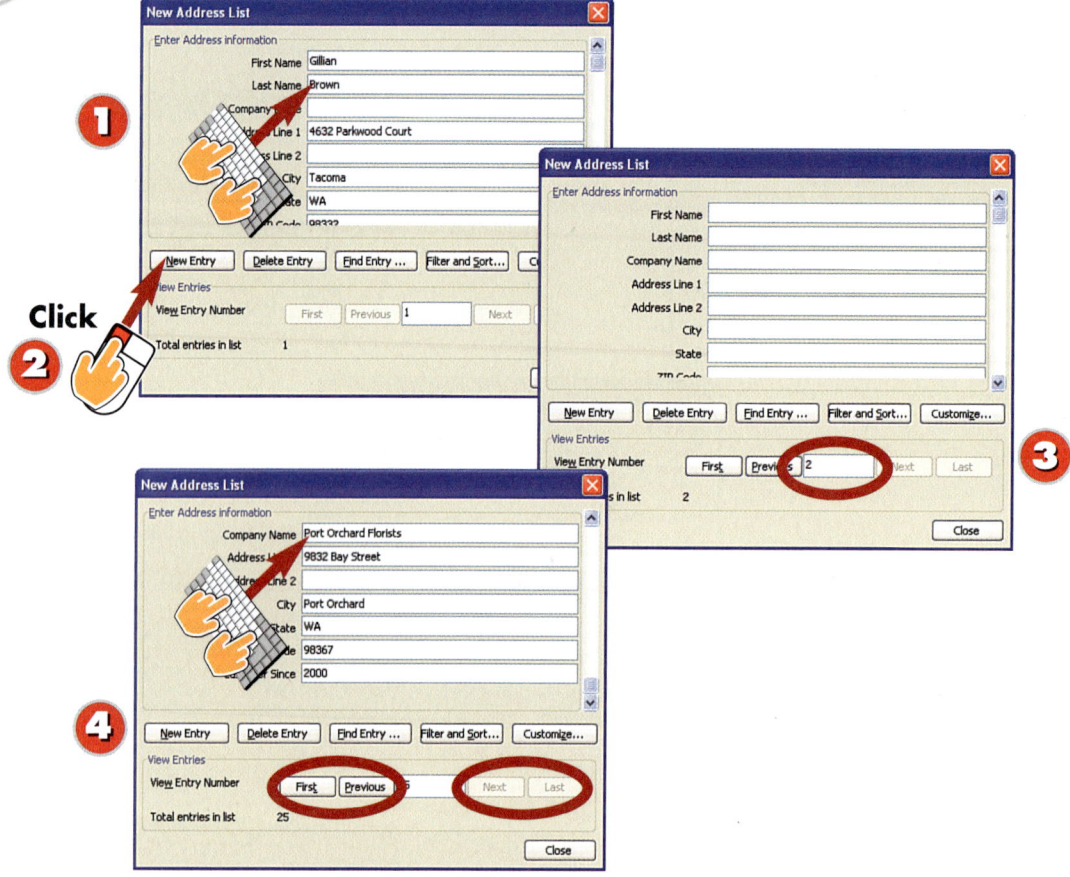

Click

1. Enter the information for the first person in your list in the New Address List dialog box, using the **Tab** key to move from field to field.

2. When you are ready to add the next entry, click the **New Entry** button.

3. Word presents a set of blank fields to enable you to enter another person's information. The number in the View Entry Number text box lists the current record number.

4. Repeat steps 1–3 to enter all the addresses in your list. Use the **First**, **Previous**, **Next**, and **Last** buttons if you need to review entries you've already typed.

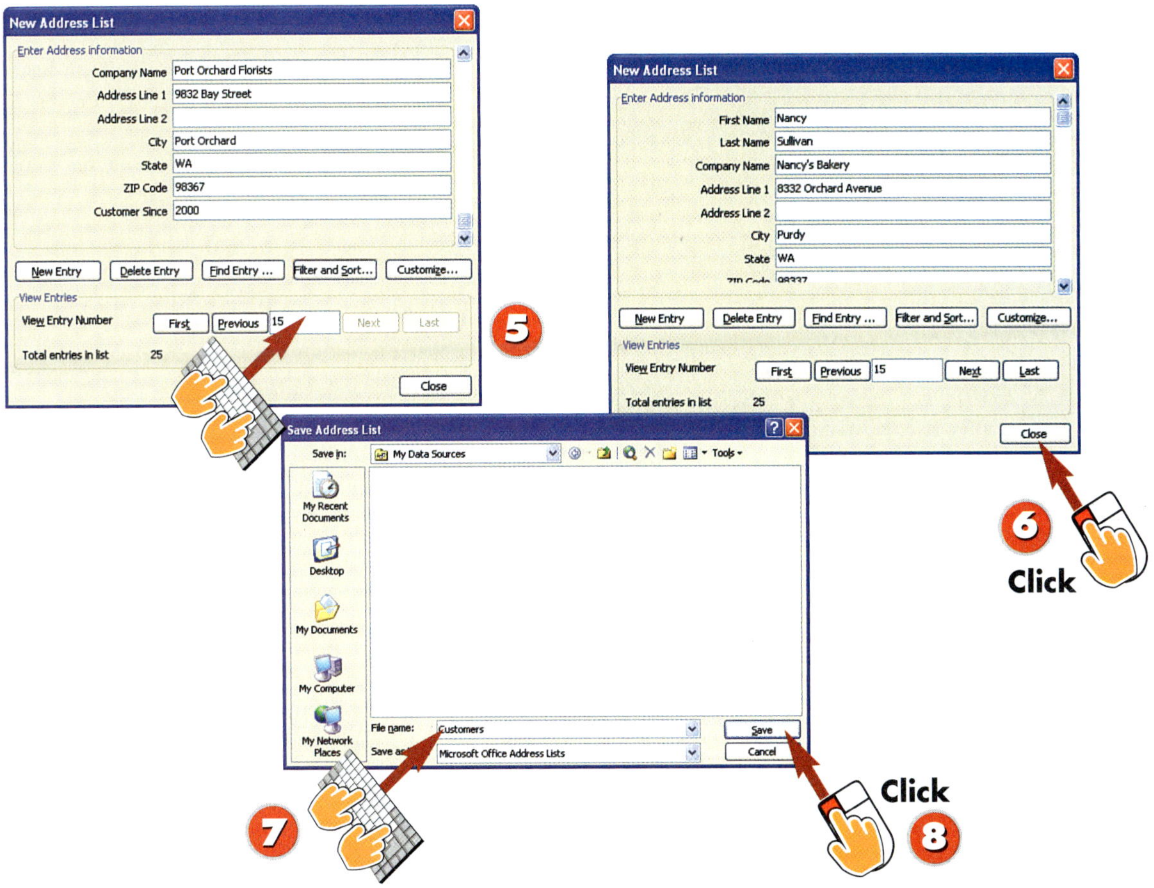

5 To go to a particular record, type the record number in the **View Entry Number** text box and press **Enter**. (The total number of records appears in the lower-left corner of the dialog box.)

6 When you've finished entering all the records, click the **Close** button.

7 Word opens the Save Address List dialog box with the My Data Sources folder selected. Type a name for your data source in the **File name** text box.

8 Click the **Save** button, and continue to the next task.

End

Saving the Data Source?
The default location for Word data source files is the My Data Sources folder (see step 7). This is a convenient location to save your data sources. However, you can save them in any folder you like.

Editing Your Data Source
The easiest way to edit your data source is to open it through the main document. First, open the **File** menu and choose **Open** to open the main document. Then, click the **Open Data Source** button on the Mail Merge toolbar (see "Completing the Main Document," later in this part) to display the Select Data Source dialog box. Navigate to your data source, select it, and click the **Open** button. When you are finished editing your records, click **OK**.

Sorting and Editing the Recipient List

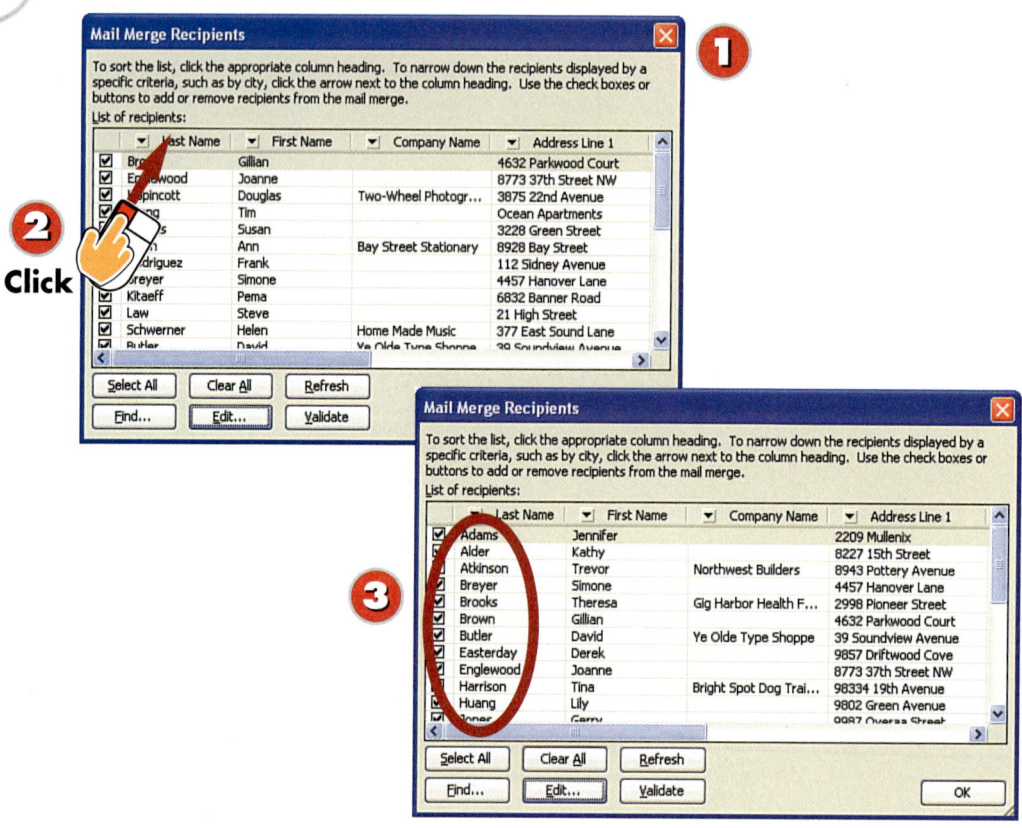

Click

1. Word presents the Mail Merge Recipients dialog box. Each row is one record, and the fields are arranged in columns across the top of the dialog box.

2. To sort the records by a particular field, click the gray column label.

3. The records are now sorted in the order you specified.

INTRODUCTION

After you have entered all the records in a data source (or opened an existing data source), Word gives you an opportunity to sort the list by any of its fields or to remove people from the mail merge.

TIP

Other Features in the Mail Merge Recipients Dialog Box

The Mail Merge Recipients dialog box also contains features that enable you to *filter* your list in a variety of ways. For example, you can choose to restrict your mail merge to people who live in a particular city or zip code. For more information, search Word's help system for the keywords **select records to include in a mail merge**.

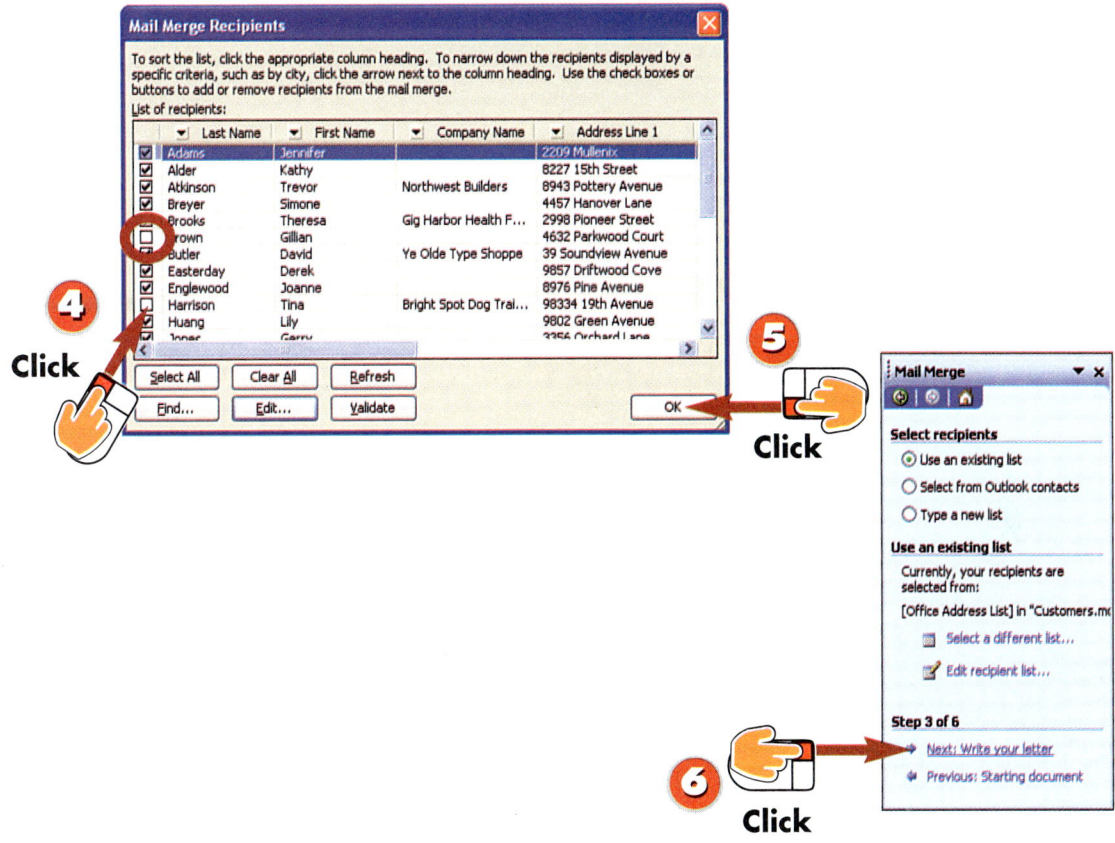

4 Clear the check boxes for any people who you do not want included in the merge.

5 When you are finished, click **OK**.

6 In the Mail Merge task pane, click **Next: Write your letter** and continue to the next task.

End

Editing Records

If you see any records that are incorrect, you can click the **Edit** button in the Mail Merge Recipients dialog box to display a dialog box where you can edit the record. When you have made your changes, click the **Close** button in the dialog box to return to the Mail Merge Recipients dialog box.

Completing the Main Document

Start

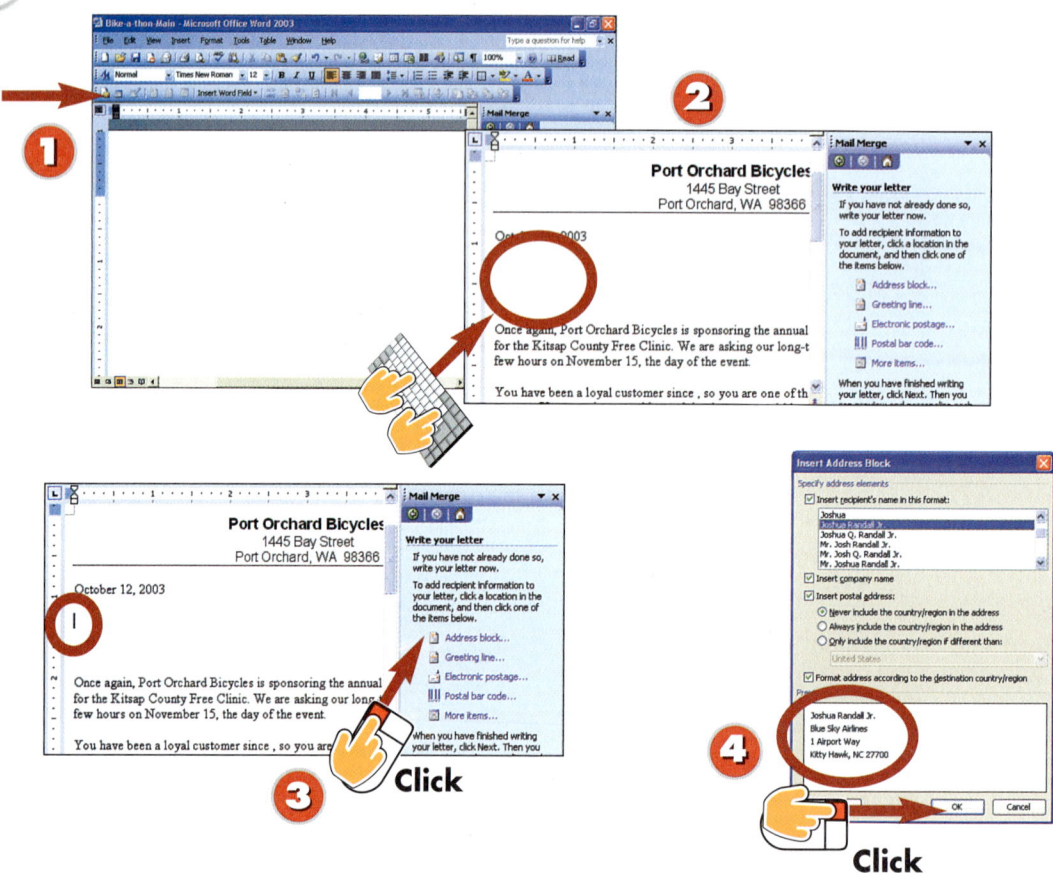

Click

Click

---

① Word displays your main document. Notice the Mail Merge toolbar that appears in the Word window.

② Type and format the letter, leaving blank lines for the recipient's address block and the greeting line.

③ Place the insertion point on the blank line for the recipient's address block, and click **Address block** in the Mail Merge task pane.

④ The Insert Address Block dialog box opens. Make the desired selections to specify how the address block will look. When the preview looks right, click **OK**.

INTRODUCTION

In this phase of the mail-merge process, you finish the main document. This entails typing and formatting the text, and inserting the merge fields that tell Word where to insert the data from your data source.

TIP

Inserting Additional Fields
In addition to the address block and greeting line fields, you can also insert fields for electronic postage, the postal bar code, and other items. If you choose the **More items** link, the Insert Merge Field dialog box opens, enabling you to select other miscellaneous fields in your data source. This link was used to insert the Customer Since code shown in step 7 of this task.

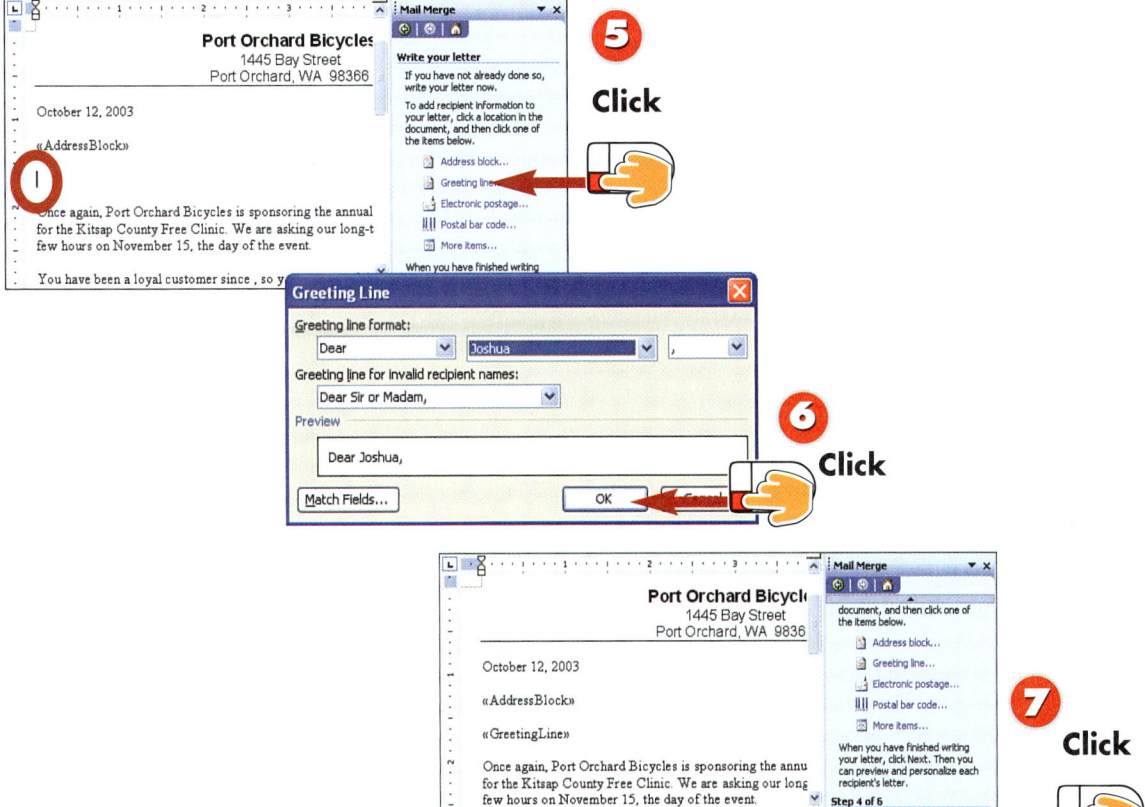

5 Word inserts the address block field in your document. Click where you want to insert the greeting line, and then click **Greeting line** in the Mail Merge task pane.

6 The Greeting Line dialog box opens. Specify how you want your greeting line to look, and click **OK**.

7 The greeting line field is inserted. Save your letter, and then click **Next: Preview your letters** at the bottom of the Mail Merge task pane. Continue to the next task.

End

Editing Fields

After you've inserted a field in your document, you can always choose different options. Right-click **field** and choose **Edit <field name>** (the name will vary). The appropriate dialog box will open to enable you to change your field options.

Restoring a Main Document to a Normal Word Document

If you accidentally used the wrong document for your main document and want to restore it to a normal Word document, click the **Main document setup** button on the Mail Merge toolbar (which automatically appears when you open your main document), choose **Normal Word document** in the **Main Document Type** dialog box, and click **OK**.

Previewing Your Merged Letters

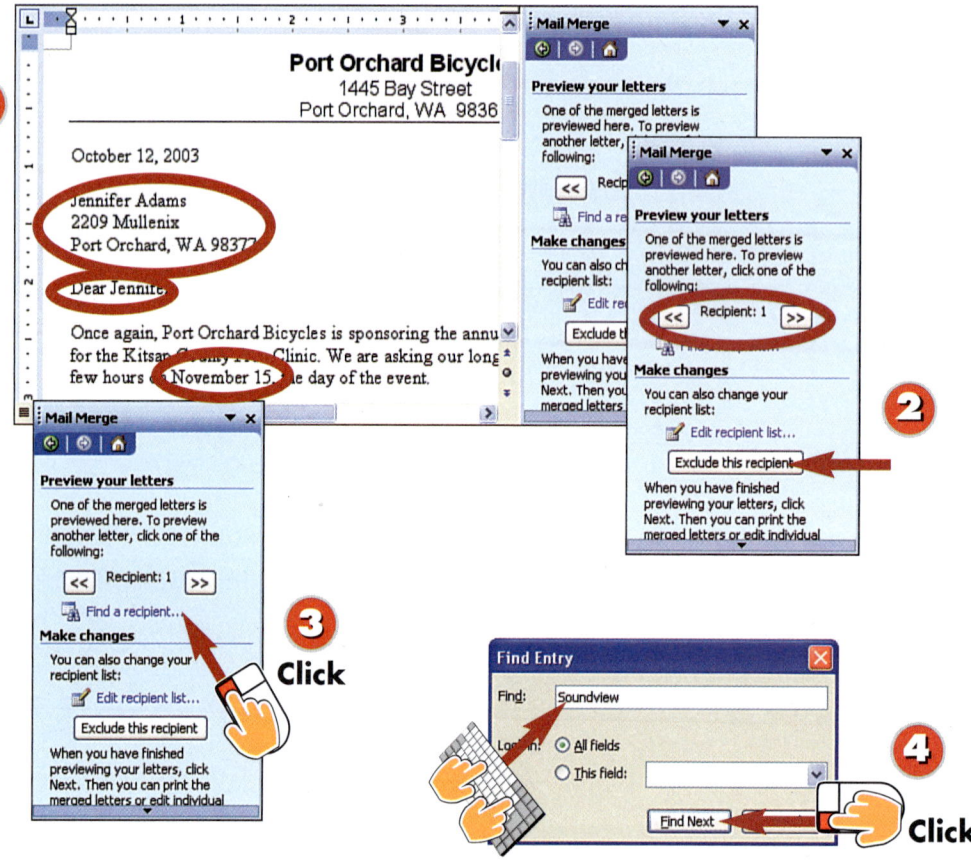

Click

Click

1. Word displays a preview of the first merged letter for you to examine. The merge fields are replaced with data from your data source.

2. Click the **arrows** in the Mail Merge task pane to view your letters one by one. To exclude a letter from the merge, click **Exclude this recipient**.

3. Click **Find a recipient** if there is a particular person whose merged information you want to review. The Find Entry dialog box opens.

4. Type some text that you know appears in the person's letter, such as the name of the person's street. Click **Find Next**.

At this step in the mail-merge process, Word allows you to see what your letters will look like when they are merged. You can browse through the previewed letters, or use the Find feature to jump to a particular merged letter you want to view. In addition, you can exclude particular records from your merge. If you find problems when previewing the letters, you can fix them before you actually run the merge.

Fixing a Problem in Your Main Document

If you see the same problem in every letter (for example, a field is in the wrong location, or it contains a typo), go back in the *Write your letter* step of the wizard, fix the main document, and then return to this step.

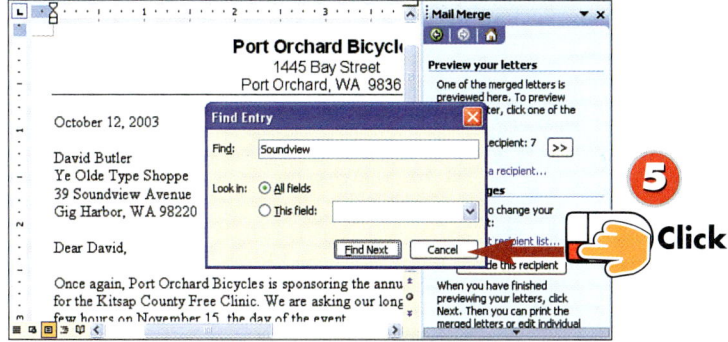

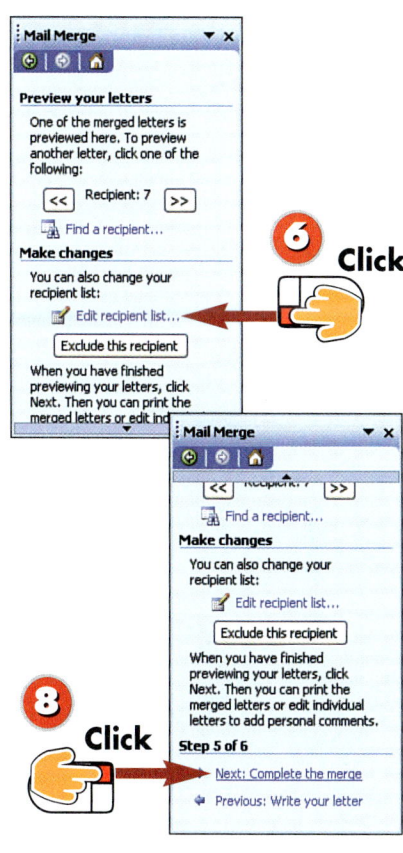

Click

Click

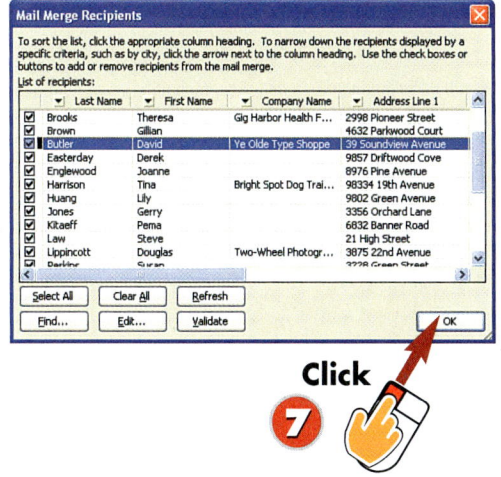

Click

Click

5   The letter to that recipient appears. When you are finished searching for particular recipients, click the Find Entry dialog box's **Cancel** button to close it.

6   If you see incorrect data in one of your letters or want to change the sort order, click **Edit recipient list** to display the Mail Merge Recipients dialog box.

7   Make any changes in this dialog box (refer to "Sorting and Editing the Recipient List" earlier in this part). When you're finished, click **OK**.

8   When you are finished previewing your letters, click **Next: Complete the merge** at the bottom of the Mail Merge task pane, and continue to the next task.

End

Speeding the Search for a Particular Letter
Notice that the Find Entry dialog box you use to locate a particular person's letter contains a **This field** option button. If you know the name of the field in which the text you typed in the Find field appears, click the **This field** option, and then select the desired field in the accompanying drop-down list.

Running the Merge

Start

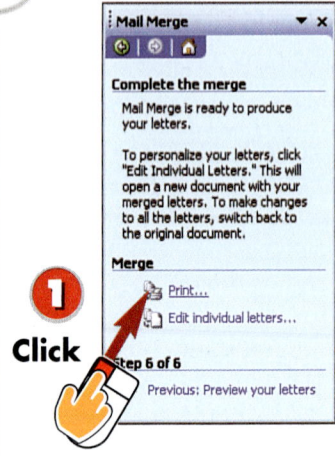

Click

Click

Click

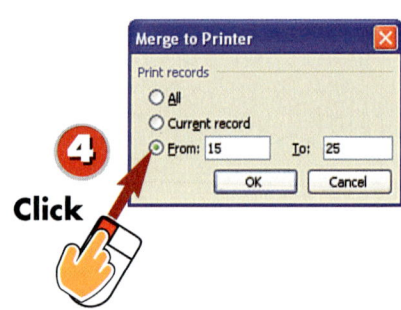

Click

1 Click the **Print** link in the Mail Merge task pane if you are sure that all of your letters are ready to be printed. They will be sent to the printer without appearing onscreen.

2 In the Merge to Printer dialog box, click the **All** option button if you want to print all of your records.

3 If you only want to print the letter that's onscreen now, click the **Current record** option button.

4 To print a particular set of letters, enter the beginning and ending record numbers in the **From** and **To** boxes. Then click **OK** to merge and print the letters.

In this final phase of the mail-merge process, you merge the main document with the data source to produce your form letters. In these steps, you can choose to print the merge letters as they are merged without leaving them onscreen (steps 1–4), or merge all of them to a new document so that you can make any further edits before printing (steps 5–8).

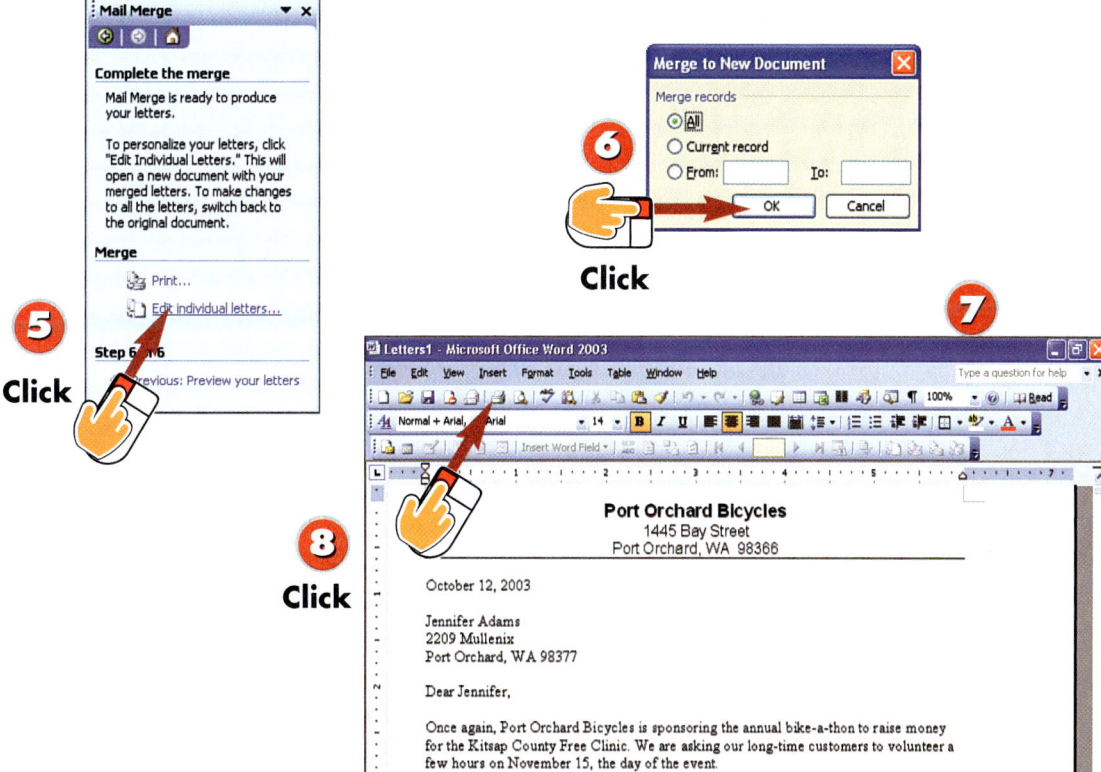

5 To create a document containing the merged letters, click the **Edit individual letters** link in the Mail Merge task pane.

6 The Merge to New Document dialog box appears with options exactly like the Merge to Printer dialog box (see steps 2–4). When you've made your selection, click **OK**.

7 Word performs the merge and displays the merged letters onscreen in a single document titled Letters1. Each letter begins on a new page.

8 Click the **Print** button on the Standard toolbar to print the letters.

Running the Same Merge Again

There is usually no need to save the letters you generate in a mail merge, because you can always merge the same main document and data source to regenerate them. Furthermore, running the merge again ensures that you merge in the most current information from your data source. When you want to run the same merge in the future, open the main document and click the **Merge to New Document** button or **Merge to Printer** button at the right end of the Mail Merge toolbar. In contrast, you *do* need to save your main document if you want to use it in the future.

Beginning an Envelope Mail Merge

Start

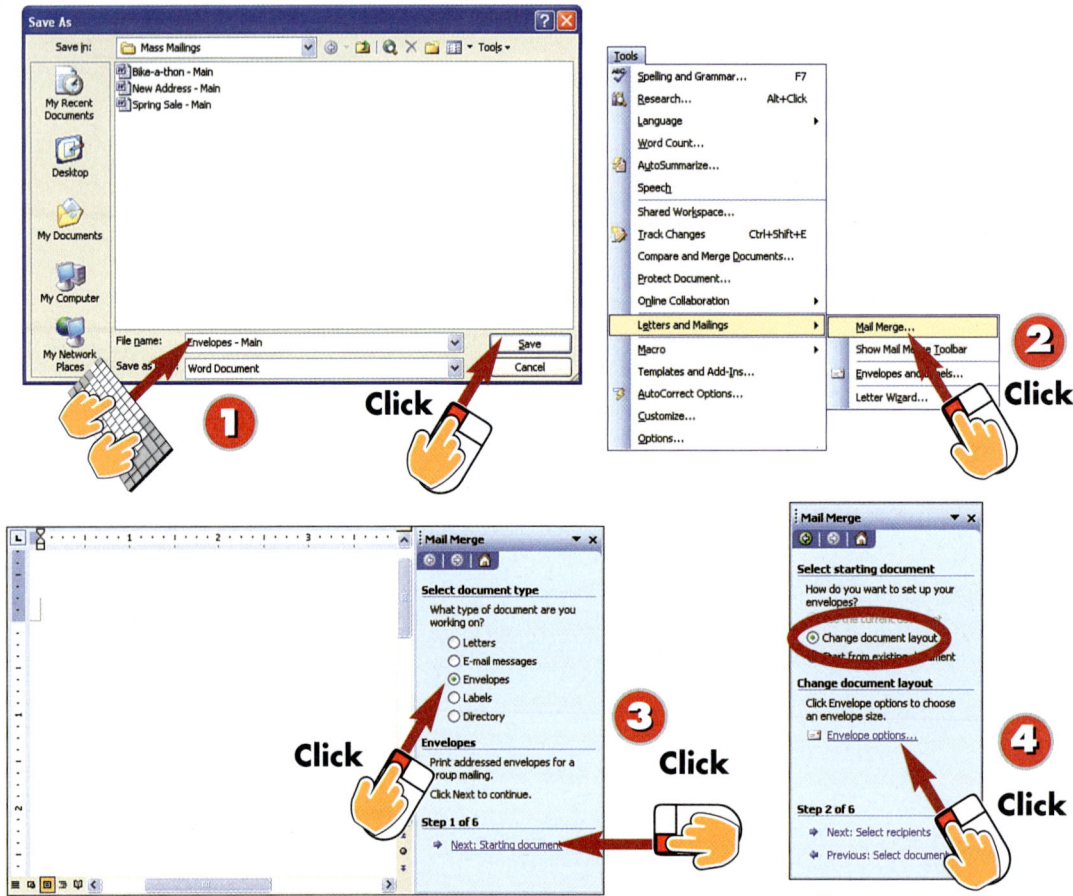

Click ... **①**

Click ... **②**

Click ... **③**

Click ... **④**

---

① Start a new, blank document and save it with a name that ends with **Main**.

② Open the **Tools** menu, choose **Letters and Mailings**, and select **Mail Merge** to display the Mail Merge task pane.

③ Click the **Envelopes** option button in the Mail Merge task pane, and then click **Next: Starting document** at the bottom of the task pane.

④ Keep the **Change document layout** option button marked, and click the **Envelope options** link.

The general steps for merging envelopes are the same as for merging letters (although the details are somewhat different). Consequently, you'll find it helpful to practice a few mail merges with letters before proceeding with this task and the next. Also note that these tasks assume that you already have a data source, so you'll open an existing one rather than creating a new one.

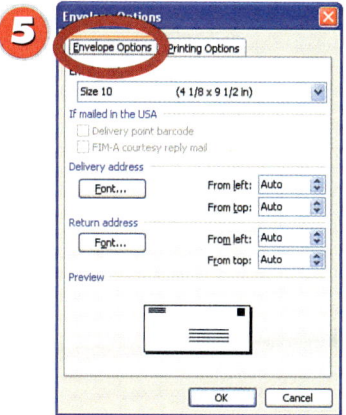
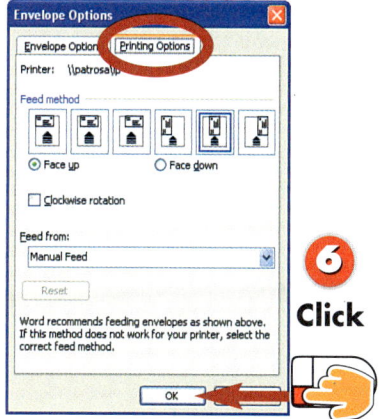

Click

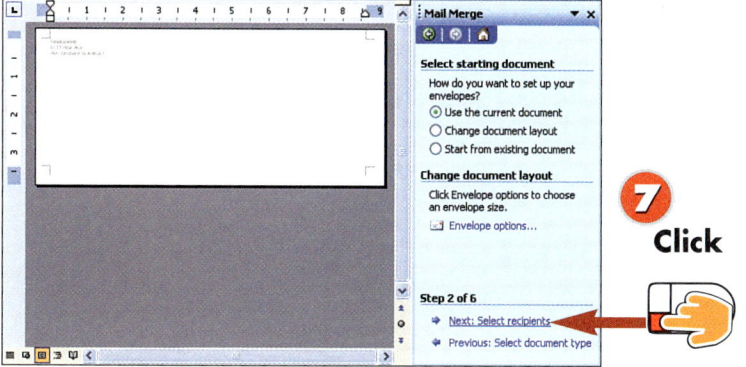
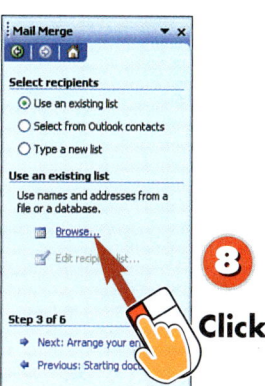

Click

Click

5 In the Envelope Options tab of the Envelope Options dialog box, choose a different envelope size if desired (the default is a standard business envelope).

6 Click the **Printing Options** tab, make any changes, and click **OK**.

7 Your document is reformatted as an envelope. Click **Next: Select recipients**.

8 Leave the **Use an existing list** option button marked, click the **Browse** link, and continue to the next task.

End

Finishing an Envelope Mail Merge

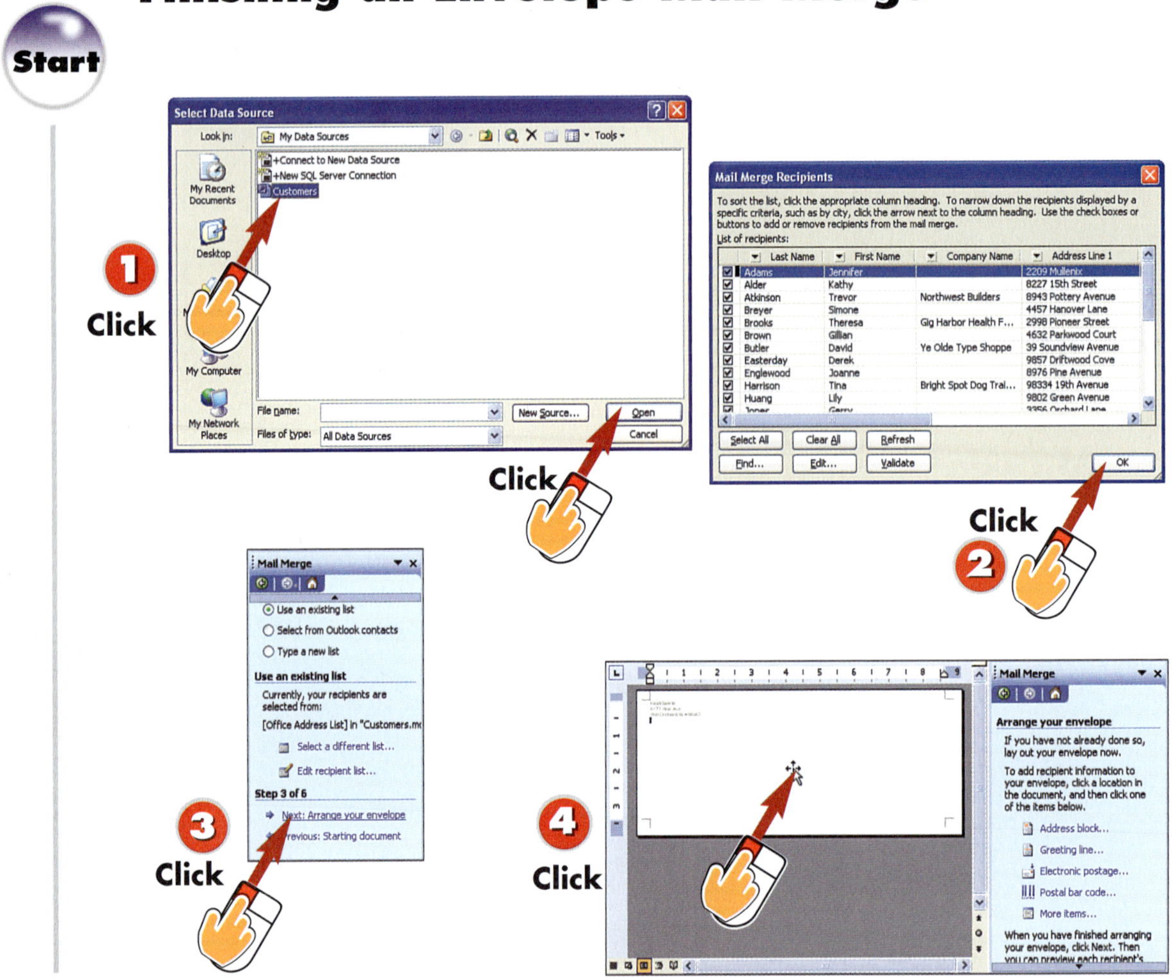

Start

1 Click

Click

2 Click

3 Click

4 Click

1 Select your data source in the **Select Data Source** dialog box, and click **Open**.

2 The Mail Merge Recipient dialog box appears. Sort and edit your address list (see "Sorting and Editing the Recipient List" earlier in this part), and then click **OK**.

3 Click **Next**: **Arrange your envelope** at the bottom of the Mail Merge task pane.

4 Click in the middle of the envelope.

Modifying the Return Address

By default, Word uses the mailing address it finds in the User Information tab of the Options dialog box for the return address on your envelope. (To display this dialog box, open the **Tools** menu and choose **Options**.) If you have preprinted return addresses on your envelopes, just delete the address after step 6. You can also edit it however you'd like (you will probably want to increase the zoom setting to see the text more clearly).

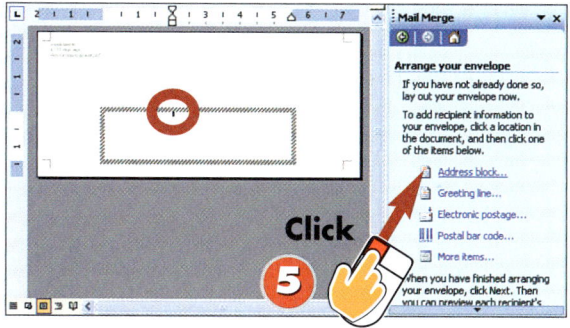

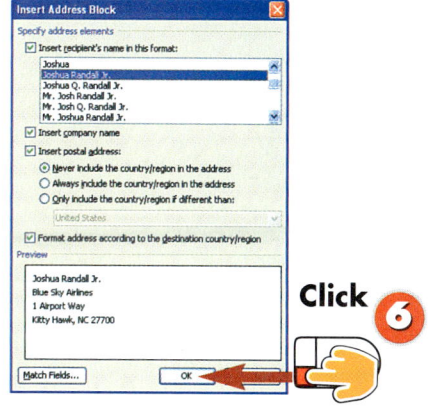

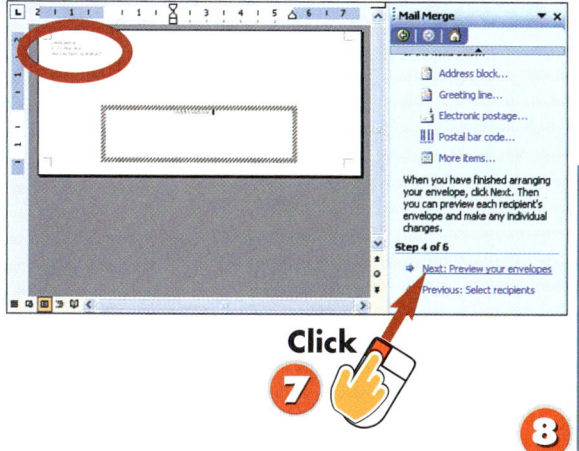

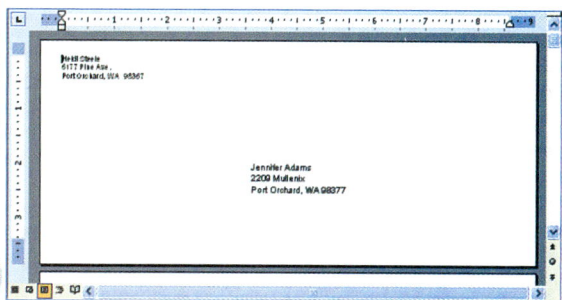

5 An insertion point appears in the text box in which the address block will go. Click the **Address block** link in the Mail Merge task pane.

6 Make the desired selections in the Insert Address Block dialog box, and click **OK**.

7 Optionally, modify the return address (see the tip on the previous page), and then click **Next: Preview your envelopes**.

8 Follow the steps described in "Previewing Your Merged Letters" and "Running the Merge" earlier in this part. Newly merged envelopes will be called Envelopes1.

Running the Same Merge Again

There is usually no need to save the envelopes you generate in a mail merge, because you can always merge the same main document and data source to regenerate them. Furthermore, running the merge again ensures that you merge in the most current information from your data source. When you want to run the same merge in the future, open the main document and click the **Merge to New Document** button or **Merge to Printer** button at the right end of the Mail Merge toolbar. In contrast, you *do* need to save your main document if you want to use it in the future.

Beginning a Label Mail Merge

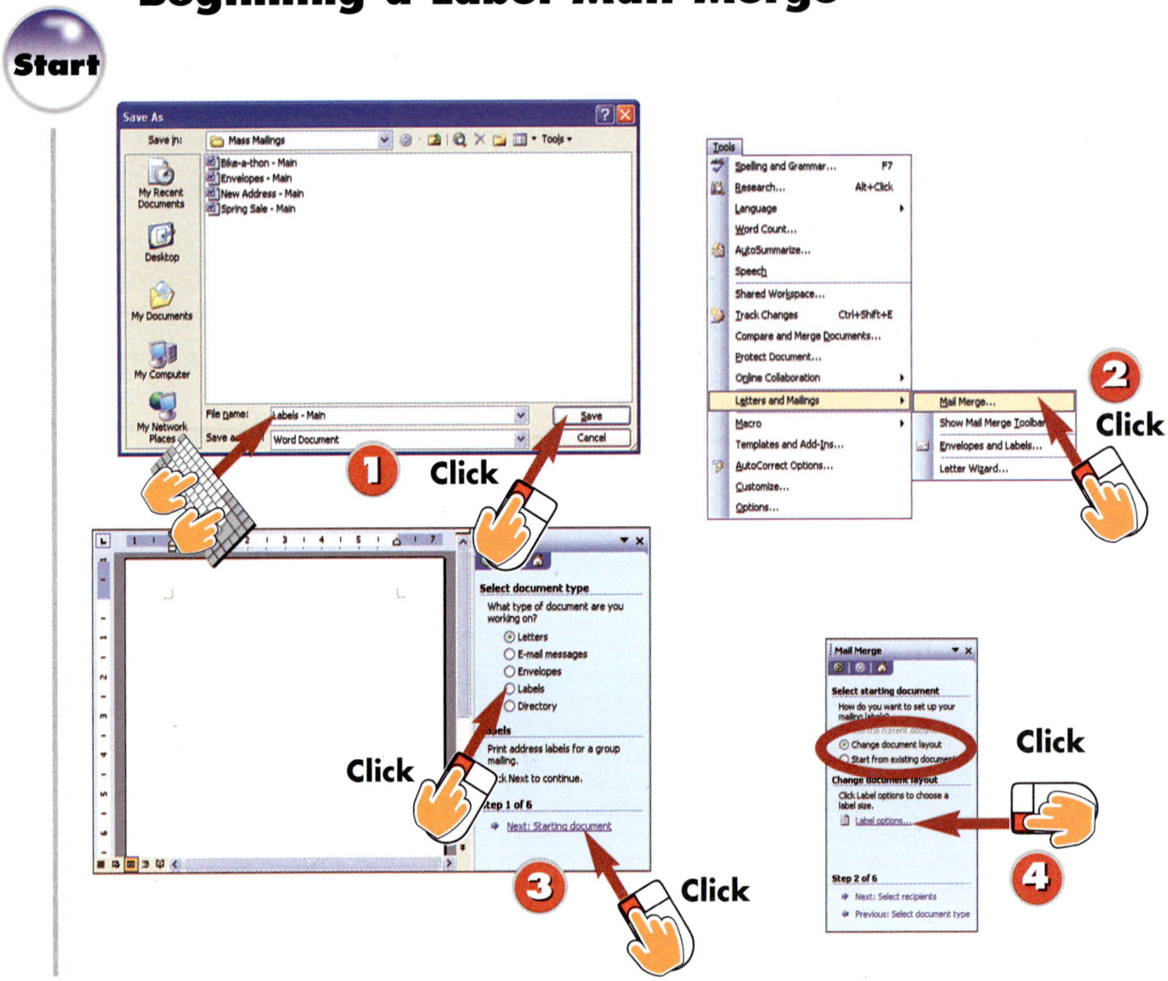

Start

Click ①

Click ②

Click ③

Click

Click ④

①
Start a new, blank document and save it with a name that ends with **Main**.

②
Open the **Tools** menu, choose **Letters and Mailings**, and select **Mail Merge** to display the Mail Merge task pane.

③
Click the **Labels** link in the Mail Merge task pane, and then click **Next: Starting document** at the bottom of the task pane.

④
Keep the **Change document layout** option button marked, and click the **Label options** link.

INTRODUCTION

As with merging envelopes (see the preceding two tasks), it's easiest to merge labels if you practice a few mail merges with form letters first. And remember that this task assumes that you already have a data source, so you'll open an existing one rather than creating a new one.

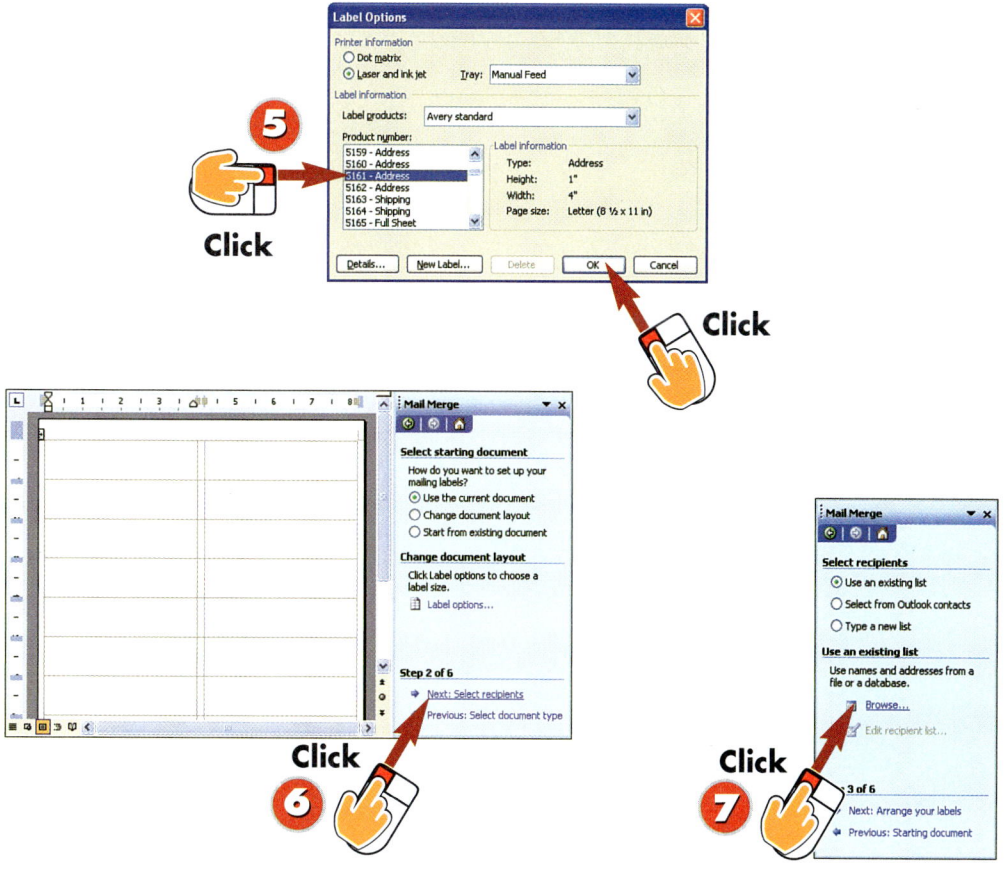

Click

Click

Click

Click

5. Select the product number for your labels, and click **OK**.

6. Your document is reformatted as a sheet of labels. Click **Next: Select recipients**.

7. Leave the **Use an existing list** option button marked, click the **Browse** link, and continue to the next task.

End

Selecting Your Labels

If you are not using Avery labels, display the **Label products** drop-down list in the Label Options dialog box (see step 5) and look for the product line that includes your labels. When you select a different product, the **Product number** list updates to reflect that company's labels. If you still can't find your labels, click the **New Label** button, manually enter your label's measurements, and click **OK**.

Finishing a Label Mail Merge

Start

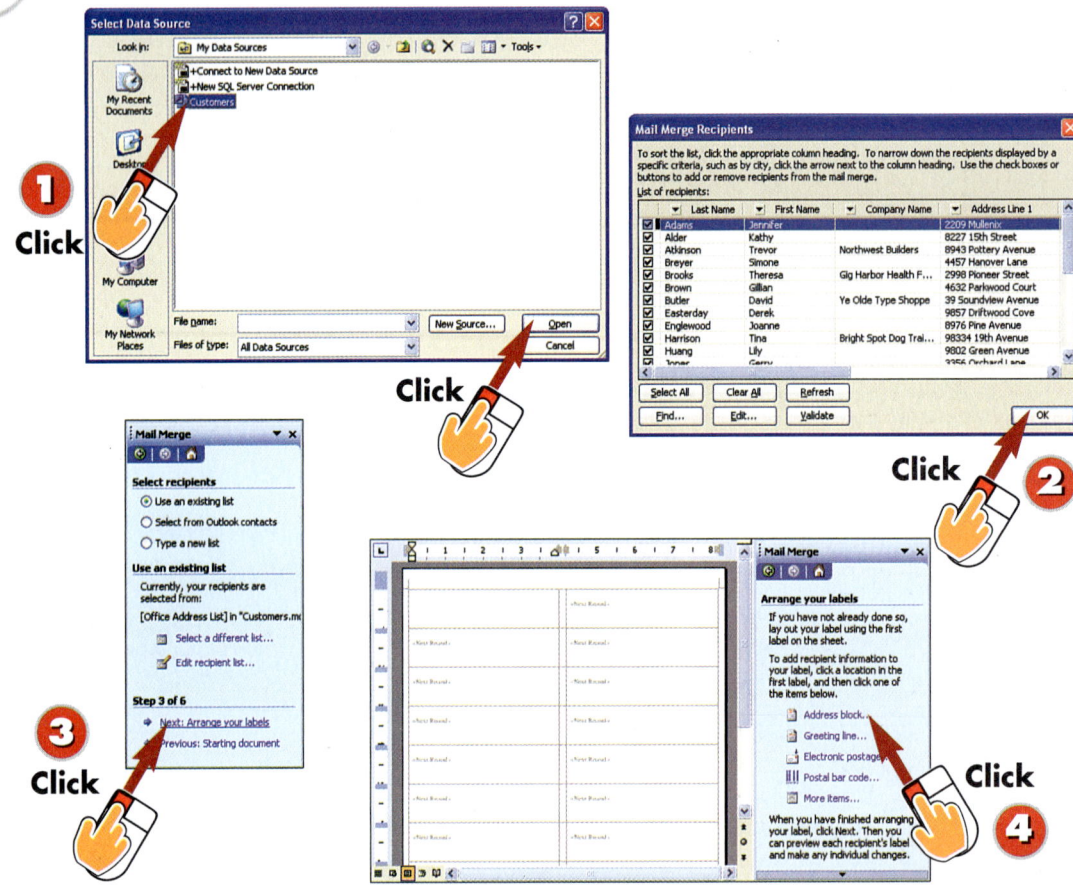

Click ①

Click

Click ②

Click ③

Click ④

---

① Select your data source in the **Select Data Source** dialog box, and click **Open**.

② The **Mail Merge Recipients** dialog box appears. Sort and edit your address list (see "Sorting and Editing the Recipient List" earlier in this part), and then click **OK**.

③ Click **Next: Arrange your labels** at the bottom of the Mail Merge task pane.

④ The insertion point appears in the upper-left label where your address block field should go. Click the **Address block** link in the Mail Merge task pane.

In this task, you complete the mail-merge process to print your labels. As with letters and envelopes, you have the option of sorting your recipient list before merging. In this task, you will insert a merge field for the address block, and choose whether you want to send the merged labels directly to the printer or display them onscreen first.

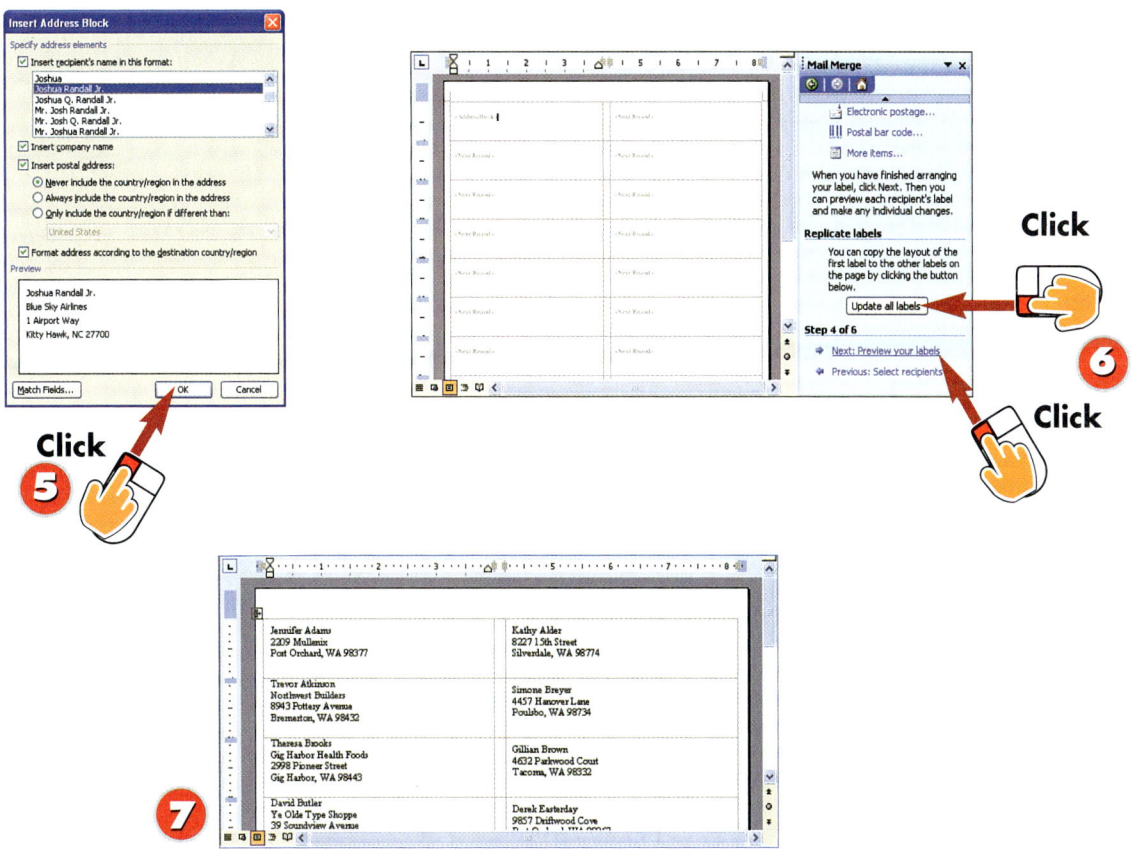

⑤ Make the desired selections in the Insert Address Block dialog box, and click **OK**.

⑥ Click the **Update all labels** button to copy the label format from the upper-left label to the remaining labels on the page, and then click **Next: Preview your labels**.

⑦ Follow the steps described in "Previewing Your Merged Letters" and "Running the Merge" earlier in this part. If you merge to a new document, the merged labels will be called Labels1.

End

Running the Same Merge Again

There is usually no need to save the labels you generate in a mail merge, because you can always merge the same main document and data source to regenerate them. Furthermore, running the merge again ensures that you merge in the most current information from your data source. When you want to run the same merge in the future, open the main document and click the **Merge to New Document** button or **Merge to Printer** button at the right end of the Mail Merge toolbar. In contrast, you *do* need to save your main document if you want to use it in the future.

Word and the Web

All the Office 2003 applications, including Word, are designed with Web integration in mind. As we rely increasingly on the Internet in our everyday work, the boundary between documents on our own computers and those on the Web begins to blur. In this part, you learn how to create links from a Word document to documents on a Web site, how to convert Web documents to Web pages, and how to convert Web pages to Word documents.

Linking in Word

Target of hyperlink

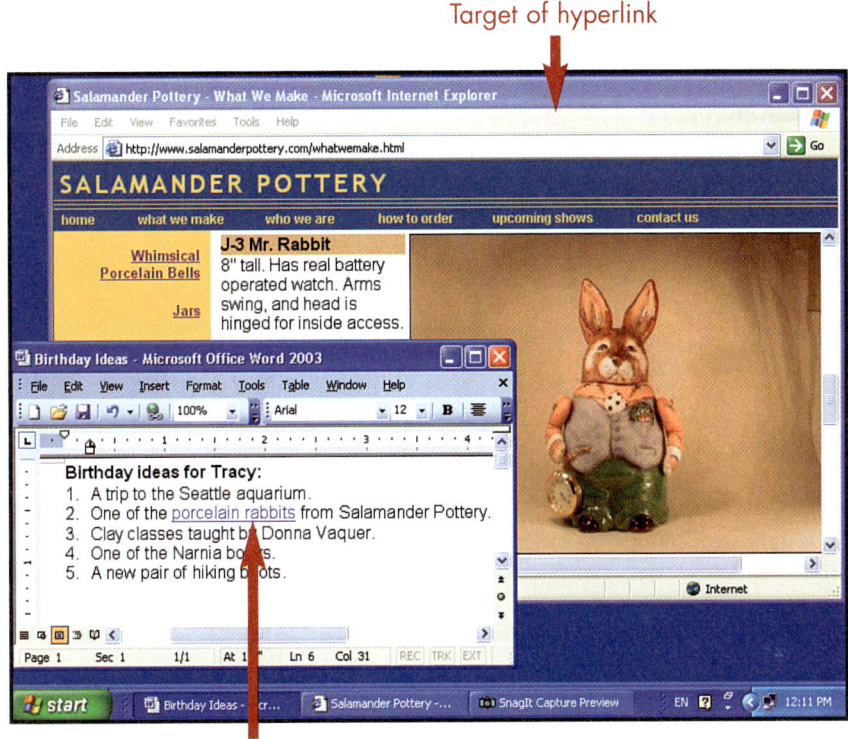

Hyperlink

Inserting Hyperlinks in a Word Document

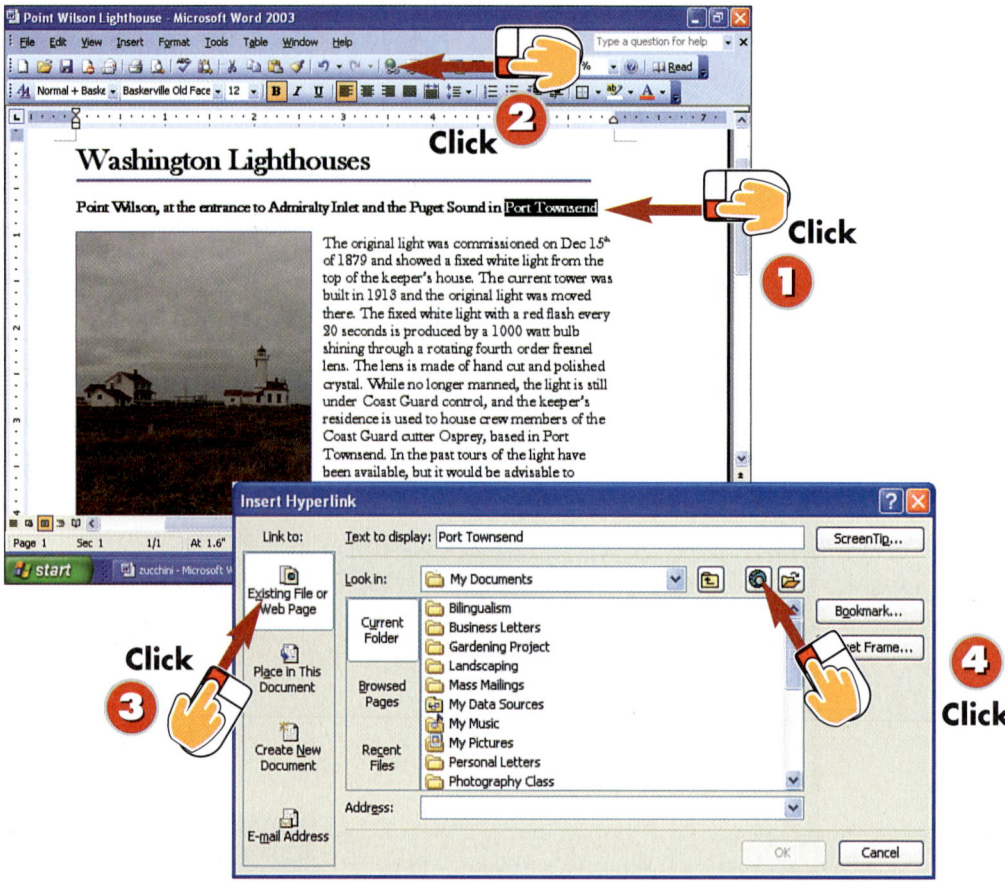

1. Select the word or phrase in your document that you want to become the hyperlink text.

2. Click the **Insert Hyperlink** button on the Standard toolbar.

3. The Insert Hyperlink dialog box opens. Click the **Existing File or Web Page** button under **Link to**.

4. Click the **Browse the Web** button. (Alternatively, type the full address of the target Web page in the **Address** text box and skip to step 6.)

INTRODUCTION

A *hyperlink* is a "clickable" piece of text or an image that leads to another location (the *target* of the hyperlink). With Word's Hyperlink feature, you can create links to other parts of the same document, to other documents, or to Web pages. In this task, you learn how to create a hyperlink to a Web page. Keep in mind that hyperlinks are only useful if your readers will view your Word document onscreen.

TIP

Modifying a Hyperlink
To modify a hyperlink, right-click it, and choose **Hyperlink, Edit Hyperlink** to open the Edit Hyperlink dialog box. Click the **ScreenTip** button to change the ScreenTip text. To remove, right-click it and choose **Hyperlink, Remove Hyperlink**.

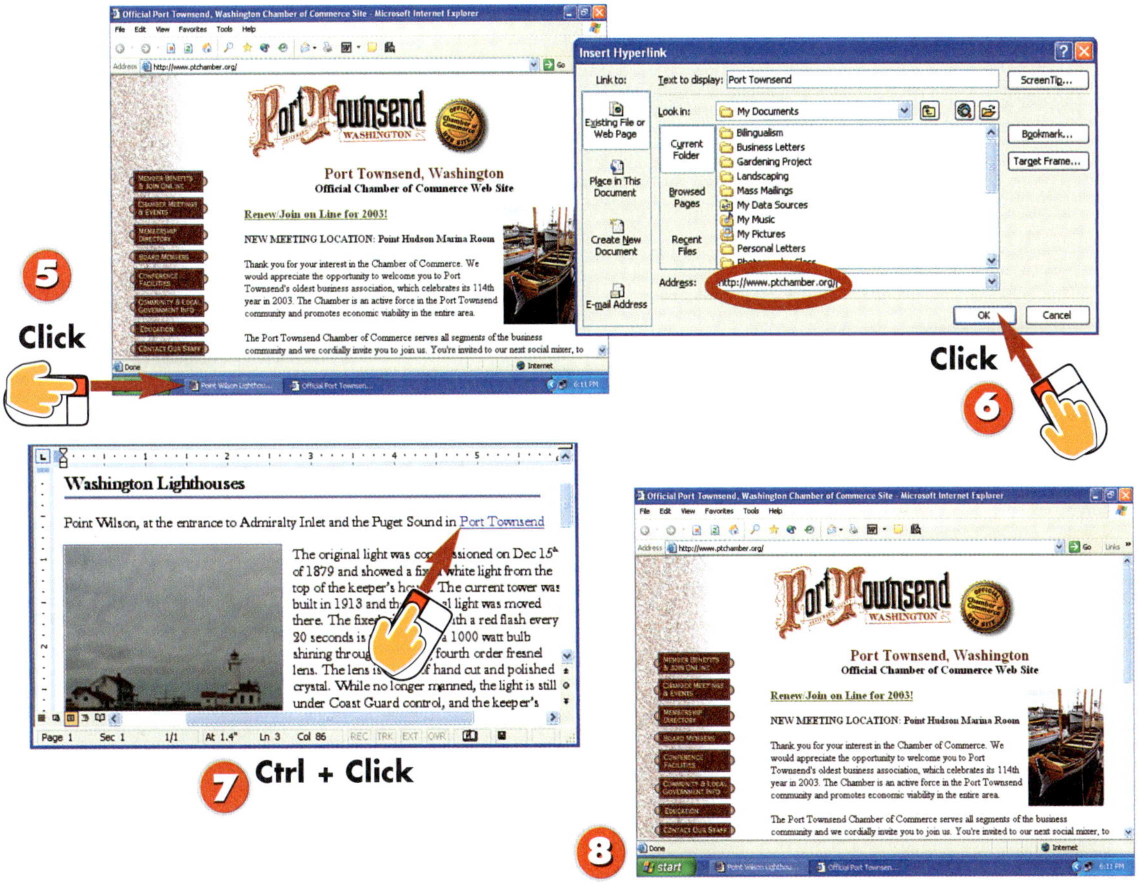

Click 5

Click 6

Ctrl + Click 7

8

5. Your browser window opens. Navigate to the target Web page, then click the Word document's taskbar button to switch back to Word.

6. The address of the Web page now appears in the **Address** text box. Click **OK**.

7. The hyperlink text is now colored and underlined. When you point to it, the address of the target Web page appears in a ScreenTip. **Ctrl+click** the hyperlink.

8. In a moment, the target Web page appears in your browser window. (You may be prompted to connect to the Internet if you have already disconnected.)

End

Linking to a Document
To create a link to a document on your network instead of to a Web page, follow steps 1-3. Then, click the **File** button in **Link to** area of the Insert Hyperlink dialog box, select the file in the Link to File dialog box, and click **OK** twice.

Be careful about using hyperlinks to Web addresses in printed documents if you do not use the Web address itself as the hyperlink text. Your readers will not only be unable to click the hyperlink to travel to the Web site, they will not even be able to manually type the Web address into their Web browsers if you don't use it for the hyperlink text. Of course, this type of hyperlink works wonderfully in documents that will be viewed onscreen.

Converting a Word Document to a Web Page

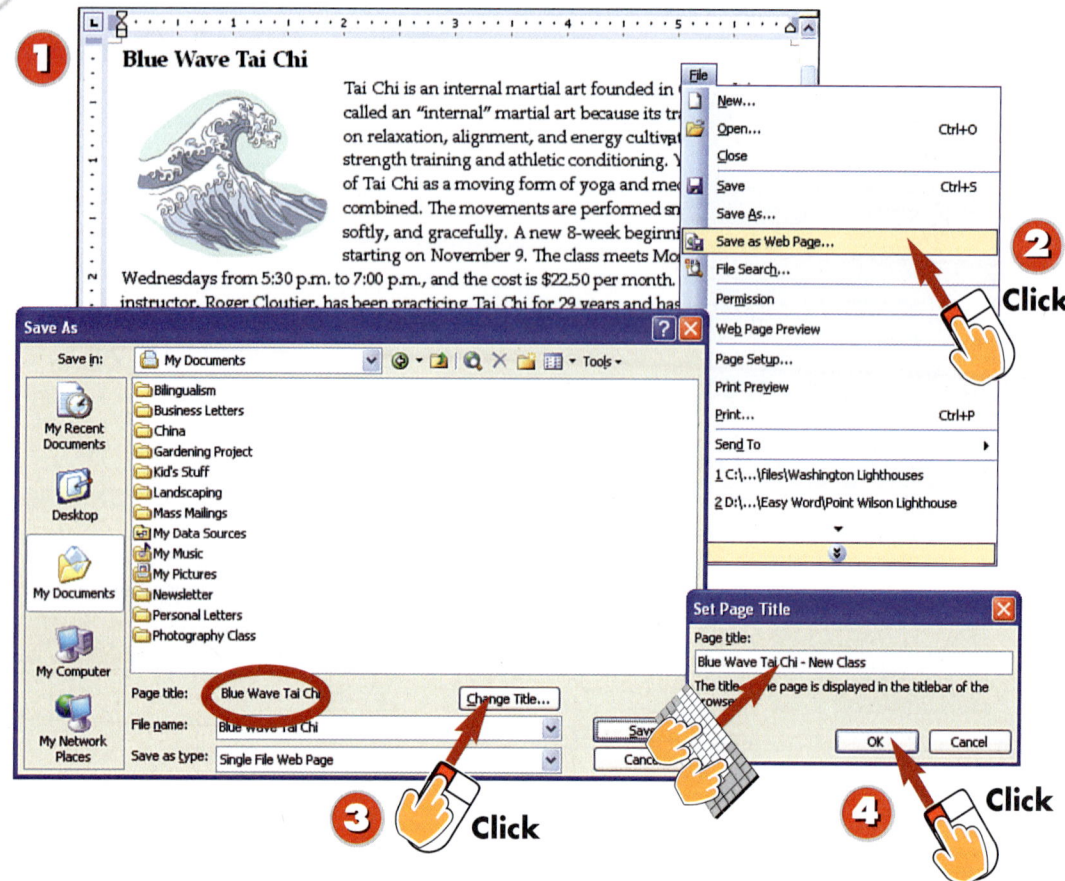

Open the Word document you want to convert.

Open the **File** menu and choose **Save as Web Page** to open the Save As dialog box.

Optionally click the **Change Title** button to revise the title that will appear in the title bar for the page.

In the **Set Page Title** dialog box, type your page title, and then click the **OK** button to return to the Save As dialog box.

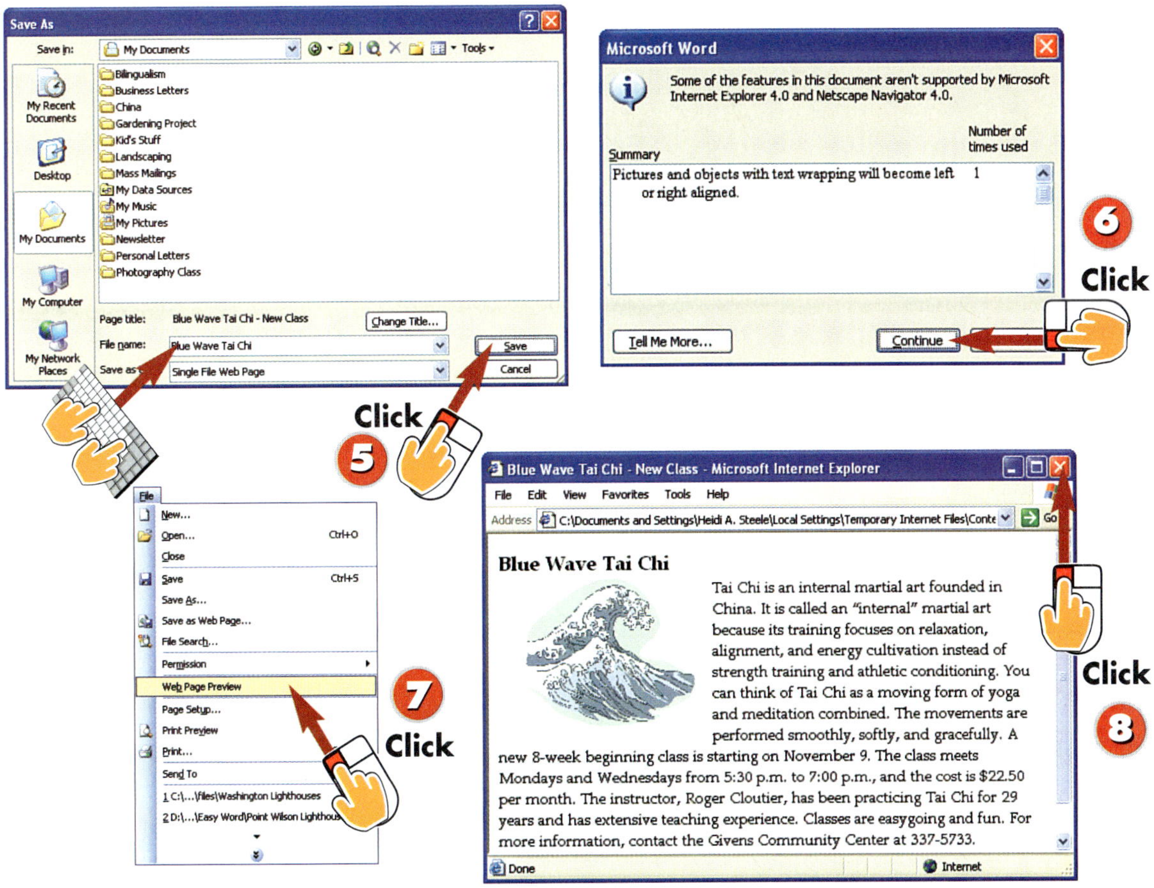

Save As dialog box shows:

Save in: My Documents

- Bilingualism
- Business Letters
- China
- Gardening Project
- Kid's Stuff
- Landscaping
- Mass Mailings
- My Data Sources
- My Music
- My Pictures
- Newsletter
- Personal Letters
- Photography Class

Page title: Blue Wave Tai Chi - New Class   Change Title...
File name: Blue Wave Tai Chi   Save
Save as type: Single File Web Page   Cancel

Click 5

Microsoft Word

Some of the features in this document aren't supported by Microsoft Internet Explorer 4.0 and Netscape Navigator 4.0.

Summary | Number of times used
Pictures and objects with text wrapping will become left or right aligned. | 1

Tell Me More...   Continue

6 **Click**

File menu:
- New...
- Open...   Ctrl+O
- Close
- Save   Ctrl+S
- Save As...
- Save as Web Page...
- File Search...
- Permission ▶
- **Web Page Preview**
- Page Setup...
- Print Preview
- Print...
- Send To
- 1 C:\...\files\Washington Lighthouses
- 2 D:\...\Easy Word\Point Wilson Lighthouse

7 **Click**

Blue Wave Tai Chi - New Class - Microsoft Internet Explorer

File Edit View Favorites Tools Help

Address: C:\Documents and Settings\Heidi A. Steele\Local Settings\Temporary Internet Files\Conte...   Go

Blue Wave Tai Chi

Tai Chi is an internal martial art founded in China. It is called an "internal" martial art because its training focuses on relaxation, alignment, and energy cultivation instead of strength training and athletic conditioning. You can think of Tai Chi as a moving form of yoga and meditation combined. The movements are performed smoothly, softly, and gracefully. A new 8-week beginning class is starting on November 9. The class meets Mondays and Wednesdays from 5:30 p.m. to 7:00 p.m., and the cost is $22.50 per month. The instructor, Roger Cloutier, has been practicing Tai Chi for 29 years and has extensive teaching experience. Classes are easygoing and fun. For more information, contact the Givens Community Center at 337-5733.

Done   Internet

Click 8

5️⃣ Specify a name and location for the page, and click the **Save** button.

6️⃣ You may see a message stating how Word will modify formatting in your document that can't be rendered by some browsers. If you do, click the **Continue** button.

7️⃣ The converted Web page appears in Web Layout view (**View, Web Layout**). To see what the page will look like when viewed in a browser, choose **File, Web Page Preview**.

8️⃣ Your browser opens and displays the Web page. Click its **Close** button when you're finished viewing the page.

 **End**

Letting Other People View Your Web Pages

To make your Web pages visible to others, you must copy (*upload*) them to the Internet or intranet site where they will live. The most common way to upload pages is via a *protocol* called FTP. Word lets you perform this task from the Save As dialog box. As a first step, choose **Add/Modify FTP Locations** from the **Save in** list to tell Word about your site. From then on, when you want to upload a page, you open it, choose **File, Save As**, select the site under **FTP Locations** in the **Save in** list, select the desired folder at the site, and click the **Save** button. Ask your network administrator for help with the details.

Converting a Web Page to a Word Document

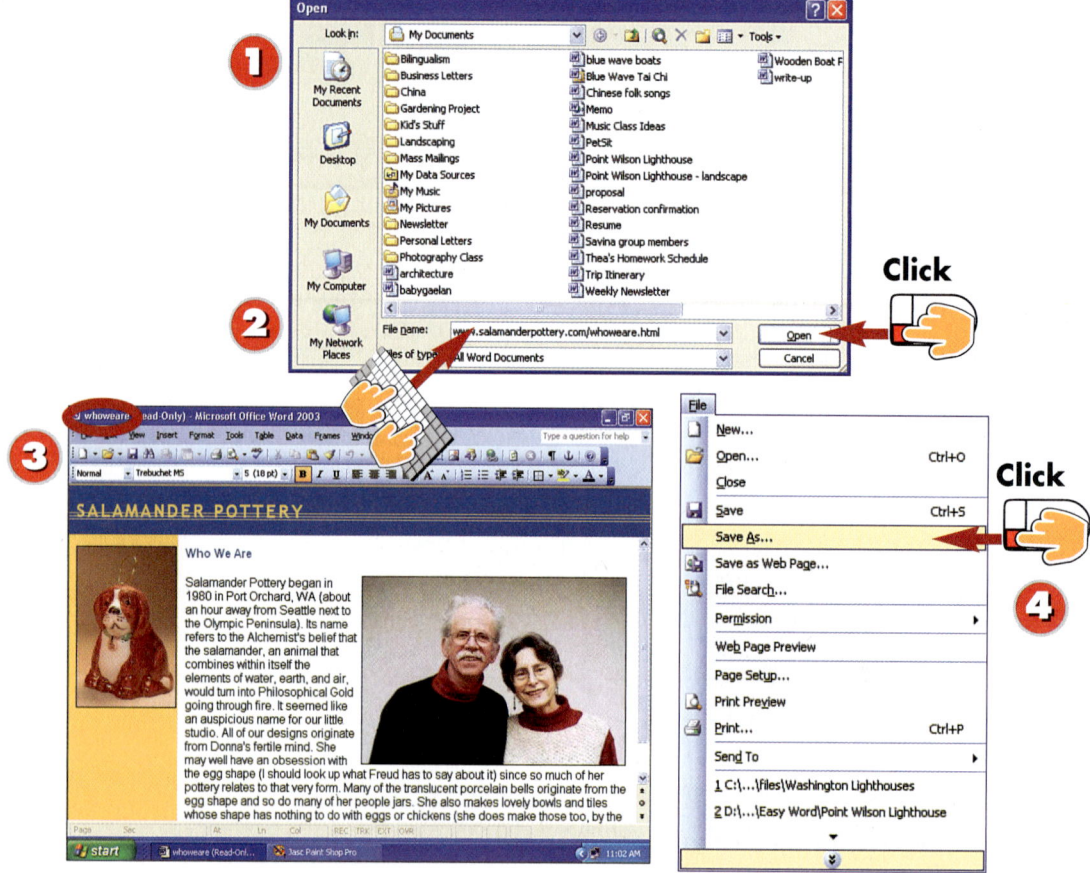

1. From within Word, open the **File** menu and choose **Open** to display the Open dialog box.

2. Type the address for the Web page in the **File name** text box, and click the **Open** button.

3. Word prompts you to connect to the Internet if necessary, and then opens the Web page in the Word window.

4. Open the **File** menu and choose **Save As** to open the Save As dialog box.

Once in a while, you may want to save a Web page as a Word document. Perhaps you found a recipe on a Web site and want to edit the text in Word, or you discovered a Web page about woodworking and want to take advantage of Word's formatting and printing capabilities to spruce it up a bit. When you convert a Web page to a Word document, Word does its best to preserve the formatting in the page.

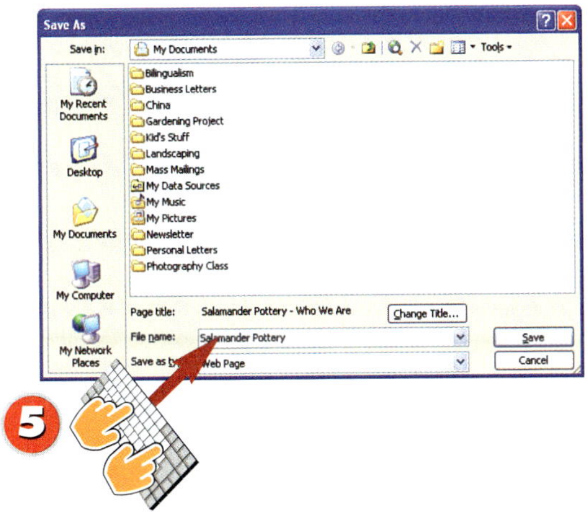

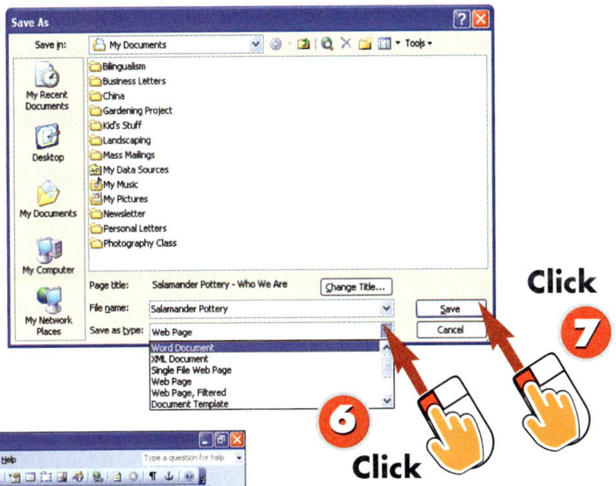

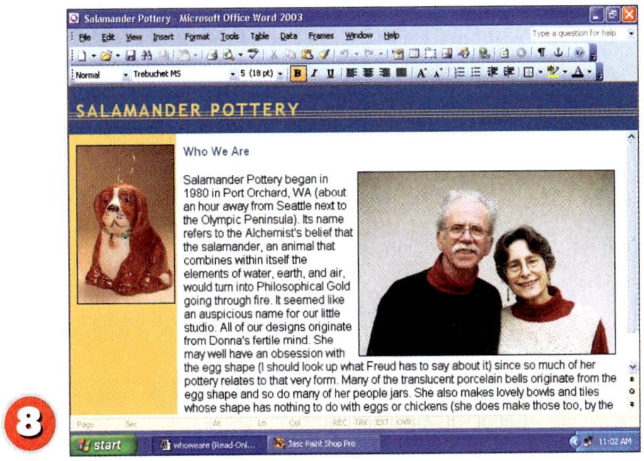

5 Choose a location for the document, and type a name in the **File Name** text box.

6 Click the down arrow next to the **Save as type** field and select **Word Document** in the list that appears.

7 Click the **Save** button.

8 The Web page is saved as a Word document.

Another Way to Open a Web Page in Word
Step 1 describes how to use Word to open a Web page directly from the Internet. You can also use your browser to save the page to your hard disk, and then use Word to open it from your hard disk. If you use this method, be sure to select **All Files** in the **Files of type** list in the Open dialog box so that the Web page will be visible. (By default, Word shows only Word documents in the Open dialog box.)

Glossary

A

alignment   The way text aligns along the right and left sides of the page. You can set the alignment of each paragraph in your document.

AutoCorrect   A feature that corrects spelling errors as you type. You can also use AutoCorrect to enter long phrases automatically.

AutoText   A feature that lets Word "memorize" long blocks of text that you use frequently so that you can quickly insert them in your document.

B–C

bar tab   A custom tab stop that creates a vertical line at the tab stop.

border   Lines around one or more sides of a paragraph (or paragraphs). Word offers a wide variety of line types and colors to choose from.

break   See **page break**.

cell   A box in a table, formed by the intersection of a row and a column.

center tab   A custom tab stop that centers text over the tab stop.

centered alignment   The text is centered horizontally on the page.

check box   A small box that you click to enable or disable an option in a dialog box. If the check box has a check mark in it, the option is currently enabled; if it's clear, the option is disabled. Check boxes are not mutually exclusive; you can mark several check boxes in a group.

context menu   A menu that appears when you right-click on something. The commands in a context menu vary depending on where you right-click.

copy and paste   To place a duplicate of the selected text somewhere else in the current document or another document.

cursor   See **insertion point**.

custom tab   A tab stop that you insert in a document. When you add a custom tab, all the default tabs to its left disappear.

cut and paste   To move the selected text somewhere else in the current document or another document.

D

data source   The file that contains the data you will merge into the "boilerplate" document (called the *main document*). See also **mail merge** and **main document**.

decimal tab   A custom tab stop that aligns text along the decimal point.

default   The assumed option, behavior, or formatting that remains in effect unless you specify otherwise.

default tab   The tab stops that appear automatically in your document. Default tabs are spaced every half-inch across the document, and they remain in effect unless you insert custom tabs (*see also* **custom tab** and **tab**).

dialog box   A small window that appears when you issue a command followed by an ellipsis (…) to get more information about how you want to carry out the command. Clicking the OK button in a dialog box issues the command; clicking the Cancel button cancels it.

docked toolbar   A toolbar that is fixed on an edge of the Word window.

download   To retrieve a copy of a program or individual file from the Internet or a company intranet.

drag   To press and hold down your mouse button as you move the mouse pointer. You typically drag to move, draw, or select objects with the mouse.

drawing canvas   An area on which you can place multiple shapes. You can easily move and resize the shapes on a drawing canvas as a group.

drop-down list   A list that stays hidden from view until you click the down arrow to its right. As soon as you select an option from the list, the list closes again.

E-F

end mark   The small horizontal bar at the very end of a Word document. The end mark is only visible in Normal view, and it doesn't print.

field   A holding place for information that can be updated. Typical fields in Word include the date field, which displays the current date, and the page number field, which displays the correct page number on each page in a document. *See also* **mail merge** and **merge field**.

first-line indent   Only the first line of a paragraph is indented.

floating toolbar   A toolbar that is located somewhere over the Word window, not along one of the edges. A

floating toolbar has a title bar, which you can drag to move the toolbar around.

font   In the Windows environment, the term *font* refers to a typeface, or character shape, such as Times New Roman or Arial.

footer   Text that repeats at the bottom of every page.

full menu   A menu that displays the full set of commands in the menu. If you are using personalized menus, you can click the down arrow at the bottom of a menu to display the full menu. If you are not using personalized menus, you see full menus all of the time. *See also* **short menu**.

G-I

hanging indent   All the lines in a paragraph except the first line are indented.

hard page break   These page breaks (also called *manual* page breaks) are inserted by the user to force a page to break at a particular spot.

header   Text that repeats at the top of every page.

hyperlink   A clickable piece of text that brings you to a different location within the current document, to another file on your own computer or network, or to a file on the Internet or your company intranet. *See also* **target**.

I-beam   The mouse pointer you see when it's resting over text. When you see an I-beam, you can click to move the insertion point, or drag to select text.

in-line   In-line images are in the same layer of the document as the text, so text cannot wrap around them.

indent   To push in the text in a paragraph from the margin. Word gives you four indent options. You can set the indentation of each paragraph in your document.

insertion point   The flashing vertical bar in a document that indicates where text will be inserted or deleted when you type or delete text.

item   In a general sense, refers to any object on your screen. Also refers to a block of cut or copied text that is stored on the Office Clipboard. *See also* **Office Clipboard**.

J–K

justified alignment   Both the left and right edges of the text are straight. Word adds or removes space between characters to form the straight right edge.

keyboard shortcut   A combination of keystrokes that you can use to issue a command instead of using the toolbars, menus, or dialog boxes.

L

landscape orientation   The document prints so that the long edge of the paper is at the top of the page.

left alignment   The left edge of the text is straight and the right edge is ragged. This is the default alignment option.

left indent   All the lines in a paragraph are indented from the left.

left tab   A custom tab stop that left-aligns text at the tab stop. The default tabs are also left tabs.

line spacing   The amount of vertical space between lines of text.

M

mail merge   The process of merging a "boilerplate" document (such as a form letter, label, or envelope) with a list of data (usually names and addresses) to generate personalized documents.

main document   The actual document that you are producing, such as a form letter, label, or envelope.

merge field   Fields that you insert in a main document telling Word where to insert the individual pieces of data (name, address, and so on) from the data source.

memory   The temporary storage area in your computer that holds the programs and documents that you currently have open (also called RAM, for *random access memory*). Memory is cleared each time you turn off your computer. If you want to return to a document later, you need to save it to disk.

N–O

Office Clipboard   A temporary storage area that holds multiple pieces of cut or copied text. You can paste items in the Office Clipboard into any Office document, in any order.

option button   A small white circle that you click to choose an option in a dialog box. If the option button has a black dot in it, it is currently enabled; if it doesn't, it is disabled. Option buttons are mutually exclusive; you can mark only one option button in a group.

OverType mode   When you turn on this feature, each character you type replaces the existing character to the right of the insertion point. By default, OverType mode is turned off, so as you type, existing characters are not replaced; they just move to the right to make room for the new text.

P

page break   The separation between one page and the next. *See also* **hard page break** and **soft page break**.

paragraph mark   This symbol (¶) indicates the end of a paragraph. A paragraph symbol is inserted each time you press the Enter key. You can see where the paragraph marks in a document are by turning on the Show/Hide button on the Standard toolbar.

personal menus   The type of menus that you see when personalized menus are turned on (the default). Word watches how you use the program and only includes in the menus the commands that you use the most frequently.

Places bar   The vertical bar on the left side of the Open and Save As dialog boxes that contain buttons for frequently used folders.

point   A unit of measurement for font size. Roughly speaking, the point size of a font measures its vertical height. There are approximately 72 points in a vertical inch. Standard business documents usually use a 10- to 12-point font.

portrait orientation   The document prints so that the short edge of the paper is at the top of the page. This is the default setting.

printer font   A font that resides in your printer. Printer fonts print correctly, but may not look onscreen exactly as they will when printed.

protocol   A set of rules that lets computers agree on how to communicate.

Q–R

recipient list   A recipient list is the same as a data source—it's the list of information that will merge into your main document. *See also* **main document** and **data source**.

record   All the information about one person in your data source. If you have names and addresses of 50 people in your data source, your data source contains 50 records. Each record is composed of individual fields for the specific pieces of information, such as first name, last name, address, and so on.

restore   To return a window back to the size it was before it was last minimized or maximized.

right alignment   The right edge of the text is straight and the left edge is ragged.

right indent   All the lines in a paragraph are indented from the right.

right tab   A custom tab stop that right-aligns text at the tab stop.

S

ScreenTip   A small "bubble" that appears when you rest your mouse pointer over a toolbar button or other screen element that identifies the item. Also referred to as a *ToolTip*.

scroll arrows   The arrows at either end of a scrollbar that you can click to scroll through your document.

scrollbar   A long bar that lets you move through your document with the mouse. Word provides a vertical scrollbar on the right side of the window and a horizontal scrollbar along the bottom of the window.

scroll box   The small box on a scroll-bar that you can drag along the bar to scroll in either direction.

select   To mark text in preparation for performing an action on it. Often called *highlighting*. When you select text, it takes on a black background. When you select an image, *selection handles* appear around its edges.

selection handles   Small squares around the edges of an image that indicate the image is selected.

short menu   A menu that displays only the commands you use the most frequently. When personalized menus are turned on, you see short menus by default. *See also* **full menu**.

shortcut icon   An icon that opens a program, folder, or file. A shortcut icon is just a pointer to a program, folder, or file. When you delete a shortcut icon, you don't remove the item to which it points.

shortcut menu   *See* **context menu**.

smart tag   A clickable piece of text that Word recognizes as a particular type of data, such as a date, a person's name, and so on. Clicking a smart tag gives you a menu with a list of actions that are relevant for that data type.

soft page break   Soft page breaks (also called *automatic* page breaks) are inserted by Word to break a page when it is full and push additional text onto the next page.

spinner arrows   Small up and down arrows to the right of a text box. Clicking these arrows increments or decrements the number in the text box.

status bar   The bar at the very bottom of the Word window. The status bar contains information such as the current page number, the total number of pages in your document, and so on.

T

tab   This term has several meanings: Many dialog boxes have tabs across the top. Clicking the tabs displays different sets of options. This term also refers to the character that is inserted in your document when you press the Tab key. Finally, the term *tab* refers to a tab stop.

target   The destination to which a hyperlink leads. The target might be a location within the current document, or it might be another file or Web page. *See also* **hyperlink**.

task pane   A vertical pane that usually appears on the right side of the Word window and contains information and options associated with a particular Word feature. By default, task panes appear automatically when you perform certain actions, such as searching for text or starting a mail merge.

taskbar   The bar on the Windows desktop (usually at the bottom of the screen) that contains the Start button at one end and the clock at the other. When a Word document is open, a button for it appears on the taskbar.

template   A rough "blueprint" for a document. A template usually contains some combination of formatting and text. Word comes with a wide variety of templates. The Normal template (also called the *Blank Document template*) is the default template that Word uses for all new documents unless you specify otherwise. This template contains the formatting for a standard business document (Times New Roman, 12-point font, single spacing, 8.5-by-11 inch paper, and so on).

text box   A small box in a dialog box in which you can type text or numbers.

text wrapping   Refers to the way text flows around an image in your document. Word provides several text wrapping options.

theme   A collection of design elements that gives a document or Web page a particular "look." Themes can include background images, fonts, horizontal lines, bullets and so on.

title bar   The bar across the top of a window that lists the name of the program and/or document that's open in the window.

toggle   A button or keyboard command that you click or press once to turn an option on and again to turn it off.

TrueType font   A font that looks the same onscreen as it does when it prints.

U–Z

upload   To send a copy of a file from your computer or network to a computer on the Internet or a company intranet.

view   The display of your document onscreen. Whenever you work with a document, you will use whatever view is best suited to the task at hand.

Windows Clipboard   A temporary storage area for data (text, graphics, and so on) that is being cut or copied. The Windows Clipboard can only hold one cut or copied selection at a time. *See also* **Office Clipboard**.

wizard   A specialized template that asks you questions about what type of document you want to create, and then generates the document for you based on your answers.

XML   An open, international standard for marking up documents to describe their structure and the data they contain. Word 2003 understands XML documents and can be used to produce XML documents, making it possible to use the content of Word documents in a company's business processes.

zoom   To change the magnification of a document onscreen. You can zoom in to enlarge a document or zoom out to shrink it.

Index

Symbols

Numbers

A

B

How can we make this index more useful? Email us at indexes@samspublishing.com

How can we make this index more useful? Email us at indexes@samspublishing.com